GROUP
DISCUSSION

Prentice-Hall, Inc., Englewood Cliffs, New Jersey 07632

R. Victor Harnack
University of Illinois at Chicago Circle

Thorrel B. Fest
University of Colorado

Barbara Schindler Jones
University of Colorado

second edition

GROUP DISCUSSION

Theory and Technique

Library of Congress Cataloging in Publication Data

HARNACK, ROBERT VICTOR (date)
    Group discussion.

    Includes bibliographies and index.
      1. Discussion.   I. Fest, Thorrel B., joint author.
II. Jones, Barbara S., joint author.   III. Title.
LC6515.H35 1977   808.53   76–40060
ISBN   0–13–365247–5

Printed in the United States of America
10 9 8 7 6 5 4 3 2 1

PRENTICE-HALL INTERNATIONAL, INC., *London*
PRENTICE-HALL OF AUSTRALIA PTY. LIMITED, *Sydney*
PRENTICE-HALL OF CANADA, LTD., *Toronto*
PRENTICE-HALL OF INDIA PRIVATE LIMITED, *New Delhi*
PRENTICE-HALL OF JAPAN, INC., *Tokyo*
PRENTICE-HALL OF SOUTHEAST ASIA PTE. LTD., *Singapore*

To our students,
from whom we have learned much

Contents

PART FOUR

SMALL GROUP DECISION-MAKING AND PROBLEM-SOLVING, *113*

Millions of words professing to help small groups achieve more productive discussion have been printed. Since, in revising this book for its second edition, we are adding more words to this supply, a description of our motives is in order.

The stream of rhetorical principles and techniques that began with Aristotle, Isocrates, and Plato has been constantly broadening and deepening. For years its main current was effective speaking on the public platform. A more recent, and parallel, stream is the scientific study of small group behavior. Since the publication of the first edition, several new tributaries have joined the main stream. We have therefore reorganized and updated the material from the first edition, and we have added completely new material: chapters on conflict and evaluation, as well as an expanded section (in Chapter 6) on nonverbal communication.

The book is divided into six parts, progressing from an overview of what small groups and discussion are about and the historical and current significance of groups to sections on group dynamics, group communication, decision-making and problem-solving, and leadership. The final section summarizes some methods we can use to evaluate and improve small group discussions. The chapter on improving small group discussion concludes with a checklist telling where to find additional material on the chapter's main points throughout the book.

A detailed definition of small group discussion is given in Chapter 2. But to help the reader understand our frame of reference from the very beginning, we include the following definition here: *Discussion is the process whereby two or more people exchange information or ideas in a face-to-face situation to achieve a goal.*

We assume that the enhancement and growth of the individual is the fundamental value of participation in groups. At times individual betterment is accomplished in a group whose primary purpose is to help individuals realize personal goals; at other times individual betterment is a by-product of working for more impersonal, task-oriented goals. We have proceeded on a goal-oriented basis, using the concept of a "bargain" struck between the individual and the group. Methods are consequently designed to implement the process of bargaining, whatever the goals of the group may be.

We have featured *real* and ongoing groups in our examples, primarily because we feel a weakness of recent research is its heavy reliance on experimental groups that meet only once or at best spasmodically. We note a change that has taken place since the publishing of the first edition: Today groups are used less as decision-making bodies and more as instruments for applying pressure (as in collective bargaining) and changing bureaucracies (such as affirmative action programs).

It will be obvious to the reader that, rather than content ourselves with describing issues to be resolved and with presenting relevant evidence for doing so, we have chosen to take a stand on many points of controversy concerning discussion theory or technique. We certainly do not expect all scholars in this area to agree with us in

Preface

every instance. We do believe our views are both provocative and soundly based in research, experience, and observation. The more inconclusive the evidence, the more tentative are our conclusions.

A book of this sort should do more than present sound and useful information; it should also challenge the reader to go beyond its pages. We have made liberal use, therefore, of footnotes and bibliographies. The exercises at the end of each chapter are also designed to stimulate the student to adopt perspectives other than our own. If in performing them the reader discovers evidence that seems to modify or change any of our conclusions, we will be more delighted than dismayed. Research is changing the field of discussion too rapidly to justify considering any answers as final.

There is far more material in this book than could possibly be used in the typical three-hour course. But, rather than provide another simplified text, we rely upon the good judgment of teachers and students to select what is of most interest, use, and relevance to them.

No authors can claim to have written a book completely unaided. We are obviously indebted to hundreds of scholars and writers who have preceded us and whose thoughts and observations we have used. Wherever possible we have indicated our indebtedness by proper citation. We wish also to acknowledge our debt to our teachers and colleagues, who have argued with us, stimulated us, and listened to us—and who have been tolerant of our mistakes. In addition, we are grateful to many publishers, who allowed us to use material from their books, and to Robert Kibler of Florida State University and Joseph M. Staudacher of Marquette University, who reviewed our manuscript and made valuable suggestions.

R. V. H.   T. B. F.   B. S. J.

GROUP
DISCUSSION

PART ONE

This book is intended to help people work more productively in discussion groups. Such productivity is in itself only a means to an end. But what is this end? Why should we concern ourselves with improving our ability in the give-and-take of discussion groups?

Group activity can, we believe, provide an opportunity for a person to develop abilities and capacities, and achieve through collective action what the individual alone cannot. Either the group processes or the end product, or both, must provide the individual with some enrichment and satisfaction not present before. The person must be better off in some way because of group membership.

When any group ceases to serve individuals and degrades them, the usefulness of that group has ended. The numerous instances in which an individual has made heroic, noble, and unselfish sacrifices for the group may seem to belie our contention that the enhancement of the individual provides the greatest good. Such actions, however, do not negate the thesis, for the act of making such a sacrifice may be the epitome of a person's accomplishment and ultimate enhancement.

We have been increasingly concerned about those critics of group behavior and collaborative activity who lament that whenever someone becomes part of a group, the individual identity becomes submerged and ultimately lost. Some are alarmed by what they believe to be a subversion of the fundamental ethic we have just discussed.

How do these critics propose to solve the problem? Some suggest a return to rugged individualism. Some hope for the emergence of a new type of personality, programmed to cope with the new pressures of society. Others look for improve-

PEOPLE
AND GROUPS

ment through the identification, understanding, and use of such mechanisms as games, transactions, and encounters.

We believe that the successful group reinforces and protects each individual's identity. What's more, we maintain that the best way to prevent people from being manipulated by or lost in a group is to improve the individual's understanding of self and others, in part by teaching the complexities and rewards of group forces, social influence, and the communication process.

In this section we will examine the processes that create and maintain the group, some of the attacks against the group, and the circumstances that have given rise to these attacks. We will briefly trace the fluctuating historical aspects that have at times emphasized the rugged individual and at other times called for highly collaborative action. We will develop what we mean by the democratic ethic of the individual, and we will show why we believe this dilemma of the individual versus the group is a conflict that can be resolved.

chapter 1

Human history is a story of the struggle of people to be individuals and to relate meaningfully to others. These two fundamental needs have been well described by Erich Fromm in his book *Escape from Freedom*.[1] Fromm asserts that the desire for freedom is a basic human drive because the condition of freedom is essential to growth. Restrict an arm and that arm atrophies; restrict the freedom of a man and that man "dies" for want of psychological growth.

Freedom, however, has a dichotomous aspect. A person's freedom may be freedom *from* external restrictions, or it may be freedom *to* relate in a spontaneous and creative fashion to the rest of the world. Fromm argues that modern man has not realized the full meaning of freedom *to* and is therefore unable to bear the awful aloneness engendered by freedom *from*. How, then, have these two human needs fared throughout history?

Men and women have always had to depend on groups. As we know, the family and the tribe existed long before recorded history, and we are all aware of the role that these groups played in the nurture of human beings. For centuries, tradition dictated a rigid social structure. Serf was bound to lord, slave to master in a structure that allowed no freedom to either party. Birth determined destiny and an omnipotent church presided over all. Neither slave nor master was free in any genuine sense; the life role of each was determined by station in life. The idea of the individual free to determine his or her own destiny was, with rare exceptions, unknown until modern times.

In such circumstances, the individual was involved in little conflict because his or her role in the social structure was definite and unalterable. Persons were provided security in life by the social structure and promised a posthumous equality and tranquility. There was little room for anxiety or doubt in such a society.

But a new idea began to emerge. One manifestation of this idea occurred on June 15, 1215, on the plains of Runnymede, where a historic document was signed. This document declared that there was a law that transcended everyone—even kings— and people as individuals could invoke this law without fear. The men who forced King John to sign the Magna Charta did not have the welfare of the common man in mind when they phrased the document; they wanted baronial prerogatives as opposed to those of the king. But they had to justify their claims in language that made generalization to include all men almost inevitable.

Events moved slowly at first but soon gathered momentum. The Renaissance began to free artists, poets, philosophers, and scientists. The hopes and aspirations of living persons now became paramount. Along with this new emphasis on the individual came increasing recognition of the importance of developing the individual's capabilities.

[1]Erich Fromm, *Escape from Freedom* (New York: Holt, Rinehart and Winston, Inc., 1941).

The Individual Versus the Group

Economic changes also helped alter the concept. Merchants, draftsmen, and traders, stimulated by the possibilities demonstrated during the Crusades, began to crack the class boundaries. The idea that people could improve their station in life was indeed radical and took considerable time to be accepted. The significant aspect, however, was the beginning of discontent with a society that preordained for every person a given niche in life and excluded most people from any chance to prove themselves capable of greater accomplishment.

This discontent with the established order became manifest in religious thought, and the Reformation and Counter-Reformation were born. These movements tended to give people freedom in religion—freedom, that is, not from their God, but from the organizational requirements of how to relate to their God. Vernon Parrington made the significant point that the "priesthood of all believers" concept made inevitable the idea that people were capable of governing themselves.[2] If persons could govern their religious life, they could certainly govern their civic life.

Hesitantly at first, people began to proclaim new discoveries and ideas. Galileo, Copernicus, Newton, and others began to question accepted notions about the nature of the world and the universe. They explored new ideas in a fashion unknown since the height of the Greek civilization and, despite considerable resistance, announced their discoveries to the world at large.

Colonial America became a haven for the nascent individualism. Here, religious freedom became a reality for most people. Although leaders such as Cotton and Increase Mather and Governor Winthrop denied religious freedom in the Massachusetts Bay Colony for Protestant sects other than their own, men such as Roger Williams, Jonathan Edwards, and George Whitefield worked to achieve religious freedom because they recognized it as inseparable from any other freedom.

Accompanying this religious freedom was an economic freedom, engendered by independent farmers, merchants, and craftsmen. The well-known success story of Benjamin Franklin demonstrates accomplishments that had been considered completely impossible a century or two earlier in Europe. Few people wore another's collar and in 1776 the real and fancied oppressions of the British monarch were rejected.[3]

INDIVIDUALISM AT ITS PEAK

The American and French revolutions marked the point when the individual, in the United States came of age. The United States was built upon these individuals, who were independent politically, religiously, and economically. Looking back to the Magna Charta, they wrote a Constitution and declared proudly that their government was one of laws and not of men.

Before we overpraise the individualism of that era, let us look a bit more closely to see what produced it and what its consequences were.

[2]Vernon Louis Parrington, *Main Currents in American Thought* (New York: Harcourt, Brace & World, Inc., 1930).

[3]The French Revolution obviously is more responsible than the American Revolution for creating the changes leading to the development of individualism. Writers such as Montesquieu, Locke, and Rousseau provided a rationale for these changes. We are using the American Revolution merely to date the peak of individualism.

Thomas Jefferson and Daniel Webster understood very well what had produced the individualism of their day. Jefferson pinned his hopes on the agrarian society. He called cities "sores on the body politic" and hoped that people would prefer to remain on the farm, where they belonged to a largely self-sustaining economic unit based on the family. In light of this fundamental premise, Jefferson's famous dictum, "That government is best which governs least," is easily understood. Since the family farm was almost completely independent of anyone else for basic necessities, the government had to do little except protect the farmer from hostile attack and ensure that such commerce as was needed operated without unnecessary interference.[4]

Webster held that property was the cornerstone of liberty. He contended that only the individual who possessed property could be truly free and trusted with public responsibility. Framers of state governments thus limited the electorate to free, adult, white, male property holders.

Individualism flourished at this time for several reasons, but a primary reason was that people did not need others very much for the ordinary pursuits of life. To be sure, people needed one another for a host of things such as the building of roads and harbors. Fundamentally, however, they were their own economic masters. The fact that the government did not interfere with the activities of the majority of citizens did not *cause* individualism. On the contrary, the relatively inconspicuous role of the government was made possible because of the small need for collaborative action.

In such a society, with its primitive economy based on the power of horse, sail, and human muscle, relationships among individuals on all levels were for the most part clear and meaningful. The family, generally large, was the basic unit of cultural and personal interchange. Families often voluntarily and spontaneously cooperated to build a barn, thresh grain, or husk corn. Many communities were composed of people drawn from a comparatively small number of families who had intermarried extensively and who shared numerous common bonds and interests.

THE FALL OF THE INDIVIDUAL

Even as individualism was coming of age, the tide of events began to destroy it. The "group" began to assert control almost immediately.[5] Industrial growth forced Northern factory owners to bring together groups of laborers; the Southern plantation owners sought slaves as workers. Despite the hopes of George Washington and virtually all the framers of the Constitution, political parties came into being. In today's political scene we frequently forget that political parties as we now know them were not provided for in the plan of our founding fathers. They fervently hoped that the government could operate without faction and contending interests, and that the people would exercise sober judgment in selecting the leaders,

[4]Adrienne Koch and William Peden, eds., *The Life and Selected Writings of Thomas Jefferson* (New York: The Modern Library, Inc., 1944).

[5]The broadest possible connotation of the word *group* is intended here. We will define and describe groups extensively in many places throughout this book. Here, the connotation of any face-to-face coming together of individuals will suffice for the definition of the word.

who in turn would ensure that the government operated in the interests of the people.[6] But political parties appeared nonetheless.

It is well known that the causes of the Civil War went far beyond the issue of slavery. The economic situations developing in the North and the South were creating sharply different kinds of relationships between workers and employers, farmers and businessmen, and, in general, the people and their government. The Civil War doomed the group structure developing in the South and accelerated the collaborative efforts for economic sufficiency.[7] Farmers' sons moved to cities to work for others, labor unions were born, private ownership began to give way to corporate ownership. The small merchant began to give way to the chain store. The last of the great personal dynasties passed from the scene when the Ford Motor Company incorporated.

Today we do almost everything in groups—the family group, the school group, the business group. The number of voluntary groups attempting to recruit membership is staggering. We decide in groups (sometimes for the sake of improving the decision and sometimes for the sake of avoiding responsibility). We exert influence by means of groups. Citizens' lobbies like the League of Women Voters, Common Cause, and Nader's Raiders are only a few of the organizations backed by millions of people seeking to influence legislation and governmental behavior.

To bring this matter closer to home, make a list of all the groups you belong to. Then add up the time you spend in some kind of collective activity during the week. The amount of collaborative activity—whether with one individual or many—in which we engage is amazing.

Groups Can Be Dangerous

One of the most important books of the 1940s was Erich Fromm's *Escape from Freedom*. In his analysis of pre–World War II Germany, Fromm offered frightening proof that groups can be dangerous. The awful aloneness, he contended, brought about by freedom *from* external restraints of government drove the people of Germany to "escape from freedom." One of Fromm's points was that a part of the basic character of the German people is a need for structure and authority; their escape from individual responsibility led them into one of the most brutal authoritarian regimes the world has ever seen.[8]

Another potential danger of groups stems from the force of group pressure. Several well-known studies by Asch[9] demonstrate that a lone, naive subject in an experimental group begins to doubt his or her own perceptions when all other group members report contradicting information. Groups have both overt and subtle means of punishing deviant behavior and bringing members into line. We will have

[6]For an example of this thinking, see George Washington's Farewell Address, September 17, 1796. One source is Burton Ira Kaufman, comp., *Washington's Farewell Address: The View from the 20th Century* (Chicago: Quadrangle Books, 1969).

[7]The best account of this point of view is that of Charles A. Beard and Mary R. Beard, *The Rise of American Civilization* (New York: The Macmillan Company, 1954).

[8]Fromm, *Escape from Freedom*.

[9]Solomon E. Asch, *Social Psychology* (Englewood Cliffs, N.J.: Prentice-Hall, Inc., 1952). See also Solomon E. Asch, "Studies of Independence and Conformity. A Minority of One Against a Unanimous Majority," *Psychological Monographs*, 70, no. 9 (1956).

more to say about group pressures and conformity when we discuss group norms and forces in Chapters 4, 5, and 14.

David Riesman and his associates, in their book *The Lonely Crowd*, [10] described the emerging character of the day as the *other-directed man*. The other-directed person was extremely dependent on the group because his definition of what is right was determined by what his peers considered right. Unlike the *tradition-directed man*, he could not rely on the established order for security; he lacked the independent judgment of the *inner-directed man*. Riesman was apprehensive about a society dominated by people whose main concern was to discover what it is popular to think and feel, whose only goal in life was getting more and more of what society thought the successful man ought to acquire, and who believed that the pathway to heaven is found by "getting on the team."

Years later, at the height of student unrest and campus demonstrations, Riesman was interviewed for an article in *Psychology Today*. The magazine's editor, T George Harris, wrote:

> Not many observers, not even in sociology, realize how sensitive Riesman has been to each innovation in student belief until today he is no longer talking about the lonely crowd—but about their children. They are very different from their teachers and parents.
>
> Throughout the conversation, you will notice, Riesman constantly points up distinctive student traits: a preference for feeling over thinking, an emphasis on the subjective, a belief in "one's own inner juices." He describes the student "cult of intimacy." Other-directed people were never like this. [11]

Writing in the same issue of *Psychology Today*, Hadden reported that the key trait that emerged from his study of college seniors was *privatism*. He wrote:

> This generation rejects meaning or authority outside of the self. If the organization slave or other-directed man saw his existence in harmony with social institutions, the new style of privatism not only cries for freedom from established institutions, it fundamentally rejects their legitimacy. [12]

Privatism, most often described as "doing your own thing," seems to be antithetical to a functioning, cohesive group. Hadden's fear was that the kind of romantic withdrawal into self exhibited by those he studied could also be an escape from responsibility to others and to society.

Privatism is not only unrealistic; it reveals as deep a dependence on groups and authority as that of the other-directed man, if only because the practitioner of privatism needs them to rebel against. It isn't feasible today to be self-sufficient; collaborative efforts are required to grow food, make clothing, provide transportation and education, offer health services, run governments. The United States is a

---

[10]David Riesman, with Nathan Glazer and Reuel Denney, *The Lonely Crowd: A Study of the Changing American Character* (Garden City, N.Y.: Doubleday & Co., Inc., 1953).

[11]T George Harris, "Editorial: The Children of the Lonely Crowd," *Psychology Today*, 3, no. 5 (1969), 26.

[12]Jeffrey K. Hadden, "The Private Generation," *Psychology Today*, 3, no. 5 (1969), 32.

nation composed primarily of white-collar workers *who do not produce anything tangible.* Many of us are teachers, lawyers, doctors, salespeople, public relations people, scientists, or managers, whose only tangible products are likely to be pieces of paper containing certain ideas. Human dependence on groups has been repeatedly demonstrated by research and analysis. [13]

THE PRESERVATION OF THE INDIVIDUAL

So we are brought back to the dilemma: How can we preserve individual choice, integrity, and dignity and still participate in productive, collaborative, and meaningful relationships with others? We think there is a way.

Start With a Liberal Education

There are three key constituents of a liberal education: understanding ourselves, understanding the groups in which we participate, and understanding the process of communication. Equipped with knowledge in these areas, we need not choose between being individuals and relating meaningfully to others. Both goals are essential to healthy individuals; both can be achieved.

Understanding Ourselves. Part of the growing-up process is wondering about identity. (Am I really the "me" I think I am? Am I the person other people see? Must I always be the way I am or can I change?)

The self-concept, what we think we are, is central to our being. It is shaped by environment, by the people who have influenced our lives, and by countless numbers of interactions, including successes and failures. Have you ever found yourself thinking "Why did I do that?" or "How could I have said that?" or "That wasn't like me"? You were going through the process of changing your self-concept. We all have differing *degrees* of awareness of self at different times. What's more, each of us has many selves.

Some of us see ourselves in terms of roles (student, teacher, wife, husband, chairperson); some focus on perceived strengths (outgoing personality, likeableness, ability to work hard); some have self-concepts based on apparent weaknesses (shyness, confused state of mind, laziness); some see ourselves in physical terms (tall, overweight, brown-eyed). Knowing where we come from, psychologically speaking, is vital to understanding ourselves; knowing where others come from is equally vital to understanding communication.

Understanding yourself is obviously a lifelong task. It is primarily an individual one. The individual does not need a group to read a book, however much book-study clubs may help. Individuals do not need a group to listen to music, to observe the beauties of the world, to think, reflect, or pray. The injunction "Love thy neighbor as thy self," assumes that a person has a healthy concept of a self that can be loved.

Even though the introspection needed for self-understanding is an individual's task, it cannot take place in a vacuum. As Keltner said,

[13]See, for example, Paul V. Crosbie, "Man's Dependence on Groups," in *Interaction in Small Groups,* sec. I-A (New York: The Macmillan Company, 1975), pp. 12–35.

Knowledge of self is developed in part from the experience of learning how other people perceive us. *If we are to understand ourselves, we must get information from other people about ourselves.* [14]

Each of of brings a unique identity to the groups in which we participate. Each of us plays a somewhat different role in different groups. The successful group participant learns to balance his or her own needs and desires and those of the group. [15] We will further develop the ideas of self-concept and personality in Chapter 5, "Group Forces."

Understanding Groups. If we do not understand the nature of groups and the ways people think and act in groups, we may not be able to relate meaningfully to others. Such understanding must be more than a textbook understanding; it must come from relating principles of group behavior to actual group experiences. Much of this book is, naturally, devoted to discussions of group behavior principles and to suggestions for actually testing and observing these principles in action.

It is essential to understand groups if we are to be successful group members. Bumbling along and hoping that "shooting the bull" will magically turn into productive discussion is futile and frustrating. We need to know specifically why some groups are more effective than others and why a collection of individuals is not necessarily a group. Reading this book is a beginning. But gaining experience by seeking out opportunities to participate and observe is an essential corollary.

We cannot emphasize enough the necessity of learning about discussion by discussing. To truly understand the potentials of a successful group, a person needs to have been a part of a group that actually accomplished something. It is distressing to hear people say, "I avoid groups because they are all talk, talk, and no action," or "I always wind up doing all the work so I might as well be on my own from the beginning." Such expressions are usually the words of a frustrated person who has been "assigned" to a group but doesn't understand what group forces are or how to use them productively. Some people, including some teachers, think that if you put people together you will automatically have "discussion." Talk, chitchat, or conversation are almost automatic when you group people, but not real discussion.

But, once a person has had the heady, exhilarating experience of being a member of a truly successful group, he or she is much more apt to be tolerant of the time and the struggle it takes for a collection of people to become a group. There is a decided sparkle and a warm climate to a successful group. We know it is worth working for and so we keep trying.

Understanding Communication. Interpersonal relationships can only be established and maintained through the medium of communication. Obvious as this truism is, it is frequently neglected. Those who wish to be effective in group situations must begin with an understanding of rational thought and continue with an understanding of the principles and methods for transmitting and receiving ideas and feelings.

[14]John W. Keltner, *Interpersonal Speech-Communication, Elements and Structures* (Belmont, Calif.: Wadsworth Publishing Company, Inc., 1970), p. 46.

[15]See Kenneth J. Gergen, "The Healthy, Happy Human Being Wears Many Masks: Multiple Identity," *Psychology Today*, 5, no. 12 (1972), 31–35, 64–66.

It is no accident that three of the fastest-growing disciplines in colleges and universities throughout the nation are psychology, behavioral science, and communication. People have begun to place increased value on the knowledge and skills inherent in these fields. Scholars from widely divergent disciplines have incorporated principles of communication as central to their work. Such disciplines include engineering, business administration, education, anthropology, political science, sociology, criminal justice, linguistics, and emerging areas such as Black Studies and Women's Studies. What's even more remarkable is that scholars in these diverse disciplines are beginning to communicate *with each other* (a comparative rarity in the academic community). Our understanding of principles of communication today is vastly richer than even a few years ago. Chapters 6 and 7 are devoted to the more important principles involved in small group communication.

These three steps—understanding ourselves, understanding groups, and understanding communication—are not panaceas; neither are they easy to achieve. But they could well be the tools Maslow had in mind when he described his "hierarchy of needs" and how people strive to achieve the highest order of need, self-fulfillment or *self-actualization.* According to Maslow, it need not be a struggle of the individual versus the group, but a mutual sustaining of each: The interests of the individual and of society are not of necessity mutually exclusive and antagonistic. The main function of a healthy culture may well be the fostering of universal self-actualization.[16]

SUMMARY

We have traced the history of the concept of the individual versus the group, and we have looked at it in terms of present-day needs. There really is no choice between the individual and the group; both must be reckoned with and both are interacting phenomena, particularly in a democracy.

In addition, we have recommended that you study the following three subjects in order to preserve individual integrity, while fully functioning in group relationships: (1) understanding yourself, (2) understanding groups, and (3) understanding communication.

DISCUSSION QUESTIONS

1.   What forces in contemporary society tend to foster individualism? What forces tend to foster conformity?

2.   What is the place of rugged individualism in our society?

3.   In your experience with groups so far, how would you characterize your most successful group experience?

4.   Describe your most frustrating group experience. How were the people or the circumstances different from the group identified in question 3?

5.   What are the circumstances or conditions that make you feel you are losing your individual viewpoint or rights? Describe what group members do or say that makes you feel that way.

[16]Abraham H. Maslow, *Toward a Psychology of Being* (New York: D. Van Nostrand Company, Inc., 1968), p. 159.

EXERCISES

1.   Make a list of those beliefs, actions, policies, attitudes, or standards in which you would be willing to conform to social pressure. Make a second list of the ones where you would not be willing to conform.

2.   Select one or more of the problems, situations, or forces you have listed in exercise 1 and organize an informal discussion with members of the class.

3.   Divide the class into three groups. Have Group A discuss one of the questions listed in the preceding section, while the other two groups observe. Have Group B look for the aspects that help the group and have Group C look for those aspects that hinder the group. Allow about ten minutes for members of Groups B and C to compare notes and prepare an informal group report to the class. Can you always distinguish between and/or agree upon the aspects that help and the aspects that hinder?

4.   With several other members of the class, conduct an informal survey among friends, or perhaps among residents of selected areas, concerning their (a) vocations, (b) the two or three things they most desire in life, and (c) the organizations or clubs to which they belong. Can you find any relationships between the three sets of data? Report your findings and conclusions to the class.

5.   Attempt to avoid all group activity and association for at least a day. Try not to engage in conversation; remain alone. For your own benefit, record how you feel during this period and when you reestablish your group relationships. Note how difficult it is to isolate yourself.

SELECTED READINGS

APPLBAUM, RONALD L., EDWARD M. BODAKEN, KENNETH K. SERENO, AND KARL W. E. ANATOL, *The Process of Group Communication*. Chicago: Science Research Associates Inc., 1974.

BORMANN, ERNEST G., *Discussion and Group Methods: Theory and Practice* (2nd ed.), chap. 1. New York: Harper & Row, Publishers, 1975.

BRILHART, JOHN K., *Effective Group Discussion*. Dubuque, Iowa: William C. Brown Company, Publishers, 1967.

CATHCART, ROBERT S., AND LARRY A. SAMOVAR, eds., *Small Group Communication: A Reader* (2nd ed.). Dubuque, Iowa: William C. Brown Company, Publishers, 1974.

DAVIS, JAMES H., *Group Performance*. Reading, Mass.: Addison-Wesley Publishing Co., Inc., 1969.

GOLDBERG, ALVIN A., AND CARL E. LARSON, *Group Communication: Discussion Processes and Applications*, chap. 4. Englewood Cliffs, N.J.: Prentice-Hall, Inc., 1975.

KING, STEPHEN W., *Communication and Social Influence*. Reading, Mass.: Addison-Wesley Publishing Co., Inc., 1975.

MASLOW, ABRAHAM H., *Toward a Psychology of Being*. New York: D. Van Nostrand Company, Inc., 1968.

chapter 2

"Shall we call a meeting," the businessman asks, "or assign this problem to different individuals?" "Would discussion or lecture be the better way to get this material across to the class?" wonders the teacher. These are some of the questions this chapter seeks to answer.

Collaborative behavior is obviously necessary, as we have said, but sometimes individual behavior is more desirable. We are dealing with the form of collaborative behavior called *discussion,* and our question is this: What are the relative advantages and disadvantages of discussion *as a method,* particularly when compared to individual behavior?

DISCUSSION DEFINED

Discussion is the process whereby two or more people exchange information or ideas in a face-to-face situation to achieve a goal. The goal, or end product, may be increased knowledge, agreement leading to action, disagreement leading to competition or resolution, or perhaps only a clearing of the air or a continuation of the status quo. The goal may be prearranged or spontaneously decided.

Many writers define discussion in much more specific terms. They include such restrictions as "under the direction of a leader," or "following a pattern of reflective thinking." We feel that little is gained by such restrictiveness.

Bormann includes another element, which appeals to us, when he says, "Group discussion refers to one or more meetings of a small group of people who thereby communicate, face to face, in order to fulfill a common purpose and achieve a group goal."[1] We like the "one or more meetings" phrase because, as we discussed in the Preface, effective groups are usually ongoing as opposed to the one-time-only gathering so often used in group methods research. Our definition, like Bormann's, includes both short-term and long-term groups.

At the risk of adding too many qualifying elements to our definition, we include Crosbie's idea that people in a small group also share a set of standards governing their activities,[2] and Steiner's concept that group members are "mutually responsive."[3]

Note that our definition does not cover large groups where interaction (including the sending and receiving of *nonverbal* messages) is impossible. There is no magic number that separates a "large" group from a small one, but we feel that the group

[1]Ernest G. Bormann, *Discussion and Group Methods: Theory and Practice,* 2nd ed. (New York: Harper & Row, Publishers, 1975), p. 3.

[2]Paul V. Crosbie, *Interaction in Small Groups* (New York: The Macmillan Company, 1975), p. 2.

[3]Ivan D. Steiner, *Group Process and Productivity* (New York: Academic Press, Inc., 1972), p. 5.

Advantages and Limitations of Discussion

becomes large when it is not possible for members who want to participate to do so freely. This generally begins when groups have more than 15 members. A comfortably sized small group has seven or eight members. When a group numbers nine or more, a good deal of self-discipline is required to ensure equal opportunity for all to participate—not just for the most vocal. We will have more to say about group size in Chapter 5.

Also note that our definition excludes groups of people who are not in the same location (such as those involved in a conference telephone call). It also excludes those who, because of the physical setting of the meeting place, cannot be face to face. Picture the rows of chairs often found in the traditional classroom and you will realize that the physical setting itself precludes interaction. We would, therefore, not define the resulting one-way communication (teacher to students) or one-to-one communication (teacher to one student at a time) as discussion.

With these definitions in mind, let's examine some of the advantages and limitations of discussion as a method. We will assume that we are writing about reasonably able, mature, sensitive, and well-meaning people because there is no purpose in assembling a group of the unfit around a conference table in order to pool their ignorance.

ADVANTAGES OF DISCUSSION AS A METHOD

We believe the following are the principal advantages of discussion: (1) two heads are frequently better than one; (2) people tend to carry out decisions they have helped make; (3) discussion can change individual attitudes and behavior; (4) discussion can frequently develop the individual; and (5) discussion can help satisfy social needs.

Two Heads Are Frequently Better Than One

Early research on discussion primarily attempted to compare the relative advantages of individual and group work. A host of experiments and tasks was employed to test this question. For instance, one experiment investigated whether individuals, after discussion, were better able to estimate the number of beans in a bottle. Other experiments dealt with whether time estimations, ethical and aesthetic judgments, and the like, were improved after discussion.[4] The majority of these experimental tasks involved making judgments or expressing preferences.

According to Dickens and Heffernan, these were the major conclusions of the studies: (1) Extreme judgments tend to become less extreme. (2) Judgments tend to improve. (3) The majority influences the individual judgments. (4) Right answers are supported more tenaciously than wrong answers.[5]

Much of this early research offers little support for the claim that two heads are frequently better than one. Results were ambiguous and in many cases showed that *averaged* individual judgments were probably as good as, and perhaps even superior to, the judgments made after discussion.

[4]For a more complete description of earlier studies, see G. B. Watson, "Do Groups Think More Efficiently Than Individuals?" *Journal of Abnormal and Social Psychology*, 23 (1928), 328–36.

[5]Milton Dickens and Marguerite Heffernan, "Experimental Research in Group Discussion," *Quarterly Journal of Speech*, 35 (1949), 23–29.

Shaw conducted some interesting research in which she had her subjects engage in what she called "the rational solution of complex problems."[6] In the experiments the subjects had to create and evaluate various hypotheses as to how certain problems might be solved. Groups seemed to be assured of a much greater proportion of correct solutions than were individuals.

Barnlund's work confirmed Shaw's findings.[7] He engaged his groups in the solution of reasoning problems that involved arguments in which personal feeling was likely to be strong. To eliminate the possibility that group superiority might be caused by the more able members bringing the others up to their level, he placed in each group subjects who had been matched according to ability. His results showed that groups were unquestionably superior to individuals in the solution of the problems.

Because the earlier research failed to show any advantage for group behavior, it pays to look at the kind of tasks these groups were asked to do: They were asked to make judgments or express preferences. But when experimenters used problem-solving situations, the results took a dramatic turn. When groups were presented with a problem to solve, they had to propose hypotheses and present rationales to defend them; contrast this with the hit-and-miss guesswork concerning the number of beans in a bottle.

Steiner made the point that many experimental groups were collections of strangers who were presented with a novel task but were not given enough time to decide how best to work together. He cautioned that comparisons should be made between the productivity of individuals and *organized* groups.[8]

In problem-solving discussions, groups have the advantage over individuals because their combined knowledge and experience can produce more hypotheses and consequently better solutions. The combined critical thinking of everyone in the group is more likely to catch and correct deficiencies in evidence and reasoning. Also, group interaction seems to have a stimulating effect upon the performance of the individuals in the group.

Another point about the differences between judgment-making activity and problem-solving activity should be noted. We must make a sharp distinction between the *making of judgments* and the *creation of criteria* upon which the judgments are to be based. Creating criteria is essentially a problem-solving activity. For example, we assign to legislative bodies the responsibility for developing and stating criteria. We call these criteria *laws* and we measure the behavior of individuals against them. But we assign the responsibility for determining whether specific behavior violates the established criteria to a different class of individuals—judges. Groups sometimes confuse the two functions; more on this in Chapter 10.

Using the review of research studies written by Lorge and associates[9] as a principal reference, Davis pulled together most of the research findings on whether individuals or groups turn out superior results. His conclusion:

[6]Marjorie E. Shaw, "A Comparison of Individuals and Small Groups in the Rational Solution of Complex Problems," in *Readings in Social Psychology*, eds. T. M. Newcomb and E. L. Hartley (New York: Holt, Rinehart and Winston, Inc., 1947), pp. 304–15.

[7]Dean C. Barnlund, "Comparative Study of Individual, Majority and Group Judgment," *Journal of Abnormal and Social Psychology*, 58 (January 1959) 55–60.

[8]Steiner, *Group Process*, pp. 64–65.

[9]I. Lorge and others, "A Survey of Studies Contrasting the Quality of Group Performance and Individual Performance, 1920–1957," *Psychological Bulletin*, 55 (1958), 337–72.

If we were to summarize the comparison of group and individual products, the gross conclusion would be that on most criteria groups *are* generally superior to individuals but that the existence and degree of superiority depend on a number of situational and task factors. . . . If the emphasis is on achieving a *correct* or *good* or *early* answer, then a group has a higher probability of achieving this aim (other things being equal) than does the single individual. [10]

People Tend to Carry Out Decisions They Have Helped to Make

Critics of the group discussion method may concede the first advantage of group discussion we cited. Of course, they say, a group of experts may produce a better solution than any single expert, but one expert will be far superior to any group of nonexperts. True, groups are better than the average individual, but they are seldom better than the best individual. So why not let the expert make the decision and give her or him the power to compel others to carry it out?

Both philosophical and practical questions are raised by this kind of authoritarian stand. But quite apart from whether people have any "right" to participate in the making of decisions that involve them, there are other demonstrable advantages in having them participate in the decision-making process.

People tend to carry out decisions they have helped to form. Consider the widely cited experiment performed by Coch and French at the Harwood Manufacturing Company. [11] The factory produced garments and employed mostly women. Although the management was liberal and progressive and always had the best type of labor relations, great difficulty occurred whenever new production techniques or equipment necessitated changing a worker's job. The traditional procedure was for management to decide on the change and then assign to an expert, such as a time-study man, the task of determining how the change would be effected and what the new piecework rate would be.

Three different procedures were used in the experiment by Coch and French: (1) The first was called the *no-participation* method and was essentially the traditional procedure, in which the employees had no voice in the planning of the change. After the decision was made, an explanation of the change was given to the workers. (2) The second method involved *participation through representation* of the workers, in which a few representatives of the employees worked with the time-study man in establishing both the most effective procedures and the new piecework rates. (3) The third method involved the *total participation* of the workers. Their ideas and opinions were sought and used by the time-study man. In each case, however, the ultimate decision to make a change was made by the management.

The results were dramatic. The no-participation group behaved as similar groups of workers had in the past. Both the participation-through-representation and the total-participation groups relearned their jobs significantly faster and soon surpassed the standard unit production level, with the total-participation group

[10]James H. Davis, *Group Performance* (Reading, Mass.: Addison-Wesley Publishing Co., Inc., 1969), p. 43.

[11]Lester Coch and John R. P. French, Jr., "Overcoming Resistance to Change," in *Group Dynamics: Research and Theory,* 2nd ed., eds. D. Cartwright and A. Zander (Evanston, Ill.: Row, Peterson, 1960), pp. 319–41.

emerging as slightly superior to the participation-through-representation group. Coch and French attributed the difference between the participation groups and the no-participation group to the fact that the former had helped set the new standards and had consequently adopted them as their own. Thus, the workers' own pressures were added to the management-induced pressures to attain a higher standard of work. [12]

An important factor that should be noted is that the Harwood Company did not give its workers the total responsibility for managing the enterprise. The decision to make a change, to introduce new machinery, or to alter the product remained a management responsibility. Not every aspect of every decision that affects a given individual ought to be given to that individual to determine in conference with others. Our complex interdependent society makes such a position impractical.

Discussion Can Change Individual Attitudes and Behavior

Discussion can be of considerable value when the object is to modify individual attitudes and behavior. Certainly, this is the central goal of the classroom and other learning groups. But changed attitudes and behavior can occur (both deliberately and inadvertently) in other kinds of groups as well.

The discussant whose mind is made up *before* the discussion is not likely to hear new ideas or to be open to change. On the other hand, few of us are completely open-minded. Most of us arrive at group sessions with at least some tentative leanings that we have already formed from our previous knowledge of the subject. We try to be objective and to listen fairly, and we like to think that new evidence or persuasive logic will cause us to shift our attitudes, opinions, or beliefs. We may feel an obligation to challenge others' beliefs but our willingness to have our own beliefs challenged and thereby run the risk of having *our* ideas or behavior changed may not be as strong.

Unless we refuse to listen, or unless all the viewpoints expressed coincide with our own, chances are we will experience some change. The change may be minor and not at all central to our ego-state, but we can recognize it as change brought about by discussion. In addition, group discussion provides an ideal forum in which an individual can work out problems of dissonance or internal conflict.

For evidence concerning the assertion that discussion is frequently a desirable method of changing individual attitudes and behavior, we cite the classic study done by Kurt Lewin and his associates at the University of Iowa during World War II. [13] During the war, when meats were rationed and in short supply, housewives refused to buy such cuts as heart, kidney, and sweetbreads, which were plentiful. Lewin's attempt to change food habits, therefore, had practical as well as scientific objectives.

The experiments were conducted among six groups of Red Cross volunteers or-

---

[12]Not everyone agrees with this interpretation. Arensberg, for example, contends that results achieved with small groups can be understood only within the larger framework of an institutional analysis. See Conrad M. Arensberg, "Behavior and Organization: Industrial Studies," in *Social Psychology at the Crossroads*, eds. J. H. Rohrer and M. Sherif (New York: Harper & Row, Publishers, 1951), pt. V, p. 14.

[13]Kurt Lewin, "Group Decision and Social Change," in *Readings in Social Psychology*, eds. Newcomb and Hartley, pp. 330–44.

ganized for home nursing. In three of these groups (ranging from 13 to 17 members) well-presented lectures pointed out the nutritional values of the meats, the desirability of cooperating with the war effort, and means to prepare the meats to mask any objectionable odor, texture, or appearance. The lecturer distributed recipes and described ways she herself prepared these meats for her own family.

In the remaining three groups the discussion method was employed. After an introduction that linked the problem of nutrition to the war effort, the housewives participated in discussion about whether "housewives like themselves" could be induced to use these meats. Naturally, the women raised questions about the objectionable characteristics of the meats and asked how these obstacles could be overcome. The same information about recipes and menus was given to these women, *but only after the women themselves had raised the problems.* At the end of the meeting the women indicated by a show of hands whether they were willing to try one of these meats within the next week.

The follow-up revealed that only 3 percent of the women exposed only to the lecture actually served one of the meats, but *32 percent of the women participating in the discussion served a meat never before served.*

Bennis and his associates devoted an entire part of their book to the subject of personal change through interpersonal relationships, on the assumption that "almost any change in behavior, beliefs, attitudes, and values is mediated by interpersonal relationships of one kind or another."[14] Using concepts developed earlier by Lewin, they have identified the process and mechanisms of change as stage 1, *unfreezing* (creating motivation to change); stage 2, *changing* (developing new responses based on new information); and stage 3, *refreezing* (stabilizing and integrating the changes).[15]

Building on these same aspects of change, Schein and Bennis have pointed out that unfreezing can occur when a person draws different items of information from different people or when he identifies with another person and sees himself from that person's perspective.[16] Schein and Bennis have also discussed the various ways that groups and organizations work *against* individual change, explaining "probably the major obstacle is that change in one person generally involves change in a whole network of relationships."[17]

Just what forces and dynamics in the group are specifically responsible for bringing about change in the individual is not clear. Majority pressure, active involvement, and discussants' skills—as well as forces within each individual—may individually or collectively be responsible. Until we can identify and study all the interacting variables, our understanding of the causes of change will be incomplete. Suffice it to say now that discussion has been demonstrated to be an effective means of changing individual attitudes and behavior.

[14]Warren G. Bennis and others, *Interpersonal Dynamics: Essays and Readings on Human Interaction* (Homewood, Ill.: The Dorsey Press, 1964), p. 357.

[15]Bennis and others, *Interpersonal Dynamics*, p. 363.

[16]Edgar H. Schein and Warren G. Bennis, *Personal and Organizational Change Through Group Methods* (New York: John Wiley & Sons, Inc., 1967), p. 281.

[17]Schein and Bennis, *Personal and Organizational Change*, p. 282.

Discussion Can Frequently Develop the Individual

Although certain personality types do not seem to profit from participation in discussion, most people do profit. Both experimentation and experience support this assertion.

First, the individual is able to learn from participation. In many ways this can be more effective than learning from reading or listening to lectures because the information and ideas contributed by others are considered in the dynamic framework of problem analysis and solution. If the individual participates fully in the discussion process, the ideas acquired should have greater meaning, since they were generated under circumstances that involved the individual more completely. According to Flynn and LaFaso, "The [discussion] form of participation is such that the material learned becomes more *meaningful* to the learner because he must constantly rephrase the information in his own terms. . . . Discussion thrusts the learner immediately into the process, and makes him the active seeker and inquirer."[18] The discussant not only absorbs information but also gains a wide range of group communication skills.

Second, participating in the discussion process will probably improve the discussant's skills in relating meaningfully to others. It would be very difficult for an individual participating in a good discussion to fail to respond to the others in the situation. The group gives individuals both stimulation and reinforcement; it offers invaluable opportunities to learn how to develop satisfactory interpersonal relationships; and it consistently demonstrates the values of collaborative efforts as opposed to competitive ones.

Finally, the discussant will be able to learn more about the people in the group. An intensive exchange about a vital matter cannot help but reveal a good deal about the individuals themselves. Since facility in taking, understanding, and appreciating the role of another person is of prime importance in the development of the individual, it follows that a greater understanding of other people in action should be of considerable benefit to the individual.

Discussion Can Help Satisfy Social Needs

We join groups to satisfy needs for affiliation, identification, and inclusion as well as to gather emotional and intellectual support. "Safety in numbers" and "strength in unity" are more than slogans. Most of us need and depend on group aid and support.

There is more than just psychological support in the fact that it is a group rather than an individual who believes in a given cause or is working to solve a certain problem. The visibility of numbers is a message in itself. More than one organization has rounded up bystanders and even schoolchildren to swell the ranks of a demonstration or march, thereby gaining the appearance of more importance and wider support.

As pointed out by Hampton, Summer, and Webber, groups do more than help the

---

[18]Elizabeth W. Flynn and John F. LaFaso, *Group Discussion As Learning Process* (New York: Paulist Press, 1972), pp. 102–3.

individual solve very specific problems: They can also protect people from making costly mistakes.[19] The new employee finds it far easier to check with co-workers than to keep running to the boss. Similarly, the student feels much more freedom to "ask dumb questions" of other students than of the teacher.

LIMITATIONS OF DISCUSSION AS A METHOD

As with most things, discussion has limitations as well as advantages. The main ones are that: (1) discussion takes time; (2) discussion requires skill; (3) discussion dilutes individual responsibility; and (4) discussion doesn't work in emergencies. In addition, the following are potentially limiting factors: status differences, value differences, majority pressure, prior commitments, and certain personalities.

Discussion Takes Time

People who work for organizations or contribute time to volunteer groups often feel that they spend the better part of their lives in meetings. You've heard the old—and somewhat bitter—cliches like "Committees keep minutes but waste hours," and "A camel is a horse designed by a committee." There is really no shortcut to the time required for a group of people to explore issues and make decisions. The more people in the group, the more time must be allotted for people just to be heard. Beyond the simple mathematical progression, however, is the increased number of communication interactions that must be accounted for when people are added to a group. More will be said about this in Chapter 6.

Time may be saved in a variety of ways through increased knowledge and skill in discussion procedures. The material in this book should help the reader effect time savings in discussion groups.

Discussion Requires Skill

A collection of people does not automatically become a group and a rambling conversation does not turn into an effective discussion all by itself. We have all observed inept discussions where goals were not clearly defined and members' contributions seemed to go around in circles instead of forward. Many different forces and problems can cause even skilled discussants to be ineffective but untrained individuals have less hope for success.

One illustration of this limitation comes through our contacts with the Federal Mediation and Conciliation Service (FMCS). Successful labor–management negotiations are a function of the skill not only of the mediator but also of labor and management representatives. Many bitter labor disputes have erupted because of poor negotiation. One FMCS commissioner summed it up when he said that an equitable agreement is not so much a function of the relative power of the contending parties as it is a function of their skill in negotiations.

---

[19]David R. Hampton, Charles E. Summer, and Ross A. Webber, *Organizational Behavior and the Practice of Management* (Glenview, Ill.: Scott, Foresman & Co., 1973), p. 217.

Discussion Dilutes Individual Responsibility

At first glance the dilution of individual responsibility may seem to be an advantage of discussion. In certain ways it is; it provides for many points of view. However, the sharing of responsibility means that there is frequently less compulsion for each member to produce something of value. A person cannot afford to be ill prepared when presenting a speech or briefing. A discussant, on the other hand, can frequently come to the group with little preparation and still participate. Since the total responsibility is not upon any one person's shoulders, the individual member is tempted to let the others carry the ball of preparation and study, while merely observing and evaluating others' contributions. If a sizable segment of a group adopts this attitude, the quality of the group discussion is considerably reduced.

There are ways to deal with the problem of diluted individual responsibility. In groups such as executive committees, where each person has a specific responsibility, the rest of the group relies on individual expertise. The tax attorney gives expert opinion concerning the way the proposed plan involves the tax laws, the production manager presents data concerning production aspects of the problem, and so on. In student groups, research assignments can be divided so that, in effect, each group member is an "expert" on one aspect of the problem. Unfortunately, delegating responsibilities to group members is not always feasible.

Discussion Doesn't Work in Emergencies

If the building we are in is on fire, there is little opportunity to discuss alternative solutions to the problem. Decisions have to be made in an authoritarian fashion. Time pressures preclude the effective use of discussion.

This, however, is a minor limitation of the discussion process. Many problems can be anticipated and most groups can plan the skeleton of a policy to guide them during an actual emergency. Also, most emergencies can be handled with some type of group action if proper communication channels are established in advance. Finally, the executive in a situation where an emergency decision must be made should make a decision and later voluntarily submit it to the group for an examination of the wisdom of both the decision and the executive's assumption of an emergency situation. Such action will protect executives from the unpleasant repercussions that may follow if the group begins to challenge their unilateral behavior.

Potential Limiting Factors

The following aspects of group life *can* be limiting factors, especially if they occur in inexperienced or immature groups.

Status Differences. Everyone has observed this limitation in operation. In teacher–student committees, teachers have frequently inhibited the potential contributions of the students; employer–employee conferences often fail for the same reason. We have observed many instances in which groups composed of military men of different ranks tended to restrict free discussion. The mere presence of the colonel causes a certain strain on the captain. (We have even observed officers who tried to make their contributions in rank order!)

The cause of this limitation is in the participants themselves and the degree to which they are affected by status differences. Some people seem particularly cowed in the presence of those of higher status, and some who possess this higher status seem to be afraid it will be overlooked. If the subject for discussion bears any relationship to the status levels of participants, those of higher status should be more competent to discuss the subject. For this reason, the opinions of those of higher status might be assumed to carry more weight. This in itself is no limitation; the limitation arises when the participants assume that the pronouncements of those of higher status should automatically be followed without further analysis or verification.

Relief from this limitation must generally come from those possessing higher status. Though we observed many discussions in which the colonel's presence inhibited the captain's contributions, we hasten to add that we have also observed many instances in which the colonel was able to dispel a great deal of the reluctance to contribute by demonstrating that he was capable of drawing people out and of listening to, as well as contributing to, free and objective discussion.

Regardless of the security, insight, skill, and tact of the higher-status person, however, we might as well recognize the influence of status differences as a fact of group life. The problem is further complicated when the person of higher status also possesses the power to reward or punish. There is no way that a teacher, with the power of the grade book, can be just one of the group, no matter how much he or she would like to be. It is impossible for a university or college department chairman to be on equal footing with department members when the chairman is the one who submits salary, promotion, and tenure recommendations.

Age plays a part in status differences. The higher-status individual is apt to be older and may view a problem from a different perspective. The older person has had more experience, not only in life generally, but also with groups and with the problem under discussion. He or she also has had greater contacts with influential people and agencies. Understandably, younger persons may get lost in a discussion group made up of older persons. They simply will not be able to match their grasp of historical antecedents or experience in solving similar problems, nor should they be expected to. We applaud the move to involve more students in the decision-making process; we feel, however, that the student's main value should be to provide input *from a student's point of view*. Students should not be expected to bring the same understandings and skills to the group as their elders. Like those of higher status, older people have the responsibility for resisting the urge to dominate and for ameliorating the situation by careful listening and patient (not patronizing) explanation.

Value Differences. Sharply differing value systems can limit the decision-making potential of the group since the members may find it impossible to agree upon common goals. Some people find it impossible to submit their values to scrutiny; their values are both personal and sacred and they refuse even to explain the rationale behind them.

Ideally, a discussion group is composed of heterogeneous participants with differing interests, attitudes, and values. Such individuals have much more to discuss than those who are in agreement about everything. More will be said about the problem of value differences in relation to conflict resolution in Chapter 11.

Majority Pressure. Majority pressure can cause groups to be ineffective. Occasionally time pressure can cause a group to make expedient rather than wise decisions; sometimes a majority can railroad decisions over the objections of minorities to the detriment of all.

Another cause of majority pressure can occur in what Janis calls *groupthink*, which is what happens when "concurrence-seeking becomes so dominant in a cohesive ingroup that it tends to override realistic appraisal of alternative courses of action."[20] Some groups become obsessed with consensus and unanimity and exert powerful social pressures on the individual who dares to question.

Skilled leadership is required to counteract this limitation. Maier and Solem, for example, found that an effective discussion leader can help a minority make itself felt.[21] All groups should be alert to ways they can integrate rather than override minority viewpoints.

Prior Commitments. Diplomats at international conferences are limited by commitments to their own countries; legislators are limited by commitments to their constituents. Whenever the membership of the group is composed of those who represent others not present, this limitation is operative. It arises not only because the prior commitment may blind representatives to alternative ways of looking at the problem, but also because they must return to the group they represent and justify their behavior or secure further directions. The union business agent who cannot "sell the membership" stands to lose both the contract and the job.

Certain Personalities. The authoritarian personality will not find most types of discussion situations a rewarding experience. This person becomes so obsessed with the rules and procedures that he or she finds the give-and-take of most informal discussion procedures frustrating. Such people often prefer a session governed by strict parliamentary procedure. They prefer an authority or expert to a group of peers and desire the stability that seems to come from clearly established policy. The type of relationship with others that they desire makes it impossible for them to have any real kind of flexibility or individual freedom. They would probably concede only the first of our advantages of discussion as a method, and then only under rigorously controlled circumstances.

Another person who does not benefit greatly from participation in the discussion process is the other-directed person. This may seem like a strange assertion since the other-directed person wants so badly to do things with others. However, such individuals may become so obsessed with harmonious relationships that they fail to follow the substance of the discussion. Because their primary focus is on personal and social adjustment, they probably won't learn much. The generation and analysis of ideas, plus the real and potential conflict involved in testing them, are things they avoid. Social acceptance may be easier and more comfortable than the hazards of exploring reality with consequent threat of alienation.

Also, some individuals can become addicted to groups and group processes and, regardless of the goal or outcome, achieve a certain kind of euphoria from together-

[20]Irving L. Janis, "Groupthink," *Psychology Today,* 5 (1971), p. 43.

[21]Norman R. F. Maier and Allen R. Solem, "The Contributions of a Discussion Leader to the Quality of Group Thinking: The Effective Use of Minority Opinions," in *Group Dynamics* (1960), eds. Cartwright and Zander, pp. 561–72.

ness. Proliferating encounter, therapy, and sensitivity training groups have spawned a whole cult of attendees who go from one group session to another, looking for the elusive magic answer. A frightening aspect is that these people may place themselves in the hands of amateurs. "Should I join a T-group, or a Transactional Analysis, a Gestalt, or a sensory-awareness group? Should the leader be a psychiatrist, an artist, a tape recorder, or one of us?"[22]

We are not negating the good that can come from these specialized groups if they are run by competent trainers, but we do worry about the phenomenon of the professional group-goer.

Thus the benefits to be derived from participation in discussion are a function of the goals for which the individual is striving. If supervisors in a factory delegate part of their decision-making capacity to the workers (as in the Harwood experiment), they give up the goal of dominating the decision-making process in favor of the goal of securing greater productivity of the workers. Most of the time the goal choices are not as specific as they appear in this example, but the insecure person (and we call the extreme forms of both the authoritarian personality and the other-directed person fundamentally insecure) would have considerable difficulty profiting in any way from the discussion situation. This person would find the modification of goals too high a price.

SUMMARY

In this chapter we defined small group discussion from the perspective that underlies this book. We showed how discussion is a valuable method of handling a variety of problems. We identified the principal advantages and limitations of the discussion method and concluded with the examination of some potential limitations. It must be obvious that under some circumstances, aspects of groups identified as advantages could become limitations—and limitations could become advantages. What's more, to maximize advantages and lessen disadvantages requires intelligent and facilitative group effort and leadership.

DISCUSSION QUESTIONS

1. What are the implications of the trend in our political life to substitute organizational for individual communications to elected representatives? For example, the present tendency would be for the Isaac Walton League to write a congressman rather than have individual fishermen communicate. Does this have any relationship to the limitations of discussion?

2. Consider what specific policies or actions can be adopted by a discussion leader to minimize the limitations of discussion.

3. In view of the cultural and social forces to which the individual is subject, what potential exists for overcoming the limitations of discussion?

[22]Morton A. Lieberman, Irvin D. Yalom, and Matthew B. Miles, "Encounter: The Leader Makes the Difference," *Psychology Today*, 6 (1973), 71. See also Renata Adler, "The Thursday Group," *New Yorker*, 43 (1967), 55–146.

4.   To what extent are the advantages and limitations stated in this chapter modified when the group members differ significantly in such matters as age, ability, experience, authority, or education?

EXERCISES

1.   Attend a meeting of a student governing body, a city council, a school board, or a similar legislative body. Prepare a 400–600 word analysis of the meeting. Base your analysis on the information in this chapter.

2.   Compile a list of realistic or practical problem situations where you feel discussion could be used profitably. Describe each situation in one paragraph; in a second paragraph justify your choice.

3.   Compile a list of cases or situations you have observed where discussion was improperly used and should not have been employed. For each case, describe the situation in one paragraph and follow it with a one-paragraph explanation or analysis of the causes of failure.

4.   Analyze the limitations of discussion covered in this chapter and prepare a list of changes in ability, knowledge, behavior, or attitude that would be required to change disadvantages to advantages.

5.   On the basis of the material in this chapter, prepare a list for your instructor of the information and skills you would like to acquire in order to become an effective discussant.

SELECTED READINGS

BENNIS, WARREN G., EDGAR H. SCHEIN, DAVID E. BERLEW, AND FRED I. STEELE, *Interpersonal Dynamics: Essays and Readings on Human Interaction*, pt. III. Homewood, Ill.: The Dorsey Press, 1964.

BURGOON, MICHAEL, JUDEE K. HESTON, AND JAMES C. MCCROSKEY, *Small Group Communication, A Functional Approach*, chap. 1. New York: Holt, Rinehart and Winston, Inc., 1974.

CATHCART, ROBERT S., AND LARRY A. SAMOVAR, eds., *Small Group Communication: A Reader* (2nd ed.), sec. I. Dubuque, Iowa: William C. Brown Company, Publishers, 1974.

FROMM, ERICH, "The Theory of Love," in *Bridges Not Walls*, ed. John Stewart, pp. 266–82. Reading, Mass.: Addison-Wesley Publishing Co., Inc., 1973.

GOLDBERG, ALVIN A., AND CARL E. LARSON, *Group Communication: Discussion Processes and Applications*, chaps. 1–4. Englewood Cliffs, N.J.: Prentice-Hall, Inc., 1975.

SCHEIN, EDGAR H., AND WARREN G. BENNIS, *Personal and Organizational Change Through Group Methods*, chaps. 14, 15. New York: John Wiley & Sons, Inc., 1967.

chapter 3

The purpose of this chapter is to examine the nature of discussion in our society by identifying its purposes and circumstances. In the previous chapters, we attempted to put value judgments upon our analyses of discussion and the individual participants. Here the emphasis is on description rather than on evaluation. Instead of describing how discussion *ought* to function, we describe how it *does* function today.

We are going to answer two questions: Why do people discuss? Under what circumstances do they discuss? The first question refers to the purposes, goals, and objectives that may be inferred from observing a given discussion. The second question refers to the conditions under which the group meets and to the different forms of discussion (explained in the last section of the chapter).

Before proceeding, here are two warnings: First, there is no magic in naming something. Giving something a name does not result in any physical change in the thing that is named, but often it affects our perception of the thing or the idea. Assigning a name can serve a useful function if we understand the basis for the classification and if that classification helps us make meaningful distinctions so that our attention is called to things we might otherwise have missed.

Second, the classifications of purposes and circumstances are not mutually exclusive; neither does a given discussion usually have only one purpose. It may have several. The reason for the classification is to enable the observer to discover the central tendencies of the discussion as a basis for analysis.

DISCUSSION PURPOSES

A convenient way to describe purposes for discussion is to group them according to those that are essentially *personal* and those that are essentially *task*. Such a division is neither exhaustive nor mutually exclusive but it provides a helpful way of viewing the process. Personal purposes are those having their origins primarily within the individual and relating most directly to the satisfaction of ego-centered needs and drives. In contrast, task purposes are those of a more objective and impersonal character. They tend to be external in origin (although they may come to have a large personal component) and relate to the substance of the discussion.

PERSONAL PURPOSES

Social Purposes

Sometimes people engage in group discussion for primarily social reasons. Most discussions over coffee, over back fences, and at parties are primarily

Functions of Discussion in Our Society

social. Individual goals in such discussions range from whiling the time away as pleasantly as possible to deliberately attempting to strengthen interpersonal relationships, promote status, or secure good will.

Beware of the tendency to sneer at this activity by labeling it as mere chitchat or socially acceptable noise or small talk required by etiquette. Perhaps the substance of most social discussion is of little moment, but it is equally true that social discussion is often the prelude to considerations of more significant subjects. Even the most inane exchange ("Hot enough for you?" "Yes, indeed.") may contain a reaching out for recognition of our existence and our humanness. What's more, the establishment of a climate conducive to effective decision-making is not an unimportant objective.

The concern with social discussion in this book is primarily with its use as a part of, or prelude to, discussions that include task-oriented purposes. However, much that is said of establishing favorable group climate and interpersonal relations could easily apply to discussions whose primary or sole objective is social.

Cathartic Purposes

Closely related to social discussion is cathartic discussion, which gives individuals an opportunity to relieve their tensions, fears, gripes, apprehensions, and aspirations in a group—in short, to blow off steam. Bull sessions or counseling interviews are examples. Cathartic discussions differ from social discussions in that they exist primarily to deal with personal rather than interpersonal problems. Cathartic discussions may lead to nothing more than an expression of personal feelings, but often, like social discussions, they are a prelude to personal or collaborative problem-solving.

Care must be taken not to dismiss cathartic discussion lightly either. The invitation to "get it off your chest" is one most people need and often seek. Surely it is preferable for people to talk out their grievances rather than to fight them out, and frequently the very airing of a grievance is sufficient to remove or alleviate the cause. For example, marriage counselors report that many a marriage has come apart because the husband and wife could not find a way to let the other know how they felt or what was troubling them. When they were able to talk about the problems, perhaps aided by a counselor, they found a basis for understanding that made further problem-solving either easier or unnecessary.

Therapeutic Purposes

The aim of therapeutic or training discussions (such as sensitivity or awareness discussions) is to help people alter their attitudes, feelings, or behavior about some aspect of their personal life or personality. Rather than working toward a group goal or product, each individual is seeking help in a supportive group setting. Stimulated by the work of Carl Rogers and others, group psychotherapy, counseling, and psychiatric treatment has become a sizable field for study and practice.

The value of therapy group sessions is unquestioned—provided the group is led by an experienced and well-trained therapist. When troubled people seek psychiatric help they are, in effect, asking someone to change their attitudes, and also their ways of thinking and responding, because they have concluded that their former attitudes and ways of thinking and responding were faulty and possibly the cause of their emotional stress. Whether the purpose is consciousness raising or assertiveness training (to take examples from the women's movement) or some other subject, the group setting can provide both insight and mutual support.

Transactional Analysis groups offer therapy in which members are helped to see how their "life scripts" have been shaped, how their Parent, Adult, and Child roles came to be, and how the Adult role can be modified and improved. Hannaford, for example, describes the use of Transactional Analysis with group counseling of elementary-school teachers and suggests this method to help free teachers from their perfectionist Parent tapes and enable them to teach with more warmth and spontaneity.[1]

This book is obviously not designed to provide extensive background in therapy discussions. Much of what is included here, however, can be applied to therapy groups as well as to other kinds.[2]

Learning Purposes

Discussion methods are useful tools in the classroom and elsewhere when the goal is the acquisition of new knowledge or skills. Unfortunately, the term *discussion* has been used to label a wide variety of teaching activities, from oral quizzes to teacher–student dialogues, so that some confusion on the use of discussion as a teaching method has resulted. What we mean by discussion as a teaching method is the use of small groups for student interaction about the subject matter being taught. The teacher may or may not be the discussion leader. A student may lead the group, or students may operate under shared leadership. The group should be arranged in a circle or around a table.

Some educators view classroom discussion as a game or as a reward for having done other "work" well. Effective learning discussions are neither games nor rewards; they have serious purposes and require considerable effort.

Surveys and research conducted by educators to evaluate and improve teaching methods have shown that when it comes to transmitting factual data, there is little difference between the results achieved from the lecture method and those from the discussion method. If an expert is available, that person can invariably cover the subject matter in a lecture more quickly and efficiently than can a group of untrained people through discussion. But how many of our problems and concerns can be settled by fact alone? Isn't true education the *interpretation* and the *application*, as well as the acquisition of facts?

The inherent value of discussion as a learning method is that it helps the participant interpret and evaluate the subject matter *in terms of his or her own emotional and intellectual experience, and his or her own abilities and needs*. There is evidence that the

---

[1]Mary J. Hannaford, "A T.A. Approach To Teacher Group Counseling," *Elementary School Guidance and Counseling*, 9 (1974), 6–13.

[2]Additional information on Transactional Analysis will be found in Chapters 4 and 5. For further insights into group therapy, consult one or more of the following: Carl R. Rogers, *Client-Centered Therapy* (Boston: Houghton Mifflin Company, 1951); Carl R. Rogers, *On Becoming a Person: A Therapist's View of Psychotherapy* (Boston: Houghton Mifflin Company, 1961); S. H. Foulkes and E. J. Anthony, *Group Psychotherapy: The Psychoanalytic Approach*, 2nd ed. (Baltimore: Penguin Books, Inc., 1965); Dorothy S. Whitaker and Morton A. Lieberman, *Psychotherapy Through Group Process* (New York: Atherton Press, 1964); and Donald S. Milman and George D. Goldman, *Group Process Today: Evaluation and Perspective* (Springfield, Ill.: Charles C. Thomas, Publisher, 1974).

learning achieved through the discussion method is not only more complete, but also more immediately usable and more readily retained, because the material has pertained directly to, and become a part of, the discussants' lives.[3]

In addition to more thorough and lasting learning, the discussion method offers the following benefits: (1) A satisfying sense of accomplishment and of belonging comes from shared ideas, problems, and experiences, which can be achieved as a group to a much greater degree than by an individual working alone. The very exchange of ideas will often stimulate new and better ideas. (2) Discussion and the freedom to speak freely and frankly permit everyone to share the control of what is going on, since the individuals in the group, as well as the teacher, can determine what the group's needs are, and—within the necessary boundaries of time and required subject matter—where it is going and how fast. This kind of independent study is much more satisfying than being told how much of what to study and when. (3) New insights into human behavior through observation of others and oneself in a social process can be rapidly developed in a discussion situation with long-lasting effect. When we develop the ability to observe the process of discussion going on around us, while being a participant, new vistas of human behavior and understanding are visible. An increased awareness of our own basic assumptions and frame of reference might even reveal that we, too, have blind spots. Herein lies real self-education and a potent incentive for change and improvement.

Among the many specific advantages to learning by the discussion method cited by Flynn and LaFaso are the following: (1) increased internalization; (2 greater change in beliefs, preferences, and attitudes; (3) increased rate of learning; (4) retention; (5) motivation and reinforcement; (6) lessening of the fear of failure; (7) provision of educationally effective interpersonal relations; (8) improved communication and human relations skills; and (9) cooperation and community.[4]

TASK PURPOSES

Decision-Making and Problem-Solving

Among the most important and pervasive purposes for discussion are making decisions and solving problems. Chapter 10 will be devoted to these key purposes.

Action

Frequently one group makes the decision and other groups are empowered to translate that decision into action. When preparing for a student body election, for example, one committee decides upon the process and timing; other committees arrange for facilities and publicity. Often the decision-making group and the action group are the same, or some of the same people are in both groups. In large organizations, action groups are apt to be given rather limited powers, such as the implementation of a specific decision made by the organization's leaders.

[3]Nathaniel Cantor, *Dynamics of Learning*, 3rd ed., (Buffalo, N.Y.: Henry Stewart, 1956).

[4]Elizabeth W. Flynn and John F. LaFaso, *Group Discussion As Learning Process* (New York: Paulist Press, 1972), pp. 102–7.

Appraisal

Some groups, such as fact-finding boards, committees of inquiry, and juries, are organized primarily for the purpose of examining a situation. Appraisal may take place either *before the fact*, in which case it is usually a prelude to policy formation, or *after the fact*, in which case it is usually intended to evaluate or to set a value judgment upon something that has already happened.

One of the best-known examples of the appraisal group is the congressional investigating committee. Sometimes creatures of a parent group, these committees are assigned the task of collecting information on some subject to form the basis of legislative action.

An appraisal group combines some of the characteristics of both decision-making and action groups. They often recommend action to be taken or decisions to be made as a result of their investigations, but the difference lies in the fact that the appraisal group is seldom directly responsible for the decision or its implementation.

Advisory Purposes

An advisory group performs most of the functions of the decision-making and action groups but does not have the power to make a decision. The advisory group differs from the appraisal group in that it is not so much concerned with investigation or evaluation as it is with policy making.

This type of discussion is very common and has received far too little attention in discussion literature. Almost all military staff meetings, many business and professional committees, and many student and faculty committees perceive themselves and are in turn perceived essentially as advisory groups. Such a group may operate as if it had the power to decide and may assume that its recommendations carry great weight. It is important, however, for advisory groups to remember that someone else holds the decision-making power and bears the responsibility.

A city human-relations commission can investigate the causes of friction between two community groups and make recommendations for alleviating the situation. But it is the city manager or the city council that decides which, if any, solutions to accept and implement. The human-relations commission may in turn be asked to help in providing educational programs, and at this point it becomes an action rather than an advisory group. Its sphere of action, however, is quite narrow and specific.

The advisory group is distinguished from the other types of task-oriented groups because of the peculiar forces that operate on its members. They are usually affected by the decision; they have an opportunity to speak their minds about the problem, assuming that the person or group in power tolerate free speech; but they cannot carry out their recommendations. This is not necessarily a disadvantage since the responsibility for decisions cannot always be shared, but it certainly creates problems that the head person or group and the rank-and-file members cannot ignore. A clever advisory group can often have things its own way, but this must be accomplished by persuasion or subterfuge, rather than as a matter of its right.

One kind of advisory group that is being used more and more on university campuses is the *search committee*. When administrative or faculty position openings occur, affirmative-action plans usually dictate a nationwide search and open recruiting, because word-of-mouth advertising is no longer considered sufficient. Usually the search committee spends months advertising, screening, and interviewing candidates. It has great power in the establishment of selection criteria and in screening out candidates. Often it reduces the field to from one to six candidates who are recommended to the person making the final selection. The committee's power usually ends with the recommendations on the finalists.

DISCUSSION CIRCUMSTANCES

Let's turn now to the problem of classifying discussion groups according to the circumstances that bring them together. Three kinds of reasons operate to form groups: (1) *casual* situations, (2) *voluntary association*, and (3) *organizational requirement*. A group that begins under one set of circumstances often continues or develops under a different set.

Casual Situations

The group formed in a casual situation usually comes about by chance and is not organized or continuing. There are many possible purposes for such a group. During the course of a day, a man may meet a couple of his associates and ask them to give him their reactions to a project he is planning, and an advisory group exists; later he might have coffee with some friends and discuss baseball, and a social group exists; still later, he might join with people at a bus stop in complaining about the irregular schedule, and a cathartic group is formed. The cathartic group might turn into an appraisal group, or, if it possessed the power, into a decision-making or action group.

Voluntary Association

An organized group whose members enlisted of their own volition for one or more of the purposes already covered would be an example of the voluntary association. This type of group differs from the casual in that the meeting has been planned and an ongoing structure and identity exist. Clearly, a casual group can grow into a voluntary association group, and the point at which it changes character may be quite hazy; but the main criteria should be evident.

Dozens of examples of this kind of group can be offered, such as the League of Women Voters, service clubs, church groups, and country clubs. Sometimes membership in such organizations borders on the mandatory for individuals seeking certain kinds of status within a community, but in the strictest sense, association is voluntary.

Volunteerism is a burgeoning phenomenon in the United States. In fact, in many communities today there are so many volunteer groups (hospital boards; agencies to help the retired, the retarded and the elderly; committees working on solutions to problems of drug abuse, consumer ethics, or overpopulation) that a new profession has evolved: *volunteer coordinator*. Because volunteer groups are becoming more and more pervasive and most of us will be associated with one or more at one time or another, we need to know more about how they function and how they differ from groups formed under other circumstances. We will come back to this point after a brief look at a third circumstance.

Organizational Requirement

Within any organization, whatever the circumstances of initial membership, there are usually a number of groups that exist to maintain and further the objectives of the organization. Such subgroups exist as a result of organizational requirement.

Look at the organization chart of any sizable business firm and you will find groups formed according to line or staff functions. The organization requires that given collections of people work together; that is their reason for being.

Differences Between Voluntary and Organizational Groups. The members of a discussion class would be considered a voluntary group. If they set themselves the task of discussing some problem concerning the United Nations, their responsibilities to the external world *for the substance* of their decision would be very limited. True, they have to satisfy their instructor that they are proceeding according to accepted principles of discussion and fulfilling the requirements of the assignment. If they attempt to represent or role play delegates of different countries, they can approximate something of the feeling of external responsibility. But contrast the forces operating on this group with those operating on the actual Security Council of the United Nations, whose members have responsibilities both to the world community and to their respective governments. They cannot act as they wish; their decisions are "for real."

Voluntary groups tend to focus more on personal goals, whereas organizational groups focus more on task purposes. Once again, however, external forces will vary. A service club deciding on a charitable project is not subject to the same external forces as is the sales department of a corporation deciding upon a new sales campaign. Similarly, the leader of a voluntary group does not have the same control as the supervisor of a work group.

Reasons for Membership. An individual may be a member of an organizational discussion group for one or both of two reasons: The subgroup may exist as a part of the larger organization, its membership resulting from the *dictates of the organization.* On the other hand, the individual may form a group within a larger structure or enlist in an existing one because her or his best interests demand it. We would call this latter instance the result of *personal dictates.*

An example in an academic setting would be a professor of history who finds himself a member of the university's history department. This happens automatically rather than as a matter of choice. Within his department he may be appointed to a variety of committees, such as a graduate or curriculum committee. However, he may offer to make himself a candidate for the university budget committee because of his own interests and concerns. We are persuaded that most of the meaningful memberships of discussion groups result from the dictates of conscience rather than the dictates of the organization. Many people hold nominal membership in literally dozens of groups, but they hold genuinely active membership in fewer, largely as a result of the requirements the individuals levy upon themselves. And we should not forget that reasons for group membership can change.

DISCUSSION FORMS

Public Discussion (Before an Audience)

Colloquy. The colloquy is an arrangement similar to a panel discussion. A number of audience "representatives" share the platform with a number of "experts." The audience representatives question or raise issues with the experts. This method is often used when one or more outside consultants are brought into an organization. To sharpen the focus of the contribution the experts make, the colloquy sometimes proceeds at once to the questioning of the experts rather than allowing them to give prepared speeches that may or may not deal directly with the particular problems of concern to the audience.

Popular radio and television interview programs, such as "Meet the Press" and "Face the Nation," embody most of the principles of the colloquy. Prominent persons in government or politics are questioned by a panel of reporters, whose purpose is usually to back them into a corner or to catch them in a contradiction. These reporters ask questions and make observations that they feel the members of the audience would ask if given the opportunity.

Debate. A debate is sometimes referred to as a form of discussion and thus should be mentioned here. Because speakers take opposite sides of a proposition, a debate provides an organized method of illuminating a subject or persuading an audience. When controversy dominates a discussion, some people say the discussion has turned into a debate and it probably has. But we would be making a mistake if we called controversy the antithesis of discussion. (See Chapter 11, on conflict.)

A typical debate will have one or two speakers on a side. Speeches of a set length will be given for and against the proposition, with the speakers favoring the proposition having the right to speak first and last.

There are three principal differences between debate and small group discussion: (1) Discussion seeks to *inquire,* but debate seeks to *advocate;* (2) debate has a prescribed format and is more formal; and (3) debaters either select or are given the pro or the con side of an issue and bring up all their evidence and reasoning to support this preselected position, whereas discussants research and reason through all aspects of an issue so that there are no sides.

Forum. The word *forum* formerly designated a public place or marketplace of a city. Since the Romans used such a place to hold open discussions on questions of public concern, the term has come to refer to audience participation in discussion. A period of time is alloted for members of the audience to ask questions of speakers or to make observations on issues. When describing a program, the word *forum* is usually hyphenated with the word describing the speaking that gives rise to the audience participation. Examples are *lecture-forum, panel-forum,* and *symposium-forum.*

Panel. A panel discussion is usually a public discussion in which the members examine some problem or issue under normal discussion give-and-take. Anywhere from 3 to 12 members may be found on a panel, but the ideal number for coherent discussion is about 4 or 5.

Symposium. A symposium resembles a panel in that it is a public discussion with approximately the same number of participants. However, the members give prepared speeches on different phases of the question. Following the speeches, the members may operate for a time as a panel, or they may open the discussion for questions and comments from the audience and become a forum.

Private Discussion

Buzz Group. A convenient method of providing for a large number of people to participate in discussion is the buzz-group technique. It consists of breaking up a large group into subgroups of approximately six members each; giving each subgroup some set time for discussion, usually 5 or 10 minutes; and then having a representative from each subgroup report to the larger group. This method is often used following a lecture, panel, symposium, or the like, as a means of generating a manageable number of questions from the audience while giving everyone a chance to participate in the formulation of the questions. It is managed, usually, by a chairperson who designates the composition of the groups, indicates the matter they are to consider, and tells them how they are to make known the results of their discussion. Sometimes counting off or similar techniques are used to ensure heterogeneity of subgroups. Sometimes the matters for discussion are predetermined and distributed to each of the subgroups.

Case Discussion. The case method of study has gained considerable popularity.[5] Applicable to a wide range of problems, it consists of presenting a discussion group with a description of a situation which the members are first to analyze and then suggest procedures for solving or handling. Sometimes the group focuses on the overall problem, sometimes on an individual in the case.

Committee. The term *committee* may refer to any group organized or appointed to accomplish some given task. It often refers to a group created by a legislative body. This kind of committee has the task of investigating problem areas and producing motions that can be examined by the parent body. Such a legislative committee is distinguished from the legislative body, which uses parliamentary rules. The committee can investigate a problem without having before it a motion, whereas the legislative body is restricted to debating motions. If the parent body wishes to investigate and deliberate without a motion, it must resolve itself into a *committee of the whole.*

Conference. When representatives of different groups come together to share information or to coordinate efforts, they are engaged in a conference. When the heads of various volunteer organizations meet to compare notes and progress reports, it can be called a conference. This term can be confusing since it is sometimes used as a synonym for a private meeting. ("Mr. Smith is in conference.") It is also used interchangeably with *convention.*

Encounter Group. The term *encounter group* is the expression most commonly used for a variety of client-centered groups. Other terms are *sensitivity training, T-groups (training groups),* or *group laboratory for human relations.* Depending upon who is using

[5]The Harvard Business School has been particularly instrumental in popularizing this method of learning. The method has also become popular in some types of adult education.

these terms, their exact definitions may vary; but their goals are usually one or more of these: (1) better understanding of oneself; (2) insight into how one is perceived by other people; (3) improvement and change in oneself; (4) better understanding of other people; and (5) better understanding of the complexities of group process. Led by a trainer or a training team, these groups focus on the here-and-now. The group itself, including its development and the personal interactions among its members, serves as both the laboratory and the only agenda. Goals and tasks, if any, are deliberately ambiguous so that the group must struggle to form and function. The trainer usually refuses to lead or make decisions, serving only as a catalyst who occasionally intervenes and calls attention to personal or group phenomena.[6]

Role-Playing Groups. A very effective method of discussion training involves role playing. Discussants are asked to assume the role of a given individual or of a set of qualities or attributes (usually handed to the discussant on a slip of paper). Roles may be worked out in advance to illustrate a particular problem, or they may be created on the spur of the moment in order to examine and experience some aspect of interpersonal relationships. Further explanation and role-playing exercises will be provided in Chapter 16.

SUMMARY

In this chapter, we have identified discussion purposes (personal and task) and three main kinds of discussion circumstances (casual, voluntary, and organizational) in which groups are formed. We concluded with a glossary of common discussion forms, both public and private.

DISCUSSION QUESTIONS

1. In the daily conduct of business, education, government, and social organizations, people engage in many discussions. How useful do you believe it would be if these groups understood and applied the distinctions made between discussion purposes? Compare and contrast the possible values of such understandings in relation to personal and to task purposes.

2. Compare and contrast the orientation, procedures, and problems of representative decision-making groups with those of similar advisory groups. Are there any misconceptions or distortions of perception to which advisory groups may fall victim? If so, how may such errors be avoided?

3. Assume you are a member of a voluntary group that is trying to preserve an endangered species of bird. What would be some of the factors that would keep you attending meetings? What advice would you give the group's leader to increase membership and attendance?

[6]For a brief history and explanation of the "laboratory approach," see Alvin A. Goldberg and Carl E. Larson, *Group Communication: Discussion Processes and Applications,* (Englewood Cliffs, N.J.: Prentice-Hall, Inc., 1975), pp. 162–74. For more extensive background, see Kenneth D. Benne, "History of the T-Group in the Laboratory Setting," in *T-Group Theory and Laboratory Method,* eds. Leland P. Bradford, Jack R. Gibb, and Kenneth D. Benne (New York: John Wiley & Sons, Inc., 1964).

EXERCISES

1. Keep a record of the nature and length of all the discussions in which you engage for a full week. What subjects or topics were discussed? How would you classify the discussions as to purpose? Do many subjects reappear in discussions having different purposes? Do you find any pattern of relationship between topics and purposes?

2. Having classified your discussions in exercise 1, try to view these through the eyes of the other participants. Do you feel that any of these persons would assign different purposes to some of the discussions? If you find differences, how would you account for them? If possible, check with some of the participants to see how they viewed the discussion.

3. Using either radio or television, listen to two contrasting programs that employ discussion in some form. Prepare a four-minute analysis of the two in which you comment on such elements as:
    a.   Purpose
    b.   Content
    c.   Form
    d.   Value to both participants and listeners
    e.   Degree to which each group approaches discussion as we have defined it.
(Possible contrasting kinds of programs would be those for entertainment, controversy, propaganda, and education.)

4. Interview two business executives about the number and kinds of groups of which they are a part because their organizations require them to be. Prepare a report for the class.

SELECTED READINGS

APPLBAUM, RONALD L., EDWARD M. BODAKAN, KENNETH K. SERENO, AND KARL W. E. ANATOL, *The Process of Group Communication*, chap. 1. Chicago: Science Research Associates Inc., 1974.

BEINSTEIN, JUDITH, "Small Talk As Social Gesture," *Journal of Communication*, 25 (1975), 147–54.

BORMANN, ERNEST G., *Discussion and Group Methods: Theory and Practice* (2nd ed.), chap. 13. New York: Harper & Row, Publishers, 1975.

BRILHART, JOHN K., *Effective Group Discussion*, chap. 1. Dubuque, Iowa: William C. Brown Company, Publishers, 1967.

CORTRIGHT, RUPERT L., AND GEORGE L. HINDS, *Creative Discussion*, chap. 2. New York: The Macmillan Company, 1969.

FLYNN, ELIZABETH W., AND JOHN F. LaFASO, *Group Discussion As Learning Process*, chap. 7. New York: Paulist Press, 1972.

GOURAN, DENNIS S., *Discussion: The Process of Group Decision-Making*, chaps. 1, 2. New York: Harper & Row, Publishers, 1974.

KLEIN, E., AND B. M. ASTRACHAN, "Learning in Groups: A Comparison of Study Groups and T-Groups," *Journal of Applied Behavioral Science*, 7 (1971), 659–83.

PART TWO

Almost invariably students in our discussion classes ask, "Are we going to use group dynamics in this course?" When we answer that we cannot avoid using group dynamics, they are puzzled. The reason, of course, is that the popular connotation of the term—and a common misconception—is of a set of techniques or gimmicks to stimulate or measure interaction.

Group dynamics is more properly defined as a field of inquiry that concentrates on forces operating on an individual within a group and on the group as a whole. We use the term in the sense that Lewin first used it and as it has been amplified by Cartwright and Zander:

> Group dynamics should be defined as a field of inquiry dedicated to advancing knowledge about the nature of groups, the laws of their development, and their interrelations with individuals, other groups, and larger institutions.[1]

We feel it is useful to consider group characteristics and forces together but to identify them as separate phenomena; hence Chapter 4 is devoted to *characteristics* and Chapter 5 to *forces*. But this separation also causes problems reminiscent of the chicken-or-the-egg puzzle. Couldn't aspects of group life, such as goals or climate,

[1]Dorwin Cartwright and Alvin Zander, *Group Dynamics: Research and Theory* (New York: Harper & Row, Publishers, 1968), p. 7.

SMALL
GROUP
DYNAMICS

be considered both as characteristics and as forces? Yes, they could. So, for those two instances, we decided to develop the subjects twice, both as characteristics and as forces.

When reading Part Two keep in mind that the forces discussed are never static, but are in constant play on the individual, the group, and the larger environment, much as are the forces in a magnetic field. The number of interacting variables is unlimited, but those we have identified can be and have been measured in objective fashion and the effects are also measurable.

To help clarify and illustrate the necessarily abstract concepts used in the next two chapters, we recommend that you visualize a specific group such as a class or club. Instead of viewing climate in merely theoretical terms, for example, think about the climate of a real group of which you are a part.

chapter 4

Discussion was defined as the process whereby two or more people exchange information or ideas in a face-to-face situation to achieve a goal. The various kinds of discussion groups were classified as to purpose and formation. As indicated, the concern of this book is primarily with groups formed as a result of voluntary association or organizational requirement, and therefore the characteristics of groups covered in this chapter are limited to those discussion groups with task or learning as their primary purposes and to those groups with sufficient permanency and stability to acquire *group* characteristics.

GOALS

Man has been described as a wanting animal. When one need is fulfilled, another takes its place. The goals of organized human effort are as diverse as individual human needs and human interests. Most group discussions involve a complex intermeshing of group and individual goals.

You may join a group because the people in it seem interesting and your goal is to make new friends. Before long you find yourself deeply involved in the work and process of the group and find that you, too, are working to help achieve the group's goal. But to make our example even more realistic, chances are that you had more than one reason for joining the group. The group itself, has main goals and subordinate goals, as well as immediate and long-range aims.

Even a particular act may be intended to move an individual in the direction of *several* goals. A single contribution in a discussion may move the discussant in the direction of all these goals and more: (1) the goal of helping the group solve the main problem; (2) the goal of being regarded as an indispensable member of the group; (3) the goal of discrediting another who did not have the information or whose reasoning was shaky; and (4) the goal of manipulating the group into a certain path.

Individuals are probably not directly conscious of much of their goal-selecting and goal-seeking activity. We undoubtedly select most goals habitually in response to familiar stimuli. The group's norms and the individual's attitudes, personal security, and prior state of well-being all act to influence the selection and means of attaining goals. Certainly, as individuals we seldom make our goals public. Sometimes we are silent because we don't feel that announcing our goals is important; sometimes we are unwilling to announce them for a variety of reasons; sometimes we don't know how to announce them; and sometimes we don't know ourselves that we seek them. Haiman called these unrevealed goals the individual's *hidden agenda*. [1]

[1]Franklyn S. Haiman, *Group Leadership and Democratic Action* (Boston: Houghton Mifflin Company, 1951), p. 89.

Characteristics of Groups

Some goal-seeking behavior does not depend on other individuals. Such goals are individual and do not require a group for satisfaction. However, if the attainment of the goal depends to some extent on the behavior of others, a group goal is obviously involved.

Whether the group's goal is implicit in the reason the group was formed (such as the case of a subcommittee that has been given its task and therefore its goal) or whether the goal evolves during the group's development, it is essential not only that the group have a goal but also that the group members join in verbalizing it. Without a goal, the group is aimless and like a ship heading for an unknown port. If the group has not taken the time to shape the goal orally, the participants run a grave risk of discovering too late that they have been working at cross-purposes.

Shaw has tackled the problem of defining what a group goal is and how it can be identified:

> It is obvious that whatever goals can be attributed to the group must reside in the members of the group. It also seems clear that groups whose members all agree upon a single goal to the exclusion of all other goals, both individual and group, are extremely rare. In the typical group, there exists at least one goal which is acceptable to the majority of the group and which can properly be identified as the group goal. . . . Thus, a group goal is an end state desired by a majority of the group members. It can be identified by observing the activities of group members or, usually, by asking the members of the group to specify it.[2]

Complementary and Antagonistic Goals

In his study of the effects of cooperation and competition, Deutsch pointed out the essential distinction between the kinds of goals that give rise either to cooperation or to competition.[3] In a cooperative situation the individuals can reach their respective goals *only if all the group members can also reach their goals.* We call such goals *complementary.* In a competitive situation, however, the goals are such that an individual can reach his or her goals *only if the others do not reach their goals.* These goals we call *antagonistic.*[4]

Let's say two people had a friendly rivalry to see which one could raise the most money for a charitable organization. True, they are competing, but the harder they compete the better off the organization is. Their individual goals are complementary to the group's goal of raising money. But suppose both people decide they want to be chairperson of the group. Here, each can succeed only if the other fails and they therefore have antagonistic goals. Should their competition for leadership become heated or hostile, it is conceivable that members of the group could choose up sides and a permanent rift occur.

[2]Marvin E. Shaw, *Group Dynamics: The Psychology of Small Group Behavior* (New York: McGraw-Hill Book Company, Inc., 1971), pp. 293–94.

[3]Morton Deutsch, "The Effects of Cooperation and Competition Upon Group Process," in *Group Dynamics: Research and Theory,* eds. Dorwin Cartwright and Alvin Zander (New York: Harper & Row, Publishers, 1968) pp. 461–82.

[4]Deutsch used the terms *promotively interdependent* and *contriently interdependent* for the terms *complementary* and *antagonistic.*

As teachers of discussion, we find the determination of student grades a painful contradiction to the goal of achieving group cooperation. No matter what criteria are used (and we prefer those designed by the students themselves) the assignment of grades introduces the element of competition, which is antagonistic to the formation of a cohesive, cooperatively functioning group.

A further discussion of the *forces* of cooperation and competition and their effects will be found in Chapter 5.

NORMS

Norms are standards or codes, explicit or implicit, that guide and regulate thinking and behavior. They are essentially criteria by which behavior is judged. Norms, of course, are not peculiar to small groups but permeate our belief systems and society as a whole.

Homans described a norm as "a statement made by a number of members of a group, not necessarily by all of them, that the members ought to behave in a certain way in certain circumstances."[5] Others such as Abrahamson feel the statement need not be verbal, implying awareness.[6] In fact, it has been our experience that as soon as some groups are made aware of the norms they have been following, they immediately try to change them.

Sources of Norms

Laws or Regulations. Norms sometimes appear as laws or regulations either formed by the group itself or dictated to the group by an outside agency. When a group adopts a set of bylaws to govern its operation, we have an instance of regulations formed by the group. In the case of a group created by a larger organization, we often find that the larger group hands down certain rules and regulations along with the charge to the smaller group.

Cultural Products. Norms are sometimes agreed-upon standards of the larger culture. The language we use, for example, and the connotations attached to the language are norms. Turning to the dictionary for the "right" definition of a word, we find a statement of the word's *normal* meaning. Even more important is the way that the connotation of a term gains currency in a culture. In the United States, the term *free enterprise* is used to signify not only a type of economy but a praiseworthy idea to which all politicians are expected to pay homage.

Still more examples of this type of norm include the clothes we wear and the places we wear them. In some groups, such as religious orders and the military, actual laws govern the wearing of clothing. Although there are no written-down laws governing the wearing of clothing for most of us, we find ourselves following certain norms that are almost as demanding as laws. Few of us would wear jeans to a formal reception.

[5]George C. Homans, *Social Behavior, Its Elementary Forms* (New York: Harcourt, Brace & World, Inc., 1961), p. 46.

[6]Mark Abrahamson, *Interpersonal Accommodation* (Princeton, N.J.: D. Van Nostrand Company, Inc., 1966), p. 78.

And speaking of jeans, the pervasive wearing of what used to be the appropriate costume for only farmers and cowboys has become an interesting norm in itself.

From requiring the wearing of celluloid collars to determining the length of sideburns, employers have a way of enforcing company norms. When new employees hear, "But we don't do things that way around here," they realize they have stepped over the invisible boundary. They find themselves with the choices of adopting (or at least living with) the norm, challenging or attempting to change the norm, or finding employment elsewhere. Their behavioral choices will depend on the importance of that norm to their own goals, their perceived capacity for changing the group, and the availability of suitable alternatives. In Chapter 14 we will discuss ways to persuade groups to change their norms.

Products of Group Interaction. Norms sometimes emerge implicitly from the interaction of the group itself. These norms concern us most because they are peculiar to each discussion group. The group itself can do little about norms that are a part of the general culture, or those handed to the group from the outside. But the group *can* modify the laws, regulations, and norms that emerge from its interaction. In one sense laws and regulations are easier to deal with since they are open for all to observe. Implicit norms are often harder to modify since they may not be recognized or verbalized.

Kiesler and Kiesler discuss norms in connection with group pressure and individual motives:

> What determines which norms will emerge in a group? . . . the motives that each individual has for joining and maintaining membership in a group will interact with the others' motives to determine the norms that the group has. The most important norms will be those that hold the group together and smooth interpersonal interaction, since motive satisfaction depends so much on these factors. Some norms become rituals and look silly to outsiders (e.g., secret handclasps). However, these norms can increase members' security, help to define the group, and give the impression of uniqueness.[7]

Values of Norms

To add to the values identified by the Kieslers (increase security, help define the group, and give the impression of uniqueness) we add this: *Norms provide psychologically meaningful shortcuts to decisions.* Norms provide us with clues to appropriate behavior and often save us the trouble of having to look at the evidence each time we make a decision. If our group has developed the norm of meeting at a regular time and place, we don't have to check with each other about the time and place of the next meeting. If we have developed a procedure of taking turns being chairperson we don't have to waste time and energy jockeying for position or competing for status. Norms can be useful time-savers.

On the other hand, if our group insists on blind adherence to norms ("We've

[7]Charles A. Kiesler and Sara B. Kiesler, *Conformity* (Reading, Mass.: Addison-Wesley Publishing Co., Inc., 1970), p. 35.

always done it this way!") without regular reexamination and reevaluation, we have an unhealthy situation. We might find ourselves meeting out of habit rather than need.

GROUP CONTROL

Next, we'll examine the areas over which group control extends and the means groups use to maintain control. Before launching the investigation, it is well to point out that control is not synonymous with evil. Groups must have appropriate control if they are to perform any useful function just as individuals must exercise some control over their lives if they are to be useful to themselves or others.

Areas of Control

Task Control. Decision-making, action, appraisal, and advisory groups all control some area of investigation or decision-making that has either been delegated to them by some outside agency or that they have arrogated unto themselves. Social, cathartic, therapeutic, and learning groups, since they exist largely to satisfy personal needs only, tend to have little task control.

When we say that the proper function of a group is to perform such and such a task, we are indicating the task area that is, or should be, the province of that group. Identification of the proper area of task control is seldom easy; we observe groups struggling constantly to gain more and more control in order to improve their status. This is not surprising, since the individuals composing those groups are often trying to do the same thing in their private lives.

One advantage of such struggles is that often the best way to secure control over some task area is to demonstrate that the group deserves the control because it is best equipped. This means positive accomplishment. A college or university provides excellent illustrations of this since it must react to constantly changing developments and, consequently, assignment of areas of control must also shift. Patterns of administrative control seem always to be undergoing reorganization.

For example, on most campuses, a constant struggle for control goes on between the student government and the administration. (There is, of course, a parallel contest between the faculty and the administration.) Students at one major university were upset because the faculty council instituted a new procedure by which students were to evaluate the faculty—at the same time a student group had been working on their own system. Both groups had similar goals but the students were incensed because they felt that the student government should have at least been consulted before action was taken. The issue—who should have control of the task area?

Control of Individuals. Without question, groups exercise control over various aspects of the lives of their members. The kind and amount of control vary from group to group and from individual to individual. Groups ask members to devote time to group activities; groups seek loyalty; groups demand individual energy and talents; and, of course, groups expect their members to abide by group norms. The evils that may result from group control arise from one or both of the following: The group may seek to exercise unreasonable control, or the individual may "make a bad bargain"—that is, a person may give up more than he or she receives from the group.

Individuals commit themselves to a group because they perceive that the attainment of their goals depends on others. They must pay something in order to secure these group benefits; but when the result of the bargain is unsatisfactory they will either have to live with a bad bargain or cease to pay. Insecure persons, for example, may be so concerned with belonging to a group that they exchange their own integrity for social acceptance.

Too much control of the individual produces a group under one-person rule or tradition-bound, inflexible procedures. Too little control produces anarchy. Neither of these extremes permits a group to function in what we have come to believe is an effective, satisfying manner.

Chapter 1 presented a number of instances in which groups sought to exercise unreasonable control over their members. Such attempts at unreasonable control are the result of norms the group develops concerning standards of behavior and thinking. The control may be exercised directly by members who possess power and influence over others, but control can also be exercised indirectly by norms that have been around so long no one knows just where they came from.

Harris tells the story of just such a family norm:

> The mother of a teen-ager related the following parental edict, which had long governed her housekeeping procedures. Her mother had told her, "You *never* put a hat on a table or a coat on a bed." So she went through life never putting a hat on a table or a coat on a bed. Should she occasionally forget, or should one of her youngsters break this old rule, there was an overreaction that seemed inappropriate to the mere violation of the rules of simple neatness. Finally, after several decades of living with this unexamined law, mother asked grandmother (by then in her eighties), "Mother, *why* do you never put a hat on a table or a coat on a bed?"
>
> Grandmother replied that when she was little there had been some neighbor children who were "infested," and her mother had warned her that it was important they never put the neighbor children's hats on the table or their coats on the bed. . . . Many of the rules we live by are like this.[8]

When groups attempt unwarranted control over the lives of their members, the norms that give rise to this attempted control should be changed. But when the norms are the result of interaction of large and complex organizations over a long time, their origins may be shrouded in bureaucratic obscurity. "I'm just doing what I was told to do," protests the employee. If we don't know who thought up the original idea or was responsible for promoting it, we will have a more difficult time in loosening the control.

Means of Control

To examine the means of enforcing control, it is necessary to look at the resources that the group has to establish its bargaining position. Our examination will be brief since the majority of these matters are a function of leadership and power relationships, to be discussed later in this book.

[8]Thomas A. Harris, *I'm OK—You're OK: A Practical Guide to Transactional Analysis* (New York: Harper & Row, Publishers, 1969), pp. 22–23. Copyright © 1967, 1968, 1969 by Thomas A. Harris, M.D. By permission of Harper & Row, Publishers, Inc.

Enforcement of control must take some form of reward or punishment, or both. These two forms have been used for a number of years in a variety of fields, and many people tend to view rewards and punishments as largely external. A man is rewarded by payment for work; he is punished by dismissal or demotion. In contrast let us cite two of the six assumptions developed by McGregor in his excellent treatment of modern management philosophy:

> 2.   *External control and the threat of punishment are not the only means of bringing about effort toward organizational objectives. Man will exercise self-direction and self-control in the services of objectives to which he is committed.*
>
> 3.   *Commitment to objectives is a function of the rewards associated with their achievement.* The most significant of such rewards, e.g., the satisfaction of ego and self-actualization needs, can be direct products of effort directed toward organizational objectives.[9]

GROUP CLIMATE

Another characteristic often discussed in books of this sort is the concept of group climate or atmosphere. According to Cartwright and Zander, however, little research has been conducted on the ingredients or effect of group climate.[10] Perhaps the reason is that a group's climate is an intangible, almost mysterious aspect of its existence. Yet the student of groups recognizes the unique mood or aura surrounding a given group. The climate can be felt as soon as one enters a meetingplace or classroom. It is a function of the kind of interdependence that exists among the members of the group; it stems from what the group is like, how the members feel about themselves and the group; it has to do with the group's leadership, productivity, personality and much more. We feel the group's climate is an important characteristic, but because we lack the tools necessary for a complete descriptive analysis, we do not develop the concept here to the same depth as the other major characteristics of groups. We will, however, also deal with climate as a dynamic force in the next chapter.

GROUP MATURITY

Like individuals, groups may be characterized by their capacity for growth and maturity, and, again as with individuals, chronological age does not automatically guarantee maturity.

Many people who read about the advantages expected from group activity are disappointed in the seeming lack of accomplishments of their groups. Students in discussion classes, for instance, observe that their fellow discussants appear to be capable, skilled individuals, but the group does not seem to function effectively. Members of a newly formed civic committee may be puzzled to discover that the group, composed of people who have experience in such groups, seems to take so long to get under way.

The answer to this bewilderment is that, despite the presence of able members, the

[9]Douglas McGregor, *The Human Side of Enterprise* (New York: McGraw-Hill Book Company, Inc., 1960), pp. 47–48.

[10]Cartwright and Zander, *Group Dynamics* (1968), p. 102.

groups in question have not yet matured. Describing a mature group is describing an effective group. Therefore the remainder of this section will concentrate on those factors necessary for a group to begin to mature and criteria whereby an observer may detect the degree of maturity of a group.

Maturation Requirements

Our discussion of maturation requirements begins with the assumption that the group is composed of otherwise able individuals. If the group contains individuals who lack the characteristics, skills, and insights requisite to effective discussion, the group will inevitably be immature. But people and groups can learn and grow together.

Justifiable Reason for Being. The cause or reason for the existence of the group must be justifiable if the group is to mature. A group provides a kind of gateway that mediates the goal striving of the group members. If either the individual goals (that the group is established to facilitate) or the group goal (that emerges after interaction) is significant, the first major requirement for maturity exists.

Sometimes the group objective is of such overriding importance that the group grows up in a hurry. Wartime emergencies are cases in point. Ernie Pyle recorded hundreds of instances in which truly mature groups were formed almost instantly.[11]

Realistic Opportunities for Progressive Successes. The cliché, "Nothing succeeds like success," is fundamentally sound. If a group is forced to tackle problems beyond its scope in the early stages of group development, the group may well fail and the members may become dissatisfied with the group and pessimistic about its future. This point is especially important to remember in discussion classes. Early group tasks should be those that the group members can undertake with reasonable expectation of success. This does not mean that the group must meet with complete success on each task. Some failures are probably inevitable (and can be very educational) but a measure of success must be present. Anyone familiar with amateur theatre groups realizes the importance of early success. After the theatre group has become mature they can attempt bizarre performances, knowing that if they fail, the failure can be taken in stride. Young, newly formed groups had better stick with the surefire hits.

Promise of Continuity. This requisite needs no emphasis. If the members see no prospect of continuity, they cannot be expected to do more than attack the immediate problem as best they can without worry about the nonexistent tomorrow. As we have already noted, this has often been the problem with experimental groups that were gathered for one discussion period only. Since they were not real groups in a continuity sense, participants had little or no stake in either the process or the outcome and merely went through the motions of functioning as a group.

We don't want to impy that "one-shot" groups cannot be effective or productive. Our point is that such groups have neither the need nor the opportunity to achieve maturity.

[11]Ernie Pyle, *Here Is Your War* (Chicago: Consolidated Book Publishers, 1944).

Promise of Intergroup Status. There is no need to cavil at the desire for status. If the group is to recruit and retain able members and keep their interest, the group must hold forth some promise of status in the world of which the group is a part. Second-rate schools, for example, have little prospect of attracting first-rate teachers unless the school can provide evidence that it is improving and the first-rate teacher can "get in on the ground floor."

Each of these requisites for group maturity is not necessarily an either–or condition. Seldom do we find a group, however, in which any of the requirements is entirely absent. The issue is whether the requisite exists in sufficient degree to make further growth probable. Assuming that a group does possess the requisites in sufficient degree, how then do we distinguish the degree of maturity in that group?

Maturity Criteria

Although the age of the group may be a general clue to its maturity, the following five criteria are more reliable indices. Each criterion is related to group effectiveness, but focuses on maturity.

Degree of Reliance on Rules and Regulations. Generally speaking, the more a group must be conscious of rules of procedure, the more immature it is. The mature group will have developed norms and traditions that enable it to operate without constant reliance on constitutions or bylaws. A history of collective effort alone will not provide freedom from codified regulations unless that history is accompanied by a growth in the degree of interpersonal *confidence*, respect, and affection. Of dozens of possible examples, here are a few:

1.   International conferences today provide interesting examples of immature groups. The conference must be preceded by exhaustive preliminary work to draw up agendas and agree on facilities, and then the conferees must follow rigidly prescribed rules.

2.   When the United States was formed it was necessary to draft a written constitution with a variety of built-in checks and balances. The country lacked the traditions, the established confidence, the respect and affection that have enabled England to operate without a written constitution. Today, our interpretation of the Constitution is so broad and flexible that we appear to operate as much upon tradition as upon the written document.

3.   Student governing groups, because their membership turns over so often, are plagued by considerations of rules and regulations. After each election, the new group usually examines and reevaluates the former group's bylaws and procedures and spends a lot of time revising and amending them to their own satisfaction. The time available for substantive discussion is thereby lessened.

Degree of Intragroup Competition for Status. Until the group has begun to achieve a degree of intergroup status and until the members have committed themselves to attainment of the group objective, there is likely to be considerable striving for status among the group members. The members of a mature group care less about intragroup status than about the accomplishment of their main mission. Again, the amount of interpersonal confidence, respect, and affection is a clue to this criterion. If these interpersonal relations are positive, the rewards for successful action will ultimately be appropriately distributed among the members of the group. Successful athletic teams almost always display very little intragroup competition for status. Someone once said, "Nothing would be impossible if people didn't care who got the credit." It requires considerable individual and group maturity to allow the group to get the credit.

Degree of Operational Efficiency. Please note our distinction between *efficiency* and *effectiveness.* An efficient group is one that makes optimum use of member resources and one in which the members are readily able to pick up clues and ideas from one another.

A group that wastes member potential by assigning people tasks or roles for which they are not particularly suited, or which are already being performed by others, shows evidence of being an immature group. Sometimes haste forces the inappropriate division of labor; in most instances, such inefficiency is born of immaturity.

The ability of members to pick up clues from other members is included under the heading of the efficiency criterion, because individuals not familiar with one another will often make many errors as they attempt to interpret one another's meaning and intentions. During the early stages of one group's development, a serious roadblock was caused by the blunt and forthright speech of one of the members. Most of the group members interpreted his behavior as antagonism toward and rejection of the group objectives and methods. Once they learned to understand him, they discovered they had been reading too much into his behavior. He was naturally an impulsive person who spoke bluntly but he expected others to be equally blunt and reject his ideas if they didn't like them. Once this was clear, the group operations became much more efficient.

Degree of Member Regard for the Group. The higher the members regard their group (assuming their evaluations are accurate), the more they perceive that the group is capable of satisfying their needs—hence the more mature the group. Loyalty and commitment are high in such a group.

Degree of Permissiveness. Sometimes this criterion is included under headings like *involvement, openness, trust, freedom from apathy,* or *friendliness.* The meaning here is simple. There is a degree in any group to which individuals feel free to speak their minds. Members of mature groups speak their minds quite freely and frankly, inhibited only by the normal restraints of tact, propriety, and common sense. They have learned the knack of disagreeing without being disagreeable; they can dislike each other's *ideas* but continue to like each other. By contrast, members of immature groups are often seen leaving meetings muttering ideas they did not feel free to express during the meeting.

For example, here is an experience an individual had when he mistakenly believed that his group had matured sufficiently to allow free expression. After expressing some views about what he considered unwise administrative practices of the organization of which the group was a part, he found himself called to account for a distorted version of what he had said. There were even statements made that the frank member should be fired. Because of this experience it was years before that group became mature enough to provide genuine permissiveness.

Authoritarian leadership, competitive wrangles, disorganized thought patterns all inhibit expression. The point is that the degree of permissiveness and openness is an excellent criterion of maturity.

SUMMARY

This chapter described five significant characteristics of groups: goals, norms, control, climate, and maturity. The list of characteristics does not exhaust the dimensions for measuring a group, nor will a knowledge of these characteristics, alone, enable an individual to understand groups. The characteristics are like parts of a motor. Taken singly they are instructive but incomplete; when understood and put back together in the dynamic unit that is the complete functioning motor, their interaction begins to round out the picture of understanding. Chapter 5 focuses on the interacting forces of the group.

DISCUSSION QUESTIONS

1.   Invite several people from other countries to a discussion to consider customs and practices in their homelands concerning the following:
   a.   The child's place in the family.
   h   Making acquaintances or establishing social interaction.
   c.   The student-to-student and the student-to-teacher relationship.
   d.   The citizen–law enforcement relationship.
   e.   Attitudes toward civic responsibility.
   f.   Attitudes toward charity.
(Avoid discussing such obvious things as differences in dress or food preferences.)

2.   What norms have developed in your current classes? Which ones are useful? Why?

3.   How would you describe the climate of your current classes? How do the climates differ from class to class? Why?

4.   Which of the groups you belong to is the most mature? How many of the maturation requirements does it meet? How does it stand in relation to the five standards for measuring maturity?

EXERCISES

1.   Compile a list of the most important groups to which you belong, excluding your family. For each group, attempt to make parallel lists of your personal goals and the group goals. Be fully honest with yourself since this will be a private exercise. Have you learned anything about your relationship to these groups? Have you learned anything about yourself and your

goals? To what degree have you modified your goals in order to retain membership in any of the groups?

2.   A collection or association of persons does not immediately or inevitably evolve into a group. Consider three to five associations in which you are involved and attempt to trace the development or disintegration to determine the critical events or points. Choose your cases so as to include one that has not yet clearly become a group and one that may be disintegrating. Do not hesitate to consider transitory associations such as seminars, review sessions, luncheon conferences, or car pools.

3.   Using the cases chosen for exercise 2, analyze the role of several individuals in changing the character of the association.

a.   Which individuals were most receptive or helpful to the development? Which were the least inclined to accept or aid group development? On what factors do you base your judgment?

b.   Which ones seemed to be the first to disassociate themselves from the group or allow it to disintegrate? Which ones seemed most desirous of continuing the group relationship?

c.   Where would you place yourself in the foregoing analyses? Do you feel you are consistently in such a position with respect to group formation?

4.   Pair yourself with another individual with whom you are well acquainted and agree to exchange the following analyses:

a.   List five to ten groups to which you belong.

b.   Rank each list in the order of importance you perceive the groups to have.

c.   Rank each list in the order of control the groups have over you.

d.   Exchange lists with your partner. What do you conclude?

5.   For each of the behaviors listed, indicate how appropriate or inappropriate a norm you think it would be for your class. Compare your list with those of other classmates.

a.   Described his reactions to what was taking place in the group.

b.   Said little or nothing in most meetings.

c.   Talked about the details of her personal life.

d.   Kissed another group member.

e.   Asked for reactions or feedback (How do you see me in this group?).

f.   Frequently joked.

g.   Said she was not getting anything from being in the group.

h.   Refused to be bound by a group decision.

i.   Asked for the goal to be clarified.

j.   Noted competition in the group and asked how it could be reduced.

k.   Was often absent.

l.   Encouraged other group members to react to the topic being discussed.

m.   Acted indifferently to other group members.

n.   Talked a lot without showing his true feelings.

o.   Challenged other members' remarks.

SELECTED READINGS

CARTWRIGHT, DORWIN, AND ALVIN ZANDER, *Group Dynamics: Research and Theory*, 3rd ed., pt. I. New York: Harper & Row, Publishers, 1968.

CIVIKLY, JEAN M., *Messages: A Reader in Human Communication*, pt. 4. New York: Random House, Inc., 1974.

MYERS, GAIL E., AND MICHELE TOLELA MYERS, *The Dynamics of Human Communication: A Laboratory Approach*, chap. 10. New York: McGraw-Hill Book Company, Inc., 1973.

SHAW, MARVIN E., *Group Dynamics: The Psychology of Small Group Behavior*, chap. 9. New York: McGraw Hill Book Company, Inc., 1971.

WENBURG, JOHN R., AND WILLIAM W. WILMOT, *The Personal Communication Process*, chap. 2. New York: John Wiley & Sons, Inc., 1973.

chapter 5

This chapter is divided into five parts. The first three were suggested by Cattell's proposal that terms used to describe groups should fall into three "panels of group description": (1) characteristics of the individuals within the group (population variables); (2) attributes of the members considered as a whole (group personality variables); and (3) relationships existing among the members (structural variables).[1] To these we have added two categories of our own: (4) intergroup forces; and (5) resultant forces.

CHARACTERISTICS OF INDIVIDUAL MEMBERS

Personality

How is a person's personality determined? Some think it depends on what a person does, others on what he thinks, and still others on what he says. Beyond these dimensions is still another—defining personality in terms of the individual's self-concept, or *who he thinks he is*. (Recall the section on the self-concept in Chapter 1.) Perhaps all these viewpoints are significant but we include them here only to indicate how complex the subject of personality is. Much has been said about individual differences and how they affect the individual's perceptions of and reaction to his environment; but our chief interest is in how different personalities serve as forces to affect the development and operation of a group.

Personality Structures or Systems. Social psychologists Harvey, Hunt, and Schroder have developed what they call *personality structures* based on the study of an individual's belief system in terms of two aspects, *content* (referents toward which we hold beliefs or attitudes) and *structure* (how we organize our beliefs).[2] They feel that most of us fall into one of four personality structures. Although a person might be categorized in more than one system, he or she will fit predominantly in one of the four.

System 1 is essentially an authoritarian individual who looks to external sources for determination of belief and behavior. This person has a strong tendency to view the world in an overly simplistic, either–or, black–white way, and has a strong belief in inherent truth. The active version likes to give orders; the passive type likes to take orders. System 1 relies heavily on authority, whether that be a person or an institution. System 1 is comfortable in clear-cut situations and likes to know what is expected of him or her and what the rules and regulations are. If a person of power

[1]R. B. Cattell, "New Concepts for Measuring Leadership in Terms of Group Syntality," *Human Relations*, 4 (1951), 161–84.

[2]O. J. Harvey, David E. Hunt, and Harold M. Schroder, *Conceptual Systems and Personality Organization* (New York: John Wiley & Sons, Inc., 1961).

Group Forces

and high status makes a statement, the System 1 individual will accept it without regard to the logic of what is said or the expertise of the one saying it.

Whereas the System 1 individual is strongly positive toward institutions and traditions, the *System 2* person has strong negative attitudes. This person is the lowest of the four groups in self-esteem and the highest in alienation and cynicism. The active version of the System 2 personality opposes authority; the passive version is merely noncooperative.

> While he denounces power figures and their use of power when he is of low status and without power, he appears to use authority and power quite rigidly and abusively once he gets them. Espousal of the cause of the weak and disenfranchised by the System 2 individual when he is of low power doesn't seem to stop him from using power unfairly once he acquires it.[3]

A *System 3* belief system has a strong emphasis on friendship, interpersonal harmony, and mutual aid. A System 3 person depends on other relevant people in the environment for clues to behavior and for acceptance and affection. System 3 needs to be needed and to control others through dependency relations. The active version champions the causes of others (usually the underdog); the passive version seeks help from others (usually people of high status, power, and expertise).

System 4 is information and problem-solving oriented and the most open-minded of the structures. Although a System 4 person is comfortable working either alone or with others, he or she is relatively independent of authority or peer approbation. The System 4 person pays more attention to people's abilities than to their status and can become ego-involved in a belief or activity without being closed-minded to alternative possibilities. The System 4 type is self-reliant and looks for objective reasons for success or failure. The active version builds theories and tests them in reality; the passive version plays with ideas and continues to collect information without putting it to specific use.

The critical difference among these personality systems is personal security. A System 1 individual derives security from leaning on authority and having a concrete orientation to a predictable environment. A System 2 person finds security in opposing established authority and being anti-Establishment. (System 2, however, is just as dependent on authority as System 1, if only because he or she needs someone or something to rebel against.) A System 3 person gets security from association with other persons and groups; a System 4 individual derives security in the reasonably predictable consequences of his or her own and others' actions.

How many individuals fall within one or another of these personality systems varies with the population being studied. As an example, 93 percent of the school administrators studied in a three-state area were System 1. Among teachers, 55–60 percent were System 1 and only one teacher (out of thousands studied by Harvey and his colleagues) was a System 2—and he was busy forming a teachers' union and quit his job the next year. No matter which population we look at, however, there are bound to be fewer of the more abstract personalities labeled System 3 or 4. In a cross section of the population, representing many different kinds of people, a typical

---

[3]O. J. Harvey, "Beliefs and Behavior: Some Implications for Education," *Science Teacher*, 37 (1970), 3.

breakdown would be this: System 1, 65–70 percent; System 2, 10–15 percent; System 3, 10–15 percent; and System 4, 3–5 percent.

What this means for the student of groups is this: Chances are high that the majority of the group members will be System 1 but chances are equally high that there will be representatives of the other systems present as well. Other implications include the fact that a System 4 individual would want to disband a group if he or she felt it had outlived its usefulness; a System 3 person would want to keep the group going.

If you are the leader of a group that is having trouble agreeing on goals or procedures, you might give thought to the differing personality structures represented among the members. You may, for instance, want to provide more clear-cut goals and more closely planned agendas for those who seem to have more need for structure, and offer alternative assignments (such as interviews and observational or library research) to the more abstract personalities.

Additional Analyses of Personality. We'd like now to conclude by briefly examining three other approaches to the understanding of personality:

1. Adding a different dimension to the discussion of personality are the four other personality types identified by Mann, Siegler, and Osmond, who divided people according to their ways of perceiving *time*: (1) For the *feeling* type, time is circular and the emotional past is all-important; (2) for the *thinking* type, time flows from the historical past and continuity and consistency are vital; (3) for the *sensation* type, time is *now*, in depth; action is the only appropriate response; and (4) for the *intuitive* type, the future is all—what *will* happen is more real than what is happening.[4]

2. Harris, in his very popular book, *I'm OK—You're OK,* uses the framework of Transactional Analysis to demonstrate life positions, of which the book title is one.[5] As originally developed by Berne,[6] Transactional Analysis analyzes the personality in terms of its three parts: the Parent, the Child, and the Adult. The Parent represents life as it is taught to us, the Child is life as we wish it were, and the Adult is life as we figure it out for ourselves. All three parts make up the whole personality.[7]

3. Renewed interest has recently been directed toward still another per-

[4]Harriet Mann, Miriam Siegler, and Humphry Osmond, "Four Types of Personalities and Four Ways of Perceiving Time," *Psychology Today,* 6 (1972), 76–84.

[5]Thomas A. Harris, *I'm OK—You're OK: A Practical Guide to Transactional Analysis* (New York: Harper & Row, Publishers, 1969).

[6]Eric Berne, *Games People Play: The Psychology of Human Relationships* (New York: Grove Press, Inc., 1964).

[7]For additional references on Transactional Analysis, see Eric Berne, *What Do You Say After You Say Hello?* (New York: Grove Press, Inc., 1972); Muriel James and Dorothy Jongeward, *Born to Win: Transactional Analysis With Gestalt Experiments* (Reading, Mass.: Addison-Wesley Publishing Co., Inc., 1971); Dorothy Jongeward, *Everybody Wins: Transactional Analysis Applied to Organizations* (Reading, Mass.: Addison-Wesley Publishing Co., Inc., 1973); and Jut Meininger, *Success Through Transactional Analysis* (New York: Grosset & Dunlap, Inc., 1973).

sonality form that has relevance to students of groups: *Machiavellianism*. As expressed by Burgoon, Heston, and McCroskey, "The label originates with the name of a famous sixteenth century Italian writer, Niccolo Machiavelli, whose motto might have been 'the ends justify the means.'"[8] The Machiavellian group member, according to Christie and Geis, is "someone who views and manipulates others for his own purposes."[9] We will return to this subject in the section devoted to leadership.

By including this material about personality, we are not advocating personality labels or analysis in any depth. Nor are we suggesting that we try to change people's personalities—even if we could. We *are* stressing both the problems and the values of individual differences. In addition, we are pointing out that the effective group leader tries to understand as much as possible the unique characteristics of group members, and tries to match people with the role or task in which they can be both comfortable and productive.

Motivation

Motivation, or why we do what we do, varies from person to person and group to group. Most of our actions, if not all, are goal seeking even though the goals may be subconscious. When people join groups, it may be because they want to work toward the group's goals; but none of us is all that unselfish, so we can be certain that the primary motivation arises because *there is something in it for us.* That something may or may not be related directly to the group's goals.

Because the motivating factors range from intangibles (prestige, recognition, friendship) to tangibles (a better grade, a promotion) it would be pointless to try to identify all the possibilities. The key concept here is that group members need to understand that no two members are working for exactly the same reasons or to the same degree. For person X, the accomplishment of the group's task may be the chief satisfier; for person Y, the interpersonal interaction may be more rewarding. Suffice it to say that groups disintegrate and people drop out if their needs are not being met.

Commitment

Closely related to motivation is an individual's commitment to the group, to the task, and to other individuals in the group. We have all met people who appeared to be committed to nothing, who were apathetic even in the presence of high enthusiasm from others; these people will obviously contribute little to a group's welfare. On the other end of the continuum (and just as troublesome to a group) are the live-wire, "let's get in there and *win*" types of people, who if not kept in some reasonable check will push too far too fast for the rest of the group to accept.

[8]Michael Burgoon, Judee K. Heston, and James C. McCroskey, *Small Group Communication: A Functional Approach* (New York: Holt, Rinehart and Winston, Inc., 1974), p. 34.

[9]R. Christie and F. L. Geis, *Studies in Machiavellianism* (New York: Academic Press, Inc., 1970), p. 1.

Ability

The relative ability of the members also creates forces on the group's operation and structure. Knowledge of the subject under discussion, skill in communication, and understanding of group forces and process are all significant abilities. Another is the capacity to perform given roles necessary for the group to succeed, as well as the capability to be flexible in assuming a variety of roles. Clearly, the more limited individuals are with regard to the kinds of roles they can perform, the greater the forces will be that limit the group to certain kinds of tasks.

Security

We described sources of security in connection with personality structures. But we feel that the individual's own, general sense of personal security is an important attribute. What's more, we believe that only those who are sufficiently secure personally can participate with profit in the give-and-take of discussion.

Any given belief of an individual can be said to be grounded at one or more points along a *reality continuum* (Table 5.1) ranging from objective reality at one end (left side of the table) to social reality at the other (right side of the table). The belief in the equality of races, for example, may be grounded in objective evidence and further substantiated by the beliefs of others such as anthropologists.

One of the most important characteristics of the secure individual is the tendency to rely on objective reality as the basis for beliefs. Obviously not all beliefs can be grounded in objective reality. Many situations are vague or ill defined, and objective standards of measurement are either unknown or simply not applicable. However, the whole objective of scientific inquiry has been to move from right to left on the reality continuum. Not long ago, historically speaking, the practice of medicine was governed almost entirely by beliefs grounded in social reality. Diseases were assumed to be caused by the devil; charms, incantations, or other forms of magic were believed to be the means of curing disease. The dramatic advance in medicine was made possible by a few who were secure enough to believe and set out to prove that the causes and cures of diseases could be objectively measured. Until recent years, almost every advance in medicine was resisted by those who preferred to ground their beliefs in social reality.

When forced to rely upon social reality, people's confidence in their beliefs will vary in proportion to their confidence in the people who provide the conclusions they are asked to accept. A given individual may not possess the competence, tools, or access to evidence necessary to observe at first hand the objective reality necessary to give support to a belief. However, others may, and there is clearly no reason for rejecting a belief simply because we cannot look for ourselves. If secure individuals

TABLE 5.1.   The Reality Continuum

Objective Reality	*Social Reality*
The individual perceives her or his belief is amenable to objective measurement, that the belief is relatively independent of the beliefs of others.	The individual perceives his or her belief may be verified only by reference to the beliefs of others or to intuitive or supernatural sources.

are forced to rely entirely upon social reality as the basis of their beliefs, and if they must act upon such evidence, they will hold such beliefs tentatively rather than dogmatically.

Finally, secure individuals are not personally distressed by contradiction. Knowing the uncertainties of observation and the hazards of inference, they are not upset to discover that new evidence or different interpretations of old evidence tend to shake old beliefs. Whether they accept or reject the new evidence will not be a function of its novelty. The acceptance will, rather, be a function of weighing the two sets of evidence against appropriate criteria of believability.[10]

Attitudes, Beliefs, and Values

According to Rokeach, an *attitude* is a predisposition to respond in certain ways; a *belief* is a hypothesis concerning the nature of objects and events and the types of actions that should be taken; and a *value* is an enduring belief.[11] We have thousands of beliefs but they stem from a few dozen values, and perhaps only five or six primary values.

It is not our purpose to recapitulate the copious research conducted by Rokeach and others but to alert the student of groups to some of the consequences of both shared and conflicting attitudes, beliefs, and values. When we feel an inconsistency between our values and our behavior, we are experiencing a state of psychological imbalance or dissonance. Humans are uncomfortable when in a state of dissonance and will change their attitudes and beliefs—even values—to achieve a state of internal balance. Change is more difficult to achieve when the person is "ego-involved" in the subject or the process of the group.

Research has shown us that people of similar attitudes are apt to like each other. Moreover, if we like each other we are apt to assume that we have similar attitudes. In describing a study by Byrne and Wong,[12] Berscheid and Walster said this:

> Subjects who possessed varying degrees of prejudice against Negroes were asked to estimate how similar the attitudes of a Negro stranger and a white stranger were to their own. Prejudiced subjects assumed that they would agree with the Negro less often than they would agree with the white stranger. Unprejudiced subjects assumed that the Negro stranger and the white stranger were equally likely to share their attitudes. It appears, then, that the subject's liking (for Negroes) influenced his perception of how similar or dissimilar another's attitudes were likely to be to his own.[13]

Differing beliefs and values can cause conflict. Barnlund and Haiman, in their analysis of levels of conflict, identified value differences as the level most difficult to

[10]A thorough discussion of all aspects of evidence, including believability, will be found in Chapter 8.

[11]Milton Rokeach, *Beliefs, Attitudes and Values* (San Francisco: Jossey-Bass, Inc., Publishers, 1968), p. 2.

[12]D. Byrne and T. J. Wong, "Racial Prejudice, Interpersonal Attraction and Assumed Dissimilarity of Attitudes," *Journal of Abnormal and Social Psychology*, 65 (1962), 246–52.

[13]Ellen Berscheid and Elaine Hatfield Walster, *Interpersonal Attraction* (Reading, Mass.: Addison-Wesley Publishing Co., Inc., 1969), p. 70.

resolve.[14] Yet the results of shared values and shared contact are apt to be a coming together of viewpoints. According to Berelson and Steiner;

> It appears to be a basic generalization about human beings that the more people associate with one another as equals, the more they come to share values and norms, attitudes and feelings, tastes and beliefs.[15]

The more we work together in our group, the more apparent will be each person's attitudes, beliefs, and values. It will also become increasingly clear that not all our firmly held convictions are based on truth or reason.[16]

ATTRIBUTES OF THE GROUP AS A WHOLE

Cattell coined the term *syntality* because he felt group research needed a concept comparable to the personality of an individual. He liked syntality because it implied togetherness as well as personality and totality.[17] Now we will identify some of the aspects that make up a group's personality or syntality.

Common Goals

When we consider the forces that operate in the group situation, one force must be the group's common goal. In Chapter 4, a justifiable reason for being was mentioned as a condition of group maturity. Here it is time to talk about the group goals as exerting forces upon the members that result in goal-seeking activity. Task commitment exerts forces upon the members to achieve the goal of completing the task. In addition to the specific tasks the group confronts, it has those goals that involve the maintenance of the group itself and the long-range goals that are fundamental to the existence of the group.

To the extent that the individuals' goals can be clearly merged with long-range group goals, the force exerted by group goals is increased. Merging of individual goals, coupled with facilitative task goals, results in the image or personality of the group that can be recognized by outsiders as well as members of the group. To

[14]Dean C. Barnlund and Franklyn S. Haiman, *The Dynamics of Discussion* (Boston: Houghton Mifflin Company, 1960), pp. 168–72.

[15]Bernard Berelson and Gary A. Steiner, *Human Behavior* (New York: Harcourt, Brace & World, Inc., 1964), p. 55.

[16]For further information on attitudes, beliefs, and values, see F. Heider, *The Psychology of Interpersonal Relations* (New York: John Wiley & Sons, Inc., 1958); L. A. Festinger, *A Theory of Cognitive Dissonance* (Evanston, Ill.: Row, Peterson, 1957); M. Sherif and H. Cantril, *The Psychology of Ego-Involvements* (New York: John Wiley & Sons, Inc., 1947); Muzafer Sherif, Carolyn W. Sherif, and Roger E. Nebergall, *Attitude and Attitude Change* (Philadelphia: W. B. Saunders Company, 1965); Howard F. Taylor, *Balance in Small Groups* (New York: Van Nostrand Reinhold Company, 1970); and Milton Rokeach, "Persuasion That Persists," *Psychology Today*, 5 (1971), 68–71, 92.

[17]Raymond B. Cattell, "Concepts and Methods in the Measurement of Group Syntality," *Psychological Review*, 55 (1948). Reprinted in *Small Groups: Studies in Social Interaction*, eds. A. Paul Hare, Edgar F. Borgatta, and Robert F. Bales (New York: Alfred A. Knopf, Inc., 1965), pp. 107–26.

separate the external forces from the internal forces in the complex structure is particularly difficult; at this point the distinction is largely semantic.

It has been interesting to observe several voluntary groups plagued by the problem of defining their fundamental group goals. A particular church group, when first formed, was intended to be primarily a learning group composed of young people from post-high-school to middle age. As such, the group did not flourish. Attendance was sporadic and small. Later the group reorganized along social lines and evolved into a young married couples' group. Both interest and membership increased and the group began to undertake a variety of tasks to help the church. The forces induced by the first set of goals were simply not strong enough to develop the group. Once the group had generated member support for social objectives, it became able to do things it was not able to do under the original set of circumstances.[18]

Task Requirements

Stability. The stability of the task requirement is a measure of the degree to which the task requirement is predictable by the members of the group. If a group is asked to come up with a decision on some matter and then that decision-making responsibility is taken away or changed to an advisory responsibility, there is bound to be considerable unrest among the members of the group. In complicated and diverse organizations, often the groups low in the hierarchy fail to find much stability in the tasks they are assigned. Group members, therefore, tend to avoid individual involvement with the task since they do not know whether their group will be allowed to see the task through.

A specific example of this kind of discouragement occurred at a university where a group of young faculty members enthusiastically began a project. When the project was beginning to bear fruit, it was taken from them by a group of senior faculty members. The younger members perceived that the older ones wanted the credit. The accuracy of their perceptions is beside the point. What is important is that those younger members hesitated thereafter to commit themselves to other group tasks.

Complexity. The complexity of the task requirement includes both the difficulty of accomplishment and the diversity of the skills required. If the group feels that success is unlikely, the members' achievement motivation will probably be less. Some support for this position is offered by Deutsch, who studied the effects of: "(1) the objective probability of prize attainment; (2) the past experience of success or failure as a group; and (3) the perceived motivation of other group members toward participating in the group. . ." upon membership motivation and achievement motivation.[19]

When the task complexity requires sharply different skills, still other forces are engaged. Many examples of this force come to mind, but one is especially dramatic. A group was considering whether or not to embark on a new set of responsibilities. A substantial minority of the group was objecting rather strenuously, and, at first, the

[18]For an extended discussion of the relationship of both external and internal goals and the forces operative on the group, see D. Cartwright and A. Zander, eds., *Group Dynamics: Research and Theory*, 2nd ed. (Evanston, Ill.: Row, Peterson, 1960), pt. 4.

[19]Morton Deutsch, "Some Factors Affecting Membership Motivation and Achievement Motivation in a Group," *Human Relations*, 12 (1959), 81–95.

rest of the members assumed that the objectors believed it would be unwise for the group to undertake the new task. The reason for the objection, however, turned out to be that the objectors feared the demands of the new task would go beyond their own capacities and they would be shouldered aside if it were undertaken. Only when they were assured of a place in the new scheme were they willing, although still reluctant, to agree to the task.

Similarly, leaders of a group often hesitate to assume tasks that require different leader skills. If such tasks are assumed, and if the leaders' skills do not measure up, pressures will very likely emerge to change the group's leadership structure.

Intensity. The intensity of the task pressure can vary from a mañana level to a crisis level. Anyone who has gone to school knows that the end of the semester seems a long time away when the requirement for the term paper is first levied.

The effect of low pressure on the group is, of course, negligible, but the effect of crisis can be revolutionary. Hamblin's experiment showed that during times of crisis the leader's influence rises sharply, and, if the leader has been unsuccessful, he will probably be replaced.[20] We have observed both results in the political arena where under stress of war or economic instability, Presidents have been given extraordinary powers. Equally obvious, many totalitarian leaders deliberately seek to create crises they feel they can manage in order to gain powers they may otherwise be denied.

The degree of intensity, which is one of the most significant forces acting upon the group, is a function of the perception of the members. Often a group is faced with what is actually a crisis situation, but the members refuse to see, or are incapable of seeing, the gravity of the situation. Bringing the group face to face with the intensity of the task requirements is one of the leader's most important challenges. We shall return to the concept of task intensity when we examine resultant forces later in this chapter.

Attractiveness. Task attractiveness is such an obvious force that we need do little more than mention it here. The attractiveness of a task is a function of the rewards that individuals can expect during, and as a result of, successful task performance. Together with intensity, attractiveness is a potent force. Even without the factor of intensity, it remains potent.

Origin of Task Requirements

The discussion to this point may suggest that tasks are always levied upon the group from outside sources. This is not true. In organizational groups the tasks are usually assigned by the larger organization. Most voluntary groups, however, levy requirements upon themselves, and many organizational groups seek to extend their area of control in such a fashion that they seem to be initiating their own task requirements. The concern here is with how the group initially is confronted with the task requirement. The task may be levied upon or created by, the group's leadership; the task may be levied upon or created by followers; or the task may be levied upon or created by the group as a whole. In each case the forces are somewhat different, so each must be examined briefly.

---

[20]Robert L. Hamblin, "Leadership and Crises," in *Group Dynamics* (1960), eds. Cartwright and Zander, pp. 571–85.

When the task requirements originate outside the group, they usually are transmitted through the group's hierarchy; when they come from within the group, they are usually created by the group's hierarchy. Thus, the group's leadership is usually in the position of prodding the group into action.

When the task requirements are created by followers, the impact on the group as a whole is generally less. If the leader is unreceptive and if the task requirement is imperative, one of two things will happen. The leadership structure will be overturned or undermined or the group's significance will diminish proportionately.

Examples of the applications of task requirements can be found in the problems that come to the staff of a university department. Such tasks as making budgets, recommendations for promotion, and curricular plans come directly from the administration and are levied upon the chairperson who must assemble his or her department or its appropriate committees and make plans. Such tasks are not usually attractive, the guidelines for their execution not always stable. The complexity varies; the intensity is usually determined by deadlines set by the dean. On the other hand, tasks such as the creation of new courses or the expansion of programs that involve hiring new staff members are usually created within the department by people higher in the leadership hierarchy (not necessarily the chairperson). Often the intensity and attractiveness of such tasks are not immediately apparent to some of the department members even though their areas of responsibility may be directly involved. In such cases the forces for task achievement are weaker than when the leadership hierarchy is backed up by outside power. The accomplishment of such tasks requires the leaders to exercise either persuasion or coercion, or both.

Members of the department who are lower in status are often in most direct contact with many students and thus are sensitive to task requirements involving organization and teaching of mass enrollment courses. The departmental leadership is usually less sensitive to such task requirements than to those levied by the administration or involving departmental budgeting and control. Hence such followers have to be especially involved and persistent if they are to have much effect upon departmental policy.

Sometimes, as is particularly characteristic of groups that have been used for experimental purposes, the tasks are assigned to, or created by, the group as a whole. For example, if a group is told when all are present that it has 20 minutes to arrive at a solution to a problem, and that the best group in the experiment will receive such and such a prize, the appreciation of the intensity and attractiveness of the task requirement does not have to be mediated by some part of the group. The task pressure is applied to each individual directly. The same thing happens when the task requirements are set by the group as a whole. As we shall emphasize later, such procedures are most likely to generate effective task pressure with a minimum of interpersonal strain. (This is one of the reasons for the stress on goal-setting procedures.) Unfortunately, genuine creation of task requirements by the group as a whole is infrequent except in small mature groups.

Task pressures are usually not accepted simultaneously by all members of the group. Some members of the group will have committed themselves to the task, but other members are either not aware of task pressures or are resisting them. Thus a complicated set of forces is present during the stage when the group is formally or informally considering task commitment. Members who have committed themselves to the task face the immediate problem of securing commitment from other members. Those who are unaware of the task pressures do not yet feel any pressure, and those who are resisting the task pressures will contend that the task goals are unnecessary, undesirable, likely to be achieved without group activity, or some combination of the three. This is the point at which those who are committed may possibly succumb to the feeling that the end justifies the means and attempt to bludgeon recalcitrant members into task commitment.

Sometimes task activity is produced not by genuine commitment to the task itself but by acceptance of personal influence of others. When this happens, we can distinguish between those who are task oriented and those who are source oriented.[21] The results of these two kinds of commitment were studied by McDavid who compared message-oriented with source-oriented subjects. He found that

> The message-oriented group differed from the source-oriented group in that members of this group (1) were generally less susceptible to group influence, (2) were less affected by manipulations of task difficulty, and (3) showed a tendency to compromise with discrepant group judgments rather than to agree completely with them when yielding did occur.[22]

Once group members have accepted the task requirements and have committed themselves to the goal of task achievement, additional forces are created. These forces can be called the *pressures for closure*. The effects of pressure for closure can be dramatic when skillfully manipulated by group members. To test the extent of these pressures, one of the authors conducted a study to determine whether a minority could use these pressures to force the majority to shift its opinion and conform to the minority, rather than follow the more usual direction of conformity.[23] Groups averaging six members each were given the task of making recommendations about a human relations problem within a strict time limit. Although it was unknown to the four naive members, two of the members were "plants" operating under instructions from the experimenter. All members read the instructions and the problem. Then they individually checked their reactions on a seven-point scale. The experimenter collected the individual reactions and reported the actual scores of the four naive members, and then the scores of the other two members. One of these corresponded to the group mode, but the other took the most extreme position.

The modal plant then began a personal attack on the deviate, who remained polite, unassuming, but firm. This was done to create group resentment toward the modal plant and thereby induce forces against a source representing the position taken by the group majority. At the same time sympathy was created for the deviate. About halfway through the period the modal plant stopped talking and pretended to consider his behavior. Then with only 10 or 15 minutes remaining, the modal plant began the shift toward the extreme position of the deviate.

---

[21]This distinction is comparable to the objective reality–social reality continuum outlined earlier in this chapter.

[22]John McDavid, Jr., "Personality and Situational Determinants of Conformity," *Journal of Abnormal and Social Psychology*, 58 (1959), 245–46.

[23]R. Victor Harnack, "A Study of the Effect of an Organized Minority upon a Discussion Group," *The Journal of Communication*, 13 (1963), 12–24. See also Henry L. Minton, Joseph A. Steger, and George R. Smrtic, "Group Opinion Change as a Function of Circular vs. Rectangular Seating Arrangement," *Psychonomic Science*, 12 (1968), 357–58.

The task had to be solved, and the solution consisted of getting group agreement on one of the seven alternatives. The results showed a dramatic shift of the majority in 16 of the 20 groups to the position taken by the minority of two. The forces for closure mounted as the deadline drew near. Most of the majority realized that something had happened to them, but they were not quite sure how to define it. The result, however, was a deliberate reversal of the effect of the majority over the minority.

We have discussed task requirements and have found that the task to be performed does put considerable force upon the group members. The nature and extent of the forces are a function of the nature of the task requirement itself, including its stability, complexity, intensity, and attractiveness. The task forces are further modified by the manner in which they are applied to the group, whether through the hierarchy, individual members, or the group as a whole. Finally, pressures for closure are created when the group members have committed themselves to task accomplishment.

Role Differentiation and Flexibility

To be successful, a group needs a variety of functions or roles performed. Whether the role is classified as performing a leadership function or a follower function is immaterial. Because these necessary roles are assumed by individuals, it was tempting to include them under the first part of this chapter, which dealt with characteristics of the individual. We resisted the temptation, however, on the grounds that the ability to perform more than one role is one mark of a successful discussant. An important measure of a group's syntality is the individuals' abilities to mesh and interchange their respective roles. An individual will assume a certain function at a certain time not only because the group needs the function at that time but also because there are needs operating within the individual.

If we agree with Slater that a role is "a more or less coherent and unified system of items of behavior,"[24] then we recognize the impossibility of characterizing every conceivable role or function. But Slater points out that the most fundamental type of role differentiation occurs between task functions (getting the group's job done) and socioemotional functions (helping members maintain the group and get satisfaction out of how the job is being done).

> Presumably, the ideal leader of a small group would be sufficiently skillful and flexible to alternate these types of behavior in such a way as to handle both problems, and maximize his status on all possible dimensions. He would be able to make both an active, striving response to the task and a sympathetic response to the individual needs of group members. He would be a high participator, well-liked, rated high on task ability, and eventually chosen leader.
> Such individuals are rare.[25]

---

[24]P. E. Slater, "Role Differentiation in Small Groups," *American Sociological Review*, 20 (1955), 300–10.

[25]Slater, "Role Differentiation," p. 308.

Haiman cites three reasons why role specialization is needed: (1) because people are different; (2) because people need stability in their relationships; and (3) because a division of labor is more efficient.[26] But he also notes that too much role differentiation works counter to group cohesiveness and friendship. He offers two arguments for not being too specialized and for being able to do more than one role: (1) individuals need flexibility more than stability, and (2) groups can become overdependent on the specialists.[27] In other words, group members need to be flexible enough to perform whatever role is needed at the time. We recall a student group in which one member became adept at summarizing. Yet when this skilled summarizer was absent, no one else even saw the need for a summary.

Climate

Everyday experience makes it clear that a group often develops a general atmosphere that determines members' reactions to the group as a whole. Some groups are businesslike, impersonal, and efficient. Others are warm, relaxed, and friendly. And still others are full of tension and suspicion.[28]

It is evident that different climates provide significant forces on individual and group behavior. Most people would agree that the ideal climate provides trust, risk taking, mutual caring, and open communication. The teacher is the principal climate-setter in his or her classroom and only recently have we begun to gauge the influence of nonverbal communication on classroom climate and the general learning atmosphere.

Gibb categorized behavior that was characteristic of supportive and defensive climates in small groups. Defensive climates included evaluation, control, strategy, neutrality, superiority, and certainty; supportive climates, on the other hand, were characterized by description, problem orientation, spontaneity, empathy, equality, and provisionalism.[29]

You will recall our brief description of climate as a group characteristic in the previous chapter and our confession that we found it an elusive and intangible attribute. How do you pin it down? Some writers, such as Bormann,[30] combine climate with cohesiveness. We feel they are related but separable concepts. We believe all groups have climates but not all groups have cohesiveness.

[26]Franklyn S. Haiman, "The Specialization of Roles and Functions in a Group," *Quarterly Journal of Speech*, 43 (1957), 165–74.

[27]Haiman, "The Specialization of Roles and Functions," p. 169.

[28]Dorwin Cartwright, "The Nature of Group Cohesiveness," in *Group Dynamics: Research and Theory*, eds. Dorwin Cartwright and Alvin Zander (New York: Harper & Row, Publishers, 1968), p. 102.

[29]J. R. Gibb, "Sociopsychological Processes of Group Instruction," in *The Dynamics of Instructional Groups*, ed. N. B. Henry (Fifty-ninth Yearbook of the National Society for the Study of Education, Part II, 1960), pp. 115–35.

[30]Ernest G. Bormann, *Discussion and Group Methods: Theory and Practice* 2nd ed. (New York: Harper & Row, Publishers, 1975).

Cohesiveness

Cohesiveness, or the tendency for group members to stick together, is the product of many factors. Membership in the group satisfies our needs and we are attracted to the task or the group members or both. The group provides us with some kind of payoff or reward that makes it worth our while to give our time and energy.

According to Cartwright, we can measure a group's cohesiveness by analyzing the interpersonal attraction among members, evaluating the group as a whole, studying the members' feeling of closeness or identification with the group, and determining the members' expressed desire to remain in the group.[31] Whether we call it *team spirit* or *one for all and all for one*, there comes a time in the life of a successful group when a collection of people has turned into a real group. There is a new surge of loyalty and a renewed willingness to work together. Davis summed it up when he said that cohesiveness occurs when "the forces acting on the members to remain in the group are greater than the total forces acting on them to leave it."[32]

Decision-Making Structure

When group members are uncertain as to just *who* has the decision-making responsibility, or when they do not know *how* a matter is to be brought to a decision, forces tending toward disintegration and dissatisfaction are increased. Mulder found, for example, that the more centralized the decision structure of groups, the better the group's performance in regard to speed, quality, and efficiency.[33] He went further to distinguish centralized structures, as such, from centralized decision-making structures. A centralized structure with all member contributions polarized around a leader is not the same thing as a centralized decision-making structure. The former concerns interaction alone; the latter concerns the actual process of making decisions. Mulder found that centralized structures, without the centralized decision-making characteristic, were more vulnerable and resulted in negative performance.

The decision structure is not so important in the actual face-to-face discussion. It becomes an issue when subgroups of the larger group are faced with a variety of decisions and they do not possess a clear understanding of how decisions are made. Then questions such as these arise: Who is responsible for this matter? Should this matter come before the whole group? If I have an idea, to whom should I direct it? When the structure for initiating, processing, and solving problems is clear and appropriate, the forces tend toward efficiency and member satisfaction.

Size

Size is a very important variable as a group force. Genuine leaderless discussion, for example, seems unlikely to occur except in *small* mature groups. As Bass

---

[31]Cartwright, in *Group Dynamics* (1968), eds. Cartwright and Zander, pp. 92–95.

[32]James H. Davis, *Group Performance* (Reading, Mass.: Addison-Wesley Publishing Co., Inc., 1969), p. 78.

[33]M. Mulder, "Communication Structure, Decision Structure, and Group Performance," *Sociometry*, 23 (1960), 1–14.

pointed out, the first consequent of increased group size is a reduction in the "interaction potential" of any given set of members.[34] The more people there are in the group, the less time each individual has to communicate. To show how the number of relationships increases geometrically as the group number increases arithmetically, we have devised the simple formula:

$$R = \frac{N(N - 1)}{2}$$

where R equals the number of relationships and N equals the number of people in the group. Thus, a group of two has only one relationship, AB, if we use A and B to identify two individuals. Continuing with alphabetic designations, we find that if we add a third person, C, we now have three relationships, AB, AC, and BC. But suddenly, the progression takes off so that a group of five has ten relationships, and a group of ten has forty-five and so on.

Many people believe that small groups are merely prototypes of large groups. Although some aspects of small and large groups are similar, differences in the communication structures alone suffice to compel the distinction. There is no more warrant to attempt to equate small and large groups than there is to equate personality dynamics and group dynamics. Recall that in Chapter 2 we defined a group as large when there were too many people to permit easy communication (both verbal and nonverbal). Although the cutoff point may vary, we feel that groups usually have these communication difficulties when they have nine or more members. But, we repeat, it is the ability to communicate freely that distinguishes the small group rather than the specific number of members.[35]

In his study of student learning discussion groups, Schellenberg found limited evidence that small groups showed slightly higher academic achievement, but he did find a "surprisingly consistent inverse relationship between group size and student satisfaction. Students claimed greater satisfaction in the smaller groups."[36]

The second consequent of increased group size is multiplication of demand for specific structure. Hamblin discovered that, as group size increases, there is a tendency for one member of the group to become a substantive leader and another to become a procedural leader.[37] That is, as the group becomes larger, the leadership roles become more specialized. It follows that the greater the specialization, the greater the need for structure to regulate behavior.

Gibb found that although increasing the size of the group brought a plus, in-

---

[34]Bernard M. Bass, *Leadership, Psychology, and Organizational Behavior* (New York: Harper & Row, Publishers, 1960), chap. 17.

[35]Steiner identifies *groups* as collections of "mutually responsive individuals," *organizations* as sets of "mutually responsive groups," and *societies* as clusters of "mutually responsive organizations." See Ivan D. Steiner, *Group Process and Productivity* (New York: Academic Press, Inc., 1972), p. 5.

[36]James A. Schellenberg, "Group Size as a Factor in Success of Academic Discussion Groups," *Journal of Educational Sociology*, 33 (1959), 73–79.

[37]Robert L. Hamblin, "An Experimental Study of the Relationship of Communication, Power Relations, Specialization, and Social Atmospheres to Group Size" (unpublished Ph.D. dissertation, University of Michigan, 1955).

creased potential for creativity, it also brought at least two minuses, increased potential for interpersonal threat and greater defensiveness. He also reported that "relative productivity decreases with the size of the group."[38]

Time and again, discussion classes are frustrated by the complexities of increased group size. Most of the early discussions in our classes are conducted in small groups of five to seven members each. When larger groups, including the class as a whole, are given decision-making assignments without instruction concerning group structure, they often flounder helplessly, trying to use the same leaderless or informal structure that had worked so well in the smaller groups. It usually takes a frustrating experience or two for students to accept emotionally (as well as intellectually) the complexities introduced by increased group size.

We have noted another interesting phenomenon in classroom discussions when groups of 15 to 20 are struggling to reach consensus or arrive at a mutually satisfactory decision. Often, those students who are most verbal increase their participation, taking the floor more often and holding it longer, while the less verbal people retreat to partial, if not complete, withdrawal. Thus the more people there are in the group, the fewer people there are who will actively participate.

Pressure Toward Homogeneity

A significant group force is the pressure toward uniformity and conformity. "We always do it this way" may not be expressed in so many words but group members who try to deviate from accepted norms or standards will find the group trying a variety of means to bring them back into line. Kiesler and Kiesler said that "the individual may conform to avoid rejection, to ingratiate himself, [or] to be 'one of the boys.'"[39] Of course there are other reasons for acquiescing to the pressure to conform. The group member may feel, for example, that if he conforms the group will remain together and accomplish its [and his] goal.

Cartwright and Zander have pointed out that not all groups exert pressures to conform. Occasionally, the need is for heterogeneity, particularly if the group members are representatives from other groups.[40] This is rare, however. The pressure is almost always toward conformity.

Group Development and Continuity

Many researchers have agreed that group development follows predictable patterns. Erikson likened the growth of a group to the maturation process in individuals.[41] According to Shaw, "Group formation does not stop with affiliation of members. The group develops over a moderately long period and probably never reaches a completely stable state."[42]

[38]J. R. Gibb, "Factors Producing Defensive Behavior Within Groups," Final Technical Report (Boulder, Colo.: Group Process Laboratory, 1956), pp. 1–16.

[39]Charles A. Kiesler and Sara B. Kiesler, *Conformity* (Reading, Mass.: Addison-Wesley Publishing Co., Inc., 1970), p. 33.

[40]Cartwright and Zander, *Group Dynamics* (1968), pp. 147–48.

[41]Erik H. Erikson, *Childhood and Society* (New York: W. W. Norton & Company, Inc., 1963), pp. 247–69.

[42]Marvin E. Shaw, *Group Dynamics: The Psychology of Small Group Behavior* (New York: McGraw-Hill Book Company, Inc., 1971), p. 101.

A variety of terms have been used to describe the stages of group development. Bennis and Shepard used two principal phases, dependence and interdependence, pointing out that when a group develops it moves from preoccupation with authority relations to preoccupation with personal relations.[43] Tuckman identifies four stages: forming, storming, norming, and performing.[44]

Forces are also created by the continuity of the group and by the relative stability of the group's membership. If the membership is continually changing, forces for integration and orientation must be satisfied before genuine task accomplishment can even be launched. The problem is that the addition or subtraction of *even one individual* significantly changes the group and makes it necessary for the initial stages of group development (what Bormann called the *shakedown cruise* phase[45]) to begin all over again. Some classroom discussion groups never get past the elementary stage of development because not all members are present at all sessions.

Leadership

Later chapters will be devoted to the subjects of leaders and leadership. However, since the focus of group forces is usually upon the leaders, let us examine a specific force we call the *leader paradox*. Sometimes the responsibilities of group leadership are comparatively minuscule, as when a group of children seeks to decide whether to play baseball or tag. Sometimes, however, the responsibilities are enormous for those people who seek, or have thrust upon them, the job of guiding a group.

If the group has any justifiable reason for being and if the members feel genuine concern, the leader faces this paradox: The pressures of task accomplishment fall most heavily upon the leader, but he or she can't accomplish them without a cohesive, cooperative group. The leader has the responsibility of maintaining a balance between what Berrien called *group need satisfaction* and *formal achievement*. Berrien's experiments showed that homeostasis (desirable equilibrium) broke down when stresses destroyed this balance.[46] What are the implications of this paradox?

If the leader succumbs to the internal forces for cohesiveness and ignores external forces, she or he may become someone whose leadership turned out to be impotent. If leaders owe their position to the group, if they are insecure in that position, or if they are still on the way up, the chances are increased that they will succumb to the internal forces.

If the leader succumbs to external forces, the members of the group may become helpless pawns if they do not control the selection of the leader, or disgruntled rebels if they have the power to replace the leader. No one who has ever worked in a large bureaucracy can have failed to experience that feeling of impotence. In such situations perhaps the most ennobling expression is "Ours not to reason why . . . ."

[43]Warren G. Bennis and Herbert A. Shepard, "A Theory of Group Development," in *Organizational Behavior and the Practice of Management,* eds. D. R. Hampton, C. E. Summer, and R. A. Webber (Glenview, Ill.: Scott, Foresman & Co., 1968), pp. 165–98.

[44]B. W. Tuckman, "Developmental Sequence in Small Groups," *Psychological Bulletin,* 63 (1965), 384–99.

[45]Bormann, *Discussion and Group Methods,* pp. 220–24.

[46]F. Kenneth Berrien, "Homeostasis Theory of Groups: Implications for Leadership," in *Leadership and Interpersonal Behavior,* eds. Luigi Petrullo and Bernard M. Bass, (New York: Holt, Rinehart and Winston, Inc., 1961), pp. 82–99.

The leader paradox exacts a price that is often more than many would-be leaders are willing to pay. Some leaders are rewarded more richly than their sinecures warrant. By the same token, the quickest way to educate foot draggers is to give them specific leader responsibilities and let them experience this paradox of leadership themselves.

RELATIONSHIPS AMONG MEMBERS

Communication

Later chapters will be devoted specifically to communication, but no discussion of relationships among members would make sense without at least mentioning the means by which relationships are possible. Naive discussants are convinced that communication occurs only when they speak. They forget or don't realize that communication is occurring all the time, whether they want it to or not. They are not aware of the subtle nonverbal messages they are simultaneously sending and receiving. What's more, they underrate the significance of the most difficult communication skill, listening.

Process

Students of small groups are often heard referring to the dichotomy of *content* on the one hand and *process* on the other. Content means the subject of the discussion, what is being talked about. Process means what is happening in the group, the forward movement or change, the way interactions are occurring, and the actual steps the group takes when trying to accomplish a task. When we study a group's process, we are interested in such aspects as who talks the most, who talks the least, and who talks to whom as examples of the series of behaviors or events that move the group or impede it.

As we will see in Chapter 15, following all the possible components of a group's process is very difficult. There are not only many variables to observe, there are also intangible aspects (such as an individual's motivation). But studying group process is usually the focus of most courses in group discussion and even a partial grasp is rewarding.

Social Facilitation

Human behavior in groups is affected by the presence of those in the group. Zajonc reported that experiments with animals and insects showed that the mere presence of another animal or insect of its own kind would cause the species under observation to eat more and work harder; other experiments showed that the amount of learning decreased because of the distraction of adding other members of the species.[47] Experiments on humans have also produced mixed results. We are sometimes stimulated by the presence of others and sometimes inhibited. We obviously behave differently in groups than we do when alone; but less obvious is the fact that we behave differently from group to group. One factor is the presence of different

[47]Robert B. Zajonc, "Social Facilitation," in *Group Dynamics* (1968), eds. Cartwright and Zander, pp. 63–73.

people; another is whether it is a competitive or cooperative situation; and still another is the difference in what is at stake.

Steiner observed that "evaluation apprehension" can facilitate or inhibit performance, depending on the ability of the individual. He says that "a skilled athlete is likely to perform best before an audience, whereas a rank amateur is not."[48]

Teachers of discussion classes must continually weigh the effect of their presence on the group. If students suffer from evaluation apprehension they may perform better or worse than they would without the evaluator's presence. Particularly in the early stages of the class's development as a group, students often unconsciously direct more of their communication to the teacher than to fellow discussants. Artificial communication patterns are the result.

Obviously, much more research needs to be done before we can fully understand all the ramifications of the presence of others—which is, after all, the primary distinction between an individual's behavior when operating alone or in groups.

Interpersonal Attraction and Compatibility

Sentiment, affection, liking, or attraction are obviously important forces in group interaction. Shaw found support for two of his hypotheses: (1) Compatible groups are more effective in achieving group goals than are incompatible groups; and (2) members of compatible groups are better satisfied than members of incompatible groups.[49] Byrne, on the other hand, felt developing a model from research on interpersonal attraction was a continuing process. He wrote:

> With interpersonal attraction as a potential research problem, one finds that observations concerning man's likes and dislikes, the basis of friendship, and the reasons for love and hate are painfully numerous and frequently contradictory. Could paradigm research possibly emerge from "absence makes the heart grow fonder," "love me, love my dog," "birds of a feather flock together," "out of sight, out of mind," "opposites attract," or "love is blind"?[50]

Interpersonal attraction develops from contact, particularly when it is buttressed by interdependent activity, homogeneous background and comparable values. Clearly, the contact must be rewarding if it is to produce interpersonal attraction. This principle need not be spelled out except to remember that the rewards need not be extrinsic. The very act of establishing meaningful relationships with others is, according to the theory we have been developing, a highly rewarding act.

Attraction for, or liking of, an object or act is just as evident as interpersonal attraction. We like things as well as people. Heider developed, as the fundamental basis of his theory, the notion of maintaining a balance between one's liking for a person and for an object.[51] If P, for example, likes O and if O likes X (some object or

[48]Steiner, *Group Process*, p. 134.

[49]Shaw, *Group Dynamics*, p. 230.

[50]Donn Byrne, *The Attraction Paradigm* (New York: Academic Press, Inc., 1971), p. 23.

[51]Fritz Heider, *The Psychology of Interpersonal Relations* (New York: John Wiley & Sons, Inc., 1958).

act), P will tend to like X also. By the same token, if P likes O and O *dislikes* X, then P will tend to dislike X.

This theory of balancing attractions is not new; Aristotle developed it rather extensively 24 centuries ago.[52] The novelty of the idea is not important, but the forces created by the balance or imbalance of attractions are significant. If the attractions are in balance, forces are created to maintain this balance or equilibrium. P will tend to reject ideas that imply either O or X are anything but what he perceives them to be. Similarly, if the attractions are out of balance, forces are created that operate on P to restore balance. Thus, if P likes O and *dislikes* X, and if O *likes* X, P is in trouble. He must find some way to reconcile this discrepancy.

If a person can recognize differences and learn to accept them without a corresponding psychologically unhealthy compartmentalizing of self, he or she is probably a mature individual. Genuine tolerance and acceptance of individuals who hold different views demand this recognition of disparity. Probably much of what passes for religious or political tolerance is simply the result of not caring very much about one's religion or politics. When people do care, and can still accept the discrepancy, this is the epitome of genuine interpersonal attraction.

Cooperation or Competition

Discussants are often advised about the virtues of cooperating with others. Some of the advice seems to make cooperation an end in itself. The hard headed approach is to say that an individual will cooperate if personal goals are perceived as complementary to those of others and will compete if personal goals are perceived as antagonistic to those of others. (Recall the discussion of complementary and antagonistic goals in Chapter 4.)

Of course, discussions are seldom dominated by only one complementary or antagonistic goal. Think of goal complexes or goal clusters that tend to dominate an individual's behavior. The relationships between goals and behavior are represented in Table 5.2.

It is important to understand the *effects* of cooperative and competitive climates on group behavior. By now it must be evident that cooperation means more than merely getting along with others. It includes interdependence and mutually helpful productivity.

TABLE 5.2.   Relationships Between Goals and Cooperation/Competition

Perceived Goals		
Members perceive that the majority of their goals are *complementary*.	Members are not sure whether the majority of their goals are complementary or antagonistic.	Members perceive that the majority of their goals are *antagonistic*.
Member Behavior		
Members cooperate.	Members are cautious and spar for position.	Members compete.

[52]Lane Cooper, *The Rhetoric of Aristotle* (New York: Appleton-Century-Crofts, 1932).

Some of the fundamental differences between cooperative and competitive behavior as identified by Davis[53] and Deutsch[54] are:

1.   Group cohesiveness is generally increased by intergroup competition
but decreased by intragroup competition. In other words, it is a stimulus for
us to work well together as a volleyball team when we are competing against
another team. But if several of us are agitating to become captain of the
team, our team spirit may come unglued.

2.   There is more sharing of roles and responsibility for action in cooperative situations than in competitive ones. That is, individuals in a cooperative
situation will not feel a compunction to perform the same acts that others
have performed so long as the actions of the others are moving the group
toward its goal or goals. We have all observed discussions go around and
around until everyone had seemingly discovered the solution to the problem for themselves. Such discussions indicate fundamentally competitive
behavior. Harnack and Goetzinger conducted an investigation in which
complete transcripts of discussions were kept. The suggestions advanced
by the discussants were analyzed to determine what happened to the original suggestion. The researchers discovered that the majority of suggestions
finally adopted, not counting routine procedural offerings, such as "Let's
arrange the chairs in a circle," were adopted after most of the discussants
had made the same suggestion, usually in different words without giving
credit to the originator.[55]

3.   Individuals will react more favorably toward the actions of others in
cooperative situations than in competitive ones. Cooperating individuals
will evaluate fellow cooperators more highly than they will evaluate competitors. We are much more apt to give each other the benefit of the doubt
when we are on the same side. But our competitors inevitably become the
enemy and must be viewed in less favorable light.

4.   There will be greater acceptance of other people's ideas and points of
view in cooperative situations than in competitive ones. That is, members of
cooperating groups will be more inclined to adopt suggestions made by
other members of the group, rather than insist on having their own way.
This type of acceptance should be distinguished from the acceptance that a
submissive individual gives to actions initiated by a dominant individual. If
the group is cooperating optimally, members will accept or reject suggestions made by others largely on the merit of the suggestion alone.

There is a danger that a cooperating group may miss significant shortcom-
ings in suggestions offered by group members; it may be generally less
critical. Another significant difference, which at first glance appears to be

[53]James H. Davis, *Group Performance* (Reading, Mass.: Addison-Wesley Publishing Co., Inc.,
1969), p. 80.

[54]Morton Deutsch, "The Effects of Cooperation and Competition Upon Group Process," in
Group Dynamics (1968), eds. Cartwright and Zander, pp. 461–82.

[55]R. Victor Harnack and Charles Goetzinger, "Determining the Sources of Influence in Discussion Groups" (paper presented at the national convention of the Speech Association of
America, December 1955).

contradictory to the previous statement, is that cooperating individuals tend to openly criticize one another more readily than competitors. Constructive criticism of another is one way of helping that person. Withholding constructive criticism allows the other person to make the same error again and again.

5.   More helpfulness will be exhibited in cooperative situations than in competitive ones. This follows naturally, for helping another attain his or her goals (if both sets of goals are complementary) is tantamount to moving toward our own goals.

In addition to these differences, Deutsch noted that cooperating individuals communicated more readily and more clearly with one another. Further, it will come as no surprise that he also found that cooperative groups were more productive and produced a superior product.

Cooperative groups are obviously preferable to competitive groups, yet cooperation does *not* mean absence of conflict, as some believe. It does mean absence of conflict intended to *block individuals* but not the presence of vigorous conflict intended to *explore ideas*. As we will discuss in greater detail in Chapter 11, conflict of this latter type is an essential ingredient to productive discussion. Groups that are all sweetness and light are in just as much trouble as those that are all agitation and turmoil.

Interdependence

An essential feature of any group is that its members are dependent, to some degree at least, on one another. This feature of interdependence is manifested in each of the group characteristics, in the group structure, and in the resultant forces operating on the group members. This feature does not distinguish one group from another since any form of collective behavior involves some kind of interdependence.

The extent of interdependence may not be apparent until we examine a few examples. Talkers depend on listeners; debaters depend on opponents; and information seekers depend on available sources of information. Considering *indirect* interdependence, it is apparent that we depend upon others for almost everything we want, but the concern here is only with the direct form of interdependence.

One way to further illustrate this feature of interdependence in groups is to use the *pathway* definition. When individuals' paths toward their goals intersect, and when they become aware of this intersection, they possess the ingredients of a group. In Figure 5.1 individuals A, B, C, and D find progress toward their goals—AG, BG, CG, and DG—depending to some extent upon each other's behavior. Thus, X represents the place where the paths of the four intersect in their progress toward their goals, and the point at which they become a group, *even though individual goals may be different.*

Kiesler and Kiesler have referred to the concept of *common fate* or *we're in this together* as being allied to interdependence. They feel, however, that both interdependence and common fate really are aspects of the more general term, *dependency*. To illustrate this point they use the example of a teenager who is still dependent on his parents but feeling pressure from his peers to weaken the relationship. The teenager may behave in ways that conflict with his parents' expectations and values.

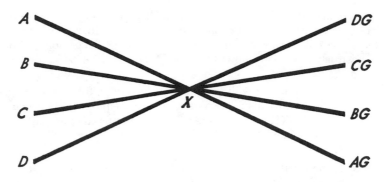

FIGURE 5.1   A "Pathway" Definition of a Group

We note that the teenager's often bizarre behavior has a dual function, although he may not realize it. It not only helps him to define his self-image as an independent person, but it also provides cues to the other—in this case the parents—that the dependent relationship is no longer desired. Indeed, the cues provided to the other that the relationship is no longer desired may be the most important part of the behavior.[56]

According to Bennis and Shepard, "dependence and independence—power and love, authority and intimacy—are regarded as the central problems of group life."[57]

INTERGROUP AND EXTERNAL FORCES

An examination of some of the characteristics of *intergroup* relationships will help in understanding how groups relate to one another. In the study of *intragroup* relationships, we pointed out that the individuals had to interact with one another in a situation in which there was some degree of interdependence. The concern here is with groups that have some formal or recognized relationship as, for example, a group that is a part of a larger organization and is therefore formally related to other groups within the larger organization.

Intergroup Climate

Like the individuals who compose them, groups can be described as having cooperative or competitive relationships with other groups. The best way to illustrate the nature of this intergroup climate is to describe briefly some extensive experiments that were carried out by Muzafer Sherif and his associates.[58] Sherif used 24 twelve-year-old boys as subjects for his experiments. The boys were placed in a camp

[56]Kiesler and Kiesler, *Conformity*, p. 79.

[57]Bennis and Shepard, "A Theory of Group Development," p. 181.

[58]Muzafer Sherif and others, *Intergroup Conflict and Cooperation: The Robbers Cave Experiment* (Norman, Okla.: University Book Exchange, 1961).

situation for several weeks, during which time Sherif and his assistants divided them into two groups and conducted a three-stage experiment. The first stage was the development of in-group feelings, accomplished by presenting to each of the two groups goals that could only be achieved by collaborative effort (complementary goals). This action stressed the degree of interdependence within the group and produced group solidarity. The second stage was the development of intergroup hostility and competition, accomplished by setting forth various goals that necessitated the failure of one group in order for the other group to succeed (antagonistic goals). In this stage a tournament, involving a variety of athletic events, was held between the two groups. The final stage was the reduction of intergroup tensions, accomplished by means of imposing superordinate goals that could be reached only if both groups worked together. The results of this third stage produced considerable friendliness and other attributes of cooperation despite the rather bitter rivalry that had been caused by the second-stage activities.

Although the anecdotes about the boys' interactions make fascinating reading, it is necessary, here, to pass over them and point out some of the alternative approaches that Sherif rejected as means of reducing intergroup conflict and tension and the reasons that Sherif rejected them.

Personal contact between members of conflicting groups is often said to be the best method of reducing conflict and promoting cooperation. In the Sherif experiments, however, contact did not result in improved relations because of a lack of goals that required intergroup collaboration.

A *common enemy* is another way to bring groups together. This has been, of course, the bond that has joined hostile nations in time of war. Schools have used the common-enemy approach to produce harmony and solidarity by means of athletic and other contests with other schools. Business, military, and even church organizations have resorted to some form of the common enemy tactic in order to weld diverse groups together within their organizations. The difficulty is that the common enemy still produces conflict that can often become bitter and wasteful. Superordinate goals need not be those of defeating someone; they can be goals of defeating some common enemy like poverty, ignorance, and disease.

Individual competition and rivalry can reduce intergroup competition and rivalry, but group solidarity is destroyed in the process and the benefits of collaborative action are harder to attain.

Leadership may be able to do much to reduce intergroup tensions, but leaders are often helpless in the face of the forces built up and sustained by their own followers.

The point should be clear. The forces engendered by the nature of intergroup climate can have a considerable effect on the nature of group operation. The nature of intergroup climate can be comprehended very much in the same way as the nature of intragroup climate, and the effects on intergroup behavior are very much the same as they are on intragroup behavior.

Intergroup Status

A group's status may be primarily a function of its area of control; the status may also be a function of the importance that others attach to the tasks performed by the group. A jury considering a murder case has a higher status, for example, than a jury considering traffic offenses. A group may gain status if its members possess status in their own right. Finally, a group may be accorded high status by virtue of the requirements for membership. This is one of the main reasons for the high status of people on the Social Register and the prime source of status for members of honorary groups such as Delta Sigma Rho or Phi Beta Kappa.

The forces produced by the status of the group affect not only those individuals who seek to gain or maintain membership in the group but also the power of the group in dealing with other groups.

Intergroup Power

By *intergroup power* we mean the extent of the influence of the group over other groups or over individuals who are not members of the group. Intergroup power is often specified by laws, rules, and regulations. Thus, a legislative body has its power specified by law, and the United States system of judicial review operates to define the boundaries of that legal power. Within an organization both the scope of control and the authority of groups listed on the organization chart are specified.

This force can be especially great when it is applied by one group directly upon individuals in another. For example, manipulative application of promotion criteria is one way in which the larger organization can break up the power of groups within the organization by destroying their solidarity. If, for example, promotion is based on behavior that requires intragroup competition, the solidarity of the smaller groups is almost impossible to maintain. Larger organizations can render small groups impotent by requiring multiple coordination between and among groups, limiting both the scope of control and the power of those groups. Classroom teachers are often mystified because student discussion groups, for which they have so carefully planned, do not seize their opportunities and assume significant responsibilities for their own learning. The reason may well be that the power of the teacher in the area of extrinsic rewards and punishments has never been relinquished. The students recognize their group's impotence and continue to resort to maintenance of personal relations with the teacher in order to maintain the status quo.

Other Institutional Characteristics

Large organizations, like the small groups that compose them, develop such things as norms, communication networks, and leadership hierarchies. These characteristics differ from those of the small group chiefly in that it is much more difficult for the individual to exercise influence over them.

Earlier in this chapter, we discussed how forces associated with the task affect the group as a whole. The group task deserves mention again in this section because it can be a force applied by sources external to the group. Many groups have tasks imposed upon them; indeed the task identified by the larger organization may be the very reason for the group's existence. Witness the wide use of special task forces by governmental, business, and educational organizations. The task force is given an assignment to investigate, study, evaluate, recommend. Usually its life is over whenever the task is finished.

Multiple Membership

One aspect of the external forces that cannot be generalized from the previous examination of group characteristics is the set of forces generated by the multiple group memberships of the several group members. Each individual member of a discussion group is almost certainly a member of several other groups. These groups also have norms, structure, and status relationships, and the individual brings them with her or him into any other group.

The limitation upon discussion imposed by the *problems of representation* was covered in Chapter 2. Individuals are often not free to act as they might wish when they have commitments as representatives of other groups. Whether this representation is formal or not, each individual usually feels to some extent the forces imposed by the other groups. The notion, "When in Rome, do as the Romans do," will free the individual only to the extent that his or her behavior cannot be observed by his fellow Carthaginians, or to the extent that internalized values and standards can be quieted or harmonized, or both. One of the authors was a member of a student–faculty group in which a first-name basis was a norm. A student in the group had just taken a class from the author and simply could not bring himself to say "Vic." He evaded the issue by using no name at all and gained attention by other means such as a tap on the elbow.

Special leader problems can occur because the leader, like the rest of the members, is also a member of other groups. The forces created by the leader's other memberships are somewhat distinctive, however. The leader of the group is usually a member of another group that stands higher in the intergroup hierarchy. In formal organizations this is worked into the recognized structure of the organization. A glance at the hypothetical segment of an organizational chart in Figure 5.2 will illustrate how this happens.

Person A is the leader and member of the group composed of himself and persons 1, 2, 3, 4, and 5. He is also a member of the group led by X and composed of D, C, D, E, himself, and X. He shares the values, sentiments, norms, and responsibilities of both groups. If the attraction of the group led by X becomes too strong and if A begins to transfer his primary allegiance to it, he becomes a poor member of the numerical group.

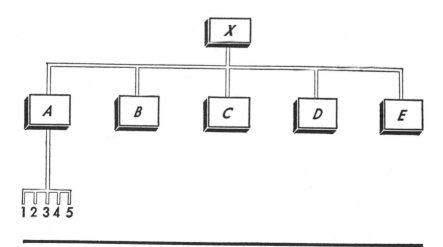

FIGURE 5.2.   Organizational Chart Segment

Kurt Lewin discussed this matter in *Resolving Social Conflicts.*[59] He pointed out that although most members of the Jewish minority were not accepted by Gentiles, *the Jewish leaders were.* This produced forces that often tended to perpetuate unfortunate intergroup relationships because the leaders had been accepted under the status quo. Similarly, Louis Lomax believes that the Negroes' lunch counter sit-in demonstrations were an expression of revolt against the leadership of the NAACP (National Association for the Advancement of Colored People) as well as a revolt against the Southern segregationists. Despite the legal gains won by the organized black leadership, Lomax contends that the leadership had lost touch with mass sentiment. The black leaders, according to this analysis, find themselves accepted by the whites and therefore "don't have the same fire in their stomachs that the students and the rallying Negro masses have."[60] A similar problem faces leaders of the women's movement who gain acceptance from the Establishment only to find they have lost effectiveness and rapport with other women, who now view them with suspicion.

RESULTANT FORCES

The forces presented thus far clearly act neither singly nor independently. Acting in concert, they tend to produce other or resultant forces. This idea of resultant forces was originally borrowed by Kurt Lewin from the concept of resultant forces in the physical sciences.[61] In Figure 5.3 we see that forces A and B are pulling object X. R is the resultant force. It is different from, yet a part of, both A and B.

Lewin contended that the forces operating upon a group tended to result in what he called a state of "quasi-stationary social equilibrium."[62] That is, the forces for change tend to be counterbalanced by the forces against change, resulting in a more or less stationary position. The group, or individual, will tend to go about operating in much the same fashion in its day-to-day behavior unless one, or a combination, of two things occurs. The forces for change can be heightened, or the forces against change can be lessened. If the forces for change are heightened without a corresponding lessening of the forces against change, the result will be increased tension. Obviously, the lessening of forces against change, particularly when coupled with heightened forces for change, will accomplish the change with the least amount of disturbance.

Bales identified the problem encountered by groups that are attempting to adapt to forces from the outside and on the inside at the same time:

The social system in its organization, we postulate, tends to swing or falter indeterminately back and forth between these two theoretical poles: op-

[59]Kurt Lewin, *Resolving Social Conflicts* (New York: Harper & Row, Publishers, 1948), pp. 190–97.

[60]Louis E. Lomax, "The Negro Revolt Against 'The Negro Leaders,'" *Harper's Magazine,* 220 (1960), 41–48.

[61]Kurt Lewin, *Principles of Topological Psychology* (New York: McGraw-Hill Book Company, Inc., 1936).

[62]Kurt Lewin, *Field Theory in Social Science* (New York: Harper & Row, 1951), chap. 9.

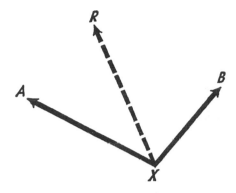

FIGURE 5.3.   Resultant Force

timum adaptation to the outer situation at the cost of internal malintegration, or optimum internal integration at the cost of maladaptation to the outer situation.[63]

Examples of these ambivalent tendencies are easy to find. Following wars, nations almost always experience a period of reaction: "Back to normalcy!" We have all observed discussion groups proceeding efficiently toward a solution of a problem and suddenly, and apparently unaccountably, going off on some tangent marked by joking and expressions of tension release. Some of the tangents upon which groups embark are appropriate "fishing expeditions," but many are mild forms of revolt against the pressures of task accomplishment and represent efforts to reestablish group harmony and solidarity.

Are groups bound to be unhappy regardless of what they do? If they respond to external forces, they seem to disrupt internal harmony, and vice versa. But not always. Successful interdependent action has already been shown to result in increased group solidarity and internal harmony. Torrance underscores the point that mild stress results in improved performance, but severe stress tends to be disruptive.[64] The ideal situation is one in which task pressures of appropriate levels of stability, complexity, intensity, and attractiveness can be tackled by a group that is mature enough to understand and accept the concomitant structure and role differentiations and can resist pressures to extend the structure beyond that necessary for successful task accomplishment. Stresses and ambivalent tendencies are inevitable even in such a group, but they are likely to be perceived more objectively and examined profitably by the group.

Often discussion groups, whose purposes are largely personal, attempt to impose some of the characteristics of task groups. In some learning groups, for example, a few of the members begin to act as if the group had to have some formal structure.

[63]Robert F. Bales, *Interaction Process Analysis* (Reading, Mass.: Addison-Wesley Publishing Co., Inc., 1951), p. 157.

[64]E. Paul Torrance, "A Theory of Leadership and Interpersonal Behavior Under Stress," in *Leadership and Interpersonal Behavior*, eds. Petrullo and Bass, pp. 100–117.

Such members are impatient with the apparent aimlessness of the group and attempt to establish definite procedures in order to improve efficiency. The reasons for this impatience vary but might be the desire to obtain status, personality compulsions, and time pressures. Usually the rest of the group will quite properly resist such unwarranted extension of group structure.

We observed an interesting instance of a group rejecting unwarranted controls imposed by its leader. The situation was a workshop on the educational implications of problems of intergroup relations. The participants were unknown to one another and were organized primarily for learning purposes. The group had spent the morning examining several aspects of the problem. In the afternoon session, the leader was a woman who had not participated in the morning session. She had a background of working with decision-making and action groups dealing with this very subject. At the beginning of the afternoon session, she attempted to organize and structure the discussion in order to be efficient. The group resented such attempted control and for about an hour the discussion was unproductive. Fortunately, she realized that her perceptions of what was required were not shared by the rest of the group. She stopped trying to impose unwarranted controls and the discussion then progressed more to the satisfaction of everyone concerned.

This ambivalence is reflected also in the literature about group discussion. Some writers clearly prefer the more nondirective, group-centered structure and lay more stress upon the personal development of the individuals. Other writers seem to be primarily concerned with procedures for controlling and structuring the group in order to improve production and efficiency. The battle-lines often seem to be drawn between those who favor democracy and those who prefer autocracy, but we see it more as a distinction between group cohesiveness and task accomplishment.

Sometimes these two forces are labeled *task* and *maintenance* functions and, as such, they will be discussed in depth in later chapters dealing with leadership. The managerial grid developed by Blake and Mouton is based on two axes: *concern for people* and *concern for production*. They report that the 9,9 position on the grid (high concern for production united with high concern for people) is "the soundest way to manage to achieve excellence."[65]

SUMMARY

This chapter has dealt with the complex array of group forces, beginning with some of the more important characteristics of individual group members, continuing with attributes of the group as a whole, relationships among members, intergroup and external forces, and finally, resultant forces. Two concepts, goals and climate, were examined both as group characteristics (Chapter 4) and group forces.

DISCUSSION QUESTIONS

1.   What would be some of the advantages and disadvantages of including people who had different personality structures in the same discussion group?

[65]Robert R. Blake and Jane Srygley Mouton, *Building a Dynamic Corporation Through Grid Organization Development* (Reading, Mass.: Addison-Wesley Publishing Co., Inc., 1969), p. 62.

2.   What have you observed to be the problems of leadership related to multigroup membership in your organization, class, college, or community?

3.   What are the forces acting on your class (or some comparable group)?

4.   In what ways does the size of your class group affect its climate and productivity?

EXERCISES

1.   Select several well-established groups of which you are a member and identify six to ten major forces to which each is subject at a given time. It may be helpful to choose groups that range from relatively immature to mature. Did you discover any forces you had not been aware of?

2.   Using your analysis of groups from exercise 1, attempt to determine how the forces relate in specific and observable ways. Check your conclusions with another member of each group studied. Prepare a report that could be the basis of discussion for either your class or one of your groups.

3.   Attempt to examine your own reactions as a group member to the forces you have listed in exercise 1. Does this introspection change your conclusions as to the nature and effect of the forces? Does it change your understanding and attitudes toward the group and its work?

4.   Recall a number of group discussions in which pressure for completion of the task significantly affected the solution or conclusion. How could the group or individual members have dealt with this force more effectively?

5.   Think about a group to which you belong in which attendance has been irregular. How far behind is the group in its development compared to where it might be if attendance had been better?

SELECTED READINGS

BEM, DARYL J., *Beliefs, Attitudes and Human Affairs*. Belmont, Calif.: Brooks/Cole Publishing Company, 1970.

BERSCHEID, ELLEN, AND ELAINE HATFIELD WALSTER, *Interpersonal Attraction*. Reading, Mass.: Addison-Wesley Publishing Co., Inc., 1969.

BORMANN, ERNEST G., *Discussion and Group Methods: Theory and Practice* (2nd ed.), chap. 10. New York: Harper & Row, Publishers, 1975.

HARRIS, THOMAS A., *I'm OK—You're OK: A Practical Guide to Transactional Analysis*. New York: Harper & Row, Publishers, 1969.

HARVEY, O. J., DAVID E. HUNT, AND HAROLD M. SCHRODER, *Conceptual Systems and Personality Organization*. New York: John Wiley & Sons, Inc., 1961.

KIESLER, CHARLES A., AND SARA B. KIESLER, *Conformity*. Reading, Mass.: Addison-Wesley Publishing Co., Inc., 1970.

LORSCH, JAY W., AND PAUL R. LAWRENCE, eds., *Managing Group and Intergroup Relations*. Homewood, Ill.: Richard D. Irwin, Inc., 1972.

SHAW, MARVIN E., *Group Dynamics: The Psychology of Small Group Behavior*, chap. 6. New York: McGraw-Hill Book Company, Inc., 1971.

PART THREE

We have been dealing with the process of communication from the very beginning of this book. In the discussion of the nature of groups and the consequent interrelationships of individuals, we have assumed that the creation, perpetuation, and modification of group characteristics are dependent on what people say to one another and how what is said is interpreted.

Effective communication in discussion involves considerably more than an understanding of the concepts covered so far, important as those concepts are, and it obviously involves more than a good vocabulary, clear articulation, and acute hearing.

To assume that two chapters on communication can accomplish what is normally difficult to accomplish in at least two books is fatuous. Many books have been written about the nature of communication in general; countless others deal with speaking, listening, linguistics, semantics, voice and articulation, and organizational communication. All these topics are relevant to small group discussion and we have included particularly useful books in the reference lists at the end of each chapter.

What we will focus on in this section is an overview of communication theory and practice, with special emphasis, naturally, on what is involved in group communication. Those factors in the group discussion situation that have a marked effect upon communication are identified and then techniques for dealing with those factors are suggested.

SMALL
GROUP
COMMUNICATION

chapter 6

COMMUNICATION DEFINED

Defining communication is no simple task.[1] Here the term is intended to apply to a special situation, however, and thus some of the limitations of its use should be identified before an attempt is made to define it.

Our consideration of communication is restricted to *interpersonal* communication. That means we are excluding communication between people and their environment, people and animals, people and machines, machines and machines, or even between people and society. Much interesting research has been done in many of these areas. Studies in the Bell Telephone and IBM laboratories have emphasized machine communication, for example, and though much can be learned from such research about means of studying and measuring human communication, we feel it is inappropriate to cover communication that includes nonhuman components.

For the most part, our use of the term *communication* is also restricted to nonwritten communication that usually takes place in a face-to-face situation. (Note that we did not say restricted to *verbal* communication because much of the communication in a typical discussion is gestural, or facial—nonverbal means.)

With these two restrictions in mind, we define communication as *the process by which people interact for the purpose of interpersonal and intrapersonal integration.* The idea of integration is used here in the psychological sense of coordinating and bringing together into a consistent whole the processes of perception, interpretation, and reaction. We agree with Stewart and d'Angelo when they say "interpersonal communication is not just one of several dimensions of human living, but is the defining dimension."[2] Some key concepts of our definition need to be spelled out in greater detail.[3]

First, communication is identified as a process, not as an act or the result of an act. Because communication is a dynamic, ongoing process, it is impossible to isolate and study an "act of communication." We can look at a building, for example, as an entity. We can measure and describe that building in many ways—size, color, struc-

[1]If this statement still seems too strong after you have finished reading this chapter, we suggest that you read Newman's excellent discussion of the problem of defining communication. John B. Newman, "A Rationale for a Definition of Communication," *Journal of Communication*, 10 (1960), 115–24.

[2]John Stewart and Gary d'Angelo, *Together: Communicating Interpersonally* (Reading, Mass.: Addison-Wesley Publishing Co., Inc., 1975), p. 25.

[3]This definition is very similar to the concepts advanced by Jo F. Richmond and Roy E. Buehler, "Interpersonal Communication: A Theoretical Formulation," *Journal of Communication*, 12 (1962), 3–10.

Communication Principles

tural properties, location, and others.[4] But we cannot similarly approach an act of communication. True, we can record the words used and examine them, but we lose a great deal of meaning when these words are taken from the process situation in which they were uttered. This process problem is further discussed when the theory of communication in the discussion situation is examined.

The term *interact* is probably clear. It includes the sum total of everything that people do and say. It also includes their appearance, tone of voice, dress, surroundings, and everything else that could conceivably affect another person.

The concepts of interpersonal and intrapersonal integration are not confusing after a moment's thought. When you talk to a friend, for example, you may attempt to convey some information to him, change his mind, or cheer him up. You may also attempt to learn something, modify your own beliefs, and strengthen your friendship. In any event the communication is purposive. Whether the purpose is conscious or unconscious is beside the point. You seek a response from your friend, and your friend's response provokes another response from you, which response provokes yet another—and we are back to our process.

This concept of communication is in keeping with the approach throughout this book. Oversimplifying the concept has been avoided. The concept has been tied to our main goal—an understanding of how individuals may best relate themselves to others in small groups. It will become clearer through this and the next chapter.

One way to identify communication is in the sense of *sharing meanings*, as Barnlund put it:

> Communication, as I conceive it, is a word that describes the process of creating a meaning. Two words in the sentence are critical. They are "create" and "meaning." Messages may be generated from the outside—by a speaker, a television screen, a scolding parent—but meanings are generated from within.[5]

Berlo emphasized this point when he said *"words do not mean at all. Only people mean, and people do not mean the same by all words."*[6]

Some of the aspects and qualities of communication have been used to measure people's ability to cope with the stresses and strains of living. How effective are the messages they send and receive? Are they taciturn? Are they verbose? Are their remarks often tangential? Do there appear to be discrepancies in the self-concept from which the communication springs? Are there distortions in meaning? Singer called communicative ability the *hallmark of emotional well-being.*[7]

One of the authors studied the communication occurring in a psychotherapy group, hypothesizing that as the patients progressed toward better mental health, their use of language to clarify their own and others' meanings would increase. The

---

[4]When we begin to talk about what the building "communicates" to people (as do some artists, architects, and other students of the visual arts), we are right back to our process problems.

[5]Dean C. Barnlund, "Toward a Meaning-Centered Philosophy of Communication," *Journal of Communication*, 12 (1962), 197–211.

[6]David K. Berlo, *The Process of Communication* (New York: Holt, Rinehart and Winston, Inc., 1960), p. 176.

[7]Erwin Singer, *Key Concepts in Psychotherapy* (New York: Random House, Inc., 1965), p. 79.

hypothesis was borne out: There was a high correlation between the therapists' assessment of the patients' progress, from mental illness to mental health and the patients' understanding of the need to ask for meaning clarification rather than assume that because they had spoken, they had communicated.[8]

Just as communication ability is vital to the functioning and well-being of the individual, so is it essential to the success of groups. It doesn't take a scientist to prove that people who are highly skilled in communication will be more effective in groups than those who are not. Highly skilled communicators will not just speak and then wait for a response; they will not be satisfied with action–reaction, as Berlo put it. Their goal is *interaction*.[9] They will carefully listen and avoid judging the listener, and only judge the message when they have heard it all. They will watch for nonverbal clues to help their understanding. When they are not sure they interpreted correctly, they will check out their impressions rather than make assumptions or inferences.

We have verification of the direct relationship between the quality of communication and the quality of product in a problem-solving group in the research conducted by Leathers,[10] who pointed out that most previous research had equated good communication with good morale rather than productivity. Now it is time to turn to some specific characteristics of communication.

CHARACTERISTICS OF COMMUNICATION

Listening

For years, listening was the least valued or understood of the language arts. Everyone listened as long as they had good hearing, and what is there to understand or learn about listening itself? It took Paul Rankin's pioneer study to show that white-collar workers spent 70 percent of their time communicating, with listening, by far, the skill most used.[11] Ralph Nichols of Minnesota University later determined that because of poor listening habits and weak memories, most people listened at 25 percent efficiency.[12] Now it is generally recognized that listening is an art that few practice well and that it is a skill that must be learned.

Because we can think faster than most people speak, we are apt to believe that we are listening well, when in reality we are tuning in and out and catching only part of what is said. In the intervening seconds when we are tuned out, we are probably thinking of something else entirely. If we are thinking about the subject being discussed, we are spending our time thinking of what we want to say in reply. This poor listening habit is probably what prompted one author to write, "There are no discussions anymore, only intersecting monologues."

[8]Barbara Schindler Jones, "Functions of Meaning Clarification by Therapists in a Psychotherapy Group" (unpublished Ph.D. dissertation, University of Colorado, 1968).

[9]Berlo, *The Process of Communication*, pp. 106–31.

[10]Dale G. Leathers, "Quality of Group Communication as a Determinant of Group Product," *Speech Monographs*, 39 (1972), 166–73.

[11]Paul T. Rankin, "Measurement of the Ability to Understand the Spoken Language" (unpublished Ph.D. dissertation, University of Michigan, 1926).

[12]Ralph G. Nichols and Leonard A. Stevens, *Are You Listening?* (New York: McGraw-Hill Book Company, Inc., 1957).

Listening in a discussion group is even harder than listening to one speaker. We must follow not only what is said, but how it relates to what else has been said so that we keep track of the thread of ideas and conclusions. Accurate listening requires thought and active effort. Passive hearing, as we might use to be aware of distant noises from the radio or stereo in the background, will not do in a discussion group. What's more, we often engage in evaluating or thinking about the speaker's motives, intent, or abilities, or thinking ahead to what we *think* the person is going to say. Good listeners think *with* the other person and do their best to understand *the speaker's* perceptions and *the speaker's* meanings. They try to grasp the entire message before evaluating or replying. Perhaps the best advice that can be given a discussant to improve listening ability is this: "Stop talking."

Nonverbal Communication

In a normal conversation, according to Birdwhistell, 65 percent of the meaning is conveyed by nonverbal cues. Words or verbal cues account for only 35 percent. [13] Mehrabian developed an equation wherein total feeling is made up of 7 percent verbal feeling, 38 percent vocal feeling, and 55 percent facial feeling. [14] Although people may argue about the percentages, no one disagrees with the fact that nonverbal messages are an important part of the communication process.

As Barnlund put it,

> Many, and sometimes most, of the critical meanings generated in human encounters are elicited by touch, glance, vocal nuance, gesture or facial expression with or without the aid of words. From the moment of recognition until the moment of separation, people observe each other with all their senses, hearing pause and intonation, attending to dress and carriage, observing glance and facial tension, as well as noting word choice and syntax. [15]

We often respond to nonverbal cues without realizing it. When we drive a car, we respond automatically to the color of the signal light without having to think about it. Similarly, when we are speaking and see our listener frown, we begin at once to try to understand and adapt to this message. If we are alert to feedback, we constantly seek nonverbal cues as to how we're doing and how the listeners are responding. But there is a subconscious level of response, as well.

For example, a group of students in a Principles of Communication class decided to try an experiment, unknown to the professor. They were members of one section of a multisectioned course that met once a week for a lecture-discussion. The group of about 20 students scattered themselves throughout the classroom, with about half on each side of the center aisle. While the professor lectured, the half of the class on the left side of the aisle gave him very positive feedback. They appeared to be listening intently, nodding their heads at important points and taking copious notes. The

[13]Ray L. Birdwhistell, as reported in Mark L. Knapp, *Nonverbal Communication in Human Interaction* (New York: Holt, Rinehart and Winston, Inc., 1972), p. 12.

[14]Albert Mehrabian, *Silent Messages* (Belmont, Calif.: Wadsworth Publishing Company, Inc., 1971), p. 44.

[15]Dean C. Barnlund, *Interpersonal Communication: Survey and Studies* (Boston: Houghton Mifflin Company, 1968), pp. 535–36.

students on the right side of the aisle, meanwhile were transmitting very negative feedback; they dozed, they yawned, they doodled and did everything but appear to pay attention. Without being aware of it, the professor began to direct more and more of his lecture to the left side of the room and even physically moved closer to the left side.

About halfway through the period, the students in on the experiment switched roles so that it was now people on the right side of the room who were most attentive. Sure enough, the professor slowly changed his field of concentration to the right side of the room. The game was over, however, when one of the "bad guys" on the left side of the room made a paper airplane and sailed it right at the professor. Before he could angrily explode, the students quickly confessed to him and the rest of the class what they had been up to.

Communication is difficult enough between people of the same culture but when messages are sent in one culture and received in another, problems of understanding and intent arise. This is particularly true when nonverbal meanings are exchanged cross-culturally. Although nonverbal communication is culturally bound and learned, we are often ignorant of the meaning of nonverbal clues in cultures other than our own. We might take offense if someone spit at us without being aware that in some cultures this act is a mark of respect. As Brown said,

> Because their etiquette is different from ours, peoples from other cultures may appear to us to be lacking in manners. What we are seldom aware of is that such peoples have their own rules that often put to shame our most formal behavior. . . . Whether you do or do not open a gift in the presence of the giver; whether you should or should not turn the plate over to look at the maker's symbol on the back; whether you put your coat on before or after you leave the host's house; whether you eat as quietly or as noisily as possible; . . . these and a thousand other questions are matters of cultural definition. None of them is inherently right or wrong, and none is good or bad manners, except as a society defines it so.[16]

A person's understanding of nonverbal communication is learned by observation and imitation, by accident, and also by being subtly corrected. (Some corrections are not so subtle, we know, as in the case of the man who was told he could have the job he had applied for, provided he shaved two inches off his sideburns.)

One other culturally based example is that of eye contact, perhaps the most forceful of all nonverbal messages. Most white Americans have been conditioned to believe that looking another person directly in the eye is a mark of directness and honesty. Most black Americans, by contrast, have been conditioned to avoid eye contact lest it be considered a signal of confrontation. A black woman of our acquaintance told of the conflicting messages her father gave her when she was growing up. On the one hand, he would say, "Look at me when I'm speaking to you," and on the other, he would also scold, "Don't you look at me in that tone of voice!" Apparently, in that family, the expression in the eye was more important than the eye contact.

Fromme and Beam, in a study of dominance and sex differences related to eye contact, found that "males tended to use personal space and approach rate to signal

---

[16]Ina Corinne Brown, *Understanding Other Cultures* (Englewood Cliffs, N.J.: Prentice-Hall, Inc., 1963), pp. 85–86.

dominance, while females used reciprocal eye contact."[17] Although the study should be replicated before generalizations are made, it is interesting that they found an exception to the popular notion that positive attitudes are associated with high levels of eye contact: The "low-dominant" males in the experiment responded to direct gaze with a more negative attitude.

Two other experiments of interest to discussion students are (1) Breed and Colaiuta's examination of nonverbal behavior in the classroom in which they determined that higher test scores were associated with increased looking at the instructor;[18] and (2) Duncan and Niederehe's analysis of how people signal each other when they have decided it's their turn to speak.[19]

The discussion student needs to become more aware of nonverbal messages and their sometimes subtle, sometimes obvious effect upon the group. Spatial arrangements convey a message and influence the quality of the group's work. For example, when a group discusses at a square or rectangular table, the people on the corners have more difficulty being recognized and getting into the discussion. When groups meet in living rooms or lounges, the person who sits in the largest or highest chair is literally and figuratively looked up to and often is given the leadership role.[20]

An interesting aspect of nonverbal behavior examined by Davis is the special and regular pattern each human develops for speaking and listening. According to Davis, "a man's conversational rhythm is one of his more stable and predictable characteristics."[21] Discussion students could profit not only from analyzing patterns of group members' participation (with the aid of video- and audiotapes preferably), but also from identifying them as sources of both rapport and conflict.

When verbal and nonverbal messages contradict each other (such as a person saying "Take your time; I'm in no hurry," and then looking at a clock) people are apt to believe the nonverbal cue is the real message. Since we are largely unaware of the nonverbal messages we send, we can hardly fake them and they are therefore considered to be honest expressions of our ideas and feelings.

If group members are not participating, reading their nonverbal communication usually helps diagnose the cause. Do they inch their chairs back away from the group? They may be saying, nonverbally, that they are uncomfortable with the people or the subject. Do they open their mouths to speak but get cut off by the more vocal members? They have given you a means of helping them into the discussion. You could say something like, "Joe wanted to make a point a few minutes ago but we cut him off." Such mutual assistance and sensitivity to individual needs are greatly enhanced by becoming more aware of the whole spectrum of nonverbal communication.

[17]Donald K. Fromme and Donna C. Beam, "Dominance and Sex Differences in Nonverbal Responses to Differential Eye Contact," *Journal of Research in Personality*, 8 (1974), 76–87.

[18]George Breed and Victoria Colaiuta, "Looking, Blinking and Sitting: Nonverbal Dynamics in the Classroom," *Journal of Communication*, 24 (1974), 75–81.

[19]Starkey Duncan and George Niederehe, "On Signalling That It's Your Turn to Speak," *Journal of Experimental Social Psychology*, 10 (1974), 234–47.

[20]For more about the nonverbal communication involved in space and time, see Edward T. Hall, *The Silent Language* (Greenwich, Conn.: Fawcett Publications, Inc., 1959) as well as Hall's newer book, *The Hidden Dimension* (New York: Anchor Books, 1969).

[21]Flora Davis, *Inside Intuition: What We Know About Nonverbal Communication* (New York: McGraw-Hill Book Company, Inc., 1973), p. 130.

A word of caution is important here. We doubt that any of us is sufficiently skilled in the interpretation of nonverbal communication to be able to generalize from person to person or situation to situation. If a person sits with crossed arms, it *may* mean the person is withdrawn or rejecting what is happening in the group. And it *may not.* If we work with the person over time and note that the crossed-arms behavior usually precedes a negative comment, then we have a somewhat better basis for our assumption of meaning. What does it mean when a discussant nods his or her head? We might assume it means agreement or assent, when the head nodder was merely intending to signal, "Keep talking, I hear you," or was perhaps having difficulty staying awake!

These *raw cues,* as Stewart and d'Angelo call them,[22] must be kept separate from our interpretation of what they mean. To be safe, we should check out possible meanings by using all three codes of language, voice, and body, and by taking careful note of the circumstances.

Feedback and Feedforward

We have made several references to *feedback* without defining it because it is a well-known term in common use. The response to a message is fed back to the speaker verbally or nonverbally. Feedback serves the function of acknowledging receipt of a message and checking the accuracy of the transmission. Public feedback may range from a nod of approval or a frown of puzzlement to a detailed rephrasing and evaluation of the communication. Our reactive communication may be private internal reactions without outward signs or public statements that can be detected and interpreted by others. We may silently "talk to ourselves" about what is happening in the group and make decisions about how and when to make our next point.

Feedback is one of the most important kinds of interactive communication; the offering of feedback is one of the most useful tools in the discussion process. You know how it feels when you bring forth what you believe is an excellent, well-thought-out point, only to have it lie there without response from the group. A speaker would often rather be argued with than ignored.

Extensive and nonevaluative feedback has become an article of faith with therapists. By feeding back to clients their thoughts and feelings, the therapist helps them discover for themselves the accuracy and significance of their own communications. In the discussion group, intelligent, spontaneous feedback helps both the original communicator and the others in the group. The original communicator receives a check on the accuracy of the communication, and the rest of the group (remember, everyone is feeding back to some extent all the time) can check the accuracy of their reception of the message. More will be said about specific ways to provide feedback in the next chapter.

Feedforward communication[23] is the initiating thought or idea that starts a communication sequence and elicits feedback. The distinguishing characteristic of this activity is that feedforward communication typically suggests the direction and content of further communication. These preliminary messages may serve one or both of two

---

[22]Stewart and d'Angelo, *Together,* p. 76.

[23]This concept was developed by Bess Sondel using a term coined earlier by I. A. Richards. For further explanation, see Gardner Murphy, "Toward a Field Theory of Communication," *Journal of Communication,* 11 (1961), 196–201.

functions. The first, and most apparent function is to alert others to what is to come. We can call this the *road sign* function. Sometimes the feedforward is explicit, such as a comment like "Today, I think we should discuss budget problems." But often the road sign function is only implied or suggested, as when a frown and a tense manner suggest that a discussant is intending to register a complaint.

Another use for feedforward communication is to get a reading as to whether or not the communicator should continue in a given direction. This is the *trial balloon* function of preliminary messages. A person who is insecure may send out trial balloon preliminary messages in order to find out what it is proper to say, in an effort not to appear foolish or incompetent.

To decode and interpret an extended message is difficult enough. Consider, therefore, how much more difficult it is to decode and interpret an abbreviated message, which many trial balloon and road sign messages are. Others in the group may misinterpret the preliminary message feature of feedforward communication and discourage or inhibit a potentially valuable contribution. Further, many others in the group will be sending out their own feedforward messages. They will, of course, be preoccupied with their own messages and may devote less energy to decoding and interpreting the messages of others.

The preliminary message feature of feedforward communication is naturally most prevalent during the beginning stages of any discussion. Many matters must be settled, at least tentatively, before the group can actually begin stating and examining serious content ideas. One mark of a mature group, as indicated, is the ability to keep the sparring for position to a minimum.

Whether wisely used or not, preliminary messages in feedforward communication deserve attention. Road signs used to indicate clearly to others the direction of further communication are potentially very valuable. Both the message sender and the message receiver have a responsibility to consider carefully all messages intended to set the stage. The more complete, specific, and stable such messages and their interpretations become, the more useful they are to the group. When trial balloons are used to discover what it is proper to think and say, both the individual and the rest of the group are obliged to help reduce anxiety motivations. If people are unsure of the ideas they wish to express, the group atmosphere should be permissive enough, and the individuals secure enough, to allow them to confess their uncertainty and thus produce preliminary messages that are sufficiently specific for them to receive meaningful assistance from the rest of the group.

Jamming

Jamming is a form of communication that disrupts or obscures other communication attempts. Essentially, jamming consists of transmitting messages that seemingly complement, but actually violate, the intent of other messages. Like feedback, jamming may be either public or private. Let us illustrate.

One time a middle-aged woman was talking to a group of junior-high-school youngsters. In order to illustrate her point, she made repeated references to baseball. Unfortunately, she knew little about the game and many of her references were erroneous. In the discussion that followed her talk it became apparent that the young people missed her point altogether because their minds were occupied with straightening out her understanding of baseball. In this instance the inaccurate illustrations triggered a series of private reactive communications—jamming—that interfered with the rest of her message. These private reactions became public after the speech, but by then the main objective of communication had been lost.

Jamming has many causes. Inappropriate humor can trigger jamming if the listeners are either overly amused or offended by something that is said. If the speaker fails to organize the message, the listener may impose an inappropriate organization and, consequently, jam the communication. For any of dozens of reasons, group members may misinterpret a message or follow some tangent.

In group discussions, both speakers and listeners have a responsibility to avoid jamming. The sensitive communicator will think of many techniques to minimize jamming by others, but message receivers should be even more concerned, for a large part of the responsibility belongs to listeners. They are the ones who do the actual jamming.

COMMUNICATION AS A PROCESS

We have already stressed the dynamic, ongoing, and interactive nature of communication and do not intend to belabor the point. A favorite means of identifying communication components and their interrelationships is by way of a model. Berlo developed his SMCR model (Source, Message, Channel, and Receiver),[24] which focused on the parts but did not indicate the process nature or the feedback component. Other well-known models have been drawn by Miller,[25] Johnson,[26] and Westley and MacLean.[27] Keltner has done a good job of spelling out these and other basic models and explaining their differences.[28] Models are a useful means of demonstrating how communication works, but because so many are available in other books and articles we will make no attempt to describe them here.

In most communication situations, a person is both a message source and a message receiver at the same time. This is more pronounced in a group communication situation. Learning how to follow both the verbal and nonverbal messages, while deciding *what* to communicate, *how, when,* and *to whom,* are precisely the ingredients that make discussion difficult.

The message is the product of coding—encoding by the message sender and decoding by the receiver. The elements of words, vocal inflections, gestures, bodily action, and more must be placed into a structure. True, we have conventionally agreed-upon definitions of words, but the difficulties of using a dictionary to find the *meanings in people* are obvious. We can, however, talk about the probability that different people will impute the same meaning to a given message, never exactly the same, but close enough to make communication possible. What's more, we can

---

[24]Berlo, *The Process of Communication*, pp. 23–39.

[25]Gerald R. Miller, *Speech Communication: A Behavioral Approach* (Indianapolis: The Bobbs-Merrill Co., Inc., 1966), p. 55.

[26]Wendell Johnson, "The Spoken Word and the Great Unsaid," *Quarterly Journal of Speech*, 32 (1951), 421.

[27]Bruce Westley and Malcolm MacLean, Jr., "A Conceptual Model for Communication Research," *Journalism Quarterly*, 34 (1957), 31–38.

[28]John W. Keltner, *Interpersonal Speech-Communication, Elements and Structures* (Belmont, Calif.: Wadsworth Publishing Company, Inc., 1970), pp. 16–21.

illustrate how structure is likely to affect meanings by the old classic: "The teacher said the student was lazy." Add commas after *teacher* and *student* and see what happens to the meaning.

APPROACHES TO COMMUNICATION ANALYSIS

Information theory, as the name implies, analyzes the message to see what happens to the information as it is encoded, transmitted, decoded, interpreted, and finally fed back to the original source. Information theory was originally developed in machine communication—electronic "brains," telephone, radio—and was a some-what simplistic action–reaction model. (In these areas the term *information* has a much more specific meaning than the one we conventionally give it.)

Field theory, as developed by Kurt Lewin,[29] is more relevant to the study of group communication. Some of its elements were delineated by Allport:

> These latter concepts for the most part refer to *systems of tension* within the person himself. Whenever Lewin feels it necessary to speak simultaneously both of these tension systems within the individual and of the pressures emanating from the surrounding field he introduces a third type of concept, such as field *forces* (motives clearly depending upon group pressures), *barriers* (obstacles to individual action owing to group restraints), or *locomotion* (changing of the individual's position with reference to the group). In reality, of course, these three aspects of his thought are not separable.[30]

Simply stated, the essence of the field theory approach is that the "given" with which we start is a person's desire to maintain integration and equilibrium. Proceeding from that given, we examine the way individuals discover what they wish to communicate and the way they attempt to interact with others in the communication process. We ask such questions as these: Why did the group start talking about irrelevant issues? Why did some members fail to present information they had with them? What happened to change attitudes? Much of Chapter 5, "Group Forces," dealt with concepts included in our understanding of field theory.

System theory is a means of relating activity and interaction. In his book *The Human Group,* Homans identified internal and external systems (norms developed from within and outside the group) and brought the subject of analysis closer to the simple events of everyday life.[31] He chose activity, interaction, and sentiment for emphasis, seeing them as a system so closely interrelated that a change in one leads to a change in the others.

[29]Kurt Lewin, *Field Theory in Social Science,* ed. Dorwin Cartwright (New York: Harper Brothers, 1951).

[30]Gordon W. Allport, Foreword to *Resolving Social Conflicts,* by Kurt Lewin (New York: Harper & Row, Publishers, 1948), p. ix.

[31]George C. Homans, *The Human Group* (New York: Harcourt, Brace, 1950). See also Henry W. Riecken and George C. Homans, "Psychological Aspects of Social Structure," in *Handbook of Social Psychology,* vol. II, ed. Hardner Lindsey (Cambridge, Mass.: Addison-Wesley Publishing Co., Inc., 1954); George C. Homans, *Social Behavior: Its Elementary Forms* (New York: Harcourt, Brace & World, Inc., 1961).

In a section of his book called "Is the Group a System?" Steiner said that it is difficult to detect a system by looking at individuals and their behaviors. What's more, we bias our perceptions when we are a part of the group we are studying. Yet he concluded with these thoughts:

> Several lines of evidence suggest that groups may legitimately be regarded as systems. When participating in groups, individuals often behave quite differently than when alone. Personality measures generally do a poor job predicting how people will behave in groups, and there are many reasons for saying that the actions of individuals are shaped by the interdependencies that prevail in groups. Finally, analysis of collective action reveals the systematic patterning of members' behaviors.[32]

Interaction process analysis is still another way of observing and analyzing groups. Robert F. Bales developed a 12-category interaction scheme whereby he could label each interaction and indicate the "who-to-whom" feature.[33] This kind of quantitative and qualitative analysis requires skill and experience to make certain that all communication acts are noted and properly categorized but it is, nonetheless, a useful tool. It will be discussed further in Chapter 15, "Evaluating Small Group Discussion."

SOME CHARACTERISTICS OF DESIRABLE CONTRIBUTIONS

When group members are communicating, their contributions may be questions, statements, or exclamations. Contributions may be long or short; they may have several purposes or just one. The eight characteristics that follow will provide a beginning checklist for the discussion student. You may want to expand the list on the basis of experience.

Relevance. Just as an individual may find his or her mind wandering into irrelevant channels, groups also go off on tangents. Before any contribution is classified as irrelevant, however, speakers should be questioned and allowed to explain how they see the connection between their contribution and the thrust of the discussion. Some people see clear connections in their minds but fail to explain; it is a mistake to assume someone is off the subject because we do not see a connection. Perhaps the intention of the contribution was to suggest a more profitable line of thought or to provide tension release. Relevance, in short, does not necessarily mean that a contribution must be "on the topic"; it does mean that a contribution must be "centered on significant task or personal needs."

Relatedness. Often a contribution is relevant—it is directed to some significant task or personal needs—but it is not related to the comments that have just preceded it or what is likely to follow. This often occurs early in the life of a group when people have

---

[32]Ivan D. Steiner, *Group Process and Productivity* (New York: Academic Press, Inc., 1972), p. 169.

[33]Robert F. Bales, *Interaction Process Analysis* (Reading, Mass.: Addison-Wesley Publishing Co., Inc., 1950).

something to say and they say it, whether or not the idea is related to what else is being said. It may be a form of role identification, a standing up and being counted. Such contributions, however, are like parts of a machine dumped on the floor. Each one is relevant, to be sure, but useless until put together. One good way to establish relatedness is to introduce your comment like this: "I'd like to go back to the point John made and add some evidence." If the contribution is to be used, someone must, sooner or later, relate it to other contributions. If the maker of the contribution cannot relate it, he or she should at least ask someone else for help.

Good Timing. This criterion is especially difficult to meet because the idea may not occur to the discussant at the appropriate time, or because he or she may not be able to get the floor when it is timely. Appropriate timing is difficult for another reason, however. Individuals differ in their speed of comprehension and in their capacity for leaping to conclusions. One individual will occasionally see the perfect way out of a difficulty, present some suggestions triumphantly, and then be dismayed when the more pedestrian discussants ignore the contribution. The fault may be the timing or failure to measure up on one or more of the other criteria. Of course, the fault can also lie with the listeners.

Sufficient Length. A contribution should be long enough to make its point. Most contributions that fail to get through are too short rather than too long. Obviously, a contribution is of little value if too little is said to make the point clear and related.

Clarity. Because meanings are in people rather than in words, we should never assume understanding or assume that because we have spoken we have communicated. Beginning discussants often have to find out the hard way that they haven't been talking about the same thing because they failed to define and rephrase significant terms. Group members must reach some agreement on meaning *to them* in order to be clear.

Informativeness. This criterion stems naturally from our point of view throughout the book that the basis of effective discussion should be a genuine attempt to clarify and share meaning. As indicated in Chapter 5, contributions should be rooted in objective rather than social reality. This criterion will be underscored again in the next chapter in the consideration of techniques for improving communication.

Openness to Evaluation. An effective contribution indicates to the hearers *how* the contribution may be evaluated and suggests the *willingness* of the contributor to have that evaluation made.

Assume that a group is discussing the future developments of the United States economy, and one member offers this contribution: "The price of gold stock is *rising* on the international stock market. This shows that the economy is headed for troubles." He has presented his evidence and his conclusion, but he has not shown the reasoning process by which he reached the conclusion. That is, economists point out that the rising price of gold stock indicates a lack of confidence in other stocks and is therefore a predictor that investors will pull back on their investments in other businesses. Of course, we often do not bother to spell out the thought processes because our hearers will perceive them for themselves. If we look up at the sky and say, "It's clouding up. I believe it will rain," we do not describe the thought process that leads us from the evidence to the conclusion, and we do not need to. Often, however, we erroneously assume that these thought processes—because they are perfectly clear to us—are understood by others. But our failure to suggest or describe them prevents the group from making an evaluation.

Evidencing a willingness to have the contribution evaluated is a virtue difficult to master. Jack Gibb's studies of what he terms *defensive behavior* demonstrate that such reactions reduce communicative efficiency.[34] His experiments indicate that one of the major causes of defensive behavior is evaluation. *Supportive behavior,* on the other hand, can be achieved when a contribution is described or clarified rather than criticized. His implied conclusion that description should replace evaluation is clearly valid when groups are organized for social, cathartic, and therapeutic purposes. However, the conclusion can apply to only a few learning groups and almost no task groups, because evaluation of contributions is a must if the groups are to reach worthwhile conclusions. Mature individuals, as members of a mature group, find it possible to criticize each others' *ideas* and still maintain cohesion and mutual support. Immature individuals cannot separate their ideas from themselves and so interpret an evaluation of their ideas as attacks upon themselves. Thus, the problem seems to be learning how to make and accept evaluations rather than how to avoid them. This issue will be further dealt with in the next chapter.

Provocativeness. Contributions should provoke further thought and feedforward communications. But some contributions, particularly those made by high-status persons, say or imply, "This is it. Two plus two equals four and no more need be said." Such contributions cut off controversy and dampen the desire to think further. Here are some more typical conversation stoppers: "But that's socialism!" "We've tried it before, and it didn't work." "It's just as simple as that." Making provocative contributions involves much more than simply avoiding conversation stoppers. It is an art that good teachers, for example, have mastered.

SUMMARY

This chapter identified communication first as a phenomenon and second as a process. The more significant characteristics of communication, listening, nonverbal communication, feedback, feedforward, and jamming, were explained and illustrated. Following a brief description of four approaches to communication analysis, the chapter concluded with eight characteristics of desirable contributions.

DISCUSSION QUESTIONS

1. Explore the implications of this statement: *The purpose of communication is social control and the effect of communication is learning.*
2. What is the relationship between group norms and communication?
3. How does the following statement relate to group discussion: *Communication produces change and change constitutes communication.* How does this concept relate to individuals within the group?

[34]Jack R. Gibb, "Defensive Communication," *Journal of Communication,* 11 (1961), 141–48.

4.   Which of the communication concepts covered in this chapter are changed when the communication process occurs in a group instead of between only two individuals?

EXERCISES

1.   Arrange for several persons to observe a discussion that can be videotaped or tape-recorded while they observe. Have each observer evaluate the contributions of one or two discussants, using the list of characteristics of desirable contributions in this chapter. After an interval of a week or two, arrange to play back the tape and have the same observers again evaluate the communications of the same person or persons observed earlier. Each observer should answer the following questions: (a) How would you rate the overall communication of the persons you observed? (b) How do your two ratings of the same individual compare? (c) What does this suggest concerning communication and its evaluation?

2.   Plan and carry out a simple experiment to permit observation of the effects of evaluation and description in two or more discussion groups. For example, it might be possible for a team of three or four individuals to work together in such a manner that two would be members of a social discussion group, with one deliberately refraining from making any evaluative contributions and the other deliberately casting most comments in evaluative terms. Observers (either external, or perhaps as members of the group) could note the effect on other group members, as well as on communication. Obviously, the majority of group members should not know that an experiment or planned observation is in process until the conclusion of the discussion.

3.   Observe the communication process in a group for the purpose of identifying and evaluating feedforward, feedback, and jamming. To what extent are these present? What individuals engage in each type of response? To what degree are the group members aware of such contributions?

4.   Sit opposite someone you wish to understand, and sit in a way that enables you to concentrate on his or her face—in a posture of attention. Think only of the other person, his or her thoughts, and nonverbal communication. What thoughts, feelings, and emotions do you see? Give feedback on the messages you receive without putting any evaluation on them. Phrase the feedback: "You feel ———— about ————." Always start the statement with *you* to show that the speaker is most important. Your goal is understanding—not evaluating or judging. After 10 or 15 minutes, change places and roles. After the exercise, compare impressions and feelings. How did the communication in this exercise differ from typical exchanges? How accurate were your readings of nonverbal meanings?

SELECTED READINGS

BIRDWHISTELL, RAY L., *Kinesics and Context: Essays on Body Motion Communication.* Philadelphia: University of Pennsylvania Press, 1970.

DAVIS, FLORA, *Inside Intuition: What We Know About Nonverbal Communication.* New York: McGraw-Hill Book Company, 1971.

GOFFMAN, ERVING, *The Presentation of Self in Everyday Life.* Garden City, N.Y.: Doubleday Anchor Books, 1959.

JOHNSON, WENDELL, "The Fateful Process of Mr. A Talking to Mr. B," in *Small Group Communication,* eds. Robert S. Cathcart and Larry A. Samovar. Dubuque, Iowa: William C. Brown Company, Publishers, 1970.

KELTNER, JOHN W., *Interpersonal Speech-Communication, Elements and Structures,* chaps. 4–7. Belmont, Calif.: Wadsworth Publishing Company, Inc., 1970.

KNAPP, MARK L., *Nonverbal Communication in Human Interaction.* New York: Holt, Rinehart and Winston, Inc., 1972.

NICHOLS, RALPH G., AND LEONARD A. STEVENS, *Are You Listening?* New York: McGraw-Hill Book Company, Inc., 1957.

RUESCH, JURGEN, AND WELDON KEES, *Nonverbal Communication.* Berkeley, Calif.: University of California Press, 1966.

SCHEFLEN, ALBERT E., *How Behavior Means,* sec. 1. Garden City, N.Y.: Anchor Press, 1974.

WEITZ, SHIRLEY, *Nonverbal Communication: Readings With Commentary.* New York: Oxford University Press, 1974.

chapter 7

The eight criteria for measuring the quality of contributions in a discussion (in Chapter 6) now form the objectives of techniques for improving communication. The techniques in this chapter, however, are not organized according to these criteria, for several reasons. No one-to-one correspondence exists between the techniques and the objectives. Some techniques lay the groundwork for meeting several objectives; some work directly toward several objectives; and often several techniques are needed to accomplish one objective. But before we develop the techniques, a few assumptions are necessary.

First, we assume that you and the rest of the group have conscientiously attempted to follow the advice given so far. Advice about communication techniques is sterile unless prefaced by the principles governing sound thinking about meaningful problems discussed in purposeful and maturing groups. Second, we assume that it is important to good communication that discussions be as free as possible from outside distraction, that discussants articulate carefully, that members be seated comfortably and in positions where they can readily see and hear one another. Finally, we assume that you and your fellow discussants understand that discussion is difficult and that effective communication is not easily attained. Improving the communication process requires hard but fascinating work with many rewards.

Our emphasis is on means of facilitating communication rather than errors that should be avoided. Concentration upon barriers to communication, upon pitfalls, traps, or blunders, assumes that communication would function ideally if the barriers could only be eliminated. That assumption is not sound. Communication is a dynamic process requiring creative input. Further, the error avoidance approach tends to make people fearful of making mistakes, and the only sure way to avoid making mistakes is to make the biggest mistake of all—to try nothing whatsoever! Therefore, suggestions will be made that should improve communication.

Discussants are beset by many, often competing, stimuli that they must sort out and evaluate. Thus, the basic objective underlying many of the techniques is to reduce complexity and bring the stimuli into manageable proportions. There are stories about high-powered executives who can simultaneously carry on two telephone conversations, read the morning mail, dictate to a secretary, and approve a production plan. But it is all most of us can do to carry on just one conversation at a time. We need to learn, therefore, how to manage stimuli more effectively.

We can learn to handle our communication problems by careful planning *before* the discussion and by paying close attention to some specific techniques *during* the discussion.

Improving the Communication Process

BEFORE THE DISCUSSION

Prepare Your Information

You have notes, documents, observations, and ideas. Good. But unless you are adequately prepared to present the information to the group, your task is only half-done. What more remains?

Organize According to Some Pattern. If you have more than one piece of information, you should select some pattern for presentation. If you leave the decision to the spur of the moment, you complicate the decisions you must make and run the risk of confusing the other discussants. Therefore, plan the organization before the discussion, and try to have the organization reflect some pattern. What do we mean by *pattern*, and how does the advice apply?

Suppose that your group is discussing ways and means of improving public-school education, and you have been assigned the task of securing information about teachers' salaries. You have secured the information and are ready to organize it. You may wish to organize the information according to a *chronological* pattern, showing what has happened to salaries over the years:

Average Teacher's Salary

Educational Level	1956	1966	1976
Elementary	$———	$———	$———
Secondary	$———	$———	$———
College	$———	$———	$———

You may organize it according to a *space* pattern, showing comparative salary figures for different parts of the country:

Average Teacher's Salary

Educational Level	Regions of the United States			
	East	West	North	South
Elementary	$———	$———	$———	$———
Secondary	$———	$———	$———	$———
College	$———	$———	$———	$———

You may decide to use a *cause–effect* pattern, showing what factors seem principally responsible for major changes from time to time:

Average Teacher's Salary

I.   Factors that have affected salary.
     A.   Improved attitudes about teaching as a profession.

     B.   Improved attitudes about the importance of education.
     C.   Rise in the standard of living, generally.
     D.   More teachers seeking postgraduate education.
     E.   More collective bargaining by teachers.

Or you may use a *comparison* pattern, showing how teachers' salaries relate to those of comparably trained people in other professions:

Average Teacher's Salary

	Compared to Other Professions				
	Teachers	*Doctors*	*Lawyers*	*Accountants*	*Plumbers*
1956	$———	$———	$———	$———	$———
1966	$———	$———	$———	$———	$———
1976	$———	$———	$———	$———	$———

   Other patterns are available, of course, and you may study them at greater length by consulting one or more of the speech and communication texts listed at the end of this chapter. Our suggestion here is to pick some reasonable pattern and stick to it rather than presenting the data helter-skelter. You may have to change the pattern once the actual discussion begins. But if you do, it will be because an alternative pattern seems to make more sense at the time, and you will be able to spot that alternative more readily if you have already been thinking in terms of patterned organization. Above all, you simplify the listeners' task if you have organized your information according to some recognizable scheme.

Provide Necessary Visual Aids or "Handouts." Some information is better comprehended visually than orally, and some information needs to be preserved, so occasionally you will want to show or distribute graphs or charts to assist others in grasping figures, statistics, or complicated relationships.

   Let's go back to the organizational patterns used to present data on teacher's salaries. The *chronological* example could probably be explained orally by indicating whether salaries have risen or fallen across the decades or whether the rate of change has been different according to teaching level. The information is not too complicated for people to grasp or retain.

   But the material as we have suggested it be arranged for the *space* patterns would be more difficult. If this is a point that is important to the discussion and you feel it might get lost if presented orally, a simple chart showing regional figures in different colors should be useful. This could be displayed or copies could be made and distributed.

   The fourth example, *comparison* pattern, could be made clearer by using a graph indicating dollar amounts in one direction and the chronology in the other. The professions could be coded by different colors or by different kinds of lines across the graph.

   In general, people can understand images (bars, graphs, straight lines, wavy lines) more thoroughly and quickly than they can a lot of statistics or involved narrative.

Discussants have to weigh the importance of the message against the time and trouble it takes to make visual aids.

Decide When to Present Your Information. This decision must be tentative, of course, since you cannot anticipate precisely the course of the discussion. But if you take some time to plan before the discussion, you are less likely to violate the timing criterion offered in the previous chapter. Planning ahead and deciding upon tentative timing does *not* mean we are advocating a formal speech. That would obviously be out of place in an informal discussion.

Plan to Perform Functions

Having some specific functions in mind to perform allows you to concentrate on and be alert to communication problems. If, for example, one of the functions you intend to perform is harmonizing interpersonal conflict, your planning will cause you to focus on feedforward messages that hint of trouble brewing. You will be able to interpret those messages readily and thus be able to respond to them before the situation gets out of hand. Deciding ahead of time that you will help the group get and give better feedback ensures improvement in this direction instead of leaving communication improvement to chance.

PREPARE TO MEET POTENTIAL COMMUNICATION PROBLEMS

Here are four questions to aid in the analysis of your group's communication effectiveness.

1.   What are the group's communication needs? Have contributions been irrelevant? Has feedback been insufficient or poorly handled? Have there been too many squabbles over different interpretations or opposing viewpoints? Remember that you are part of the group so that the question about the group's communication needs also includes your own problems.

2.   What have I done to meet those needs? Before you can answer this question, and indeed, before you can answer the first question, you must take a sharp look at your own attitudes toward the communication process. An individual's attitudes can affect his or her perception of an appropriate role in the discussion situation. Here the concern is with your attitudes about *what* should be said, to *whom* it should be said, and *how* it should be said. If you believe that communication is easy or has little value, you will tend to see few problems. If you believe that it is unlikely to be improved, you will tend to be blind to what you have done or what you may do to improve.

3.   What can I do now? This chapter describes several ways to improve the communication process. Of course, we would all like to be exceptionally good in all aspects of communicating. But realism tells us that we should expect to focus our attention, at least initially, upon those things we do best. Focusing upon either task or process needs is often the best way to limit the scope of the undertaking to manageable size. Some, for example, will find it easy to diagnose and improve communication that involves the group's

task. Particularly if the topic is highly interesting to us, we can easily cope with problems of relevance, relatedness, and clarity. For any number of reasons, however, we may be more inclined to focus upon process needs and will probably concern ourselves more with such problems as creating a permissive climate and equalizing participation.

4.   What can I train myself to do or do better? Each of us must broaden and refine our capacity so that we are no longer performing only those functions we do well or focusing on only a part of the group's communication needs. Our initial predispositions and the nature of the needs of our particular group may suggest a place to start. Beyond that, each person should diagnose his or her own strengths and weaknesses and set some learning goals for improvement. There are many opportunities to take courses and enroll in special, short-term workshops. In addition, the student of discussion should deliberately seek out opportunities to learn by doing, in a variety of groups.

These, then, are some suggestions for things to do before the discussion. If you follow these suggestions, you can reduce the communication complexities of the actual discussion situation for three fundamental reasons. First, you will make certain decisions and preparations in advance that you need not make during the discussion. Second, you will anticipate communication problems and will therefore be in a better position during the discussion to interpret messages indicating their presence. Finally, you will focus your attention on stimuli that are both important to you and the group and that you feel you can respond to. You will gear yourself to become group minded rather than wrapped up in your own needs and problems.

DURING THE DISCUSSION

Because discussion is dynamic, all problems cannot be anticipated. To assume that any of our anticipations are final answers is, therefore, unrealistic and naive. We must be particularly alert to whether the grounds for our anticipations continue unchanged during the discussion.

We feel the following suggestions can solve or alleviate the most crucial communication problems. Unless otherwise indicated, each technique applies equally to source–encoder and decoder–receiver.

Assessing Relevance and Relatedness

Relevance and relatedness were explained in Chapter 6. We'll discuss three techniques that help to meet these twin objectives.

Ask How the Contribution Fits. Both the one talking and the listeners must keep asking the question, How does this fit? Both must attempt answers. The problem-solution pattern described in Chapter 10 provides a structure for determining relevance, but this structure often will not be enough. Before striking out into new territory, speakers should warn their listeners. If their ideas are vague, but they nonetheless feel they are beginning to grope toward something valuable, they should ask for help in establishing relevance.

Listeners have special responsibility. They must ask how the speaker's contributions fit, and they must ask how their subvocal reactions fit. If they are feeding back, fine; but if they are jamming, they should catch the tendency quickly.

If a group is brainstorming a topic, there is no need to worry whether or not the contribution fits. (For an explanation of how brainstorming works, see Chapter 10.)

Be careful, however, of injudicious application of this technique. Improperly used, the question can stifle productive discussion. If discussants are struck by an idea and begin to explore it, either publicly or privately, and then discover that they cannot answer the question, they may abandon the line of thought before the group has sufficient opportunity to examine it. On the other hand, a listener may hear a contribution, ask how it fits, decide it does not fit, and *then dismiss the thought without further evaluation.* Let's examine each of these circumstances a bit more closely.

If we knew more about human thought processes in general and creativity in particular, perhaps we could tell when our minds are simply wandering and when we have the kernel of a promising idea. Considering our ignorance, however, it seems wiser to play our hunches when intuition tells us that we may have caught hold of something, rather than dismiss the thought because we cannot relate it at the time. Even if the idea proves ultimately to be irrelevant to the discussion at hand, it may be an idea we want to pursue privately or with another group at another time. When you are faced with this situation, do one of two things. If there seems to be any possibility that the idea might prove relevant, ask the group's indulgence in allowing you to try out the idea. Second, if the relevance seems highly unlikely, for the time being pigeonhole the idea, either in a corner of your mind or on paper. When you are alone, take the idea out again and turn it this way and that, giving it as fair a trial as possible.

Listeners who dismiss a contribution because they cannot see how it fits are simply shirking their duty. If it does not seem to fit, stay with the contribution until the speaker has finished. Grant the assumption that speakers sense a relevance or they would not be talking. If, when the speaker has finished, you still cannot fit the idea in, or if you are unsure of the fit, simply ask the speaker, and the others, how they see the idea fitting in. You may be the only one who has not found the fit, but others may be as puzzled as you. Or, others may only have assumed that the idea was relevant.

Use the Hook-on Technique. One way to ensure that your comments are related is to use what we call the *hook-on technique.* Hooking on consists simply of prefacing a contribution with a reference to a contribution that has gone before. For example, if the person who just finished speaking has suggested a solution to a problem, you might begin like this: "John has suggested one way of solving the problem, but I would like to go back to the problem itself before we evaluate any solutions. I don't think we have analyzed it deeply enough." If you had not taken the trouble to recognize John's point and relate yours to it, others might reasonably have inferred that you were quarreling with John's proposed solution, when actually your contribution has no direct bearing at all upon his solution.

Many hook-on statements are supportive and offer agreement or add-on ideas that augment the basic premise. "In line with what Jane said . . ." is an example.

To hook on when you intend to talk directly about the contribution that has preceded yours is easy. Trouble arises when your contribution aims in a different direction. If hooking on is difficult, either the preceding contribution was out of line or your contribution is out of line. If it is the other contribution that is offbase, your first task should be to try to relate it or help the contributor to relate it. If you find that your contribution doesn't fit, you should either wait until it is appropriate to introduce it or double back as in the first example.

Hooking on applies to listeners as well as speakers. They must seek the bridge between what is being said and what has been said. If speakers perform their task well, the listener's problems are lessened. But if you as listener must discover the bridge yourself, do not assume that all the others have found the same bridge. Give feedback as quickly as possible. If you are right, your feedback will clarify and emphasize the contribution. If you are wrong, you have checked your own potential to jam.

Give One Point at a Time. If a discussant suggests at one time a new goal, an obstacle to another goal, and a solution to meet still a third goal, everyone is likely to become confused. The contribution has become a small oration. But to give three reasons *for one point* at the same time is a good policy. Others may agree with one or two of the reasons but wish to disagree with the third. You may need to present all three reasons for any one of them to have meaning. The important thing is to keep all parts of the contribution related to one main point.

To stick to just one point is often very difficult. Complicated subjects with complicated interrelations tempt us to talk about everything at once. But so far as possible, we should resist the temptation because if contributions are to be properly received and decoded, the contributor must help maintain the focus.

Creating Clarity

"Be clear! Be clear! Be clear!" These were Napoleon's famous three rules for transmitting messages. But, although this threefold injunction serves to emphasize the importance of clarity, probably it no more helps produce clarity than the injunction "Be objective!" helps produce objectivity. To guarantee clarity is frankly impossible, as pointed out in the previous chapter. Since meaning is a process that involves everyone in the discussion situation, being clear must require something more than plain speaking. Weaver and Ness point out that it is not sufficient that the *speaker* know what he is talking about. The purpose of informational speaking is to achieve understanding *in the mind of the listener.* [1]

We are more apt to be clear if we remember the following: (1) Speak naturally. Informal group discussion calls for natural, not artificial speaking. (2) Use simple, concrete words. Some discussants throw up a smoke screen to cover their ignorance. Some are too indifferent to genuine communication to use words that other people will understand. (3) State the point. As a general rule you should state the point you intend to make and then offer examples, reasoning, and other support for the point. If you lead up to the point you run the risk of having your listeners miss connections between ideas because they may miss the main direction. Whether you state it first or last be sure you do state the point. Never leave your listeners wondering what you are trying to establish.

[1] Andrew T. Weaver and Ordean G. Ness, *An Introduction to Public Speaking* (New York: The Odyssey Press, Inc., 1961), p. 89.

There are five specific techniques that are particularly useful in the attainment of clarity. We'll discuss each of them here in some detail.

Seek the Purpose. Seeking the purpose is different from determining relevance and relatedness. It requires both speaker and listener to ask this question: What goals does the speaker seek to accomplish as a result of making the contribution? The nature and effects of goal-seeking behavior have been discussed, particularly as they concern group climate, in Chapter 4.

In your role of decoder–receiver, you must be careful not to allow your own goals to cause jamming. You must seek the speaker's purpose to be *able* to decode and interpret the message. If you cannot discover the purpose, ask the speaker to explain. Seeking the purpose for reasons of clarity is an excellent method of sensitizing others to goals. You may accomplish much more than just clarity, important as that is.

Seek the Pattern. Recall the importance of organizing messages according to some pattern. Your planning before the discussion will help organize thoughts during the discussion, but you must continually keep on organizing ideas. One way is to announce at the beginning of your contribution *how* you plan to develop the rest of the message. For instance, "I see three reasons why we should reject that solution. First . . ." or "Let me offer one example and one statistic to support that point." Announcing your organizational pattern is one valuable use of road sign messages. You set the bounds of your own message and you alert others to *what* is coming and to *how* they can expect it to arrive.

Seeking the pattern is more difficult for the listener, however. The listener has little difficulty if the speaker announces a pattern and then sticks to it, but not many discussants either announce or follow a pattern. Active and critical listening for ideas should come first. Discovering the pattern or helping the speaker formulate a pattern are of less importance.

Seek the Other Person's Meaning. Both speaker and listener must look for the other person's meaning. Your knowledge of purpose and pattern will help, as will your knowledge of backgrounds, habits, and peculiarities of other individuals. The total context of the message will help you judge the other person's meaning. When you speak, you should obviously warn listeners if you use a word in a nonconventional manner. When you listen, watch for hints of a word being used nonconventionally.

An amusing incident illustrating the failure to keep this question uppermost happened when we were conducting a training program for a group of businessmen. We gave them copies of a case study, which they read and then began to discuss. Something was wrong, however, because the discussion was disjointed. We discovered the trouble when one of the businessmen said, "What I can't figure out is why the auditors were going over his books." That was it. We had written something about a speaker and his auditors. By *auditor* we meant a listener; they meant an accountant. Neither we nor they had stopped to think what the other might mean by the word. Little was lost by the error because we were teaching communication and we had a first-rate example of what happens when people do not ask what the other person means.

Rephrase. The best way to make molehills out of mountains of communication difficulties is the technique of rephrasing the contributions of others. Rephrasing consists of putting another's idea into a different set of words. If every group set as its first operating rule, the principle that no one be allowed to disagree with another's argument until he or she rephrased that argument *to the satisfaction of the originator,* progress would be much greater. This practice illustrates the use of feedback at its best.

You must ask and answer three questions about rephrasing to use the technique effectively. Who should rephrase? What should be rephrased? How should contributions be rephrased? The first question is most easily answered. Anyone who feels unsure of the intended meaning of a contribution may rephrase and certainly anyone who wishes to take issue with a contribution should first rephrase it.

Rephrasing does *not* mean parroting what someone else has said. It is possible to parrot without thinking or understanding but rephrasing requires both.

Obviously, we cannot rephrase every contribution made, so we must establish some ground rules for judging which contributions merit rephrasing. If a contribution is unclear to some members, someone should probably rephrase it. But an equally important consideration is the degree to which the contribution is central to the discussion—how much difference it makes. Although all contributions should be considered important, few can be considered *central* to the discussion and the key issues. It is wise, therefore, to rephrase most central contributions, even though you do not seriously doubt their intended meaning. Be less concerned about messages involving supporting details, questions for exploration, illustrations of a point, and the like.

When you rephrase another's contribution, keep the intended meaning in mind and refrain from extending the argument. If you want to add something, make sure you have cleared up the problem of meaning first.

One useful method of rephrasing is to relate an abstract statement to more specific and observable instances. If you stay on the abstract level, you may find that you simply substitute one set of ambiguous words for another, and no one will be any closer to a workable understanding. Suppose a discussant says that the federal government has become too large and powerful. In rephrasing this contribution, you might mention certain powers and certain areas of governmental control and ask if the speaker would include these as examples of undesirable size and power. After a few exchanges, you may discover that there is no objection to the activities of the Securities and Exchange Commission, the Federal Communications Commission, or the Federal Reserve Board, but the speaker does object to several instances of governmental influence over price and wage settlements. By pinning down the abstraction to specific instances, you are able to discover a relatively specific area of control to which the speaker objects. Now you and the rest of the group may better examine the implications and validity of the position.

In the example just given, the discussants required an exchange of contributions to complete rephrasing. This often happens when we discuss abstract and complicated subjects. If the original contribution is more specific, your rephrasing can usually be a simple preface to your own contribution. In either case, however, persist in your rephrasing until the other person acknowledges its accuracy.

The spirit in which such attempts at clarification should be undertaken must be positive, not hostile. You are trying to pin down the *meaning*, not *the speaker*. You must put forth some effort, too; don't throw out the challenge, "Define your terms!" and then sit back and wait for the other person to do all the work. It should be in the spirit of genuine helpfulness; you are trying to help the discussant, the rest of the group, and yourself to agree as precisely as possible on just what is meant. Finally, in the process of pinning down the meaning of a contribution, the contributor some-times finds that his or her contribution had sound but little substance. It is embarrass-ing to find that one's words are empty. Therefore, unless people are capable of making (or taking) a joke at their expense, let the matter drop as quietly as possible.

Watch for the Loaded Word. We all know that words elicit connotative meanings besides their literal conventional meanings. Sometimes such words provide humor, as in the well-known case of the "declension" of the word *obstinate*: I am firm; you are stub-born; but he is a pigheaded fool. More often, however, such words provide com-municative troubles because of the feelings surrounding them. If we want to label someone on the faculty of a school, we may call him a teacher, a professor, an educator, a pedagogue, an instructor, a scholar, or a host of other names that stu-dents use out of faculty earshot. The literal meanings of the various words are similar, but the loaded (connotative) meanings in each suggest something different about the attitude of the user and sometimes highlight some particular characteristic of the classification. The word *teacher*, for example, may emphasize the classroom functions of a faculty member, but the word *scholar* may point up research functions. Some people say that the only difference between a teacher and a professor is that the latter carries a briefcase.

The wisest way out of the difficulty is to use ordinary words whose meanings are as neutral as possible. When conventional loadings are present or when we intend something special by the word, we should be aware of what we are doing and use the vocal equivalents of quotation marks to warn listeners that a special meaning is intended. As listeners we should be alert to the loadings, and, when we feed back and rephrase, we can substitute more neutral words to see whether they work as well.

Promoting Openness and Permissiveness

Creating conditions in which people feel free to express their thoughts is the subject of much of this book. Since permissiveness and openness are marks of mature groups, here are a few ways to improve the communicative process by promoting them.

Concentrate on Content. Concentrating on others' motives is unwise. You should concentrate instead on the content of what others say. The intent of the message is far more important than the package it comes in. Concentrating on content helps pro-mote permissiveness because it helps you react to *what* is said rather than *how* it is said or *who* is doing the talking. This procedure encourages objective analysis of ideas.

Criticize Your Own Ideas. Just as the people who can laugh at themselves set others at ease, so those who can criticize their own ideas help create the permissive climate that allows genuine evaluation. To criticize your own ideas you must listen critically *when you talk* and you must be willing to be criticized. If discussion or new evidence shows you that you should change one of your ideas, speak up and suggest the modification yourself. If the group reaches the thinking-out-loud stage, and you offer a suggestion that began in promising fashion but ended with the proverbial thud, simply say, "No, I see now, that won't work."

When group members know each other well, discussions are characterized by a high rate of self-rejected ideas. So far as we know, no one has ever tallied self-rejected versus other-rejected ideas because no one really cares who rejects a poor idea. For a time, we were members of a small group of people who had worked together for a long time and were also good personal friends. The degree of permissiveness was such that a new secretary, working in an outer office, who overheard one of our discussions began to worry about what she interpreted as fighting. After she learned to know the people better, she told one of us that she had never heard a group speak so frankly to one another. Few groups will reach the degree of permissiveness or openness that this one had reached, but none can begin to reach that level if criticism of ideas is avoided. The best place to start evaluating ideas is with your own.

Criticize Specifically. When you criticize another's ideas, criticize specifically. If you criticize vaguely, you do the other person two injustices. First, you do not show exactly what you object to; second, you imply that there is more you do not like. We are most concerned here with the second injustice. If others are uncertain of the extent of your criticism, they may become more hesitant and the permissiveness you have been trying to build by "being kind" vanishes. You are not being kind when you criticize vaguely.

Avoid Unnecessary Evaluation. Do not busy yourself correcting other's grammar, mispronunciation, or other insignificant details. If the other person's mistake has genuinely impeded communication, you may handle the matter by attempting to rephrase. Otherwise, such corrections are irritating and tend to focus attention on niceties of expression instead of on substance. Again, a dampening of permissiveness results.

Praise Generously. Sometimes we become so engrossed in thinking together that we forget to praise good ideas. We act as if not criticizing the idea is praise enough. It isn't.

Listen Empathically. Empathic listening is the most important single technique for promoting permissiveness. Note that we did not say *sympathetic*; we said *empathic*. What do we mean? The word *empathy* has been introduced before. It involves feeling and reacting as we believe someone else is feeling and reacting. It means identifying with another person. When we watch a play on the stage, we empathize with the protagonist. We struggle with him; we are elated when he triumphs. In the old days of traveling tent shows, playing the role of the villain required courage. Apparently more than one excited and empathic spectator decided to settle the issue on the spot and pulled out a gun to protect the hero and heroine. A clear example of empathy can be noted today when an especially vicious tackle is made on the football field; you can hear a collective "ooh" from the spectators empathizing with the tackled player.

What is meant, then, by empathic listening? It means putting yourself in the speaker's shoes; struggling with the person as he or she tries to shape words to thoughts; searching mentally while the speaker tries to make precise distinctions; in short, imagining that you yourself are speaking. Do not interrupt; do not supply a word unless asked for it; but empathize silently.

Although you are silent, if you listen empathically, you cannot help revealing by gesture, posture, and facial expression that you are concerned with the speaker's effective statement. We have yet to hear of a good public speaker who does not hunt for those faces in the crowd that say, "I am with you; keep it up." The same principle is true in the discussion group. Listening empathically helps the speaker, *and it helps you listen more accurately.* Moreover, it helps promote permissiveness because it encourages others to express themselves.

Communicating Totally

What do you communicate? Everything that others in the discussion group can see or hear constitutes what you communicate. You must suit the action to the word and the visible expression to the feeling. As you participate in discussion you reveal yourself as a creative, interested, and interesting human being, or you reveal yourself as something less. As we explained in the previous chapter, nonverbal communication becomes a problem when words and body language contradict.

Sometimes these contradictions occur because our words and feelings do *not* match. Perhaps we are saying what we feel is socially acceptable, and the words we'd like to say are buried inside. In other instances, nervous or distracting habits serve to detract from what the speaker means to convey. One of us was asked to serve as a consultant to a group of civil defense experts whose job involved going to various cities to interest civic and volunteer groups in organizing in case of war or natural disaster. One gentleman had prepared an excellent presentation, complete with audio and visual aids, but during the dress rehearsal, a fatal flaw was revealed. He was talking about how much damage would be inflicted upon a certain small town if a bomb or missile were dropped. He described how many lives would be lost and how much property damage would occur within a specified radius and all the while he had a sweet smile on his face. The verbal and visual effects were completely incongruous. No one listened to his words because they were trying to figure out why he was smiling. His lack of experience with public speaking caused him to smile out of sheer nervousness—and he was unaware that he was smiling. He was advised to practice in front of a mirror and he was coached to shift from self-consciousness to message- and audience-consciousness in order to control the stage fright.

However, we do not advise most people to stand before a mirror and practice gesturing. But we do suggest that you so involve yourself in what you are saying and feeling that you *want* to communicate totally, and we suggest that you become so secure personally that you *can* communicate totally. Also, become aware of inappropriate nonverbal communication. The person whose foot jiggles constantly or who repeatedly clicks a ballpoint pen not only betrays nervousness, but also detracts from everyone's ability to concentrate.

SUMMARY

In this chapter we have shown that effective prediscussion planning reduces complexities. Discussants should organize their material according to some pattern, provide necessary visual aids, and decide the best time to present the information. Discussants should predict the group's probable communication needs, examine their own attitudes and behavior to judge what they have done to meet those needs, and determine what they can do on the spot and what they can train themselves to do.

During discussion, members have more tasks. They must assess the relevance and relatedness of what they and their colleagues communicate by asking how each contribution fits, by hooking on to what others say, and by confining themselves to one main point each time they contribute. Several suggestions were given on how groups can create more clarity in their communication. In order to promote openness and permissiveness, discussants should concentrate on the content of contributions, criticize their own ideas, criticize others specifically rather than vaguely, avoid unnecessary evaluation, praise generously, and most important, listen empathically. Finally, the discussant must communicate totally, remembering that what others see may have more impact than what they hear.

DISCUSSION QUESTIONS

1.   Why do most people seem more willing to admit that they communicated poorly than that they reasoned poorly?

2.   What is the relationship between quantity and quality of communication?

3.   Which nonverbal communications are the most helpful? Which are distracting or otherwise nonproductive?

4.   How can we improve the communication in our group (or class)?

EXERCISES

1.   Develop a personal program for improving your communication based on the suggestions offered in this chapter. One possible approach is to select one or two aspects or points and direct your efforts toward improving them. Then move on to others. Supplement your own analysis of your strengths and limitations by conferences with a competent colleague or with your instructor.

2.   Reflect on your experience as a member of discussion groups, recalling instances where an idea that had significant substantive merit was weakened, disregarded, or lost because of poor communication. What factors account most often for such reduction in effectiveness?

3.   Pair yourself with a colleague and replay a tape recording of a group discussion in which you both participated. Each should first analyze the

other's communication and then immediately replay the tape and analyze his/her own. Compare your self-analysis with your analysis of your colleague. Do you note any places where your communication behavior during the discussion was affected by your prediscussion preparation? Exchange the analyses you have made of each other and discuss them. What new insights have you gained? Do you anticipate any modifications in your communication behavior as a result of this experience?

4.   Analyze your communication behavior in terms of one or more of the following possibilities:

a.   Feedforward. Can you recognize preliminary messages? Can you use such communication when it comes from others? Which type, road sign or trial balloon, do you use most frequently? Why? How useful do you find it?

b.   Feedback. To what extent do you provide feedback? How helpful do you feel your feedback is to others? To what degree are you conscious of providing such responses? Do you deliberately attempt to modify your feedback or is it always spontaneous? Do you feel that others respond to your feedback? Do you respond to theirs? Do you welcome it?

c.   Jamming. To what extent do you jam the communication of others? What causes you to do this? To what extent do you believe that your jamming has affected adversely your interpersonal relationships, achievement, or progress? How do you think you can reduce your jamming? Do you have any evidence that others jam your messages? How do you think you can reduce their jamming?

SELECTED READINGS

EGAN, GERARD, *Face to Face: The Small-Group Experience and Interpersonal Growth,* chaps. 5, 6. Monterey, Calif.: Brooks/Cole Publishing Company, 1973.

GOLDBERG, ALVIN A., AND CARL E. LARSON, *Group Communication: Discussion Processes and Applications,* chap. 4. Englewood Cliffs, N.J.: Prentice-Hall, Inc., 1975.

KELTNER, JOHN, *Elements of Interpersonal Communication,* chap. 3. Belmont, Calif.: Wadsworth Publishing Company, Inc., 1973.

MONROE, ALAN H., AND DOUGLAS EHNINGER, *Principles and Types of Speech* (6th ed.). Glenview, Ill.: Scott, Foresman & Co., 1967.

MYERS, GAIL E., AND MICHELE TOLELA MYERS, *The Dynamics of Human Communication,* chap. 10. New York: McGraw-Hill Book Company, Inc., 1973.

NICHOLS, RALPH G., AND LEONARD A. STEVENS, *Are You Listening?* New York: McGraw-Hill Book Company, Inc., 1957.

POWELL, JOHN, Society of Jesuits, *Why Am I Afraid to Tell You Who I Am?,* chaps. 1–4. Chicago: Argus Communications, 1969.

PART FOUR

The next four chapters deal with a subject that has fascinated people for centuries—the human mind. We have no idea how many volumes have been written about the nature of thinking, and it would be presumptuous for us to suggest that our analysis could adequately delineate the scope of what is known or conjectured about thought. Our aim is to organize and present the essentials so that they are useful in actual discussions. The reader who wishes to explore this subject further will find a list of readings at the end of each chapter.

A book about discussion should include a section on thinking. Some people believe that thinking is largely an individual matter and that its adaptation to group discussion should be treated in connection with such matters as group structure or communication. There are reasons for disagreeing with this position. It is disturbing to note the number of people who do not apply the same rigorous standards to their thinking in discussion groups as they do in other situations. Such people may hold themselves to strict standards in a research project, an essay, or a speech, but may exhibit the most casual reasoning in a discussion. As pointed out in Chapter 2, the process of thinking seems to be affected by participation in discussion. From the early social facilitation experiments of F. H. Allport to present-day studies of conforming and deviating behavior, evidence for this has been accumulating. Finally, the process of thinking is essentially a social one.

We are not saying that thinking takes place only in groups or even that the *best* thinking takes place in groups. Much of what is productive, valuable, and rewarding is a product of solitary work. The point here is twofold: (1) thinking is better understood as an interactive process, both between individuals and between individuals and the objective world; and (2) certainly, effective groups require effective thinking. Most of the advice given in these four chapters will apply equally to individuals working alone or to groups of individuals working together.

SMALL GROUP
DECISION-MAKING
AND PROBLEM-SOLVING

chapter 8

Evidence furnishes the building blocks of belief—the basis of thought. One of the principal distinctions between a session that is merely "shooting the bull" and one that is effective discussion lies in the amount and quality of evidence.

DEFINITION OF EVIDENCE

Black's Law Dictionary defines evidence as

> Any species of proof, or probative matter, legally presented at the trial of an issue, by the act of the parties and through the medium of witnesses, records, documents, concrete objects, etc., for the purpose of inducing belief in the minds of the court or jury as to their contention.[1]

This definition serves as a starting point from which to spell out the nature of evidence. Note the important phrase *for the purpose of inducing belief.* Facts and opinions exist independently of the use to which they may be put; the moment they are used to induce belief, they become evidence and must be examined as such. Many discussants believe that information and evidence are the same thing. Information may be used broadly to cover a variety of purposes; one example would be for background or orientation. Information only becomes evidence when it is used for the purpose of inducing belief, when we marshal it to support a point of view or to help us win an argument.

KINDS OF EVIDENCE

Evidence may be conveniently classified under three headings: fact, statement of observation, and inference. Each is defined briefly and then compared and contrasted with the others. Then the importance of making the distinction is illustrated.

Fact. The word *fact* is short and we all use it regularly but there is no succinct way to define it. *A fact is something the majority of people with access to the information accept as true as of now.* Note the qualifiers in that definition: It takes a *majority* of people to accept it (but not necessarily all); they need only accept it as true *as of now* because everyone knows new evidence that may change what we now believe to be true is being discovered all the time. For example, it took Pasteur to change surgeons' minds about the need for sterilization against bacteria; it took astronauts actually going to

---

[1]*Black's Law Dictionary*, 3rd ed. (St. Paul, Minn.: West Publishing Co., 1933), p. 695.

Evidence:
The Basis of Thought

the moon and bringing back rock samples to change geologists' minds about the composition of the moon's surface.

Another way to define a fact is to say it is any observable object or act that either has been or can be verified. The term observable does not restrict the definition to what may be observed by the unaided senses or what has been directly observed by the person stating the fact. We can't all go in person to check out the truth of factual statements. So, we have come to rely on people who have observed and on verification by respected people or other sources such as encyclopedias, which report what has been verified.

Smith divided facts into three kinds, according to their sources:

> Some facts are obtained through direct observation. Some come to us as a result of general agreement among people who did observe them directly. Still others come to us through authorities or experts in a particular field. We call these, respectively, *observed* facts, *agreed* facts, and *authorized* facts.[2]

Statement of Observation. A statement of observation is a report of an alleged observation. Usually when people speak of the need to get the facts before making decisions, they mean that they want symbols of facts or statements of observation.

Even when made as accurately and conscientiously as possible, a statement of observation is only, at best, a guide to the facts reported and not a substitute for the facts themselves. The observer must of necessity leave out many or most of the characteristics of the facts. That is, he must abstract from the many things that might be reported and concentrate upon what he considers the important or essential characteristics. Further, many reporters of observations have difficulty discriminating among the aspects of what they observed and expressing what they observed so that other people can understand. Most men, for example, have much more difficulty identifying and describing different colors than women have. For another example, consider how hard it must be to report a performance of an orchestra, with only slippery and grossly inadequate words at your disposal.

Inference. An inference is a statement that goes beyond observation and asserts that which has not been (or cannot be) observed by the one who makes the statement. An inference goes from the known to the unknown. All statements about the future must be classed as inferences since the maker of the statement cannot observe what has not yet occurred. Even statements about causal relationships must be classed as inferences because all we can see is the proximity of time or space, not the relationships themselves. And, of course, conclusions, judgments, and interpretations must be labeled as inferences. Every decision that we make during the course of living is therefore an inference. When we decide to leave the house at one o'clock in order to arrive at the airport on time for a two-thirty flight, we have made all kinds of inferences. We infer that we are allowing enough time for the trip, for delays caused by traffic, for checking in at the airline desk and for walking to the gate. We especially infer that the flight will leave and that it will be on time. Every time we drive, we infer that the other drivers will pay reasonable heed to driving regulations.

Confusion occurs when we draw inferences without realizing it and allow our

[2]William S. Smith, *Group Problem-Solving Through Discussion.* (Indianapolis: The Bobbs-Merrill Co., Inc., 1965), p. 76.

inferences to become "facts." For instance, if you see a friend walking down the street with a suitcase in his hand, a natural inference is that he is going on a trip. You might even report "Joe's going on a trip" to another friend and that is exactly how rumors get started and are perpetuated. It is quite possible that Joe is taking the suitcase to be repaired, or is using it to carry books to the library, or he is returning the suitcase to the person he borrowed it from. We're sure you can think of many other possible inferences in this situation. It seems to be human nature, however, to grab for the first possible inference without checking it out for fact and without recognizing that many other inferences are possible.

One use of inferences is not so apparent. *We must make inferences even when we attempt to report a fact.* We infer that some characteristics are more important than others and abstract them for the purposes of our report. Every reader of detective stories is familiar with that crucial clue that is overlooked by everyone except the master detective, who makes the appropriate inferences about its importance. Doctors must rely upon inferences; from the patient's temperature and skin color, the doctor draws an inference as to what the disease is. He makes a tentative diagnosis but the identification of the disease does not become *fact* until laboratory personnel have completed their analysis.

COMPARISON OF FACT, STATEMENT OF OBSERVATION, AND INFERENCE

Using concepts developed by Irving Lee, Haney suggested the following criteria for distinguishing the making of statements of observation from the making of statements of inference:[3]

Statements of Observation	*Statements of Inference*
1. Can be made only after observation.	1. Can be made at any time.
2. Must stay with what one has observed—must not go beyond.	2. Can go beyond observation— well beyond. We can infer to the limits of our imaginations.
3. Can be made only by the observer.	3. Can be made by anyone.

Haney's criteria for making statements of observation suggest that, if the maker of the statement abides by these criteria, the statement of observation will presumably be valid. The same is not true of the criteria for statements of inference. The next chapter will develop in detail the methods for assessing the degree of probable truth that our inferences possess.

Irving J. Lee of Northwestern University was fond of using the following example to make the distinction between facts, statements of observation, and inferences.[4] He

---

[3]William V. Haney, *Communication Patterns and Incidents* (Homewood, Ill.: Richard D. Irwin, Inc., 1960), p. 21.

[4]Lee used the term *statement of fact* for what we have termed *statement of observation*. We are following Haney's practice in this matter.

would bring an apple to class and, showing it to the class, ask them if there were seeds in the apple. Most people said that there were, if they could assume that the apple had not been tampered with. Lee would then ask if it were a fact that there were seeds in the apple, and again most people said it was a fact, but a few would begin to hedge. Finally, he would cut open the apple and point out that only then could statements of observation be made about the seeds. The seeds themselves were facts; talk about them, when they could be observed, was a statement of observation; and talk about them, when they were hidden in the apple, was inference.

General semanticists insist that we should be careful to avoid two fundamental confusions. First, statements of observation are not the same as that which is observed. The word or symbol is an arbitrary convention used to stand for a fact, but it is not the fact itself. Second, inferences should not be confused with statements of observation.

There is such insistence upon separating facts, statements of observation, and inferences because three fundamentally different methods are used to verify them. Facts simply exist; they are neither true nor false. (The next time you hear someone say "This is a true fact!" try asking him or her to point out some false facts.) Verification of facts is determined by independent observations of their presence, in which case statements of observation may be made about the facts; or by independent observations of their effects, in which case inferences may be made concerning their existence. Statements of observation may be verified by others using the statement as a guide or "map of the territory described" to determine whether the map guides them with reasonable accuracy to the fact. If, for example, you say that your house is located at 15th and Pine, your statement becomes a literal map that can be verified by looking. If this is not possible, the statement of observation must be assigned a degree of probability by making inferences about the one who reported the statement. (Recall the old saw, "Figures can't lie, but liars can figure.")

We can assign a degree of probability to an inference by examining the reasoning process that led the maker of the inference from observation to conclusion or from one inference to another. We can finally verify an inference by observing the outcome of predictions made by the inference. The next chapter gives a more detailed explanation of the reasoning process by which inferences are evaluated, and it examines the whole concept of probability.

A fourth kind of evidence should be noted here and that is *opinion*. Although much opinion is offered in most discussions, we must be careful to distinguish it from fact. Opinions are judgments or evaluations and even when they are presented as *expert opinions*, from authorities in a given field, they should be separated from fact.

SOURCES OF EVIDENCE

When you ask a college freshman where he gets material or evidence for a term paper, he almost invariably replies, "the library." The library is the first place he looks. Although libraries are certainly full of evidence, they are not the only source and it would be a more efficient use of the student's time if he did some thinking and planning *before* he headed for the library.

When a discussant is preparing to deal with a particular subject, the first source of evidence might properly be *his or her own experience*. What is already known that could be shared with the group? What else should be known or might the discussants like to know? Here at the point of identifying gaps in knowledge or experience, discussants can plan on how to get more evidence. Part of the plan might include a *visit* or *field trip* to observe. If the subject is how to improve the country's penal system, discussants could profit from a firsthand visit to a jail or prison to see for themselves what conditions are. Next, they might *interview* a police officer, a lawyer, a judge, a warden, and a parole officer. The discussants will find that their interviews are easier to conduct and report if they plan them in advance so that comparable questions can be asked of all interviewees. Tape-recorded interviews are most useful because they can be referred to again and because the more important parts can be shared verbatim with the group.

Two other sources of evidence are *oral presentations,* including lectures, radio and television programs, tapes and films, and *written materials* of all kinds from pamphlets to encyclopedias. Every good student is familiar with such indispensable tools as the card catalogue and the *Readers' Guide to Periodical Literature.* Students also know how to take notes that include directly quoted material and summaries and abstracts of information. The discussant has two needs for such evidence: First, to refer to during the discussion; and second, to share in written form with other members of the group. Some discussants find it useful to put their evidence on cards, the way debaters do, so that ideas, facts, and opinions can be better organized for quick and easy reference.

It is not sufficient for a discussant to present evidence to the group as something "I read in a magazine the other day." To properly evaluate the evidence, the group needs to know who wrote it or said it, in what publication it appeared, when, and upon what occasion. On the other hand, discussants need not be as formal as debaters, who are required to document publishers, as well as page and line numbers. The key point is that the group should have enough information to evaluate the worth of the evidence and to be able to locate the material for themselves.

Another pitfall is adding our own ideas and opinions when we are abstracting material for evidence. We should not edit the material we find, but present it faithfully as intended. Even the substitution of a word or two can radically change someone else's meaning. For example, the phrase *equality of the sexes* has a far more restricted meaning than *women's lib.* When we are interpreting someone else's ideas, we need to be especially careful not to slip in loaded language, even unintentionally. Later in this chapter we will comment further on the effective presentation of evidence to the group.

GATHERING EVIDENCE

Many groups seem to feel that announcing the topic for discussion to the members will be sufficient to start the research ball rolling, and many otherwise conscientious discussants charge off in all directions, looking haphazardly for evidence. We have divided our suggestions on how to proceed into those that are the group's responsibilities and those that individuals should perform. The steps should be followed in approximately the order listed when the group is faced with a new problem. When the problem is one of those recurrent varieties that the group understands quite well, some of the steps may be eliminated.

Group Responsibilities

The initial thinking stage should normally be carried out in a preliminary meeting of the discussion group. It is usually unwise for a group to attempt to deal with a significant problem in only one meeting. Even if the individual members have known about the discussion topic for some time, their individual preparation is likely to be inefficient, duplicating in some areas and lacking in others, and indifferently researched by some members, if not most. Significant problems almost always require at least two meetings, and more complicated problems may require a considerable number of sessions during which these steps may have to be repeated several times if continued investigation reveals something lacking.

Insight into the Problem. The first step is for the group to begin discussing the problem as if it were intending to go all the way through a problem-solving sequence. The purpose of this step is for the group members to begin to see the ramifications of the problem to be solved. In this preliminary problem examination the group should be especially careful to stress goals and should remember that at this stage it is not trying to solve the problem, but to find and earmark trouble spots for further investigation.

Canvass of Available Evidence. In an amazing number of instances the members already possess much of the necessary evidence or they know how to find it. Groups that meet regularly to solve problems are obviously most likely to have a ready supply of usable evidence. If, for example, the trustees of a college are meeting to determine what procedures ought to be followed to improve the financial support of the institution, it would indeed be surprising if they did not already possess most of the facts they need to know.

Determination of Needed Evidence. The gap between what is known and what is needed should become increasingly clear as the group moves along with its analysis and the members indicate what evidence they already possess. The members should be careful to note the kind of evidence needed, especially the kind that they might be most able to discover.

Whenever a group comes to a point in which someone says, "I wish we knew the answer to that," or "I wonder if more information on that point is available," it is wise to make a note of the expressed need. The group can decide at the end of the session if the need is still felt and, if so, which group members will be responsible for doing the research. Groups more often err on the side of too little evidence; but it is also important to remember that it is never possible to gather all the evidence there is.

Assignment of Individual Research Responsibilities. This is an important step and one that is often neglected by discussion groups. In Chapter 2 we noted that the spread of responsibility is a limitation of discussion and that one way of reducing this limitation is to make specific assignments to group members. There are two obvious advantages to making specific research assignments. First, it encourages individual responsibility and commitment to the group objective.[5] Second, it increases the likelihood that the group will have the evidence it needs when it next convenes.

---

[5]A study by Shaw provides experimental verification for this assertion. David M. Shaw, "Size of Share in Task and Motivation in Work Groups," *Sociometry*, 23 (1960), 203–8.

In many groups this assignment of individual responsibilities is unnecessary since the composition of the group indicates pretty clearly who has the responsibility for what evidence. The people have been placed on the committee because of the special knowledge they possess.

When making the assignments, it is wise to let the members volunteer for specific tasks while one person keeps note of who has undertaken what task. The more eager will volunteer first and the reluctant members will feel increasing pressure to carry their share. By this time the enthusiasm of the members ought to be high if the preceding steps have been skillfully conducted. Coupling this motivation with the effects of volunteering makes it seldom necessary to cajole anyone into assuming some of the research burden. Anyone who has tried this method knows how much easier it is than having the chairman contact group members individually, asking them to throw their energies into the solution of a problem whose nature they neither understand nor care about.

There is one disadvantage to dividing research responsibilities in this fashion. The person who investigates one aspect of the problem only may suffer from tunnel vision and fail to see the entire picture. What's more, having become a specialist in this one aspect, the discussant may find that he or she keeps trying to work that subject into the discussion whether or not it's relevant or related. People like to show off their knowledge. Narrow subject specialists may also become advocates for one position or one solution simply because they understand best what they have researched. A possible countermeasure to this risk is to make sure that all group members acquire some general background in the problem area before they start to specialize. Another antidote is to see that all group members have two or more aspects to investigate.

Individual Responsibilities

The assignments have been made and now the individuals must go to work. They must begin discovering needed evidence and creating ideas for problem analysis and solution. If the discussants are not already competent researchers, they will find considerable information about potential sources of evidence in most good texts that deal directly with the problems of research. The process of gathering and preparing the evidence so that it will be useful to the group has four steps:

> *1. General understanding.* Unless members are already thoroughly acquainted with the nature of the problem to be solved, they ought to spend some time investigating the nature of the overall problem before beginning to look for the specific evidence that is the assignment. The group's discussion of the overall problem will probably have been somewhat vague and incomplete since the members were approaching it with little previous preparation. Looking at the whole problem will help the individual in three ways in addition to the earlier point about the dangers of narrow specialization. First, the discussant will be better able to fit his or her specific assignment into the total picture. Second, he or she will be prepared to understand and evaluate the contributions made by others with different assignments. Third, he or she may discover some evidence or ideas that may have escaped the notice of those investigating the other aspects of the problem.

2.   *Specific research.* This is obviously the next step. The individuals must hunt for the best evidence available to them. If discussants are uncertain of the value of a given piece of evidence, they should retain rather than discard it, and let the rest of the group be the judge of its value. Better to have the evidence on hand than to have to say, "Oh yes, I saw something about that but I didn't copy it down."

3.   *Assimilate the evidence.* This is an important step. If the researcher does not thoroughly understand the meaning and implications of the evidence, it is unlikely that the rest of the group will. Assimilating the evidence means that the researcher must understand the use to which the evidence may be put; it also means that he or she must be aware of the implications the evidence has for further investigation, which might produce radical changes in the group's conception of the problem or means of solving it.

4.   *Prepare the report.* Although some texts recommend that the individual prepare a complete outline of the problem-solving sequence before coming to the discussion, the disadvantages of this practice outweigh the advantages. Such practice tends to rigidify each individual's thinking about how the problem should be analyzed and solved and results in each person tending to go his or her own way when the group discusses. Thus, collective thinking is rendered even more difficult.

We will have more to say about the presentation of evidence in the last section of this chapter.

REPORTERS OF EVIDENCE

When facts and statements are considered as evidence, we must look at how a group receives the evidence. When a group is examining a problem, the evidence seldom presents itself. Individuals must bring the evidence to the group and often it must pass through many interpretations before it becomes available for consideration. Let's look at the three kinds of evidence (fact, statement of observation, and inference) in light of how each kind may be brought to the attention of the group.

Reporters of Fact. The group may often want to observe the facts directly rather than simply act upon statements of facts. Thus, a group considering slum clearance will usually want to go out and look at the slums to be cleared and possibly examine the results of successful slum clearances elsewhere. In other cases, the object to be observed may be brought to the group, as when documents, records, letters, and similar matters are presented for firsthand observation. Such is the use of the "exhibits" introduced as evidence in court during a trial.

Usually someone brings the facts to the attention of the group. When that happens, we must concern ourselves with the communication surrounding the presentation of the fact or the circumstances under which it is observed. Communication about an object can affect our perception of it as in Figure 8.1. When we look at the figure, does it make any difference whether we say, "Look at the vase," or whether we say, "Notice the two faces?"

FIGURE 8.1.   What Do You See?

The issue here is not the variability of perception. We are simply underscoring the observation that words affect perception. Words condition us to fall into what psychologists call a *pre-set*. In other words, we see what we expect to see. Similarly, the conditions under which an object is perceived can clearly affect the perception of it. The kind of light available, the relations of the object to other objects or events, and so on will influence perception and in some cases will create such dramatic confusions as the reversing of black and white.

Reporters of Statements of Observations. The statements of observation used by a group may be either furnished firsthand by one of the members of the group or may be reported secondhand, thirdhand, and so on. The number of times a statement of observation is removed from the original observation does not affect its classification as a statement of observation, when we consider it as evidence. It does, however, affect the verification of the statement because of the number of layers that must be uncovered before we reach the original. The way in which a simple observation can be distorted by the "rumor mill" should be caution enough about this matter.

Reporters of Inference. When inferences are used as evidence, most people think that the inferences must have been made by some authority *outside* the group. But often members of a group introduce their own inferences as *evidence* rather than as *reasoning* based on information commonly available. The supervisor of a department, for example, may meet the president of the company and discuss the accepted bases of promotions within the organization. The supervisor may return to the executive committee and report some inferences that certain kinds of promotion justifications will not be accepted by the front office. The supervisor may further infer that if the group sends forward a promotion request, it will almost certainly be denied because of the kinds of justifications the group has available. Someone else on the executive committee may have talked to the president or to another high-ranking official and come back with a contrary set of inferences. The members of the committee must decide which set of inferences possesses the greater degree of probability. They must consequently decide which, if either, they will accept as evidence. They may wish to accept neither, insisting on further examination or the gathering of more evidence.

As with statements of observation, the inference may be reported firsthand by some member, or some outside authority, or it may be reported secondhand, third-hand, and so on. The same problems of evaluation are presented by successive removals from the primary source.

HOW EVIDENCE IS DISCOVERED

Evidence, as we have seen, usually exists and remains to be discovered or developed. Sometimes the evidence is created by inference or experimentation conducted by members of the group. But regardless of how the evidence comes into being there must be an initial step of discovery. Existing evidence must be located; facts forming the basis of the inference must be observed; or the hypothesis guiding the experiment must be formulated. Every so often, we literally or figuratively stumble over evidence that may be of use to us or our group, but usually discovery is the fruit of purposeful seeking. The following four factors increase the likelihood of evidence being discovered and enhance the possibility of its being valuable.

1. *Competence.* Evidence seekers must be competent. Discoveries by the incompetent are rare and usually run-of-the-mill. People bringing evidence to a group perform two functions. They first must discover or formulate the evidence. When they do this, we call them *researchers*. Next, they must bring the evidence to the attention of someone else. When they do this, we call them *reporters*. If they lack competence in either area, the group will be handicapped.

2. *Access to potential evidence.* Another indispensable requirement of research is access to potential evidence. Researchers must be in a position to observe; they must have the books and other sources of information available.

A citizen's right to know is currently an important issue in our nation. More and more states are passing "sunshine" laws requiring official bodies to open meetings to the public and the press, and "freedom of information" regulations that open public (and in some cases private) records to interested persons. Where do we draw the line, for example, between behind-the-scenes negotiations and the citizens' right to know the full story of their nation's foreign policy?

If discussants find roadblocks between them and their desired evidence, they should not necessarily take no for the answer. A check with the instructor (in the case of class projects) or with authorities (for other groups) would be wise; the roadblock may rightfully and legally be removed.

3.   *Will to observe.* One of the requirements for creativity is the ability to see and follow up on what one sees. Creativity is no passive process in which one waits for lightning to strike; discovery of evidence requires energy and imagination. Some people have potential evidence "right under their noses" and still do not have the will to observe. Hence, they pass it by. Others seem to be too lazy to look.

There are, doubtless, many reasons why some potential researchers lack the will to observe. The astronomers of Galileo's day who refused the invitation to look through the telescope for themselves did so because they believed that the very act of looking constituted heresy.

4.   *Flexibility to observe.* Even if researchers possess the attributes just described, they may still be incapable of first-rate discovery if they are not flexible enough to observe potential evidence. *Flexible* does not mean "weak-willed." It means that the researcher must be capable of perceiving distinctions that are meaningful.

Our symbol system affects, to a considerable extent, what we see. We tend to notice what we can label and lacking the labels, tend to be blind. All of us probably have had the experience of learning a new name for something, a bird perhaps, and then being astonished to discover how many birds of this type seemed suddenly to appear. The birds had been there all the time, but we had not noticed them until we learned the name, and then it seemed as if the species had suddenly multiplied.

An essential part of competence in a field is the knowledge of the symbol system of the field. To the extent that the symbols are varied and flexible, the researcher is aided in the perception of potential evidence. The novice in a field usually possesses only general terms, which tend to obscure differences by concentrating on the characteristics that individual members of a species hold in common.

Some Eskimos apparently have as many as seven different words to identify what most of us simply refer to as *snow*. Their experience with snow has led them to make distinctions, and to label those distinctions, with much greater precision than most people find necessary. A skiing enthusiast in the United States, however, will be able to make distinctions between various conditions of snow even though he or she may have to rely upon qualifying adjectives when labeling the distinctions. Again, skiers have a greater need to distinguish different types of snow than have other people.

Researchers need a broad and flexible language and must be capable of going beyond the bounds set by their language: They must be able to create labels to communicate the knowledge of the new discovery, or the scope of their discoveries will be restricted.

Another aspect of flexibility to observe is *freedom from attitudinal blind spots*. An elderly man, who had spent all his life in the fertile farm country of the Midwest, visited Colorado. Looking upon the marvelous mountains and rugged countryside, he said, "Humph! Won't grow much corn." His attitude toward farm country blinded him to seeing the beauty of the mountains. Similarly, many regard the sight of row upon row of green corn sprouting from rich black earth as a beautiful sight; to many others, the same sight is merely dreary.

Most people tend to look for virtues in their friends and flaws in their enemies.

Further, people tend to be suspicious of what they do not know and consequently quite certain they will not like it. Parents are familiar with the child who is convinced he does not like a certain food even though he admits he has never tasted it. Most children outgrow this tendency to dislike foods they have never tasted, but other types of ignorance-produced dislikes are more pernicious. Many people are quite uncertain about what a university is and what goes on within its campus, yet they are very certain that they do not like it and seize upon scraps of evidence that, they believe, offer proof that universities abound with "intellectuals," "eggheads," and people of low moral character.

Possibly no aspect of modern life is more emotion-packed than the matter of race relations. We offer two examples of attitudinal blindness drawn from this area.

Sherif and Hovland conducted a classic experiment designed to measure the effect that attitude had upon the perception of statements.[6] The subjects were given 114 statements about Negroes. Each statement was typed upon a separate card. The subjects were instructed to sort the cards into eleven piles ranging from those statements that were very favorable to blacks to those that were very unfavorable to blacks. In another version of the experiment, the subjects were told to arrange the cards as before, but with no restriction as to the number of categories into which the cards were to be sorted. The results showed that both the subjects who admitted to being strongly prejudiced *in favor of* Negroes and those who admitted to being strongly prejudiced *against* them tended to polarize their judgments. That is, the subjects tended to perceive a fairly large number of statements describing their own position, very few neutral statements, and a large bulk of statements strongly opposing their own position. When the number of categories was unspecified, the strongly prejudiced subjects often used only three categories; even in these cases, they put more statements in each extreme pile than they put in the neutral pile. Subjects whose feelings were not extreme tended to level off the number of statements in each pile and tended to use more categories. As might be expected, given cards showed up in a variety of positions on different scales. The conclusions were that those who feel strongly about an issue will tend to see things as good or bad. They perceive that people are either for them or against them—not neutral.

The second example is taken from a study conducted by Allport and Postman.[7] The picture shown in Figure 8.2 was one of several that the subjects in the experiment were asked to look at for a few seconds. The experimenter then turned the picture face down and asked the subjects to report what was in the picture. In a distressing number of reports, the black was perceived as the probable aggressor, and as being shabbily dressed, whereas the white man was seen as well dressed. The razor even found its way into the black man's hands in many of these distorted reports. We used this picture in a training session for adults brought to the University of Colorado campus from all over the country. The results were following predictable paths until a white man from the South accurately described the two men in the picture and placed the razor properly in the white man's hand. "How do you account for a razor

[6]Muzafer Sherif and Carl I. Hovland, "Judgmental Phenomena and Scales of Attitude Measurement: Placement of Items with Individual Choice of Number of Categories," *Journal of Abnormal and Social Psychology,* 48 (1953), 135–41.

[7]Gordon W. Allport and Lee Postman, *The Psychology of Rumor* (New York: Holt, Rinehart & Winston, Inc., 1947) pp. 64–74.

FIGURE 8.2   From the *Psychology of Rumor* by Gordon Allport and Lee Postman. Copyright 1947 by Holt, Rinehart and Winston, Inc. Reprinted by permission of Holt, Rinehart and Winston, Inc.

in the white man's hand?" the Southerner was asked. "Why, he obviously just took it away from the Negro," was the answer.

All of us are subject to attitudinal blindness in one form or another. One of the main advantages of discussion is that, unless all members of the group have the same blind spot, they can frequently help one another to become aware of the phenomenon as it happens. Developing freedom from attitudinal blindness in ourselves is difficult. First, we must become aware of our attitudes and the potential effect they may have on our behavior. Second, we must work to modify attitudes that appear to run counter to available evidence. Third, we must develop an attitude of skepticism about our feelings when we do not know much about the object of our attitude.

BELIEVABILITY OF EVIDENCE

Now let's look at the means whereby discussion group members can evaluate the evidence they are asked to accept. We have developed criteria in relation to logical believability, personal or source credibility, and emotional believability.

Logical Believability

The criteria in this category are those that are used to assess believability of evidence independently of the personal characteristics of the reporter or the hopes and desires of group members. Such criteria are toward the objective-reality end of the continuum discussed in Chapter 5, and are generally to be preferred over other criteria for believability.

Opportunity to Observe. This criterion is obviously similar to access to evidence. When using this criterion, the group should ask, "Did the originator of the evidence have the opportunity to observe?" When a statement of observation is presented as evidence, the originator must have had this opportunity. When inferences are presented as evidence, the maker of the inference may have personally observed the facts that give rise to the inference, or he or she may have been using the observations of others. In the latter case, the group must inquire whether the maker of the statement of observation had opportunity to observe, and whether the maker of the inference had access to reliable reports of the observation.

Removal from Firsthand. How close the evidence is to a firsthand report is the issue here. Evidence passed along by word of mouth is chiefly suspect because of the possibility of distortion. Evidence coming to us from most news stories or from journals that make a practice of condensing the information is also suspect. To keep up with the current demand for up-to-date news, the news media gather and print news quickly; they tend to select and highlight information to capture reader attention. As a result, newspaper reports are often wrong or misleading. If the group has not the time, inclination, or opportunity to get the original report, the character rather than the number of the intervening reports must be examined. The personal characteristics examined in the next category of criteria present the means whereby this is done.

Effective Reasoning to Produce Inferences. Often the inference that constitutes the evidence is supported by a description of the reasoning process that led to the inference. When this is done, the group members may examine the reasoning and thus decide the believability of the inference for themselves. (The means for checking the reasoning process are described in the next chapter.)

Source Credibility

The criteria in this category are used to assess the believability of evidence through an examination of the characteristics of the reporter, the originator of the evidence, any additional channels through which the evidence has passed, or any combination of the three. As is evident from the discussion of logical believability, the logical tests are difficult and sometimes impossible to apply. The secure individual prefers to ground beliefs directly in objective reality, but when such grounding is not possible or desirable, he or she prefers to turn to people in whose capacities for observation and judgment he or she has confidence. Such grounding falls somewhere along the middle of the reality continuum.

According to Kelman, a communicator has credibility "if his statements are considered truthful and valid, and hence worthy of serious consideration."[8] Commenting on the two bases for credibility identified by Hovland, Janis, and Kelley, expertness and trustworthiness,[9] Kelman said,

[8]Herbert C. Kelman, "Processes of Opinion Change," in *The Process of Social Influence: Readings in Persuasion*, eds. Thomas D. Beisecker and Donn W. Parson (Englewood Cliffs, N.J.: Prentice-Hall, Inc., 1972). Excerpted from the *Public Opinion Quarterly*, 25 (1961), 58–78.

[9]C. I. Hovland, I. L. Janis, and H. H. Kelley, *Communication and Persuasion* (New Haven: Yale University Press, 1953), p. 21.

. . . an agent may be perceived as possessing credibility because he is likely to *know* the truth, or because he is likely to *tell* the truth. Trustworthiness, in turn, may be related to overall respect, likemindedness, and lack of vested interest.[10]

Personal Qualifications. When discussing the competence of the researcher, we noted how competence is achieved. Here the question is this: How can the members of the group assess the competence of the person in question?

If the reporter is a member of the group or is acquainted with members of the group, the degree of competence is probably well known. However, the group should be especially careful to distinguish between the person's *status* in the members' eyes and his or her actual competence to provide evidence.

If a reporter is unknown to the members of the group, his or her qualifications are usually determined by an inquiry about training and experience in the field of concern. The group may learn about the reporter's qualifications from someone who knows him or her well and is qualified to judge, or even from the reporter in question. External evidences of qualification such as educational degrees earned and articles published may help the group assess the reporter's qualifications; such sources as *Who's Who, Dun and Bradstreet's Weekly Review, Directory of American Scholars* can be used. A librarian can suggest dozens of such references. Even such sources as positions held in an organization can suggest qualifications. Reporters who are concerned about the persuasiveness of their evidence will usually take pains to indicate their qualifications as part of their report.

One strong warning should be inserted here. The fact that an individual may be qualified in one field does not automatically mean that he or she is qualified in another. The President of the United States or a United States senator may give advice and draw inferences in fields in which he or she is essentially a layman, and be considered of high credibility because of the office held. Such prominent individuals are entitled to their opinions; yet sometimes they are not qualified to offer certain evidence as authorities.

Personal Bias. This refers to bias either toward the evidence itself or toward the group for which the evidence is intended, and may be both positive and negative. Let's examine how bias can be detected and accounted for.

If reporters are biased *in favor of* the group that is to receive the evidence, there is reasonable assurance that they will attempt to provide the best evidence possible. The opposite holds true for reporters biased *against* the group. For example, the state central committee of a national political party may ask a county chairperson to assess the party's chances in the coming election. Assuming that the chairperson is qualified for the position, he or she will probably give an accurate report to the state central committee. This report may be considerably less encouraging than the optimistic statements that the chairperson has been releasing for the local press. The reporter's attitudes toward a group may be determined from statements professing attachment. However, a more accurate evaluation can be made by looking at his or her record of reliability, consistency, and accuracy.

Considering bias toward the evidence itself, we must ask the question, What has

[10]Kelman, "Processes of Opinion Change," p. 41.

the reporter or the researcher to gain if the evidence is believed? If our answer is that the researcher would gain nothing except a reputation for accuracy, the person is probably "disinterested" and the evidence presented is probably accurate (again, assuming the reporter is qualified). Advertisers are fond of citing studies made by "independent research laboratories." If the laboratories are indeed independent, we expect that their evidence is believable. However, we question the advertiser by asking, "What have you left out of the laboratory's report, and have you confused your own statements of observation with your own inferences, or encouraged us to make further inferences?" For this reason, many people prefer to turn directly to reports from independent laboratories such as Consumer's Union and agencies like the Better Business Bureau.

When the reporter has much to gain if the evidence is believed, the evidence is almost worthless unless we are able to find other means of assessing its believability. However, in one case evidence from a biased source may be a proverbial gold mine. When the evidence reported by a biased source (if believed) is used counter to the reporter's interests, it is called *admission against interest.* Thus, in a court of law, when a known enemy of the accused offers testimony tending to show the accused's innocence, such evidence is more persuasive than if presented by a neutral or favorable witness.

Evidence of Scholarship. Evidence, whether written or spoken, should be effectively presented. It should also be well documented and well qualified. We call such qualities *evidence of scholarship* because they are the commonly used criteria of good research reporting in any respectable field.

Effective presentation includes good organization so that the pieces of evidence are seen in proper sequence. It also includes the use of language, statistics, tables, and illustrations that are intelligible and meaningful to the reader or hearer. If the presentation reveals a reporter concerned with accurate and effective transmission of ideas, his or her disposition toward both the evidence and the group receiving the evidence is revealed, and the group is provided with strong clues concerning the reporter's ability and motives. If the effectiveness of the presentation is veneer thin, a group skilled in communication principles will soon expose the sham. If the presentation is shoddy, considerable doubt may be raised about the reporter's competence and motives, and the total believability of the evidence may suffer.

A well-documented report is obviously valuable to the group when the members are assessing the quality of the minds through which the evidence has passed. The documentation of the report reveals the pains the reporter has taken to get as close as possible to the original sources of evidence and provides guides for the group that wishes to explore for itself. Like effective presentation, documentation lends credibility to the reporter.

A well-qualified report carefully separates statements of observation from inferences and claims no more and no less than is warranted.[11]

---

[11]For further background on source credibility, see B. Barry Fulton, "The Measurement of Speaker Credibility," *Journal of Communication,* 20 (September 1970), 270–79; Jack L. Whitehead, "Effects of Authority-Based Assertion on Attitude and Credibility," *Speech Monographs,* 38 (November 1971), 311–15; and Kenneth Andersen and Theodore Clevenger, "A Summary of Experimental Research in Ethos," *Speech Monographs,* 30 (1963), 59–78 (reprinted in *The Process of Social Influence,* eds. Beisecker and Parson, pp. 223–47.

Emotional Believability

The criteria in this category center around the social end of the reality continuum. Such criteria are based on the *wish to believe*. When discussing the secure individual, we said that beliefs should be grounded in social reality only if some measure of objective reality is not available, and that such beliefs should be held tentatively. That is our position here. The criteria for emotional believability are presented primarily to help the reader understand the grounds of much that is accepted by discussion groups. An understanding of the criteria may help group members reject, wherever possible, such means of inducing belief.

Consistent with Our Beliefs. "A foolish consistency," said Ralph Waldo Emerson, "is the hobgoblin of little minds." Too many little minds accept or reject evidence on the basis of whether or not it is consistent with what they already believe or want to believe. New evidence that corroborates old evidence and new evidence that tends to move the grounds of belief toward the objective-reality end of the continuum are valuable additions to the store of evidence available to the group, but the fact of consistency does not, by itself, render the new evidence more logically sound. Copernicus's evidence about the relation of sun and earth was not consistent with existing belief; non-Euclidean geometry was obviously inconsistent with Euclidean geometry. In neither of these cases were the inconsistencies detrimental to the logical quality of the new evidence.

The main value of new evidence that is inconsistent with what we already believe is that the inconsistency itself may spur investigation. Furthermore, discussants in the true spirit of inquiry deliberately seek evidence from all viewpoints—not just that which corroborates their preconceived ideas.

Consistent with Mass Belief. This criterion is similar except that the "Fifty million Frenchmen can't be wrong" notion is added to it. Advertisers, politicians, children, and university faculties are all guilty at times of using the claim, "Everybody's doing it," to justify their actions. We can think of no better retort than the typical one used by most parents—"but that doesn't make it right." Often such evidence looks deceptively like statements of observation that seem logically valid. We conduct hundreds of polls and surveys annually to determine what people say they think about almost everything. The data are presented in statistical form and the report contains much statistical terminology such as probable error and significant shifts. They look very logical, and indeed many are, if they are trying to make accurate generalizations about what people think or believe. But when such surveys purport to prove what is *desirable* or *right*, they must be rejected. It is not easy to tell a reporter whose evidence shows a preponderance of opinion favoring a position that the evidence does not convince you of the desirability of that position. Remember the discussion about group pressure in Chapter 1.

Emotional Relationship to Reporter. A variety of interpersonal relationships lead people to believe or disbelieve evidence quite apart from the validity of the evidence. A person's evidence may be believed because he or she is an authority figure who holds power over us; another's evidence may be disbelieved because he or she is our subordinate. We may accept the evidence offered by a loved one and reject evidence offered by one we dislike. In short, our feelings about a reporter, though independent of his or her qualifications, bias, and reportorial skill, often form grounds of belief.

Emotional State of Group Members. It is certainly not a novel discovery that believability is influenced by the emotional state of the hearers of an argument. Aristotle put it precisely when he said, "we give very different decisions under the sway of pain or joy, and liking or hatred."[12] The emotional state of group members is one of the criteria of believability but it is clearly not a sensible means of accepting or rejecting evidence.

PRESENTATION OF EVIDENCE

How evidence is communicated plays a big part in its acceptance and in how it is used by the group. It is not sufficient to merely throw a bunch of statistics at the group and expect group members to beam with gratitude.

Assuming that the evidence you want to present is both relevant to the subject and related to what people have been talking about, what is the best way to communicate it? One of the best ways is to introduce it by explaining how you see its relevance and relatedness. Use the hook-on technique, if possible (this was covered in Chapter 7). Next, introduce your evidence in summarized form and give your documentation. Here is where many people stop; but they have not done the whole job unless they emphasize where the major point of the evidence fits the point in the discussion. This might best be done by restating the key ideas and offering to respond to questions. You, as the researcher, have much more evidence at your command than you can possibly use in the discussion, and rather than go on at length, offer to fill in any gaps in the material as requested by the other discussants.

Another part of your task as the presenter of evidence is to help the group reach agreement on the meaning and interpretation of the evidence. Suppose, in a discussion on improving public-school education, you have introduced some evidence that challenges the validity of the educational testing and grading systems. You describe some experiments conducted in an elementary school and report the statistical results of the studies. You are not finished until you have led the discussion on what these statistics *mean* to the group and to the subject of the discussion. You might offer your tentative interpretations of the findings ("It looks from this as if the students in the pass/fail classes learned more than those who got letter grades.") But helping the group come to an interpretation of the data is most important.

What happens when two types of evidence that contradict each other are presented? Some people use this situation as an excuse to reject both pieces of evidence. It is far better to evaluate both and come to agreement on which of the two is more valid or reliable.

---

[12]Lane Cooper, *The Rhetoric of Aristotle* (New York: Appleton-Century-Crofts, 1932), p. 9.

SUMMARY

This chapter has dealt with the building block of belief: evidence. We defined evidence and discussed kinds and sources, as well as how to gather evidence, including certain responsibilities of both the group and the individuals. Next we covered reporters of evidence and their necessary qualities. Believability of evidence was analyzed in some detail and the last section dealt with some suggestions on how to present evidence to the group.

DISCUSSION QUESTIONS

1.   What problems do we encounter when we seek to determine the competence of individuals as sources of evidence or opinion?

2.   How should we evaluate the current evidence available concerning the effects of cigarette smoking on the human organism?

3.   What evidence should be considered when seeking to determine the loyalty of a United States citizen engaged in any nonsensitive work?

4.   What should be the evidence on which a teacher bases grades?

EXERCISES

1.   Observe a discussion group as it explores a problem requiring some research on the part of most members. Keep a running record of (a) the things that are accepted as evidence, (b) the things that are rejected as not being appropriate evidence, (c) the types of evidence mentioned, (d) the manner in which the evidence is used, and (e) any methods used to verify or evaluate any of the evidence used or mentioned. Following the discussion, conduct a survey of the members in an effort to determine the extent to which they sought evidence and the sources to which they turned. What do you observe? What bearing do you feel the recognition and the handling of evidence may have had on this group's work?

2.   Select some current controversial issue being discussed and reported in the mass media. Analyze several reports from a variety of sources to determine the quantity, nature, and quality of evidence being presented by both sides. To what degree are types of evidence confused? To what extent are the primary reporters of the evidence to be trusted? How would you rate the believability of the evidence?

3.   Analyze magazine and television advertising for use of inference. What is the difference between the message as it is presented and the meaning the advertiser wants you to infer?

4.   Much evidence that we use in group discussion is verbal, consisting of spoken words, written materials, and mathematical representations. Consider other forms of evidence, noting their frequency and effect. Does this analysis suggest anything concerning our sensitivity to evidence and its impact?

133   *Evidence: The Basis of Thought*

SELECTED READINGS

BORMANN, ERNEST G., *Discussion and Group Methods: Theory and Practice* (2nd ed.), chap. 4. New York: Harper & Row, Publishers, 1975.

CROWELL, LAURA, *Discussion: Method of Democracy*, chap. 4. Chicago: Scott, Foresman & Co., 1963.

GOURAN, DENNIS S., *Discussion: The Process of Group Decision-Making*, chap. 5. New York: Harper & Row, Publishers, 1974.

GULLEY, HALBERT E., *Discussion, Conference and Group Process* (2nd ed.), chap. 5. New York: Holt, Rinehart and Winston, Inc., 1968.

HOVLAND, CARL I., AND WALTER WEISS, "The Influence of Source Credibility on Communication Effectiveness," *Public Opinion Quarterly*, 15 (1951), 635–50. Reprinted in *Experiments in Persuasion*, eds. Ralph L. Rosnow and Edward J. Robinson. New York: Academic Press, Inc., 1967.

ROKEACH, MILTON, *The Open and Closed Mind*. New York: Basic Books, Inc., Publishers, 1960.

chapter 9

An automobile is traveling down a street. There is snow on the road and more is falling. As he drives, a man is thinking: "This road is getting slippery, I'd better slow down. I wonder what that fellow up ahead is doing; he's been skidding around a bit. There's a hill ahead so I'd better shift down before I come to it. Can't afford to lose traction. Oh oh! That car is coming down the hill too fast. He's skidding sideways. I can't slam on the brakes; I must pump them gently. Thank goodness, I got by him. That was close."

The driver in this example was doing what we must all do virtually every waking moment of our lives—observing and drawing inferences from observations. We draw inferences for two purposes—to *predict*, that is, to determine the existence of something we cannot observe, and to *control* some future event. The driver, for example, was trying to predict road conditions and the actions of other drivers. He was also trying to control his own car by slowing down, shifting down, and tapping his brakes. He could not be content with simply observing and describing what happened; he had to go beyond what he could observe.

The process of drawing inferences is the process of reasoning. To make reasonable decisions, one must first separate observation from inference or reasoning, as shown in Chapter 8. Second, one must observe carefully and accurately. Third, one must reason carefully to predict and control what one can not observe.

FOUNDATIONS OF REASONING

The concepts of *relationship* and *probability* are two fundamentals that must be understood before we examine the forms and rules of reasoning.

Reasoning and Relationships

Since reasoning goes beyond what is observed, the reasoner must discover some relationship between what is observable and what is not. Thus, if a production manager who has a reputation for accurate reporting tells the group that several people have reported displeasure with the new payroll plan, his colleagues may reason that he is probably telling the truth. Let us describe the reasoning that led to the conclusion that the production manager's statement was accurate:

All (or most) of Mr. X's statements have been accurate in the past.

This is one of Mr. X's statements.

Therefore, this statement is quite likely to be true.

Thinking and Reasoning: The Process of Thought

This is admittedly a very simple type of reasoning, but it will suffice for the purpose at the moment. Note that the group reached a conclusion without bothering to corroborate Mr. X's statement by independent investigation. Instead, a *relationship* was established between Mr. X's past statements, which had been corroborated, and the new statement. This, then, is reasoning: the process of establishing useful relationships.

Three kinds of relationships are possible: *causal, correlative,* and *classificatory* relationships.

Causal Relationships. A causal relationship is an agent–reactor relationship. One factor (the *agent*) brings into existence or modifies another factor (the *reactor*). One thing causes another. Fire, under certain circumstances, causes water to boil; anger causes people to make statements they would normally not make; and authoritarian leadership often causes resentment.

We attempt to establish causal relationships whenever we wish to control one event by manipulating another. For example, when the federal government attempts to control inflation by placing ceilings on prices and wages, it is acting upon the assumption that higher prices and wages *cause* inflation. Many argue that this is not a wise procedure because prices and wages are *not* in themselves causes of inflation. The basis for the dispute is clear. If prices and wages *cause* inflation, then manipulating them will control inflation. But if prices and wages *do not* cause inflation, then manipulating them is futile.

This reasoning process may be called *effect-to-cause* reasoning. That is, people in the federal government began with the phenomenon of inflation, reasoned that the cause was higher prices and wages, and attempted to control the cause. The use of a causal relationship may quite easily proceed in the opposite direction. For example, college faculties and administrators are trying to predict the *effect* that will be brought about by the anticipated decrease of students. Two questions are raised by this process of reasoning. First, what will be the consequences of decreased enrollments? Second, what can be done to modify potentially undesirable effects? That is, how can the undesirable effects of decreased enrollment be *controlled* by introducing new causes of desirable factors?

Correlative Relationships. Both correlative and causal relationships are "natural"— they are discovered rather than created. But a correlative relationship is one in which the presence or degree of one factor allows the *prediction* of the presence or degree of another factor.

Sometimes we simply want to know the answer to this question: If we know whether or not one thing exists, can we predict whether or not another thing exists? Though the relationship between the two is frequently called a *sign* relationship, it is included under the heading of correlative relationship for purposes of convenience. When the birds fly north, we say it is a sign of spring. That is, the *presence* of the birds leads us to conclude the *presence* or imminence of spring. This certainly does not imply that the return of the birds *causes* spring.

Let us note some further examples of correlative relationships. There tends to be a positive correlation among children between physical size and intelligence. There is a correlation between the speed at which an automobile is traveling and the distance required to bring it to a stop. There seems to be a positive correlation between leadership and the ability to make quick decisions.

One distinction between correlative and causal relationships is particularly important. Establishing a correlative relationship does not justify assuming a causal relationship. Physical size and intelligence *may* be causally related, as may leadership and speed of decision-making. There is certainly a causal relationship between the speed of an automobile and the force necessary to bring it to a stop. The point is, however, that data showing only a correlative relationship do not allow us to make statements concerning cause and effect.

The establishment of a causal relationship makes possible an attempt to control one thing by controlling another. The correlative relationship, on the other hand, does not permit control since it is not established that one thing affects the other. We can, however, *predict* the existence or nature of one thing from a knowledge of the other when we have established a correlative relationship. For example, we can predict that after the driver applies the brakes, a normal automobile that is traveling at the speed of 20 miles per hour will cover 44 feet before stopping. That is, there is a correlative relationship between the speed at which the automobile is traveling and the distance required to stop. The distance required to stop can be *controlled* by establishing a causal relationship between the size and nature of the brake shoes and the stopping potential of the automobile.

Classificatory Relationships. A classificatory relationship is an arbitrary one created by the act of naming. Classifying according to some characteristic that things possess in common is essential to communication; it enables us to talk about many things at once. Any discussion of campus life, for example, would be halted at once if it were necessary to name each student on the campus. We can, however, talk meaningfully about college students by using such classifications as superior students, seniors, or resident students.

Think of the different ways that you may be classified—for example, as an adult, a United States citizen, or as an upper-division student. None of these classifications tells all there is to know about you as an individual. But if an individual is properly a member of a class, each classification describes one or more characteristics.

Classifying can be dangerous because of the tendency to believe that the classification tells more than is actually the case. The fact that a person has a college degree is not necessarily evidence of his or her being highly educated. The classification only tells that the person attended and graduated from a university or college.

The classificatory relationship is similar to the correlative in that neither relationship permits control from partial knowledge; only prediction is permitted. The two relationships differ in that the correlative relationship is a natural one, but the classificatory relationship is imposed by the act of naming.

To summarize and contrast the three types of relationships: (1) A *causal relationship* is a dynamic one wherein one factor actually affects another factor; (2) a *correlative relationship* is one in which two or more things are related in such a fashion that we can predict the existence or degree of one from knowledge of the other; and (3) the *classificatory relationship* is created by grouping things according to some common characteristic and giving a name to the grouping. The first two relationships are natural since their existence must be discovered. The third relationship is one of convenience: It enables us to talk about many things at once. Only the causal relationship allows us to control; the correlative and classificatory relationships only allow us to predict.[1]

Reasoning and Probability

Inasmuch as reasoning involves going from the observable to the unobservable, we are confronted with the problem of establishing the likelihood that our reasoning is correct. This means that reasoning is the process of establishing the *probability* or, if you wish, the *betting odds* that subsequent experience will confirm the truth of our inference. The business of modern statistics is to provide mathematical means of establishing these probabilities.

A favorite means to demonstrate probability is by using the toss of a coin. If you toss the same coin 20 times, what is the probability that heads will appear 10 times or 50 percent of the time? Then if you toss the same coin 20 more times, what is the probability that heads will appear the same number of times as during the first 20 tosses?

A moment's reflection reveals that even the simplest of statements is, of necessity, only a probable truth. Yes, even a statement of observation must be considered as a probability inasmuch as there exists the possibility that our senses have been deceived. To be sure, the degree of probability in many such statements is so high that we can operate as if the statement were certain truth, but we must keep in mind that for years people believed that the earth was flat because it *looked* flat.

INDUCTIVE REASONING

The inductive form of reasoning allows us to make generalizations, possessing a degree of probability, that we can apply to specific instances. For example, we asserted in Chapter 2 that two heads were frequently better than one. This statement asserted a causal relationship between discussion and an improved product or solution. This statement was derived from an examination of a number of instances in which discussion proved to be superior to individual effort in the solving of problems.

Inductive reasoning occurs when we *build up to* a generalization from specific instances—as when we observe that this, this, and this together add up to that conclusion. Inductive reasoning is the process of investigating, analyzing, and enumerating individual cases in an attempt to establish a general principle or law. If research reveals that high-school debaters at ten high schools made superior scholastic records, we can infer (with relatively high probability) that debaters make good grades at all high schools.

---

[1]We have already indicated that the process of naming *can* affect the thing named by virtue of the feelings engendered by names; that is, calling a program *socialized medicine* is likely to cause certain people to view the program with considerably more suspicion than they would were it called *health insurance*. Calling a person *brave* has frequently been noted to "cause" him or her to become braver. From a logical point of view, naming a thing does not alter it, although it may seem to from a psychological point of view.

The essence of induction, then, lies in the use of a relationship to produce a generalization that will probably hold true for several instances. It is not reasoning at all if we assert, "We observed a discussion group that performed better than individuals working alone." Such a statement is nothing more than a statement of observation. It *is* inductive reasoning if we conclude, "Upon the basis of this observation, and others, we conclude that discussion groups are superior to individuals in the solving of problems."

We would have perfect induction with perfect reliability if we could examine all the instances involved. This is usually impossible so we must rely on examination of representative samples to make an inference or generalization.

Induction and Multiple Relationships

Thus far we have proceeded as if all relationships operated on a one-to-one basis: as if there are only one cause and one effect, only two things correlated in a given situation, or only one characteristic of a class. Obviously, situations are seldom so simple. Usually several factors act as causal agents; usually several factors are correlated. Successful performance in school, for example, is usually caused by at least three factors: native ability, previous training, and the ability to apply oneself to the task of learning.

In handling multiple relationships, we must do what was suggested in handling any relationship. We must first decide the purpose for ascertaining the relationship. Do we wish to predict, or do we wish to control? If we wish to predict, we may find a critical relationship that will enable us to make predictions with a high degree of probability. We need not worry about other possible relationships if we are satisfied with the quality of our predictions. If we wish to control, we generally seek to reduce the number of factors we have to work with, and confine our attention to key causes and control them.

Practical aspects force us to another method of limiting the factors in a given situation. For example, a teacher may wish to improve the performance of a student. The teacher is obviously incapable of doing anything about the student's native ability. A knowledge of this ability, as gleaned from IQ tests, may prove helpful in predicting the student's performance, but it will not help change the student's behavior. However, the teacher might be able to affect the student's performance by suggesting supplementary readings or methods of study.

Still we must be very careful not to assume that we have exhausted the possibilities when we have discovered one relationship that seems to have some degree of validity. Perhaps the most dramatic illustration of this is found in industry. For years managers assumed that workers were motivated primarily by the amount of money they received and the threat of dismissal. A variety of studies revealed that workers were far more motivated by management appreciation and by humane treatment than by money or threat of dismissal. Here the managers' assumption of cause delayed improvement of relationships between management and labor for years.

Example and Analogy

Many texts discuss reasoning by example and reasoning by analogy as separate forms. Actually, they are nothing of the sort. They may both be classified under the heading of inductive reasoning and both use either the *method of agreement* (where recurring similarities are noted in order to produce a generalization) or the *method of difference* (where dissimilarities are noted in order to produce a generalization).

Examples may serve two functions. They may be used to illustrate a point, or they may be used to support a conclusion. We are concerned with the latter function. If a discussant reports, "Peabody College uses the pass/fail plan of grading and finds it satisfactory," the group has been presented with one situation using the method of agreement—a situation containing the pass/fail plan and satisfaction with the grading system. If, in a discussion of gardening problems, a person says that she finally got rid of the cutworms in her garden by the application of product X, she is presenting an instance of the use of the method of differences. That is, all the factors were, presumably, constant before and after the application of product X except that the cutworms disappeared after application. If individuals allege that their examples are typical of many that might be offered, they are simply presenting to us, in digest form, the results of their survey.

The use of analogy or comparison can best be comprehended as a part of inductive reasoning. Like any generalization, the analogy depends on a deductive rationale that says, in effect, if two situations are alike in all relevant aspects save one, they will be alike in that aspect also. Thus, saying that worker participation in decision-making will work in our factory since it worked in the Harwood manufacturing plant means we believe that all the relevant circumstances in the two factories are comparable except that the Harwood plant uses worker participation in decision-making. This is an illustration of the method of difference.

Contrary to the expressed opinion of many, analogy, the method of differences, is a valuable method of inductive reasoning. Actual testing is probably the best method of determining whether or not a given idea will work in a situation, but pertinent comparisons may be the best method short of actual testing to determine in advance whether we wish to try the new method. This reasoning should be sharply distinguished from the "everybody is doing it" reasoning. Comparisons should not be used to prove that it is good because others are doing it, but to prove that it might be good here because it apparently works in a comparable place.

Bormann uses the example of a man with an obsession about women being "lousy" drivers to make the point that induction can occur on *nonrational* grounds. The man described is so convinced of the "fact" that all women drive poorly he is alert to every possible driving error and even when he learns it was a male driver who failed to signal properly, he rationalizes that the man "drives like a woman." Bormann explains such obsessions are more apt to be wrong than right. They are the bases of superstition and prejudice.[2]

DEDUCTIVE REASONING

The other major form of reasoning, deductive reasoning, is the process of relating two statements in such a way as to produce a third. Whereas inductive reasoning attempts to produce generalizations that hold true for a number of specifics, deductive reasoning attempts to make use of such generalizations in order to

[2]Ernest G. Bormann, *Discussion and Group Methods: Theory and Practice*, 2nd ed. (New York: Harper & Row, Publishers, 1975), pp. 124–25.

make application in a given case. Induction builds on instances to establish a princi-ple or law, deduction starts with the principle or law and applies it to specific in-stances, then reaches a conclusion. Induction aims at *probability*; deduction aims at *proof*.

The syllogism is normally regarded as the essence of deductive reasoning. Al-though it is important that we grasp the essential concepts involved in the use of the syllogism, this form of reasoning is not as important to effective thinking as many other aspects of the reasoning process. We will, therefore, only briefly describe the principal kinds of syllogisms.

The Categorical Syllogism

The following is a categorical syllogism:

All cases of cancer are dangerous.

This is a case of cancer.

Therefore, this case is dangerous.

In the categorical syllogism, the first statement or major premise is a categorical or unqualified statement, making classifications with no exceptions. The second state-ment or minor premise applies the rule to a specific case.

The major premise must apply to all cases. If the words *all, every, only,* and so forth are not present, they must be implied. A term in the conclusion must not have a broader meaning than it has in the premise. From two negative premises no conclu-sion can be drawn and if one premise is negative the conclusion must be negative.

The Hypothetical Syllogism

The hypothetical syllogism is one containing a condition in its major prem-ise. The *if* clause is called the *antecedent*, the other clause is the *consequent*. The previous example of a categorical syllogism can be changed to a hypothetical syl-logism:

If this is a case of cancer, it is dangerous.

This *is* a case of cancer.

Therefore, it is dangerous.

In the hypothetical syllogism, the minor premise must affirm the antecedent or deny the consequent; if these are done, the syllogism is correct. If the reverse is done, no conclusion can be drawn.

The Disjunctive Syllogism

The last form of syllogism discussed here is the disjunctive, which presents alternative possibilities. The major premise is an either–or statement; the minor premise excludes one of the possibilities; and the conclusion affirms the remaining alternative. Here is an example:

This man is either innocent or he is guilty.

He is innocent.

Therefore, he is not guilty.

The disjunctive syllogism is nothing more than the systematic elimination of possible alternatives and is used whenever it is difficult or impossible to prove the crucial factor directly. The major premise must be all-inclusive and the alternatives it contains must be mutually exclusive.

Uses and Values of Deduction

Discussants seldom talk to each other in syllogisms. Most of us use the form that is called the *enthymeme*, which is a short-circuited or bobtailed syllogism. One of the premises or even the conclusion may be omitted, with the speaker assuming that the listener will fill in the missing part or parts. Here is an example: "Bill would like to be student body president, but he hasn't had much leadership experience."

It is easy to make up phony syllogisms because a syllogism may be perfectly valid even when the premises assert utter nonsense. For example:

All men are Chinese.

Susie is a man.

Therefore, Susie is Chinese.

The syllogism does have two fundamental values, however. With a knowledge of syllogistic form and operation we are able to identify the factors necessary to form valid arguments. In addition, the deductive process enables us to create the questions or the hypotheses that we employ the inductive process to answer.

COMMON FALLACIES IN REASONING

Confusion of Fact and Inference. In Chapter 8 we identified and distinguished between fact and inference and noted that it is difficult to keep the facts separate from ideas we infer and the way we feel about the facts. We need to remind ourselves that facts are verifiable and if we haven't verified them (or if an authority upon whom we can rely has not verified them) they are not facts but inferences.

Faulty Analogies. Sometimes the things we are comparing are really not comparable, and what we have is a faulty analogy. Many people have been convinced that the United Nations will fail because the League of Nations failed. True, the two organizations have some elements in common, but they have enough different aspects to make the analogy useless.

Confusion of Causation and Correlation. Because event A came before event B, it is tempting to think that A caused B. There may be a correlation but we cannot assume causation until it is proved. We know that in the summer more ice cream is sold and there are also more automobile accidents. There may be a correlation (because of warmer weather) but hardly causation.

Hasty Generalization. When we have too few samples to warrant the general principle we reach by inductive reasoning, we may be guilty of hasty generalization. One or two bad experiences with people of a certain race or religion leads some people to form stereotypes and become prejudiced. One or two samples are hardly sufficient to form an opinion about anything.

Oversimplification. We are guilty of oversimplification when we attribute to a single source or cause what has actually resulted from many sources or causes. It is easy, for example, to place the blame for all the world's problems on a single source such as communism. It is easy but ridiculous reasoning.

Non Sequitur. Literally "it does not follow," a non sequitur occurs when a causal relationship is falsely assumed or alleged. It doesn't necessarily follow, for example, that because automobiles have been identified as major polluters of the environment that car manufacturers will automatically modify their engines or exhaust systems. Neither does it follow that capital punishment is a deterrent to crime.[3]

STEPS TO LOGICAL CONCLUSIONS

In conclusion to both this and the preceding chapter, here is an examination of the steps that a group must take if it is to come to logical conclusions.

1.   *Determine whether the objective is to predict or to control.* Failure to observe this first step has wasted uncounted hours for many groups. How often have you heard a group arguing about what might be the cause of a given problem when all they needed was sufficient evidence to predict what was going to happen? If the personnel staff of a company is discussing means of screening prospective employees, they are faced with the job of prediction. They need not worry about *why* an individual scores high or low on a test that they consider an index of success on the job; they simply need to know whether test performance can be expected to correlate with performance on the job. If, however, they are discussing means of upgrading employees or are concerned that the test may have discriminatory effects against certain people or groups, they have the task of control and must be concerned with "why" questions.

2.   *Be certain that the argument is understood.* Failure to observe this step has caused countless groups to be hopelessly split over semantic difficulties. As previously said, every group should adopt as its first operating rule the idea that no one has a right to agree, disagree, modify, or ignore another's argument until that person can phrase the argument to the satisfaction of the originator.

[3]For a more extensive examination of fallacies, see Monroe C. Beardsley, *Thinking Straight* (Englewood Cliffs, N.J.: Prentice-Hall, Inc., 1956).

3. *Cast the argument into its proper form.* Organize ideas into logical sequence, using one or more of the forms suggested.

4. *Examine the evidence.* Determine both the general accuracy of the evidence of fact and opinion that is submitted and the relevance of the evidence to the case at hand.

5. *Check the inductive method employed.* Determine whether the inductive method is capable of producing the relationship claimed in the argument and also determine the degree of probability that may be attached to the premises.

By following these steps we may be assured that we (1) know where we are going; (2) know what we mean; (3) know whether we can draw a conclusion from the premises; (4) know how sound our data are; and (5) know whether our premises square with the world of fact. If we discover a flaw in steps 3, 4, or 5, we can then turn to step 6.

6. *Present counterevidence and reasoning* The unwary discussant is often tempted to present counterevidence and reasoning whenever he or she hears something that appears to contradict his or her beliefs. However, presenting counterarguments *before* the other steps have been taken can only lead to trouble. Presenting them *after* the other steps have been taken *can* be a real contribution to group thinking.

SUMMARY

In this chapter we have examined the foundations of reasoning, including three kinds of relationships (causal, correlative, and classificatory) and reasoning and probability. We discussed the qualities of, and differences between, inductive and deductive reasoning. Six common fallacies in reasoning were outlined followed by six steps to logical conclusions.

DISCUSSION QUESTIONS

1. To what extent in American political life should we judge people by their associates and organizational memberships?

2. How valid is the adage, "Five percent of the people think; 10 percent think they think; and 85 percent want a slogan so they won't have to think"?

3. How can we determine the truth of the notion that speech and thought are identical and that "if you can't say it, you can't think it"?

EXERCISES

1. Experiment and experience indicate that most people believe their personal and public lives are governed by reason. During the next week, observe the behavior of as many individuals as possible, noting three factors:

(a) the frequency and intensity with which they state or imply that they are reasonable or that their actions and conclusions are based on reason; (b) the degree to which they appear to be governed by forces other than reason; and (c) their reactions when their reasoning is attacked. What conclusions do you reach? Compare your analysis with that of several other class members. To what extent do you feel any generalizations are warranted?

2.   Observe a discussion for the purpose of analyzing the reasoning employed. Identify the major forms and the particular methods being used. Evaluate the participants' choices of these forms and methods. Evaluate the soundness of the reasoning.

3.   Select an editorial or short article that urges support for an organization, policy, or program. Analyze the reasoning following the first five of the steps to logical conclusions developed at the end of this chapter. What do you conclude concerning the quality of the reasoning? What reasoning would you use to combat the editorial or article?

4.   Examine the transcript of a discussion or interview that the public might observe, noting examples of both sound and unsound reasoning. Consider how the reasoning may be adapted to appeal to the general public. How would you strengthen the examples of sound reasoning? How would you refute or counter the examples of unsound reasoning?

SELECTED READINGS

BORMANN, ERNEST G., *Discussion and Group Methods: Theory and Practice* (2nd ed.), chaps. 5, 6. New York: Harper & Row, Publishers, 1975.

CROWELL, LAURA, *Discussion: Method of Democracy*, chap. 5. Chicago: Scott, Foresman & Co., 1963.

GOURAN, DENNIS S., *Discussion: The Process of Group Decision-Making*, chap. 6. New York: Harper & Row, Publishers, 1974.

GULLEY, HALBERT E., *Discussion, Conference and Group Process* (2nd ed.), chap. 6. New York: Holt, Rinehart and Winston, Inc., 1968.

chapter 10

Decision-making and problem-solving discussions are at once the most common and the most difficult. They are common because to make a decision or solve a problem is often the very reason for the group's existence. They are difficult because the process, to be successful, is inevitably complex.

Human decisions seem to be made by either discussion, debate, or default. We inquire and investigate, we argue and challenge each other, and sometimes we avoid making a decision—which is, of course, just as much of a decision as making one.

First, we'll look at the similarities and the overlapping aspects of decision-making and problem-solving, and then we'll distinguish between them. Decisions must be made when we come to choice points or alternatives. The decision, once made, is the end of a process. (Often, of course, it is the beginning of still another process.) Decision-makers want to achieve something. They select the alternative that will move them closer to their goal.

As communicators we are constantly involved in decision-making within ourselves or with those around us. Although decisions have to be made in all interpersonal communication situations, the process itself is seldom something we think about consciously. Whether we are merely deciding when and what to talk about or who to elect to chair a committee, we make many decisions without really being aware of how the decision is made or what effect it has on us.

Too frequently the processes of decision-making and problem-solving are regarded as "natural"—that is, people are either born with the ability or they are not. But, as is true with most human behavior, such abilities can be acquired and learned. Most of us have learned how to make decisions just by making them and then living with the results. We watch how other people do it; then we plunge in, developing our own skill through trial and error. After a while the process becomes almost subconscious and is carried out more by habit than design.

Some people are known for their snap decisions, which they may come to regret later. Some people, on the other hand, seem incapable of deciding anything. They agonize over details and sway from one alternative to another, usually to the considerable annoyance of their associates. Still other people appear to be making snap decisions, but in reality they have quietly thought through the matter and have thoroughly prepared for the ten seconds in which it seems they spontaneously make their choice.

The significance of any decision is determined by the presence of commitment. Commitment is not visible; only the behavior that results from commitment is visible. We have all had the experience of having someone tell us they would do something, only to find it not done. Often the lack of action was because the individual was not really committed in the first place. Phony agreements in which no real commitment is made have plagued mankind throughout history.

Problem-Solving:
The Pattern of Thought

Though decision-making is not as complex a process as problem-solving, it also has a pattern. First, we become aware that we are at a choice point, in which we must choose one behavior alternative from a group of such alternatives. Next, we examine the alternatives and predict the consequences of choosing each one. Last, we make our selection among the alternatives—in other words, we make our decision. The second of these three aspects is where we most often run into trouble, because we are not always able to find out all we need to know about the alternatives and their potential consequences. Too often we grab the first alternative that occurs to us.

Fisher maintained that groups do not *make* decisions but that decisions *emerge* from group interaction. After going through the phases of orientation, conflict, emergence, and reinforcement, each characterized by a different pattern of interaction, the group finds it has made a decision. According to Fisher, it is often difficult to identify the exact point at which the decision is made; the essence of consensus is getting the group's commitment to decisions already made.[1]

Scheidel and Crowell developed a "spiral model" to show that consensus decisions are cumulative rather than linear. Their research showed that groups do not move systematically from idea to idea, but retrace concept development, continually modify ideas, and backtrack to reconfirm positions agreed upon earlier.[2]

Freud claimed that human motivations cause decisions to be made without concern for rationality. We mix the objective, impersonal aspects of the decision with feelings about its desirability or attractiveness or with subjective notions of how other people will accept the decision. The most logical, rational decision will be of no use if the emotional aspects are not weighed just as carefully as the facts.

Consider this example: An older woman's small house is gradually being surrounded by tall apartment buildings. Logic dictates that she should sell her house and move to a more compatible family residential area; the change in the neighborhood, with increasing numbers of people, has brought noise, confusion, and a shortage of parking spaces. Emotion, however, ties her to the house that was built by her father where her own children were born, and where she has lived for many years. Her decision is to stay despite the noise and inconvenience.

There are many stages in problem-solving where decisions must be made. What problem should we work on? How best can we divide the research? Which solution shall we pick? These, and many more, are decisions that need to be made along the way to solving a problem. More will be said in Chapter 14 about the various ways groups make decisions.

PROBLEM-SOLVING THINKING

Almost everyone is familiar with the classic problem-solving or reflective-thinking steps formulated by John Dewey years ago:

1.   Location, formulation, and definition of the problem to be solved.
2.   Analysis of the problem in terms of difficulties.

---

[1]B. Aubrey Fisher, *Small Group Decision Making: Communication and the Group Process* (New York: McGraw-Hill Book Company, Inc., 1974), pp. 139–45.

[2]Thomas M. Scheidel and Laura Crowell, "Idea Development in Small Discussion Groups," *Quarterly Journal of Speech*, 50 (1964), 140–45.

3.   Reformulation of the problem in light of analysis.
4.   Examination of various methods to resolve the problem.
5.   Evaluation and analysis of various solutions to discover the best one.
6.   Choice of plan of action.[3]

The discussion field owes a great deal to Dewey but here we want to stress that an apparent misunderstanding of Dewey's original concepts has caused some communication scholars to misappropriate his reflective-thinking pattern. Dewey was endeavoring to *describe* the reflective-thinking process (what usually occurs when people effectively solve problems); others have turned his description into a *prescriptive* organizational pattern to govern the structure of the discussion itself.[4] Throughout this chapter, we hope the reader will also view the phases of problem-solving as descriptive rather than prescriptive.

Dewey made problem-solving virtually synonymous with thinking. Using his analysis, we can set forth the following three characteristics of problem-solving thinking:

1.   Problem-solving thinking involves forming connections between ideas. Thinking that involves only a kind of kaleidoscopic assortment of ideas and associations is not problem-solving thinking. Apparently, the majority of our mental time is occupied with some form of activity that is little more than daydreaming. While walking down a street, we may notice the sights, sounds, and smells, and perhaps we are pleased or disturbed by them, but we do not consider such awareness, which makes no attempt to form patterns, *thinking.*

2.   Problem-solving thinking aims at a conclusion. It is purposeful. During the walk just mentioned, we might notice that the smell of a particular tree reminds us of some place we used to live and we might form mental images of the place. We thus have the connection between ideas, but our thinking is not aimed at any conclusion. Most social and cathartic discussions, for example, may involve the thinking that forms connections between ideas, but this thinking usually does not aim at a conclusion.

3.   Problem-solving thinking presupposes a perceived disequilibrium. Suppose a man gets into his car one morning in order to drive to work. When he turns the key in the ignition, nothing happens. The car refuses to respond and the man's normal routine has suffered a jolt. What does he do? He decides that he must either get the car working again or find some other means of getting to work. He tries the former. Since he doesn't have time to call the garage and have them send someone out to fix the car, he checks under the hood to see if he can spot the trouble. But his mechanical skills are not equal to the task. How else might he get to work? The bus has just gone by; he cannot take time to call a taxi; and it will take too much time and energy to walk. However, some of his neighbors work where he does and

---

[3]See John Dewey, *How We Think* (Boston: D.C. Heath & Company, 1933).
[4]See R. Victor Harnack, "John Dewey and Discussion," *Western Speech*, 32 (Spring 1968), 137–49.

they also drive. He decides to walk to a nearby intersection, in the hope that a cooperative neighbor will drive by. When one does, and he gets a ride, his immediate problem is solved and the disequilibrium has been removed. His long-range problem of getting the car fixed is postponed.

The point in this example is that the problem-solving process had to be triggered by some discrepancy between desire and capacity. Had the car started and functioned normally, the man would have had no problem and consequently would have done no problem-solving thinking.

LOCATING THE PROBLEM

Sometimes locating the problem *is* the problem. Many people, when confronted with the problem of a car not starting, decide the problem is getting the car fixed. But this is a *solution* to the principal problem of finding transportation. It is not as productive to work on the problem of how to build a better mousetrap as it is to consider how best to get rid of mice.

It takes a certain amount of creativity to look for and correctly identify problems. Some people may feel that they have enough problems already and wonder why anyone needs to go around looking for more. Others consistently ignore, evade, or escape tough problems that should be faced and solved. Still others seem perpetually trying to create problems where none exist. We have no suggestions for the kind of person whose behavior has become extreme in either fashion, but intelligent groups can be of real value in discovering problems rather than evading or creating them.

Now let's look at certain kinds of groups that evade or distort problems. Then we will examine what we call *realistic* groups and see how they identify problems.

Insulated Groups. People who wish to evade problems often join with other like-minded persons and the resulting groups are usually voluntary with social or cathartic purposes. Members of such groups seem to feel that assuring one another that "God's in His heaven—all's right with the world," is one way to make it so. Many of the groups that have sprung up to resist the pressures for racial integration in the schools seem to be examples of insulated groups. They spend more time arguing that blacks "don't really want integration," that the trouble is caused by "radical" elements and "outside agitators," and that if "outsiders would leave us alone, time will take care of things." The controversy over whether children should be bused to different schools to achieve racial balance often centers on the "evils of busing" rather than on achieving equal educational opportunities.

Witch-Hunting Groups. At the other end of the spectrum are groups that focus time and energy on imaginary or petty themes. Such groups are always demanding investigations of some sort, are certain that the country's moral fiber is decaying, and write countless letters to editors. Most superpatriotic groups, we believe, fall into this category, but, witch-hunting organizations are found almost everywhere.

People who gravitate to insulated groups very probably do so for the same reasons that others join witch-hunting groups. In both cases real problems are frequently ignored, in the first case by not seeing them, and in the second by creating diversionary problems. Perhaps the individual whose name comes immediately to mind as archetype of witch-hunting is the late Senator Joseph McCarthy of Wisconsin. In their excellent book, *McCarthy and the Communists*, Rorty and Decter point out how McCarthy nearly paralyzed a nation with his tactics, and when he did stumble across what might have been a genuine problem, he showed no inclination to follow up his widely publicized accusations.[5]

Realistic Groups. Realistic groups are generally free from restraint, catholic in interests, and information oriented. Realistic groups come to grips with problems that demand solution. Some of the clues that realistic groups use to discover problems can be described as *differences that matter:*

> 1. Discrepancies between expectation and results are signs of potential problems. One can expect to overshoot the mark on occasion, but persistent or gross miscalculations should prompt inquiry. Did we expect that the new office building would permit better work, only to discover that the money seems to have been spent in vain? The increased efficiency or productivity we expect seldom are realized. We may build a new arena but we still have the same gladiators.
>
> 2. Unexplained by-products are signs of potential problems. For years, managers of industries assumed that the annual Christmas bonuses were the epitome of enlightened labor-management relations. But some managers began to notice considerable resentment on the part of the workers and finally discovered that the employees resented the paternalistic manner in which the gift was given; they felt the gift should be theirs by right in their salaries. Could some strikes have been averted if this attitude had been spotted earlier?
>
> 3. New developments are signs of potential problems. For instance, new military weapons cause concern because government planners figure that it is only a matter of time before potential enemies will produce something similar that we must then prepare to defend against.
>
> 4. Fluctuations in the reliability of old measuring sticks are signs of potential problems. All of us use, more or less habitually, a number of guides to predict things. The Dow-Jones average, for example, has long been a barometer of the stock market trends. "As Maine goes, so goes the nation," used to be a favorite election night barometer.

There are other clues to the presence of problems, but the four just named are among the best. Realistic groups will discover other clues that are particularly suited to their needs. The point to be remembered is that a group does no one a favor by concealing problems or diverting attention from them.

ELEMENTS OF A PROBLEM

In order to understand problem-solving, we must have a precise grasp of what is involved in that disequilibrium discussed earlier. There are three elements,

[5]James Rorty and Moshe Decter, *McCarthy and the Communists* (Boston: Beacon Press, 1954).

which Keltner has called the *goal–obstacle–encounter* triad.[6] Let's look at each element.

Goal. A goal is any condition an individual perceives as capable of removing the effects of an undesirable situation. Clearly, if people are content with the situation in which they find themselves, they will have no problem. But if they envision some condition different from the present one, the first element of a problem is present. The goal may be simply one of escaping from a given situation, or it may be one of attaining some specific condition or thing the individual wants. A goal may be a genuine gain to the individual seeking it, or it may prove to be no more satisfying than the present circumstances. *Good* problem-solving, therefore, will not treat goal selection casually. The process of goal setting will be treated in greater depth later in this chapter.

Obstacle. An obstacle is any condition or thing that prevents or hinders the individual from reaching the goal. There is no problem if no particular effort or ingenuity is required to reach the goal. If nothing is standing in our way, our problem solves itself.

Encounter. It is here that we find what Keltner called "the point of encounter, when one becomes aware of obstacles between him and his goal."[7] The elements of time and place and circumstances bring us to an encounter with both our goals and the obstacles that prevent us from achieving our goals.

Now a further process of evaluation and integration begins. Problem solvers have two possible fundamental courses of action. First, they may try to find some way of overcoming or circumventing the obstacle in order to reach the goal. If they can find no way to get around the obstacle, or if all ways are too expensive, involved, or time-consuming to be worthwhile, they must change the goal. Of course, they may keep the goal and postpone resolution of the problem until they have mustered sufficient resources, but that is essentially changing the goal from an immediate matter to a long-range one.

Suppose that Paul, a high-school graduate, wishes to go to college in September (goal) and finds that he is qualified in all respects except that he does not have enough money (obstacle). He realizes the extent of his problem when he reads the college catalogue (encounter). He looks for various means of raising the money (scholarships, loans, and part-time jobs) and discovers that he will not be able to manage. He may then decide to work for a year or two to save enough money to make up the difference. He has changed his goal slightly by making it read *college in two years* and has devised a potential means of achieving that goal. The steps whereby this problem was solved constitute the essence of problem-solving, to which we turn after a closer look at goal setting.

---

[6]John W. Keltner, *Interpersonal Speech-Communication*, (Belmont, Calif.: Wadsworth Publishing Company, Inc., 1970), p. 157.

[7]Keltner, *Interpersonal Speech-Communication*, p. 156.

Goal Setting

The most critical aspect of the entire discussion process is goal setting. It is important for both problem-solving effectiveness and desirable interpersonal relationships.

Business goals may seem clear. Make money! But complications appear. Although making money may be an appropriate long-range objective, there are short-range goals that must be considered. Should the goal be production efficiency and lower costs, or should it be the creation of mass demand and a new image? Or both? Should the company attempt to lead public taste, or should it adapt to established trends? There are also research goals. William Whyte contends that business organizations often seek to mold their research scientists so that they conform to the goals of the organization and produce immediately practical results.[8] But these very goals are self-defeating, he believes. Allowing the research scientists to pursue their hunches might result in more desirable long-range gains. As cases in point, he cited General Electric and Bell Laboratories as both outstanding in industry and among the only research laboratories where scientists were given virtually free rein.

This brings us to the matter of differing values. Very often we cannot do a good job of establishing clear objectives until we have identified our values and shared them with the group. Even learning groups in a discussion class will find a marked lack of cohesion and progress if, for example, they are composed of both highly motivated achievers and those content to just slide by.

If the discussants are either uncertain of their goal or divided as to its nature, this confusion will be reflected in the quality of the solution. We have observed countless postdiscussion analyses that revealed considerable difference of opinion concerning the goals. In one such analysis a recording of the discussion was played and the discussants were amazed to discover that they had said little, if anything, directly about the goals although they were all certain that goals had been discussed and agreed upon.

One of the authors was a member of a city commission in which goals became the rock on which the group actually broke apart. One faction of the commission contended that the group could not proceed with its work until goals were set so the group knew where it was going and how. Another faction maintained that if the group plunged into a variety of activities, the goals would emerge and become evident; it would therefore be a waste of time to set goals in advance. For a time, the group tried a compromise approach. It spent some time during each meeting determining long-range goals and priorities, and some time working on immediate problems. The widely varying perceptions and the ambiguous nature of the tasks, however, became too much for the group and after one particularly bitter confrontation, the officers resigned. The rest of the group was disbanded by the city council.

Two key questions must be asked about the goal. Is it *desirable?* Is it *attainable?* The more important question is the first. If the goal is not one that would relieve the tensions the group is examining, there is little point in asking the second. The first question should be answered early in the discussion; the second may not be

[8]William H. Whyte, Jr., *The Organization Man* (Garden City, N.Y.: Doubleday & Co., Inc., 1957), pp. 225–38.

answered until much later in the process. Too many desirable goals have been brushed aside because people were either too lazy or not sufficiently ingenious to overcome the damning effect of that old assertion, "It can't be done." Since so many things that are routine today couldn't be done yesterday, it is better to err by attempting the impossible than to reject the desirable.

By way of summary, here are some of the reasons goal setting is either not done or done poorly:

1. Goals are set too high.

2. Goals are not properly agreed upon or communicated.

3. The group fails to get commitment to the stated shared goals.

4. The group is held accountable for things beyond its control.

5. Goals are accepted uncritically.

6. Old goals are retained even after they have proved inadequate or impossible to achieve.

7. No thought has been given to the need for goals or how they could be reached.

PHRASING THE DISCUSSION QUESTION

Discussions usually begin with a question about some problem. The question form is used to indicate the need to *inquire* rather than assert. A resolution for debate takes a position and the debate centers on arguments either for or against the proposition. Discussion questions, by contrast, are open-ended and do not include positions. Here are examples:

Debate: Resolved, That public funds should be the primary means of financing parochial and secular private elementary and secondary education in the United States.

Discussion: How can financial aid best be provided to parochial and secular private elementary and secondary schools in the United States?

It is important to distinguish between a *topic* and a discussion question. Millions of discussions have been held on such topics as "Pollution" or "Population Control." But they could not become profitable problem-solving discussions until the general topic became an open-ended question such as, What should the United States government policy be toward controlling water and air pollution? or What should be the United States' role in the problems of world population? A topic such as "The Rent Strike" can be turned into a suitable discussion question by selecting the aspect of the "felt difficulty" of most interest or concern and giving it a perspective as to *whose* problem it is: What should be the university's policy toward private housing?

It has been said that a question well phrased is half-solved. A vague or ambiguous question will lead only to a vague or ambiguous solution. Take the time to use words carefully and the whole discussion will go better. Once formulated, however, the question need not be treated as if it were carved in stone. The question that actually launches discussion may be substantially different from the one finally answered.

This shifting should not disturb anyone so long as everyone knows just what question is being discussed at the time. Thus, when we speak of the question for discussion, we do not necessarily restrict ourselves to the original question that launched the discussion.

Criteria for Effectively Worded Discussion Questions

The Wording Should Reflect the Discussion Purpose. There are four basic kinds of discussion questions: questions of *fact, interpretation, value,* and *policy.* Here are examples to help clarify the distinctions:

> *Fact:* What is the true cost of living?
> What is existentialism?

> *Interpretation:* What was the central theme of the book *Moby Dick?*
> How can *liberal education* best be defined?

> *Value:* Which automobile has the best safety record?
> Which proposal for reorganizing the college administration should we adopt?

> *Policy:* How can the teacher training program on our campus be improved?
> How can population control best be implemented in the United States?

The key question involved in problem-solving discussions is always a policy question. The other types of questions will inevitably arise in the course of a discussion. For example, in early stages of research, we often discuss the facts and interpretations involved; in choosing the initial problem area and in making selections of alternative routes to travel, we engage in discussing value or evaluation questions.

Many discussion groups are not expected to deal with the entirety of a problem. Learning groups and appraisal groups usually do not examine an entire problem, and, of course, social and cathartic groups seldom make any pretense of dealing with the entire problem. Learning groups examine such questions as, What *has been* the role of the federal government in providing for the health costs of the American people? and What is the present state of juvenile delinquency? Appraisal groups are frequently assigned the task of determining whether or not a problem actually exists before a decision-making or action group is handed the task of solving the problem. Thus whenever the scope of the discussion group is limited, the scope of the discussion question should be similarly limited.

The Wording Should Focus Attention on the Real Problem. Many discussions are launched by taking note of some manifestation or symptom of a real problem. This often is a good way for public discussions to attract attention; many problem-solving groups get started by identifying what disturbs them about their lives or society. But effective problem-solvers quickly turn the symptom into a question that gets at the real problem. A community recently became very disturbed when a school board ruling prohibited certain kinds of Christmas pageants and activities on the grounds that they violated the concept of separation of church and state. A public discussion was held on the topic, "Keep Christ in Christmas!" but it missed the point of the problem at issue: how to establish criteria by which religious or semireligious activities could be evaluated for appropriateness.

Sometimes groups work from the wrong end and discuss solutions rather than problems. Effective discussions can be held, for example, on many aspects of capital punishment or euthanasia. But discussants should not lose sight of the fact that these are *solutions* to larger problems.

The Question Should Specify Whose Behavior Is Subject to Change. A production committee might tackle the problem, How can production be improved? It might be understood that they are talking about their own job efficiency, but other departments might also have been involved in the concept. A more specific question is, What management practices should be adopted in order to increase worker efficiency? This question focuses attention upon the problem—worker efficiency—and specifies the group whose behavior is directly affected by the solution—the managers.

As another example, the question, What should be done about juvenile vandalism? may be a good opening for a discussion, but it should not be the question finally answered. The question might be phrased this way: What should be done (by parents) about (limiting the occurrence of) juvenile vandalism? The phrase *by parents* specifies whose behavior is to be changed, and the phrase *limiting the occurrence of* focuses attention upon the real problem to be examined. The question might also have read, What should be done (by the courts) (to juvenile vandals)? Our first question could ultimately be phrased in a dozen different ways. Each phrasing would to some extent modify the problem being examined and the scope and nature of possible solutions.

The Question Should Not Suggest Potential Solutions. If a question asks the discussant to agree or disagree with a particular solution, the problem-solving process has been short-circuited. Unfortunately, many questions that purport to stimulate problem-solving are phrased so that they include solutions. The question, Should the federal government adopt a program of compulsory health insurance? is simply a debate proposition. If discussants attempt to examine the problem for which federal health insurance is a proposed solution, they do so with a view of accepting or rejecting this particular solution, rather than creating a solution to the problem of how best to deal with the nation's health problems. A better question for the purposes of stimulating problem-solving is this: What should be the role (if any) of the federal government in providing for the health costs of the American people?

Often a particular group is not expected to begin at the beginning and proceed all the way through a problem. Sometimes one group will study the problem and may propose one or more solutions, and a different group will be asked to evaluate and select from the proposed solutions.

The Question Should Avoid Loaded Language. What alternatives exist to the mayor's well-conceived parking plan? clearly indicates the biases of the question framer and the fact that the group will not be expected to find alternatives. How can capital punishment be justified? is a value rather than a policy question and implies a negative perspective even before the discussion begins.

GROUP PROBLEM-SOLVING

Before we detail our version of appropriate problem-solving steps, we remind the reader of what we said earlier about description versus prescription. We do not expect nor do we advocate that groups follow these phases in a rigid one-two-three fashion; such a method would usually stifle attempts at creativity and prevent profitable sidetracks. Bormann explained it this way:

> People trained to evaluate groups with the expectation that groups proceed through a series of ordered, programmed comparisons find themselves frustrated and disappointed when they meet with *people* who ramble, discuss irrelevancies, get into arguments, withdraw from participation, and take flight from touchy personal questions relating to the decisions. . . .
> . . . Not all groups can apply rational procedures without incurring dissatisfaction and frustration, but at the proper point in a meeting, rationality can be expected or demanded. Difficulties arise when participants demand rationality from a group throughout its deliberations. [9]

The secret of successful use of problem-solving steps, then, comes not from following such steps slavishly, but from being aware of their existence and using them as a guide. They are also useful as a checklist that the group can refer to when in difficulty. Reviewing the phases may reveal that one or more of them have not been followed or were handled inadequately.

Problem-Solving Phases

There are essentially three phases in the structure of problem-solving that we have devised. They are (1) problem description (2) criteria setting , and (3) problem solution. Within each phase is a series of specific suggestions.

Problem Description

Problem Formulation. In this initial stage the discussants should attempt to identify the elements of the problem confronting them. (Recall the earlier section of this chapter on the elements of a problem.) Finding and clarifying the elements of a problem usually involve defining critical terms as the problem is developed. We should never assume shared meanings until we have discussed them. Don't be put off by the expression, "Oh, that's just a matter of semantics!" (Aren't all discussions matters of semantics?) One of the authors witnessed a class discussion group trying to solve the problem, How can the courts improve upon the process of selecting jurors? The group had become convinced by earlier research and discussion that the jury system did, indeed, need improvement and they were now trying to figure out how it could be done. The group had discussed for 40 minutes before it occurred to one person that they were not all talking about the same problem. It turned out that they had failed to define what they had considered to be an obvious term, *select,* and who was

---

[9]Ernest G. Bormann, *Discussion and Group Methods: Theory and Practice,* 2nd ed. (New York: Harper & Row, Publishers, 1975), p. 282.

doing the selecting. Jurors are first selected by a court official from a directory or authorized list. They may also be excused or *selected out* by either attorney before the trial. What's more, prospective jurors themselves may ask not to be selected.

Problem Analysis. At this point, the goals and obstacles must be examined, as well as the present circumstances or status quo. Most problems have a variety of goals and a variety of obstacles. Rigorous standards of reasoning and treatment of evidence are needed to determine exactly what the current situation is and exactly what must be solved. Since evidence and reasoning have already been dealt with in previous chapters, we merely insert the caution that evaluating a solution is difficult if the requirements of the solution are hazy. For example, solutions to the problem of economic inflation are considerably hampered by lack of understanding of and agreement concerning the causes of inflation and the relative effects of such alleged obstacles as wage increases, price increases, and market expansion.

The status quo, the obstacles, and even the goal are seldom fixed. When examining the present situation, for example, we must not only note where we are in relation to our goal, but we must also estimate where we will be if no significant change is made. When examining the obstacles, we must not only be aware of the existence of the obstacle and its immediate effect, but we must determine whether or not it will continue in its present stage if nothing is done. The same sort of analysis is required for the goal.

Problem Reformulation (If Necessary). If the analyses in the first two stages of the problem-description phase indicate a need to rearrange the nature of the problem to be solved, the problem should be reformulated. Actually, this may occur at almost any point in the discussion. It frequently is undertaken after solutions have been proposed, tested, and discarded and the discussants have become frustrated with their lack of success.

A problem statement is, after all, a question that is raised in order to direct inquiry. The more we know about something, the better the questions we are able to ask about it. Good problem-solvers reformulate their problems in light of their discoveries. Here's an example. An automobile manufacturing company was running out of drying sheds in which to store their freshly painted cars. At first the problem seemed to be simply the need to build more sheds. Land was expensive; buildings were expensive; and construction was time consuming. But one person had a better idea: If the paint dried faster, more cars could be accommodated in the existing sheds. This problem reformulation led to the discovery of faster-drying paint so that the company was able to expand its production without building more drying sheds.

Criteria Setting

Before we generate solutions to a problem something else needs to be done: We must identify criteria or yardsticks by which the effectiveness of alternative solutions can be measured. Much time and wheel-spinning can be saved if the criteria are established *before* the solutions are proposed. For example, if your problem involves the selection of students to run for student government offices, you would decide before you begin what qualities an individual should have to fill the positions. These qualities would be the criteria against which you would check all available applicants. If your problem involved finding a new apartment, you would decide, before you started looking, what you need in terms of size, arrangement, cost, and location.

The selection of the criteria requires careful consideration, but criteria should be realistic. Aim for satisfaction rather than perfection. If criteria are set too high or are too idealistic, we impede rather than assist problem-solving. Some people use the search for the perfect solution as an excuse for procrastination and letting the problem go unsolved.

Problem Solution

Solution Proposal. Unwary discussants are often tempted to make the proposal of a solution the first step in problem-solving, yet the logical advantages of delaying solution proposal are obvious. Not until the problem has been clearly understood does it pay to become concerned about the solutions. But when the problem is clear and solution proposals are in order, it is wise to introduce as many solutions as possible.

Many beginners have great difficulty separating solutions from goals. When asked what should be done about something, they tend to respond in terms of the formula, "We should do . . . ." They then assume that their goal is to achieve this solution rather than to recognize the solution as a means to a goal. In the previous example about the automobile paint, the goal for the first problem was more drying sheds; the solution was a means of finding the land and money to build them. In the problem reformulated, the goal was accommodating more cars in the existing space; the solution was faster-drying paint.

Because of prediscussion commitments to given solutions, some discussants tend to regard their particular solution as a goal to be achieved. Such thinking short-circuits the problem-solving process and turns potential inquiry into debate over proposed solutions without benefit of genuine problem analysis. Whatever problem description and analysis the discussants may do is often a means of "stacking the deck" in favor of their particular solution. Prediscussion determinations of preferences are neither unusual nor necessarily bad. Difficulty arises only when discussants confuse the real problem goals with the solutions they favor, consequently failing to look at the problem objectively.

Solution Testing. The various solutions proposed must be measured to determine which one, or which combination, will most nearly achieve the goals without creating additional problems. Again, this requires the application of sound evidence and reasoning.

Ideally, we would try out all our proposed solutions before selecting the best but this is obviously impossible and impractical. Therefore, we do our best to think through on a hypothetical basis. What is apt to happen if we put solution A into effect (rather than solutions B or C)? What will be all the imaginable results and ramifications?

Action Testing. A solution must be put into action because that is the only way of determing whether it will work. Problems have a habit of recurring, since solutions are seldom perfect or lasting, and consequently the whole problem-solving process should be regarded as a cycle rather than a one-way, one-time process.

CREATIVE PROBLEM-SOLVING

The most baffling aspect of thinking is creativity. We know quite a bit about judgment and discrimination, for many standardized tests have been constructed to measure such skills. But tests cannot really measure creativity. They present the test taker with two or more choices and ask him to choose the correct or better answer. But the *test maker* rather than the test taker must create the alternatives. In problem-solving discussion, however, discussants must both create the answers and judge between them. At least one researcher has defined creativity as "an aptitude for the resolution of problems."[10]

Creativity is needed particularly at two points in problem-solving—goal setting and solution proposing. Determining the obstacles and status quo is largely the process of discovery. Analyzing effects and relationships is reasoning. Judging proposed goals and proposed solutions is again a matter of reasoning. But arriving at goals and thinking up proposed solutions to analyze and judge require creativity.

A major study was conducted at the University of California at Berkeley to determine why some persons are more creative than others. Writing in the *Saturday Review*, Donald W. MacKinnon reported some of the tentative conclusions that he and his colleagues reached about creative people. MacKinnon first warned that paths toward the development of an individual's creative potential are many and varied. Characterizing the creative person is, therefore, extremely difficult, but MacKinnon's tentative conclusions suggest that the creative person is marked by the following:

> His high level of effective intelligence, his openness to experience, his freedom from crippling restraints and impoverishing inhibitions, his esthetic sensitivity, his cognitive flexibility, his independence in thought and action, his high level of creative energy, his unquestioning commitment to creative endeavor, and his unceasing striving for solutions to the even more difficult problems that he constantly sets for himself.[11]

As MacKinnon indicated, it is extremely hazardous to attempt to pin down the characteristics of creativity in some convenient little formula. We can, however, highlight three fundamental characteristics. The first two were suggested by Erich Fromm and the third is our deduction from literature and from our own experience:[12]

> 1.   Creativity is characterized by *the capacity to be puzzled.* If discrepancies in what one observes are brushed aside, if experience is made routine, if "accidents" are not noted, a person is not likely to be creative. Intelligence, curiosity, sensitivity to experience, flexibility, and freedom from restraint are all implied by the capacity to be puzzled. Both studies of creativity and anecdotes about creative people and their acts are replete with illustrations

[10]Michel Stievenart, "Influence of Guilford's Model of the Intellect on a Study of Creativity," *Revue Belge de Psychologie et de Pedagogie*, 34 (1972), 65–78.

[11]Donald W. MacKinnon, "What Makes a Person Creative?" *Saturday Review*, February 10, 1962, p. 69.

[12]Erich Fromm, "The Creative Attitude," in *Creativity and Its Cultivation*, ed. Harold H. Anderson (New York: Harper & Row, Publishers, 1959).

of the capacity to be puzzled. Some of the most revealing examples of the capacity to be puzzled are found in Wertheimer's *Productive Thinking*, which we strongly recommend to the reader.[13]

2.   As Fromm points out, *the ability to concentrate* is all too rare in a society filled with so many distractions and with work days so segmented. Many people who possess the capacity to be puzzled, as well as the intelligence and dedication required for concentration, find it well-nigh impossible to create the environment necessary for sustained concentration. Concentration, however, requires more than available time and freedom from interruption. It also requires a capacity for reasoning and close examination of details and differences.

3.   Finally, creativity is characterized by *the ability to complete*. The individual who possesses the ability to be puzzled and the ability to concentrate may still be an intellectual dilettante if he or she does not have the ability to complete. Some people have great difficulty finishing anything. Despite the stress placed upon intelligence, creativity does not imply highly intellectualized unemotional activity. Running throughout most research on the subject is the idea that creativity involves the total self without any artificial dichotomy between intellect and emotion. Rollo May uses the term *ecstasy* to describe the nature of what he means by inspiration and suggests that "reason works better when emotions are present. . . ."[14] Of course, emotion and emotionalism are not the same, nor are excitable name calling and comparable outbursts conducive to effective reasoning or creativity. Genuine creativity, rather, involves the whole person, whether he or she is working alone or with others. In summary, it is important both to complete and to be a complete person.

The concept of creative problem-solving was originated by Alex Osborn[15] and is currently studied at the annual Creative-Problem-Solving Institute conducted at the University of New York at Buffalo and elsewhere. The essence of creative problem-solving is the idea of suspended or deferred judgment. When someone suggests a solution to a problem, the all-too-human response is apt to be "We tried that and it didn't work" or "Yes, but that would cost too much." What could be more dampening to a creative spark?

Osborn developed *brainstorming* to help individuals and groups avoid the pitfalls of solutions that were rigid because of prior bias or premature evaluation. Using Einstein's assertion that imagination is more important than knowledge, Osborn suggested that groups have brainstorming sessions in which they think up solutions to a problem and any criticism or even preliminary evaluations are ruled out. Today, many regard brainstorming as the best means of releasing creativity in a group.

[13]Max Wertheimer, *Productive Thinking*, enlarged ed., ed. Michael Wertheimer (New York: Harper & Row, Publishers, 1959). See also Max Black, *Critical Thinking: An Introduction to Logic and the Scientific Method*, 2nd ed. (Englewood Cliffs, N.J.: Prentice-Hall, Inc., 1960); and a variety of articles in the *Journal of Creative Behavior*.

[14]Rollo May, "The Nature of Creativity," in *Creativity and Its Cultivation*, ed. Harold H. Anderson, p. 65.

[15]Alex F. Osborn, *Applied Imagination: Principles and Procedures of Creative Thinking* (New York: Charles Scribner's Sons, 1953).

Here is how it works. A group is presented with a problem that is specific, clear-cut, and preferably familiar. Group members are given the following ground rules: (1) *Quantity of ideas is important.* The more solutions, the better. The thirty-third idea is apt to be more creative and feasible than the first or second. (2) *No idea is too wild.* Imaginations should be permitted to run free. It is easier to tame ideas down later than to create them in the first place. A wild idea, however impractical, might be the idea that triggers the concept that will work. (Osborn's example here was of the destroyer in enemy waters that was about to be blown up by mines floating toward it. The ship was in a position where it could not maneuver and all normal techniques for dealing with mines were useless. In understandable desperation the captain called for a brainstorming session. One sailor had the wild idea of having the crew line up and try to blow the mines away from the ship. That helped another sailor suggest that they use the ship's fire hoses to divert the mines around the ship. It worked.) (3) *Don't criticize any ideas.* Brainstorming groups are warned not to snicker or indicate even nonverbally that they think an idea is silly. The "cold water" this kind of behavior throws on a potentially creative idea is almost impossible to combat. In brainstorming, the evaluation of solutions and the classifying into priorities of excellence or feasibility are carefully separated steps. The group will evaluate all the ideas generated in its brainstorming session in a separate session or the evaluation may be conducted by an entirely different group. (4) *Combination and improvement are sought.* In addition to contributing original ideas, members of brainstorming groups are encouraged to point out how suggestions by others could be improved upon or how two or more ideas could be combined into a better one. This is called *hitchhiking* on someone else's idea. (5) *Record every contribution.* Tape recorders, stenotypists, or shorthand experts may be used, but if they are not available one or two of the participants should take turns getting down the essence of each contribution. It is important that free-flowing ideas not be impeded by this process but it is equally important that the group have a record of its entire output. One method is to assign outside people, rather than group members, to put the gist of each contribution on a chalkboard, easel pad, or flip sheet. This has the advantage of providing a visible stimulus and quick review.

Brainstorming has proved very effective in many situations. Business and industry have created better products, better packaging, and better solutions to all kinds of problems through this technique. It is not, however, the answer to all problem-solving situations; the more complex the problem the less likely it is that brainstorming will be of assistance. What all groups can benefit from is (1) the notion of deferred judgment and the separation of idea generation from evaluation, and (2) the concept that discussants should come up with as many solutions as possible and resist the temptation to settle for the first or second solution that occurs to them. What's more, there is a certain infectious chain reaction that occurs when one good idea sparks another. In the climate of brainstorming, where criticism is ruled out, and where people are inspired by the ideas of others, there are apt to be many more and much better solutions.

Osborn advocates that groups be given the problem they are going to brainstorm the day before their session because "periods of incubation invite illumination."[16] In

---

[16]Osborn, *Applied Imagination: Principles and Procedures of Creative Problem-Solving* (New York: Charles Scribner's Sons, 1963), p. 315.

other words, put the problem on the back burner and let it simmer in the subconscious. Similarly, we suggest that when a group is faced with a knotty problem it is wise not to attempt to solve the problem in one sitting. If the group members progress through the problem description phase and then stop for a while, they will find they are much more creative in the next session. If the group will quickly retrace the steps taken in the first session when they meet again, members will often demonstrate amazing creativity that has been percolating since the first session. Many of the half-formed notions stimulated by the first meeting will be worked out and articulated by the time the group meets again, and totally new and better ideas may also be forthcoming.

CONFLICT

Paradoxically enough, conflict is one of the best means of encouraging creativity. Properly used, it is one of the highest forms of cooperation. Improperly used, conflict will cause the more timid to retire into obscurity and encourage the more vocal to engage in fruitless wrangles. One of the chief advantages of discussion is the opportunity to have one's ideas tested by conflict with others, thus stimulating better ideas.

However, it must not be forgotten that self-repression stifles creativity. Fear of criticism is frequently a condition of self-repression. For this reason, problem-solving seeks to separate problem formulation from problem analysis and solution proposal from solution testing. People should have a chance to propose their ideas as freely as possible, and the conflict that is a part of analysis and evaluation should not force the creator of an idea to defend it just because it is his or her brainchild. The structure of problem-solving should contribute toward creativity by encouraging expression rather than repression.

We have briefly discussed conflict here because it is integral to both problem-solving and creativity. But since it is so important to an understanding of discussion as a whole, the entire next chapter will be devoted to conflict.

SUMMARY

In this chapter we have examined the following aspects of problem-solving: Dewey's reflective-thinking steps, and characteristics of problem-solving thinking; locating the problem; elements of a problem; goal setting; phrasing the discussion question; problem formulation; criteria setting; problem solution; creative problem-solving, including brainstorming; and a brief look at how conflict affects problem-solving.

DISCUSSION QUESTIONS

1.   What are the implications for problem-solving when people are placed in small groups?
2.   In our efforts to stimulate originality and creativity in each group member, how shall we ensure some degree of order in the discussion and

progress to a practical solution of the problem? What can the individual group member do to enhance his or her creative contributions to discussion? How may we aid others in this respect?

3.   Consider the effects our patterns of daily life and thought have on our problem-solving and the reciprocal or circular nature of this relationship. Consider the actual and potential effects such conventional behavior may have on our approach to social, economic, and political problems.

4.   Biologically and psychologically, people have changed little if any in the last 3000 years. However, society and its technology have literally exploded in terms of knowledge and complex interrelationships. What, if any, problems does this present? How can we proceed to adjust to and/or solve these problems? What assumptions must we make?

EXERCISES

1.   Arrange for a group of four to ten individuals to explore the nature and perception of problems. Ask each person first to compile a list of problems that are both important and possible to solve. Have people group these problems into three categories: those of a personal nature; those related to his or her organization or work or related activities at the local level; and finally, those of a city, state, or regional nature. Meet as a group to compare lists and explore agreement as to the existence and importance of the problems. Attempt to phrase discussion questions out of several of the problems about which there seemed to be general agreement. Does the attempt to state the problem affect the perception of the problem?

2.   With one or two of your close friends, discuss a semipersonal or limited problem of mutual concern. Make a tape recording of your discussion. Next, ask each person to think over the discussion and jot down specific points or reactions to the problem-solving procedure. Play back the recording and then compare your initial individual evaluations to those you form after hearing the playback. What do you conclude individually and collectively?

3.   Play the tape recording used in the previous exercise or a tape of another problem-solving discussion for a group of students (other than those who participated in the taped discussion) and ask them to identify those contributions that involved (1) problem location; (2) goal setting; (3) question phrasing; (4) problem description; (5) problem reformulation; (6) criteria setting; or (7) solution proposals. Were any aspects omitted? What patterns or roles emerged among the participants who engaged in these problem-solving activities?

4.   Plan a short experiment to illustrate the effects of various approaches to problem-solving. Choose a problem that will challenge the interest and abilities of a group of 12 to 15 cooperating participants, and for which constructive solutions might be developed within a period of 30 to 45 minutes. Separate the large group into thirds, giving each person a written statement of the problem and any directions required, including the time available for the discussion. Ask the first subgroup to attack the problem by

group discussion, using the phases of problem-solving developed in this chapter; ask the second subgroup to attack the problem by brainstorming; and for the final subgroup, have each person formulate his or her suggestions or solutions individually and independently. Ask each group, as well as each of the persons working individually, for a short, written summary, including all the ideas or solutions generated. Bring the subgroups together for reports from each relative to participants' feelings of satisfaction, the procedures employed, the number of proposals generated, and judgments as to quality of proposals or solutions. Use the results as the basis for a discussion by the entire group.

5.   Evaluate the following as effectively worded questions for problem-solving discussion. Rephrase them in line with the criteria developed in this chapter.

How can student cheating be eliminated?
Should day-care centers be provided?
How can we control TV broadcasting?
How can we secure better teachers?
Was Hamlet insane?

SELECTED READINGS

BORMANN, ERNEST G., *Discussion and Group Methods: Theory and Practice* (2nd ed.), chap. 12. New York: Harper & Row, Publishers, 1975.

BRILHART, JOHN K., *Effective Group Discussion*, chap. 7. Dubuque, Iowa: William C. Brown Company, Publishers, 1967.

CROWELL, LAURA, *Discussion: Method of Democracy*, chaps. 6, 7. Chicago: Scott, Foresman & Co., 1963.

FISHER, B. AUBREY, *Small Group Decision Making: Communication and the Group Process*, chap. 7. New York: McGraw-Hill Book Company, Inc., 1974.

GOLDBERG, ALVIN A., AND CARL E. LARSON, *Group Communication: Discussion Processes and Applications*, chap. 7. Englewood Cliffs, N.J.: Prentice-Hall, Inc., 1975.

GOURAN, DENNIS S., *Discussion: The Process of Group Decision-Making*, chaps. 3, 4, 6, 7. New York: Harper & Row, Publishers, 1974.

KELTNER, JOHN W., *Interpersonal Speech-Communication*, chap. 8. Belmont, Calif. Wadsworth Publishing Company, Inc., 1970.

OSBORN, ALEX F., *Applied Imagination: Principles and Procedures of Creative Problem-Solving*. New York: Charles Scribner's Sons, 1963.

chapter 11

Conflict is both the boon and the bane of discussion. Conflict is a boon because it is the best means of stimulating provocative ideas and zestful interchanges; without some measure of conflict, discussions would be flat and lifeless. Conflict becomes a bane, on the other hand, because it requires skillful leadership to make it constructive rather than destructive; to the immature, naive discussant, even the hint of conflict can be frightening.

We define conflict as a struggle between opposing forces, such as a clash or divergence of opinions, interest, or aims. To keep within the discussion context, we limit the use of the term to *verbal controversy*.

For generations, at least within the predominant culture, people have been taught to be nice little ladies and gentlemen and avoid conflict. It may be all right to argue heatedly at the city council meeting over the desirability of rezoning a piece of property, as long as we are kept within prescribed limits and procedures. But when we gather for social or learning activities, most of us steer away from controversial subjects for the sake of peace and harmony. Nobody loves the individual who argues about everything, but there is also no one more boring than the "Pollyanna" who thinks everything is just wonderful; and there is no one more harmful to a good discussion than the self-appointed peacemaker who tries to smooth over every disagreement just when it is getting interesting.

Conflict is absolutely vital to discussion. Why should we waste our time agreeing that the sky is blue or that the professor gives difficult tests? It is only when we disagree about something—when we look from different perspectives or when we make different interpretations—that there is really anything to discuss. Just as life would be dull if it were all placid and free of tension, so discussions are blah if everyone agrees with everyone else about every subject, or, worse yet, *pretends to* in order to avoid conflict.

Uncertainties and tensions seem to keep people on their toes and functioning better; solving the problems involved gives a sense of accomplishment that can be gained no other way. When problems defy our efforts at resolution, however, we become depressed and frustrated. As Hayakawa put it, "Conflict is essential to growth. Conflict that cannot be resolved, however, results in more or less serious emotional disturbance."[1]

CAUSES OF CONFLICT

Think back to your last experience with conflict. Perhaps it was a forthright, out-and-out battle with someone. Perhaps it was merely an uncomfortable feeling

[1]S. I. Hayakawa, *Symbol, Status and Personality* (New York: Harcourt, Brace & World, Inc., 1963), p. 41.

Conflict: The Stimulus of Thought

that all was not well between you and another person or a group of other people. No matter how serious or complex the conflict was, try now to analyze what brought it about. This is not always easy to do because of unconscious or subconscious feelings, opinions, or values. We may not be sure of the sources or causes of the conflicts in which we find ourselves.

Let's take an example. Helen is a college sophomore, enrolled in a liberal arts curriculum. She is bright but not really motivated to study; she can get passing grades with little effort. After returning from an extended skiing trip, Helen decides to catch up on some of the class assignments she missed. She finds that all of her professors are cooperative except one. Professor Zilch informs her that she has missed a midterm exam and he permits no makeups. What's more, what she has missed to date guarantees her an F in the course no matter how well she performs during the balance of the semester. Helen argues with the professor but he is unyielding. Helen gets angry and tells Professor Zilch what she thinks of his arbitrary grading policies.

If we should ask Helen to identify the sources of the conflict, she would undoubtedly blame her adversary, the professor. It is obvious that he is a factor but if we really want to understand the conflict we must analyze Helen and her attitudes about education and about authority. If we peel off the surface layers of behavior we may discover that Helen feels guilty about her own lack of effort all the while that she is berating and blaming the professor. We may also find that Helen escaped to college to get away from a stern, authoritarian father and that the real source of the conflict is her relationship with him.

Stuart Chase described blocked goals as a primary source of conflict and identified four other conditions that tend to stimulate conflict:

1. Truculence against foreigners—what anthropologists call the In-Group–Out-Group struggle.
2. Islands of strangers inside a parent culture.
3. Communication failure.
4. Overstimulation of the competitive spirit.[2]

Some social scientists view the cause of conflict as wants and needs on the one hand and *scarcity*, or not enough of something to go around, on the other. Coser, for instance, defined social conflict as "a struggle over values and claims to scarce status, power and resources in which the aims of the opponents are to neutralize, injure or eliminate their rivals."[3] Incompatibility or incompatible activities and personality differences are also seen as sources of conflict, as are high levels of frustration experienced by individuals or groups.

Another important source of conflict is the pressure to conform and the resistance of the deviate individual or group to that conformity. The late 1960s and the 1970s have provided us with many examples of groups that started out resisting conformity, only to wind up with a new set of criteria for conformity (the hippies' long hair and the blacks' Afros).

[2]Stuart Chase, *Roads to Agreement* (New York: Harper & Brothers, 1951), p. 28.

[3]Lewis A. Coser, *The Functions of Social Conflict* (New York: The Free Press, 1956), p. 8.

We have already discussed the strong pressures groups can put on their members to conform, and the pressure toward homogeneity was identified as an important group force in Chapter 5. Deviates, or members who go against group norms, can be viewed as troublemakers who must be brought back into line, or as a constructive source of conflict whose behavior forces the group to reevaluate the content or process element involved.

As described by Vernor and Levine, when the deviate is joined by even one other group member, the deviate position is not only verified, it becomes a minority subgroup that is much better able to withstand majority influence.[4] We will have more to say about this later in this chapter in the section on subgroups.

WHERE CONFLICT OCCURS

Conflict occurs within the individual, between people, within the group, and between groups.

Within the Individual. Whenever we must make a decision between alternatives, we experience internal or intrapersonal conflict. When the choices are equally attractive it is not as painful as having to select either "the devil or the deep blue sea." This concept, developed by Kurt Lewin and others, has been labeled *Approach/Avoid Theory.*

Approach/Approach means that we have a choice between two positives. When one has plenty of money, deciding between Paris or Rome as a vacation site is a pleasant exercise.

Approach/Avoid means that pleasure and pain are mixed or that achieving a satisfying goal entails some sacrifice or risk. A desire to try skydiving requires the courage to step out of a high-flying airplane. In some neurotic people, there can be a strong tendency to approach and avoid the same goal, as in the case of a person who wants very much to be a concert pianist but is too inhibited to perform in public. Fear is one of the strongest sources of avoidance behavior.

Avoid/Avoid means that the alternatives are equally bad. In this type of conflict, which psychiatrists call the *double bind,* you can't win. To a husband or wife in conflict, for example, breaking up the family is no better an alternative than continuing to live under tension. When both alternatives facing us are threatening, we will try to avoid any decision at all. But if we cannot escape, such conflicts can cause acute anxiety and even, in extreme cases, the psychological escape of mental illness.[5]

There are many ways of analyzing the existence and consequences of opposing or conflicting forces within the individual. Some of them are balance theory, cognitive dissonance theory, congruity theory, and consistency theory.

[4]Allan Vernor and J. Levine, "Consensus and Conformity," *Journal of Experimental Social Psychology,* 5 (1969), 389–99.

[5]For more about these theories see Bernard Berelson and Gary A. Steiner, *Human Behavior* (New York: Harcourt, Brace & World, Inc., 1967), pp. 168–70; John Dollard and Neal E. Miller, *Personality and Psychotherapy* (New York: McGraw-Hill Book Company, Inc., 1950), pp. 352–68; and G. R. Miller and M. Burgoon, *New Techniques of Persuasion* (New York: Harper & Row, Publishers, 1973).

Between People. Interpersonal conflict, as we have seen, has its roots in many situational or psychological aspects of human nature or behavior. It may be conscious or subconscious, manifest or latent. Smith distinguishes between *intrinsic* and *extrinsic* conflict: Intrinsic conflict refers to differences of opinion over ideas, over methods of operation, over what is true and what is not. Extrinsic conflict comes from dislike for the person with whom one disagrees.[6]

According to Haiman, "extrinsic conflict arises from the need to save face, the need to maintain an appearance of free will, supercharged emotions, and the tendency to attribute evil to one's opponents."[7]

Within the Group. The journalist Walter Lippmann wrote, "When everyone thinks alike, no one thinks much." Conflict among group members is both inevitable and invaluable, as we have already noted. It may occur between individuals, or between factions; it may be one individual against the group.

Groups tend to follow predictable patterns of growth and behavior. Bormann described *primary* and *secondary* tensions in this light:

> Primary tension is the social unease and stiffness that accompany getting acquainted. Students placed in a discussion group with strangers will experience these tensions most strongly during the opening minutes of their first meetings. The earmarks of primary tensions are extreme politeness, apparent boredom or tiredness, and considerable sighing or yawning. When members show primary tension, they speak softly and tentatively. Frequently they can think of nothing to say, and many long pauses result.[8]

Secondary tensions, according to Bormann, are the conflicts between group members that result from social and task structuring. Disagreements over policies or methods or competition for social status within the group would be examples of secondary tensions.[9]

It is the interpersonal conflict within the group that is of greatest concern to us and to which we will return.

Between groups. This area of conflict is the most visible in today's society. Students and teachers, management and labor, blacks and whites, Republicans and Democrats perennially choose up sides. Some intergroup conflict, like ritualistic management and labor negotiations, are planned and virtually scripted. Others are spontaneous and unorganized.

One of the most interesting and complex instances of intergroup conflict in recent years has been that between the Establishment and the counterculture. Far more

[6]William S. Smith, *Group Problem-Solving Through Discussion* (Indianapolis; The Bobbs-Merrill Company, Inc., 1965), p. 67.

[7]Franklin S. Haiman, *Group Leadership and Democratic Action* (Boston: Houghton Mifflin Company, 1951), p. 196.

[8]Ernest G. Bormann, *Discussion and Group Methods: Theory and Practice*, 2nd ed. (New York: Harper & Row, Publishers, 1975), pp. 181–82.

[9]Bormann, *Discussion and Group Methods*, pp. 185–86.

than a mere generation gap, this struggle has influenced American economic, political, interpersonal, and philosophic systems. Chesebro felt that different assumptions regarding decision-making, interaction, and goals between the Establishment and the counterculture make rhetorical conflict inevitable.[10]

KINDS AND LEVELS OF CONFLICT

Deutsch distinguished between *destructive* conflict, which has a tendency to expand and escalate, and *productive* conflict, which prevents stagnation and is the root of personal and social change.[11] Fisher identified *affective* conflict as that stemming from emotional clashes and *substantive* conflict as that involving intellectual opposition on the content of ideas or issues.[12]

Haiman identified four levels of conflict: *meaning, evidence, reasoning,* and *values.*[13] The meaning or semantic level is the easiest to resolve because it involves only a misinterpretation or misunderstanding of a word or words. One of the authors observed a group discussing whether or not teachers should have the right to strike. One woman insisted that teachers did not have the right to strike, and when pressed by the group for her reasons, said, "No teacher should have the right to *strike a child.*" Once the term *strike* was clarified, the conflict disappeared.

Clashes related to evidence or facts and to reasoning or how we think about the facts are more difficult to resolve. Well-meaning people can disagree. They can read different publications or listen to different speakers with varying biases. It is touchy business to try to tell people they do not have the "true facts" or that their reasoning is faulty.

But conflicts in values are the most difficult to resolve. Each person's value system is unique, deep-seated, and, to a certain extent, unassailable. Each of us has been conditioned to believe in and value certain things, ideas, or people over others. Values are slow to change. The group that finds itself embroiled in a conflict based on differing values has an extremely difficult, if not impossible, task in achieving resolution.

Win/Lose Conflicts

A characteristic attitude toward conflict is that resolution is possible only if one person or faction wins and the other loses. Games that result in a tie are considered unsatisfactory. It is true that some conflict must inevitably be cast in *win/lose* terms whether the winners are determined by force, arbitration, majority vote, or the toss of a coin. But under these conditions, the conflict is not resolved because the differences that caused the conflict have not been eliminated. The best that can be

---

[10]James W. Chesebro, "Cultures in Conflict—A Generic and Axiological View," *Today's Speech,* 21 (1973), 11–20.

[11]Morton Deutsch, "Conflicts: Productive and Destructive," in *Conflict Resolution Through Communication,* ed. Fred E. Jandt (New York: Harper & Row, Publishers, 1973), pp. 155–97.

[12]B. Aubrey Fisher, *Small Group Decision Making: Communication and the Group Process* (New York: McGraw-Hill Book Company, Inc., 1974), p. 105.

[13]Haiman, *Group Leadership,* pp. 182–88. See also Dean C. Barnlund and Franklyn S. Haiman, *The Dynamics of Discussion* (Boston: Houghton Mifflin Company, 1960).

said for a win/lose outcome is that a temporary settlement or an agreement to move ahead despite the conflict was reached.

A *lose/lose* outcome occurs when people refuse to acknowledge that conflict exists or they are unwilling to examine or discuss it. Sweeping it under the rug, once again, is only a temporary solution. Until the group is willing to be open and honest about their differences, everyone loses.

The ideal conflict resolution results in a *win/win* situation. This can be achieved by persistent, in-depth discussions that eventually integrate the varying viewpoints. We are not talking about *compromise,* which has the connotation of having to give up something, but of *consensus,* which is working out an agreement or solution that incorporates the thinking of all parties to the conflict. Integration and consensus provides everyone in the group with a decision or solution with which they can agree, at least in part. There are no losers in the win/win kind of resolution and all participants, therefore, feel commitment to carrying out the group's decisions.

Not all groups can achieve a win/win resolution, however. Win/win only works if the participants are both willing and able to change. It also requires giving others the benefit of the doubt and ourselves the reminder that we could be wrong. Of course it is important some times to "stand up and be counted," but not in the context of "I'm right and you're wrong." In group discussions, we must continually ask ourselves how important is the issue we are preparing to fight about. Is having our way worth the cost of potential harm to ideas, feelings, relationships? Conflicts for self-preservation are basic and natural but many conflicts in small groups turn out to be fights for superiority.

Our culture has been highly influenced by competitive and win/lose attitudes from sports activities to the free enterprise marketplace. The win/win concept is difficult for some people to fathom, particularly if they have never seen it work. Perhaps this is why recent strikes by sports teams have failed. Since football players have been instilled with the idea of *winning* as the goal, they cannot conceive of operating any other way. They are not used to negotiating, give-and-take, or the notion that partial victories also have value.

ADDITIONAL ASPECTS OF CONFLICT

Polarization

When the lines of conflict become rigid and set, polarization occurs. When two persons or two groups become convinced that "truth is on our side," differences that may have been slight originally take on extreme proportions and the two factions are apt to view each other as either stupid or evil or both.

Discussants who have become polarized can easily fall into the either–or, black–white, two-valued orientation trap. According to Condon,

> Under times of stress and great tension, the number of possible responses is reduced. As we tend toward signal reactions we may reduce the choices to two—"you are either for me or ag'in' me," "you are either an American or an un-American."[14]

[14]John C. Condon, Jr., *Semantics and Communication* (New York: The Macmillan Company, 1966), pp. 56–57.

When polarization occurs, communication is seen as both the problem and the solution. We call it a *breakdown in communication* when factions either miscommunicate or stop communicating; yet we are apt to prescribe more communication as the answer. But increased communication may intensify rather than reduce conflict; it may even contribute to and help exaggerate the polarization. Fox, for example, discovered that polarized groups do not communicate positively through interaction alone but that they can learn positive communication through perception training.[15]

Power

Power will be discussed in depth in connection with leadership, but it deserves consideration as a part of an examination of conflict. In the small group, who exerts influence over whom? Which group members most often have their suggestions followed and their ideas supported? Power is, of course, a relative quality. The top dog can coerce, persuade, or tease the bottom dog only so far as the bottom dog is willing to be coerced, persuaded, or teased. There is a great deal of power in simple noncooperation.

In most small group discussions, power is of a social rather than a coercive nature. We allow ourselves to be influenced because we like the influencer or want to be liked by him or her. The attractive, articulate person appears to have an innate power over others. But conflict can easily occur when the innate power of some is resented by others or when it appears that the power is being misused. The "haves" and the "have nots" in a power context are invariably poised on the edge of conflict. There is seldom a question of sharing power. In his analysis of the Establishment versus the counterculture, Chesebro wrote that "those who confront power do not seek to share; they demand to supplant."[16]

You may find you have power without having sought it. Perhaps your status or position causes the group to defer. But even in a group of peers, the people who have some necessary information or resources, or even the access to them, are given a certain amount of power because the group is dependent on them.

Subgroups

Whenever groups of eight or more are attempting to make decisions or solve problems, there is a high possibility of the group splitting into subgroups (often pairs) simply because not everyone can speak when they want to. The reason seems to be that it is better to converse on the side than not at all. But whenever three or more people form a group, coalitions also can form over issues or ideas. In open, flexible groups, these smaller units are temporary and new combinations are forming while old ones are dissolving.

Coalitions can be troublesome to a group, however, if they result in polarized positions, often over means rather than over basic goals. The leader or leaders of the group must unite and integrate coalitions in order to arrive at consensus.

[15]Denamae Fox, "The Influence of Perception Training on Communication Between Polarized Groups of Officers and Inmates at the Colorado Women's Correctional Institution" (unpublished Ph.D. dissertation, University of Colorado, 1972).

[16]Chesebro, "Cultures in Conflict," p. 11.

Fisher pointed out that this phenomenon of coalition forming emphasizes the importance of having at least three members in a group because in a dyad "conflict is either destructive or unmanageable," and is typically resolved "by one member dominating the other."[17]

CONFLICT RESOLUTION

As we have seen, conflict is valuable to groups and we need to weigh its worth at the time before automatically embarking on a path to resolve it. If we view all conflict as destructive, we will turn our efforts to compromising, mediating, appeasing, or bargaining. But if we find the conflict zestful and stimulating, we may be willing to let it continue and may even be willing to help it along.

Attitudes about conflict are also reflected in the way we handle attempted resolutions. For example, what is the best way to try to deal with a terrorist? Skyjacking became a popular activity when airline officials paid ransoms to save the lives of threatened passengers and crews. However, the number of skyjackings decreased when a different approach to the problem was instituted: airport security and baggage examination. Terrorists are dealt with by counterforce and reprisals in Israel and in Arab countries, whereas in England, unarmed Scotland Yard officers refuse to attack or make deals with terrorist kidnappers and instead wait them out until they eventually have to surrender.

Burton defines conflict resolution as "a final solution freely acceptable to all parties, one that does not destroy any important values, one parties will not wish to repudiate in the absence of changed circumstances."[18]

Recent research has turned up a large number of theories on how conflict can be resolved or at least managed. *Game theories* view conflict in terms of strategies employed by the participants; *systems theories* deal with sets of forces that interact with the decision-making system; *bargaining theories* emphasize the negotiation aspects; and *organizational theories* look at conflict in terms of organizational behavior and internal stress points.

Students of international conflict have looked at the problems of escalation and how to undo its effects. In his book *An Alternative to War or Surrender,* [19] Osgood developed a system he called GRIT (graduated and reciprocated initiatives in tension-reduction), which was used by President Kennedy in at least two international crises.

At the height of the Berlin confrontation in 1962, Soviet and American tanks were lined up snout-to-snout for two days at Checkpoint Charlie. Tensions were building up and nuclear possibilities were in the air. Suddenly an order came from Washington, and the American commander unilaterally pulled his tanks back a few blocks. Instead of taking this as a sign of weak-

---

[17]Fisher, *Small Group Decision Making,* pp. 117–18.

[18]John W. Burton, *Conflict and Communication: The Use of Controlled Communication in International Relations* (London: Macmillan and Co., Ltd., 1969), p. 171.

[19]C. E. Osgood, *An Alternative to War or Surrender* (Urbana: University of Illinois Press, 1962).

ness, within a few hours the Russians pulled back almost the identical number of blocks. And this reciprocating pull-back was repeated several times.[20]

The GRIT technique was also used by Kennedy in the Cuban missile crisis. Instead of bombing the missile sites as some of his advisors were urging, he used a naval blockade. Within a few days the Russian missiles were withdrawn from Cuba. It does not appear that the United States has used the Osgood method in its international relations since.

In addition to knowing that groups make decisions (and thereby resolve conflicts) by force, arbitration, mediation, consensus, and integration, what can a discussion group do to make conflict productive? First, we will identify some attributes that groups can strive for, then we will detail some specific techniques.

Attributes That Help Resolve Conflict

Clear Goals and Purposes. As we have mentioned in other contexts, goals and purposes must be articulated and not taken for granted. We have to make certain that what we hope to accomplish is clearly understood and *accepted* by all participants.

Openness in Communication. If our group is mature we can frankly discuss our process problems and profit from constructive suggestions. We can ask ourselves why we are in conflict and explore ways to analyze and express it better. We can evaluate our own listening abilities and habits and determine if we are adequately withholding judgment until we understand the complete intent as well as the content of the message. The purpose of open and more effective communication, however, is *to secure understanding,* not necessarily agreement. This is an important point. Sometimes in conflict situations we feel we have communicated with each other if we can agree, and we feel that disagreement means we have not communicated. What we are doing in these instances is denying the right of others to disagree with us.

Fair and Clear Procedures. Conflict is impossible to resolve if our group is floundering procedurally. Are we sufficiently well organized to accomplish our task? Do we know how the decision will be made and by what or whose authority? Have we specified some ground rules, such as avoiding attacks on personalities?[21]

Acceptance. Some people mistakenly believe that a discussant is supposed to attack and criticize every idea offered. Supportive comments are just as important and they help provide a nonthreatening, relaxed climate. We not only need to accept other people and their ideas but also their right to be different from us. What's more, we need to make the charitable assumption about others' intentions and motives.

---

[20]Elizabeth Hall, "Prediction: Nixon and the U.S. Are Going to Become Gradually Negative for Both Russia and China, Simultaneously, (A Conversation With Charles E. Osgood)," *Psychology Today,* 7 (1973), 54–72.

[21]See, for example, George R. Bach and Peter Wyder, *The Intimate Enemy: How to Fight Fair in Love and Marriage* (New York: Avon Books, 1968).

Some Specific Techniques to Resolve Conflict

Look For and Stress Common Ground. When we are in disagreement, we are apt to emphasize our points of difference and virtually forget that there are some aspects of the issue upon which we can agree. Recognizing that we are together on some points gives us a foundation upon which to build.

Treat Contributions as Group Property. The successful group encourages people to forsake pride of ownership and handle ideas as if they belong to the group rather than to the individual who first proposed them. If the idea belongs to the group, no one has to defend it or feel personally threatened if the idea is criticized.

It is interesting to note that some psychologists and psychotherapists use this approach with their patients. They deal with the whole family unit as the patient and not just with the troubled individual who most needs help. In this way, all interacting forces are out in the open and the conflict is neither avoided nor concentrated on the "sick" member.[22]

Treat Contributions as Hypotheses. If a group can agree that all its ideas are to be considered hypotheses rather than assertions of fact or belief, it can develop a true spirit of inquiry. It takes skill to discuss on this somewhat abstract level and it means that the group, for the time being, will not insist that any of the members' contributions be factual or verifiable. The group must also work out an agreement on what evidence it will accept as substantiation of a hypothesis—how much evidence and what kind. If such a procedure can be established, the group has a method for discussion and evaluation that reduces the personal elements and focuses directly on ideas.

Restrict Communication Until Points in Conflict Are Thoroughly Understood. Some conflict goes unresolved because the subject is changed and the group goes off on another tangent. One technique that Irving Lee liked was to allow the advocate of each conflicting position to explain without interruption. Then other participants are permitted to ask questions, but only three specific kinds of questions: (1) those requesting clarification; (2) those asking for information concerning the uniqueness of the proposal or position; and (3) those asking about means of investigating or verifying the speaker's assumptions or predictions.[23] This process forces group members to listen better and to see the nature of the conflict more clearly.

Compartmentalize the Issue in Conflict. Perhaps the issue is too complex for easy resolution. If so, break it into subpoints and tackle one at a time.

Play the Devil's Advocate. If a viewpoint is being ignored or rejected without a full hearing, take up the cause whether you personally agree with it or not. By forcing more depth to the discussion, this will prevent the loss of a potentially good idea.

[22]See Rachel Chazan, "A Group Family Therapy Approach to Schizophrenia," *Israel Annals of Psychiatry and Related Disciplines*, 12 (1974), 177–93.

[23]Irving J. Lee, "Procedure for Coercing Agreement," *Harvard Business Review*, 32 (1954), 39–45.

Try Role Playing. Ask people who have conflicting viewpoints to role play each other's position. Being forced to think up arguments for the opposition is one way to increase understanding and empathy and reduce conflict.

Tape-Record Some Sessions. Play back the tape of all or a part of a session, stopping frequently so that people can analyze what was happening at the time and reveal what their unexpressed feelings were. (Example: "I got very irritated because I didn't think we had talked through the problem enough and Jim seemed to be trying to steamroller us into a solution.")

Don't Let Ideas Just Lie There. Not all suggestions have to be followed and not all points have to be classified as good or bad. But *some* response, whether verbal or nonverbal, is necessary for the sake of the group's well-being. Nothing is so deflating as being ignored. (Recall the section on feedback in Chapter 6.)

Ask Questions. Since discussants are inquiring rather than advocating, frontal attacks on ideas should usually be avoided. Opposing positions can be expressed as questions rather than assertions. One of the most important questions that can be asked is *why*. (Why do you feel that is true? Why does this problem exist?) The questioning technique clarifies issues and exposes the real nature of the conflict.

Use an Observer/Consultant. It is difficult to analyze the conflict in a group when you are in the thick of it. Either assign one group member to remain outside the group and report later or ask an outside expert or consultant to observe your group and make recommendations.

Postpone the Item Until Later. Sometimes when people have time to think back over a conflict, they can come up with solutions that previously eluded them. A cooling-off period is often useful.

SUMMARY

This chapter has dealt with an overview of what conflict is and why it is essential to good discussion. We discussed some causes of conflict, and then looked at kinds and levels. Following brief descriptions of polarization and power as related to conflict, we turned to conflict resolution, including attributes and specific techniques that help resolve conflict.

DISCUSSION QUESTIONS

1.   Some conflict is inevitable in productive discussion. Conflict almost always does violence to customs. Starting from these two statements, consider the nature of conflict, its potentials, and the possibilities of managing it to ensure productivity.

2.   How best could conflict resolution be taught in schools? How and when should it be introduced?

3.   Refer to the section on personality structures in Chapter 5. How would persons of each type be apt to handle conflict?

EXERCISES

1.   Arrange to attend a meeting that includes controversial items on its agenda. If possible, tape-record the session. Analyze the discussion for kinds and levels of conflict.

2.   Divide the class into three groups. Group A plans a role-playing discussion of some social problem, and designs a sufficient number of roles for members of group B, who will actually discuss the problem. The roles planned by Group A should grow out of goals each role player is to seek. It is essential to include a variety of antagonistic as well as complementary goals. Prepare a separate role description for each participant, with directions to identify the role in general but not to reveal the details of the role or position. These should emerge in the discussion. Allow Group B to discuss for approximately 20 minutes. During this discussion, Group C should be observing and attempting to discover the causes of individual comments and behavior. Members of Group C should analyze their individual impressions in a discussion in front of the class. Members of Group A can be called upon to corroborate role intent, and members of Group B can be called upon to explain how they felt when their individual goal-seeking produced conflict.

3.   Divide the class into pairs and one at a time, let each person describe to his or her partner the individual with whom they are most in conflict (without naming names). Compare similarities and differences in behavior. Compare feelings involved.

4.   Arrange for the class to play some games (such as Starpower or Ghetto) that deal with the use of power and conflict.

SELECTED READINGS

BERNE, ERIC, *Games People Play: The Psychology of Human Relationships.* New York: Grove Press, Inc., 1964.

BLAKE, R. R., AND J. S. MOUTON, "The Intergroup Dynamics of Win-Lose Conflict and Problem-Solving Collaboration in Union-Management Relations," in *Intergroup Relations and Leadership,* ed. M. Sherif, pp. 94–140. New York: John Wiley & Sons, Inc., 1962.

BOULDING, KENNETH E., "Conflict and Defense: A General Theory," *Journal of Conflict Resolution,* 6 (1962).

JANDT, FRED E., ed., *Conflict Resolution Through Communication.* New York: Harper & Row, Publishers, 1973.

SCHELLING, THOMAS C., *The Strategy of Conflict.* Cambridge, Mass.: Harvard University Press, 1960.

Speech Monographs, 41, no. 1 (March 1974).

SWINGLE, PAUL, *The Structure of Conflict.* New York: Academic Press, Inc., 1970.

THELEN, HERBERT A., *Dynamics of Groups at Work.* Chicago: University of Chicago Press, 1970.

PART FIVE

Without doubt one of the most fascinating aspects of human relations is leadership. Hundreds of serious studies have focused attention on leaders in virtually every walk of life. Millions of people have been exposed to what has been called *leadership training*, in circumstances ranging from traditional classrooms to workshops and seminars designed to develop specific leadership abilities. The Boy Scouts, the Camp Fire Girls, and the PTA all claim to provide training in leadership. There is what amounts to a national mania for selecting and publicizing leaders in all fields. Leaders in business receive chamber of commerce awards, movie stars receive Oscars, TV stars receive Emmies, students receive scholarships, sports heroes receive "All-American" designations. Such leaders are selected and publicized in ceremonies ranging from the pomp of a presidential inaugural to the hilarious dunking given a successful football coach.

Despite its excesses, our concern with leaders is well founded. People know that leadership is an important ingredient of success in any field. Religions must have their Muhammads; governments their George Washingtons; businesses their Henry Fords; and discussion groups their leaders. In reality, this entire book has been about leadership, because the more you understand group characteristics and forces, the more able you are to influence the group.

In this section, we turn to specific theories and functions of leadership and then look at the ways leaders modify groups and move them to action. What kinds of leaders are there? How do they rise; what methods do they use? Equally important, what standards can best be used to judge their effectiveness? And what roles, in all of this, do followers rather than leaders play?

To avoid confusion, we shall use the word *leader* in the singular. But we do not wish to imply by this that we believe every group must have but a single leader.

LEADERSHIP

chapter 12

This chapter is confined to the study of leadership in small groups. Our examination is more of a sketch than a complete portrait.

DEFINITIONS OF *LEADERSHIP* AND *LEADER*

In an attempt to pin down the complex nature of leadership into a specific definition, we sometimes ask students to call out those qualities that leaders must possess, and we then write them on the chalkboard. The board is soon covered with an amazing array of virtues. If any one individual could possess them all, he or she would have to be a paragon if not a person capable of walking on water. This exercise, incidentally, helps us make the case for shared leadership, a subject we will return to in the next chapter.

We also ask students to write a description of both attributes and behaviors of a specific leader whom they admire. Then, in small groups, the students compare their lists and find some similarities but more differences. As an example, one student might feel that concern for people is an essential ingredient of leadership, but another student might feel that the quality is not only unnecessary but also a possible hindrance to effective leadership.

Exactly what leadership is (and what makes a good leader) then must be in the eye of the beholder. It cannot be described without understanding the nature and purpose of the group and many of the characteristics and forces we have previously discussed.

Although Stogdill's monumental work on leadership may not help us find a simple definition of the concept, in it he has identified the most frequently used perspectives from which experts in the field have defined and analyzed leadership. They are leadership as (1) a focus of group processes; (2) personality and its effects; (3) the art of inducing compliance; (4) the exercise of influence; (5) act or behavior; (6) a form of persuasion; (7) a power relation; (8) an instrument of goal achievement; (9) an effect of interaction; (10) a differentiated role; and (11) the initiation of structure.[1]

If a concise definition of leadership is necessary, we see leadership as virtually synonymous with the act of influencing. But the influence may be strong and overt, as in the case of a take-charge person, or it may be facilitating and subtle, as in the case of a moderator or counselor.

Students of leadership have been plagued by the problem of distinguishing *attempts to influence* from actual influence. Clearly, if one is repeatedly unsuccessful in attempts to influence others, he or she can scarcely be called a leader. On the other hand, if we limit leadership acts only to those acts that are successful, our analysis of

---

[1]Ralph M. Stogdill, *Handbook of Leadership: A Survey of Theory and Research* (New York: The Free Press, 1974), pp. 7–15.

Theories of Leadership

this aspect of the discussion process would have to wait for some evidence of success before we could even identify attempts at leadership. Therefore, *attempted* influence will be inserted into the definition.

Thomas Jefferson noted that governments derive their just powers from the consent of the governed. Even in totalitarian states the government must seek approbation of the governed if it is to be effective. Hence, before calling an attempt to influence an act of leadership, we must assume that the followers have sanctioned the attempted influence, even though many forces may be brought to bear by the influencer to secure compliance. Therefore, an order, which the follower has no choice but to obey, is not an act of leadership.

The term *communication*, like the term *leadership*, is broad. It includes bodily actions and the use of nonverbal as well as conventional language; but when the term is used here, it does not include the kind of communication involved in "pace setting." For example, certain men and women are known as fashion leaders because their preferences in clothing influence others to copy them. Here, the term leadership excludes such influencing, which is largely emulation, since it is not accomplished by means of what is commonly called communication. The importance of communication in the understanding of leadership was underscored by Fisher when he called leadership "an emerging process precipitated by the interstructured communicative behaviors of all group members."[2]

Returning to the context of the discussion group, almost every assertion and many of the questions a discussant makes and wishes to have the others believe can be identified as acts of leadership. This means that almost every discussant exercises some measure of leadership. But some people exercise more leadership than others and some are more successful than others in directing a group toward attainment of its goals. Let us look at such people more closely.

A leader is a focal person whose contributions to the accomplishment of the group's goals are significantly greater than the individual contributions of the majority of others in the group. This is a functional definition. It is important, however, to distinguish between *leadership*, a series of functions that all groups need, and *a leader*, the person who is performing one or more of the functions at a given time.

Just as only one individual in a group can sometimes be called a leader so also sometimes *no* individual can be singled out in a group as contributing measurably more than any of the others. In the first case, we have a single-leader group; in the second, a leaderless group. The latter notion has interested a number of researchers in the field and has raised considerable dispute concerning the relative merits of such a group structure. Haiman, for example, has contended that only the leaderless group can be a truly democratic group.[3]

Most of the time leadership structures fall somewhere between the two extremes. Leaders may be singled out in a group yet seldom does one leader completely dominate a group. Typically, in most informally organized decision-making groups, about a third of the members can be called, at some point or other, leaders by our definition. Almost all group members will, at least occasionally, perform certain acts of leadership.

[2]B. Aubrey Fisher, *Small Group Decision Making: Communication and the Group Process* (New York: McGraw-Hill Book Company, Inc., 1974), p. 69.

[3]Franklin S. Haiman, "Concepts of Leadership," *Quarterly Journal of Speech*, 39 (1953), 317–22.

THE RISE OF LEADERS

Why do leaders emerge? Why do groups normally see fit to select leaders? Why do larger organizations lay so much stress on identifying and cultivating the leadership talent in the groups that compose the larger group? A better understanding of the rise of leaders will create a basis from which to talk about the character of leadership, or about the effects of different types of leadership.

Leaders Do Emerge

Although some would argue that we are suffering from a shortage of real leaders in the United States today[4] and that the young have no real heroes to admire or emulate, we will not enter that debate because our focus is on small face-to-face groups and not on national or international scenes. We feel that in a group that interacts long enough to begin to develop any distinctive group characteristics, leaders do emerge. Occasionally, as we have observed, situations exist that can be called leaderless. Genuine leaderless groups seldom exist, except when the group is small, essentially temporary, and when there are relatively few status or skill differences. The *leaderless* group, in which no leaders by our definition can be detected, and the *shared leadership* group, in which several leaders can be identified, must be clearly distinguished. Groups that interact sufficiently to demonstrate group characteristics—above and beyond the characteristics of the individuals who compose them—inevitably include a leadership structure.

Evidence for the emergence of leaders is abundant. No business organization of any size fails to make provision for filling, and refilling as necessary, its leadership positions. In the public sector also, in military organizations, educational institutions, and government agencies, leaders are recruited, trained, placed, and promoted. Even in informal groups there is definite evidence of a leadership structure. Thrasher's study of gangs, which was conducted in the 1920s, found leadership structures in all groups.[5] And Whyte's famous "street corner society," is a gold mine of information about the emergence of leaders.[6]

In the Minnesota Studies described by Bormann, the majority of leaderless group discussions (LGD) produced leaders in the following way:

> The basic principle governing the emergence of leadership in the LGD is that *the group selects its leader by the method of residues*. The group does not pick a leader, but instead eliminates members from consideration until only one person is left.[7]

Typical LGDs first eliminate nonparticipants and those who talk little and then those who are "perceived as being uninformed, unintelligent, or unskilled." Next to be

---

[4]See "In Quest of Leadership," *Time*, 104, no. 3 (July 15, 1974).

[5]Fred Thrasher, *The Gang* (Chicago: University of Chicago Press, 1927).

[6]William F. Whyte, *Street Corner Society* (Chicago: University of Chicago, 1943).

[7]Ernest G. Bormann, *Discussion and Group Methods: Theory and Practice*, 2nd ed. (New York: Harper & Row, Publishers, 1975), p. 254.

eliminated from contention as possible leaders would be those perceived as too extreme or too inflexible, followed by those who were too bossy or too dictatorial.[8]

Shaw referred to earlier studies correlating an individual's location in a communication network with his or her likelihood of emerging as the group's leader. He concluded that "the person who occupies a central position in a communication network has a high probability of emerging as the leader of the group," and similarly, "when the network consists of positions of approximately equal centrality, a leader is less likely to emerge."[9]

Trait Theory

Early investigations of the phenomenon of leadership assumed it was possible to discover a profile of traits that would identify people as leaders or nonleaders. Such studies usually began with an analysis of acknowledged leaders to determine what traits they possessed in common. Dozens of such traits, ranging from those that are presumably inherited to those that are acquired, were described. Intelligence, energy, dominance, assertiveness, extroversion, judgment, physical size, and personality adjustment were among those catalogued.

The trait approach soon proved itself inadequate to explain *why* a particular leadership structure, or any at all, should exist. The best summary of the limitations of the trait approach was offered by Gouldner, who listed five indictments: (1) The list of traits seldom distinguishes between essential and less important traits. (2) Often the traits are not mutually exclusive. (3) Seldom do the studies distinguish between the traits necessary for a leader to emerge and those that enable the leader to maintain the position. (4) Usually, the trait studies assume the leader possessed the traits *before* becoming the leader. (5) The studies frequently assume personality is simply the sum of various individual characteristics. Any concept of the dynamic relationship of characteristics or of personality structure is left out.[10]

Clearly, the trait approach is as inadequate for understanding the psychology of leadership as the technique approach is for working successfully with groups. A good illustration of this is an account of what happened to a young assistant minister who attended a short training course during which he was taught a variety of new techniques for working with groups. He was particularly impressed with a training technique in which trainers provide no direction to trainees until the group has interacted and conceived its own sets of goals. He determined to try this technique with his large Sunday school class of college students. The first Sunday they met, no one stepped forward to guide the session. Everyone sat and whispered until someone suggested they sing some hymns. Good. The idea came from the group. They sang hymns for the rest of the period. The next Sunday much the same pattern was repeated. The third Sunday, however, no one came. The minister had failed to realize, of course, that the circumstances that made the technique successful in his training course were not the same as the circumstances under which he conducted

---

[8]Bormann, *Discussion*, pp. 254–55.

[9]Marvin E. Shaw, *Group Dynamics: The Psychology of Small Group Behavior* (New York: McGraw-Hill Book Company, Inc., 1971), p. 140.

[10]Alvin W. Gouldner, ed., *Studies in Leadership* (New York: Harper & Brothers Publishers, 1950), pp. 23–25.

his class. And his knowledge of the principles involved in the differences in motivation in the two groups was not sufficient to diagnose the problem.

Although the trait approach will not explain why leaders emerge, it does enable us to predict who are most likely to emerge as leaders in a given organization. As Shaw said, "The leader of the group, to a greater extent than other group members, exemplifies traits related to ability, sociability, and motivation."[11]

Situation Theory

In an attempt to understand why leaders emerge, researchers began to turn from studying the traits of leaders to studying the *situation* in which leadership operates. As early as 1935, Pigors suggested that the following variables must be considered when examining any leadership: (1) the goal or common cause, (2) the leader, (3) the followers, and (4) the situation.[12]

It was determined that as situations varied, so did the kind and amount of leadership required. The traits or abilities that made a person a successful leader of one group did not necessarily carry over to another group.

More recently, Fiedler, in his "contingency model," developed the idea that the leader's behavior is contingent on the demands of the situation. He identified the power inherent in the leader's position, the nature or structure of the task, and the personal relationships of the leader with the other group members as the three key factors needed to understand the situational approach.[13] Analyzing these factors attempts to explain which leadership style is most appropriate for which situation and why.

Need Theory

According to need theory, leadership arises out of the necessity for the group to have given functions or roles performed in order to attain its objective. The leaders who emerge are those who have the ability to assess what the group needs and to successfully perform those roles that the group considers important. The leader stands out from other group members because he or she is most capable of providing the means for the group to fulfill its needs.

Group Needs. Every group has two sets of needs, both of which must be satisfied if the group is to operate successfully. One set of needs we call *task needs,* or getting the job done; the other set is *maintenance needs,* or how we feel about the job and the way it is getting done. A group's task needs are those that relate to ideas or the substance of the discussion; maintenance needs relate to the process of interpersonal interaction that organizes and maintains the group. Specific task and maintenance needs will be developed in Chapter 13.

[11]Shaw, *Group Dynamics,* p. 269.

[12]Paul Pigors, *Leadership or Domination* (Boston: Houghton Mifflin Company, 1935).

[13]Fred E. Fiedler, *A Theory of Leadership Effectiveness* (New York: McGraw-Hill Book Company, Inc., 1967).

Need for Dominance/Submission. The study of leadership, however brief, would not be complete without examining man's need to dominate or submit. Even the most elementary of animal forms has its pecking order, wherein some animals take over and others fall into line. Humans are conditioned, according to Haiman, to be either dominant or submissive. "It is obvious that some people are more desirous of leadership than others, and that this desire is the major factor in the development of behavior which eventually satisfies that need for them."[14]

Ardrey developed the notion of the *alpha* individual, or the most dominant member of a group. He described many behaviors reminiscent of the trait theory of leadership, and quoted Alfred Adler's description of a basic drive in humans:

> Whatever name we give it, we shall always find in human beings this great line of activity—the struggle to rise from an inferior position to a superior position, from defeat to victory, from below to above.[15]

Leader Skills. The major problem in a group, once it has recognized and appraised its needs, is to match available abilities and essential functions. The nature of the leader skills required for assessing group needs may be inferred from the discussion of group needs, but again we must emphasize the concept of perception, of the group, the leader (existing or potential), and outside agencies. Although we dismiss the trait theory as an explanation for the rise of leadership, we know that relevant differences exist among people. Thus the questions are these: Who distinguishes the differences? What is the basis of distinction? The first question is easily answered. The leader holds the position either as a result of the preferences of the *group members* or by virtue of selection through some *outside agency*. (The concern here is not with the "leader" who imposes his or her will upon a group by use of force or sanctions and compels unwilling obedience.) The role of leader is seldom, however, assigned to unsuspecting candidates; it is usually sought. So let us answer the second question by noting what the potential leader does to enhance the likelihood of being selected.

The aspiring leader must demonstrate that he or she possesses the skills necessary to cope with the perceived group needs. This may be done by cultivating and publicizing the skills themselves, by manipulating the situation or the perception of the situation to create needs with which the person is equipped to cope, or by doing both. Any political campaign will furnish illustrations of these practices. Is knowledge of foreign affairs essential? "Our candidate has such and such experience and qualifications." Do the problems demand mature judgment? "Our candidate is older and more experienced."

When aspiring leaders must look outside the group for assignment to a position of leadership, they will normally tend to emphasize those skills and traits related to task needs. When they must turn to the group for selection, they will tend to stress interpersonal needs. Hollander concluded that two things are particularly important for an individual to attain leadership. He must be seen "as competent in the group's central task . . ." and in a general way must be "perceived as a member of the

[14]Franklyn S. Haiman, *Group Leadership and Democratic Action* (Boston: Houghton Mifflin Company, 1951), p. 18.

[15]Robert Ardrey, *The Social Contract* (New York: Atheneum Publishers, 1970), p. 104.

group." That is, the potential leader must interact long enough with the others for them first, to assess his ability and second, to accept, trust, and appreciate him. [16]

Normally the leaders who are selected by a mature group will be most likely to possess the skills and attributes necessary to perform satisfactorily both task and maintenance functions. A mature group thus does not minimize its task needs. At the same time, its members are in a position to determine the capacity of any aspiring leader to satisfy its maintenance needs. (See the discussion of group maturity in Chapter 4.)

Leader Resources. In addition to skills, the leader often possesses other resources. A person's command of these resources can be an important factor in selection, and certainly an important factor in perpetuating the leader's position. He or she may possess, in any degree or combination, the resources of *information, money, prestige,* and *power.* (We will discuss power in a separate section, later in this chapter.)

Any member who has the information needed to solve a problem or who can discover that information more readily than another has an inside track in the leadership race. In the classroom, for example, the student who has previously taken a class from the instructor has a certain advantage in the leadership struggle because of the real or fancied belief of others that the experience provides knowledge about the instructor's preferences and foibles that will help the class make appropriate adaptations to the instructor's requirements. By the same token, once any member has attained the position of leader, she or he has greater access to this informational resource through a position in the communication structure.

Money is a particularly valuable resource in voluntary groups. At school, the student who owned a car used to be almost always a social leader, but automobile ownership today is too widespread to be, in itself, an index of leadership. A few years ago an annual income of $50,000 was cited as a minimum for anyone who wished to "move up in society." Individuals have held high positions in political parties largely because they could afford to spend their own money to attend conventions and meetings and to mount their own campaigns.

Prestige may result from achieving a position of leadership in a group, but it may also be a resource that enables an individual to be selected as a leader. Major fund-raising organizations often use honorary offices in order to have prestige names upon their letterheads. Prestige operates as a resource because of the group's need to achieve status as a group, and one way to achieve status is to have leaders who already possess prestige.

Leader Desire. In addition to possessing skills and resources, the aspiring leader must be willing to use them to lead. Too often, unfortunately, willingness is the only qualification some leaders possess. Although some leadership positions are essentially sinecures, especially in groups that have few task purposes, most leaders have to work at their jobs. We have all seen instances where the person who felt most keenly about the group's task was the one who performed most of the leadership functions.

---

[16]E. P. Hollander, "Emergent Leadership and Social Influence," in *Leadership and Interpersonal Behavior,* eds. Luigi Petrullo and Bernard M. Bass (New York: Holt, Rinehart and Winston, Inc., 1961), p. 196.

Besides being motivated by a desire to accomplish the group's goal because of exceptional interest in it, the leader is motivated by the promises of status and other rewards. The group values certain roles, and the skills necessary to perform those roles, more highly than it does others. In our society, for example, both the sanitation engineer and the doctor perform functions designed to further the health and well-being of the members of society. We regard the functions performed by the doctor as the more important, however, and he is correspondingly rewarded more highly in terms of both money and prestige. Similarly, in a discussion group we tend to reward more highly the functions of initiating and directing than the functions of critical listening and the giving of feedback. Although the group needs both sets of functions, performance of the former is likely to be rewarded far more conspicuously than performance of the latter.

IDENTIFYING LEADERS

Earlier in this chapter we outlined the need theory of leadership, distinguished between task and maintenance needs of a group, and indicated how such needs develop in the course of interactions among the group's members. As specific needs become apparent, leaders are sought among persons who apparently possess the requisite skills, resources, and desires to satisfy those needs. More precisely, though, how does a group identify its leaders?

There are as many ways of identifying as there are of defining leaders. We see what we are oriented to see, and the scheme we use to identify leaders will necessarily reflect our conception of what we believe a leader to be. In the literature we have examined, we have encountered at least nine fundamental frameworks for studying leaders. Although these frameworks overlap, they are useful. Without the means to analyze leadership structures of a given group, we can do little to modify the operation of that group.

Consistent with the psychology of leadership thus far developed, we will present three methods here, each providing a slightly different dimension for analysis.

Job Analysis

A job analysis is one in which the analyst studies the group needs and matches them with the skills and traits of prospective or actual leaders. This is essentially the procedure used by military organizations as well as by most business corporations. Whenever large numbers of jobs and people must be matched, some analysis of this type is probably mandatory.

The main disadvantage of this method of analysis, particularly in predicting appropriate leadership, is that several needs and corresponding traits do not operate independently of each other. Even if the analysis is able to determine accurately the requirements, the combination of traits is not a simple additive process; it is an interactive process. Another disadvantage is that an outside analyst will probably tend to concentrate solely upon task needs and corresponding personality traits to the exclusion of interpersonal needs.[17]

---

[17]See Erich P. Prien and William W. Ronan, "Job Analysis: A Review of Research Findings," *Personnel Psychology*, 24 (1971), 371–96.

Sociometric Analysis

The pioneering proponent of this method of analysis has been Helen Hall Jennings.[18] The method consists of asking group members either to indicate their preferences for leaders or to indicate their judgment of those who have been most successful as leaders; sometimes it asks them to do both. Group members are typically asked to rank "the three people who have exercised the most leadership," and "the three people whom you would most like to have as leaders," and perhaps "the three people with whom you would most like to work in some future activity." In the last two instances, the members are often given some specific activity as the basis for their choosing. A three-two-one weighting scheme is conventionally employed to arrive at the leadership score of the chosen person. That is, a first-place choice is given a score of three, a second-place a two, and a third-place receives a score of one.

The sociometric procedure is descriptive only. It does not permit the analyst to determine why given people were chosen or to evaluate the quality of leader performance apart from the index of popularity. Golembiewski stated that more attention should be paid to the source and intensity of choices because these may be more important than the sheer number of choices received.[19]

Sociometric analysis is a widely used technique that is particularly valuable whenever one wishes to differentiate between the formal and informal leadership structure of a group. Formal leaders are those who officially hold positions and informal leaders are those people who are preferred by group members. The two structures are usually at variance. When we have used sociometric analysis in our classes, for example, there is almost always a wide gap in scores, indicating that the "has been leader" people are not those in the "would like to have as leader" group.

Two additional drawbacks of this method should be underscored. The accuracy of the rankings is seriously affected if the group members do not feel free to be frank in their ratings. Though this shortcoming is apparent, the second may be less so. The accuracy of the rankings is also seriously affected by the nature of the stresses upon and within the individual and the group and by the manner in which these interact to affect the group's internal relationships at the time of the ranking.

As an example of group stresses, we recall one particularly cohesive class group that refused to single out any individuals who had been leaders or they would like to have as leaders. Their point was that everyone in the class had in some way contributed to the leadership. Their fear, although not expressed, was that identification of some class members over others would destroy the cooperative, shared leadership climate. We bowed to their wishes and abandoned the sociogram exercise, on the theory that the class may have been right and there was perhaps more to be lost than gained.

Process Analysis

As identified in Chapter 6, a process analysis consists of examining the one who communicates, the persons with whom that person interacts, and the nature of

[18]Helen Hall Jennings, *Leadership and Isolation*, 2nd ed. (New York: Longmans, Green and Co., 1950).

[19]Robert T. Golembiewski, *The Small Group* (Chicago: University of Chicago Press, 1962), p. 133.

the communication or interaction. Robert F. Bales developed a 12-category interaction scheme whereby he could label each interaction and indicate the "who-to-whom" feature.[20] Such an analysis reveals not only the amount of participation, which correlates highly with other measures of leadership, but the nature and direction of communication. When studying a discussion group, it is possible to work out ratios by time periods for actions both initiated and accepted in a variety of the categories. This method enables the analyst to identify the source, nature, and direction of influence during the course of a group's progress through phases of problem solving.

Process analysis, however, has two fundamental disadvantages. First, it is extremely difficult to score interactions precisely enough to make accurate diagnoses. Any observer must be thoroughly trained both in discussion methods and observation techniques. Secondly, process analysis looks only at one segment of a group's life. To the extent that the discussions examined are representative of the group's interactions over longer periods of time, the process analysis will accurately portray the leadership structure. Seldom, however, does one find any given discussion or set of discussions representative enough to warrant extensive generalization.[21] We will further examine the methods of process analysis developed by Bales and others in Chapter 15.

DIMENSIONS OF LEADERSHIP

In the previous section elements of group operation and leadership were picked up, turned about, and examined individually, but no effort was made to fit all their edges together and lock them into place like pieces of a jigsaw puzzle. Indeed, the task of trying to perceive the nature of leadership is rather one of trying to find matching pieces in a pile of pieces from several puzzles, and there is no assurance that all the parts are there. Let us now examine five pieces of the puzzle that are important dimensions of leadership.

Power

Power is the capacity of one individual, or group, to induce forces that affect the behavior of another person, or group. In terms of two-person relationships one person initiates an act (some kind of communication) to induce certain forces that stimulate another's compliance and thereby influences (leads) him. *At the same time,* the act of leadership also induces certain forces to resist and takes place in a context that includes the goals of both leader and follower as well as the strength of their motivations to reach those goals. Take the example of a mother calling a child to dinner. The child is hungry but he is interested in a TV program. The child is aware that obedience will bring praise and a pleasant atmosphere, but he is irritated by the interruption and wishes to exercise his independence. The mother calls again, this time inserting a threat of punishment. Resistance mounts higher in the child; now his

[20]See Robert F. Bales, *Interaction Process Analysis* (Cambridge, Mass.: Addison-Wesley Publishing Co., Inc., 1950).

[21]See R. Victor Harnack, "Problems in Measuring Discussion Process," *The Journal of Communication,* 3 (1953), 13–16.

pride is at stake. He may continue to resist until he is dragged bodily to the table, or he may decide to instigate a set of counterforces to test his own power. He feels too sick or tired to eat, he says. With any kind of skill he will soon have one or both parents paying attention to him and consoling him. In all probability he will reward his parents in due course by coming to the dinner table *on his own terms.*

Several facets in the previous illustration of attempted leadership are important. First, the conception of power is a dynamic one that includes the total situation. Second, resistance to influence is distinguished from the use of countervailing power. Finally, regardless of the power introduced into a given act of leadership, there usually remains a reservoir of power that may be tapped if the first attempts fail.

Before discussing each of these facets of power, let us clarify the meanings of the terms *power* and *authority.* They are frequently used interchangeably. Here, however, *authority* means something very similar to the area of control discussed in Chapter 4. *Power* means the capacity for control, not the scope of control. One may, for example, have authority to decide a particular issue but one may or may not have the power to enforce the decision.

The Dynamic Nature of Power. Most people make the mistake of talking about power as if it were something that can be used or withheld by the person possessing it. This is only partially true. It is more accurate to say that, when Ann wishes to influence George, George can *receive* something as a consequence of his own reaction. This is why the term *induce* was used in our definition of power. Thus, to speak of the power of Ann over George implies that, given a particular set of circumstances and considering the direction of the influence, Ann's act of leadership will, with a certain probability, stimulate George to act in certain ways in order to gain reward or avoid punishment, *either or both of which may be created by George himself.*

This distinction is not simply a matter of pedantry. If power is understood only as something possessed by an individual, then one perceives only those rewards and punishments that are largely extrinsic to the performance of the indicated act. Employers obviously have extrinsic power in that they may be able to pay well, poorly, or not at all for the performance of their employees. But to leave it at this is to overlook an employer's power to create circumstances in which his or her employees will work well *because they enjoy the very act of working.*[22]

Reciprocal Power Relationships. Resistance to influence is often apparent; at the very least it may be a form of inertia, or it may be overt and very active. It is a mistake to consider power only in terms of the power of leaders over their followers; the capacity of followers to shape the behavior of their leaders can be great. This power may be expressed in terms of a series of subgroup conversations, of a revolt in the ranks, or of countervailing power used to limit either the authority or the extrinsic rewards dispensable by leaders, or both.

Let us first cite evidence of the extent to which a leader may be influenced by those

[22]This is the whole thesis of McGregor's well-known book. See Douglas McGregor, *The Human Side of Enterprise* (New York: McGraw-Hill Book Company, Inc., 1960). See also J. Morse and J. W. Lorsch, "Beyond Theory Y," *Harvard Business Review,* 48, no. 3 (May-June 1970), 61–68.

under him or her or, to put it the other way around, the extent to which followers have power over the leader.

A study by O. J. Harvey dramatizes this process.[23] Members of an Army airborne division were divided into groups of three men each; members of each group were studied and questioned so that the experimenters knew which man was the formal leader, and which the informal leader actually preferred by the group members. The men were then led into a completely darkened room and seated in such a fashion that an opaque panel separated the official leader from the members. They were all shown two flashes of light—one pair of lights was shown to the leader and another pair to the members, but they all thought they were seeing the same pair of lights. For 30 trials both sets of lights were kept a constant 24 inches apart; but in the "influence session" the leader was shown flashes of light up to 60 inches apart. The members were still being shown flashes of light 24 inches apart. For some leaders the increase was gradual, in steps of 6, 15, and 36 inches, but for others the increase was absolute, that is, the distance was changed directly from 24 to 60 inches. During all the trials, of course, all three men were reporting aloud their judgments of the distances between the lights and were allowed to converse with one another. All the leaders were distressed by the contradiction between what they were seeing and what the other two were reporting. All the leaders were influenced by the members' judgments. The one who conformed most to the evaluations of the other members was the unpopular formal leader, particularly when his lights jumped immediately from 24 to 60 inches apart.

Although there are obvious discrepancies between the experimental situation in the Harvey study and the normal discussion situation, the study bears out the principle that members of a group can exercise power over their leader. Additional support for this conclusion is not difficult to find. Collective action, as exemplified by labor unions, is an obvious attempt by employees to secure power that will counterbalance the power of employers. By using this power, the unions have sharply restricted both the scope of control and the exercise of power by employers. Various job-security regulations, pay procedures, and hiring practices have been instituted to restrict the use of rewards and punishments by management. Indeed, the ostensible objective of most labor disputes is securing tangible benefits for workers; however, securing greater power for labor unions and their leaders is often the main objective. Strikes have been called with no apparent intention of relieving a grievance; they seem rather to have been called simply to demonstrate power.

Although personality will be discussed as a separate dimension of leadership, it should also be noted as a source of power. In an article about Matina Horner, who assumed the presidency of Radcliffe College at the age of 33, Dennis Krebs, a professor of psychology, is quoted as saying:

> Bertrand Russell said power is the ability to move people. Well, there's the kind of power, here at Harvard, to hire and fire and to make decisions no one can overturn. That's political power. I don't think Matina has that power. On the other hand, there is the ability to move people through the force and influence of your personality, the persuasiveness of your ideas,

[23]O. J. Harvey, "Reciprocal Influence of the Group and Three Types of Leaders in an Unstructured Situation," *Sociometry*, 23 (1960), 57–68.

your capacity to accumulate emotional and intellectual credits. This, I think, may well be Matina's power here.[24]

The Power Reservoir. A leader usually does not actively use all the power he or she possesses. Some of it almost always remains in a reserve that may be called the *power reservoir*. The very existence of this reserve can often condition the behavior of both leaders and followers, as Kirk H. Porter demonstrated in his description of the problems involved in administering university departments:

> Insofar as the chief officer has power officially to recommend salary increases, to recommend promotions, to recommend the appointment of new staff members, to appoint student assistants, to sign or refuse to sign requisitions for this or that, to approve or disapprove teaching loads and assignments, or the introduction of new courses, he possesses power whether he misuses it or not. No measure of kindly and impartial behavior can dispel the fact.[25]

Because of the power reservoir, Porter contended democracy in university departments is impossible even though both the department head and his or her faculty try to be as fair-minded and decent as possible. However, in view of reciprocal power relationships, department heads are just as dependent upon their chiefs. Usually an untapped reservoir of power, which may not always be used, exists on both sides. When leaders have to dip into their power reservoirs, and particularly when they have to employ coercive power, one may well infer that the position of the leader is sustained by imposition rather than by willing cooperation. On the other hand, if leaders do not occasionally use some of the powers that they normally keep in reserve, the followers may come to believe that these cannot or will not be used. As a result, one then sees numerous instances of followers "seeing how far they can go" in order to test the leader's strength.

As we all know, power is sometimes misused and abused. Adler saw aggression as "the way an individual mistakenly pursues the goals of personal superiority and power," and linked an underdeveloped sense of social interest with maladjustment.[26] Marcuse said the the use of terror was an ineffective tactic for groups seeking power:

> Terror has been effective historically only if the terrorizing groups are already in power. Think, for example, of the Jacobin terror during the French Revolution. That was terror exercised by the group holding power, not by a group fighting for it. Groups trying to gain power have never been able to use terror effectively for any length of time. Look at the anarchists and nihilists in Russia. It didn't help one bit.[27]

[24]Vivian Gornick, "Why Radcliffe Women Are Afraid of Success," *New York Times Magazine,* January 14, 1973, pp. 10–11, 54–62.

[25]Kirk H. Porter, "Department Head or Chairman?" AAUP *Bulletin,* 67 (1961), 341.

[26]Alfred Adler, "Individual Psychology," *Psychology Today,* 3 (1970), 42–67.

[27]Sam Keen and John Raser, "A Conversation With Herbert Marcuse," *Psychology Today,* 4 (1971), 35–66.

We would add: Look at the lack of solution to the terrorism and unresolved long-term problems in Ireland. Gardner, on the other hand, claimed that the notion of top leadership as possessing and using capricious power is a fantasy:

> Actually, the capricious use of power is relatively rare except in some large dictatorships and some small family firms. Most leaders are hedged around by constraints—tradition, constitutional limitations, the realities of the external situation, rights and privileges of followers, the requirements of teamwork, and most of all the inexorable demands of large-scale organization, which does not operate on capriciousness. In short, most power is wielded circumspectly.[28]

Personality

We have already discussed personality as a potentially limiting factor in Chapter 2 and as a group force in Chapter 5. We urge you to review those sections because we will build on what has been said before rather than repeat.

Now we need to be concerned about the effect of individual personalities on leaders and leadership. As you can already perceive, this is a subject overlaid with variables. Leader A's personality may benefit this group and hinder that one. Leader B may possess few if any characteristics normally associated with leadership skills, yet because of the time, the place, the group and/or the task, B may exert surprising influence.

Despite our earlier rejection of the trait theory of leadership, we do not deny that personality characteristics of different individuals contribute to their effectiveness as leaders. Some characteristics, such as enthusiasm, self-confidence, insight, and ability in the task, seem to be consistently needed from situation to situation, but other characteristics seem to be more dependent upon the situation in which they are employed. A fairly universal leader characteristic that we have encountered is a sensitivity, an empathic quality, that permits the person to assess and understand what the group needs and wants, and to help the group members clarify and express their aspirations. We have seldom seen a pessimist in a leadership position; consistently effective leaders have a vision of success and are convinced that solutions are possible.

Schutz said that "the leadership functions in the small group are the same as the ego functions within an individual personality."[29] He described the leader as one able to put the group's needs ahead of his or her own and complete whatever the group leaves undone, no matter how distasteful the assignment.

Personality also enters into both Machiavellianism (defined in Chapter 5) and charisma. Let's look at both of these in relation to leaders and leadership.

Bochner and Bochner used four-man groups to study the effect on group behavior of certain orientations toward human nature. People who possessed the manipula-

[28]John Gardner, "The Antileadership Vaccine," Annual Report (New York: Carnegie Corp.) 1965.

[29]William C. Schutz, "The Ego, FIRO Theory and the Leader As Completer," in *Leadership*, eds. Petrullo and Bass, pp. 48–65.

tive or Machiavellian orientations were included in the study.[30] The Bochners discriminated (as earlier researchers have done) between "high Machs," who were excessively task oriented and treated others as objects to be controlled rather than individuals, and "low Machs," who were highly affective and tended to get carried away in irrelevant interaction. The Bochners found that "group composition based upon Machiavellian profiles had a decided effect on group interaction, particularly task-related communicative acts."[31] They also noted that "Machiavellianism can be considered a *group trait* as well as an individual trait, and as such has a pervasive effect on interaction and reaction."[32]

When we consider Machiavellianism, as well as other concepts such as authoritarianism and closed-mindedness,[33] we find ourselves edging along the continuum of leadership styles to the iron-fisted leader who coerces rather than facilitates. Whether the control and manipulation are highly evident or so subtle that they are outside the group's awareness, this type of leadership is obviously not with the "consent of the governed." Where would you place the boundary between ethical and unethical practices when the leadership is with neither the consent nor the *knowledge* of the follower? Would you argue that the end justifies the means?

Charismatic leaders seem to have the kinds of personalities that inspire and enchant. The word, *charisma*, has only recently been added to the popular vocabulary but it was apparently needed to describe an elusive quality, an aura, that gives certain people almost automatic veneration from their followers. We usually associate charisma with individual influence or authority over large numbers of people; yet we have all observed, even in small groups, the person who captivates and charms the group seemingly with neither the intent nor the desire to do so. People with this personality trait have a special responsibility to help the other group members maintain objectivity and avoid becoming blinded by their attraction.

Since both the leader and the followers affect the nature and success of attempts to exercise influence, we must also be concerned with the personalities of followers. How susceptible to influence are the followers? Although all groups need effective listeners, there is little room for the classic "yes man" who rubber-stamps others' ideas and has none of his own. At the other extreme of follower personalities is the highly competitive arguer who constantly challenges the leader and everyone else. Understanding each member's personality and motivation, bringing out the best he or she has to offer, and forging all the members into a group personality are major tasks of the leader.

Communication

The rest of this chapter will deal with leadership styles and methods. It will become apparent that the amount and kind of communication among group mem-

---

[30]Arthur P. Bochner and Brenda Bochner, "A Multivariate Investigation of Machiavellianism and Task Structure in Four Man Groups," *Speech Monographs*, 39, no. 4 (November 1972), 277–85.

[31]Bochner and Bochner, "A Multivariate Investigation," p. 284.

[32]Bochner and Bochner, "A Multivariate Investigation," p. 284, emphasis added.

[33]See T. W. Adorno and others, *The Authoritarian Personality* (New York: John Wiley & Sons, Inc., 1964); Milton Rokeach, *The Open and Closed Mind* (New York: Basic Books, Inc., Publishers, 1960).

bers is a product of the amount and kind of leadership. The communication of the authoritarian leader, for example, will be more directive than the communication of other types of leaders. What's more, a greater proportion of the total communication occurring within the group will be directed to the group leader. By contrast, the more permissive or democratic leader will evoke more generalized and diffused communication patterns.

Many studies have analyzed communication networks within organizations,[34] and it is well known that the person who has access to the information—such as the person who occupies a central point in the hierarchy or network—has a vital leadership resource. People are bound and shaped by the complex relationships of which they are a part, but it is also true that people determine these relationships.

Able leaders must also be able communicators. It is not enough that the leader be articulate and clear; the leaders we remember through history are those who could also capture the essence of their vision and put it into words for others to follow. Commenting on the fact that President Nixon failed to say anything memorable when he touched glasses with Chinese leaders in the Great Hall of the People in Peking, Marvin Jensen said,

> Possibly this widespread lapse of leadership stems from a basic misunderstanding of a leader's role. Too many see a leader as a plan-maker and problem-solver, but somehow the plans never gain complete acceptance and the problems linger unresolved. The need is not someone to persuade us and give us a plan, but someone to inspire us and call us to our own best selves.[35]

Structural Rigidity

The leadership hierarchy that emerges in a given group may take a variety of forms. It may be a hierarchy with widely shared leadership functions, small status differences, and considerable viability. At the other extreme a hierarchy may be sharply pyramidical, that is, with rigorously assigned leadership functions, great status differences, and considerable rigidity. The degree of structural rigidity can affect leadership in two ways. We will discuss each.

Leadership Flexibility. The more sharply defined the leadership functions and the more pyramidical the hierarchy, the less likely it is that members low in the structure will be able to initiate action. The leaders themselves will tend to have sharply defined areas in which they legitimately exercise their leadership. This means that attempts at leadership must travel up the hierarchy before they may be relayed back down. We have all observed discussions that tended to polarize around a central figure. Members of such groups direct all their remarks to the leader, and when members and the leader interact outside of group sessions the behavior is similarly polarized. At the same time, members take little responsibility for initiating action. If they do show initiative, they have undoubtedly cleared their idea or proposal through the leadership hierarchy before the discussion session. And not in-

---

[34]See Shaw, *Group Dynamics*, pp. 137–48 for a summary of research.

[35]Marvin E. Jensen, "Leadership and Language," *Iowa Journal of Speech*, 3 (1972), 32–40.

frequently, the leader may voice the idea to the group directly without acknowledging its source even though it originated with a member.

Member Attachment to the Group. The psychological attachment of any member to such a leader-dominated group is largely personal—directed to the leader. Since a sharply defined hierarchy limits *lateral interaction*, members are not likely to feel drawn to their peers in the group as a whole; consequently, they are not apt to feel responsible for maintaining a healthy group atmosphere. In such groups participation is likely to be quite formal and concerned primarily with task needs. If members do not highly esteem their leader, if they find him or her inaccessible, or both, the quantity and accuracy of the communication they send up through group channels will suffer.

William Read sees a new tradition emerging in large organizations, however, in which the chain of command is being replaced by a sideways structure. The old up-and-down structure in which the brains in an organization are clustered at the top is being superseded by one in which highly skilled and talented specialists may be found off to one side instead of in the mainstream of the organization.[36]

Spatial Considerations

One last dimension of leadership to be analyzed briefly is the effect of distance, elevation, and other spatial considerations. A person who sits outside the main group or at the corner of a table where eye contact is not possible with everyone will seldom emerge as the group's leader. The women who attended one League of Women Voters discussion group discovered that the largest overstuffed chair in the hostess's living room was invariably the "leader chair." Whoever sat in the chair found the focus of communication and attention was upon her, whether she wished it or not. The group became more comfortable and the leadership was more easily shared when the overstuffed chair was moved out for the evening. Similarly, it is no accident that the judge's bench is elevated so that the people in the courtroom literally look up to the person of highest status. We have already commented upon nonverbal communication and the physical setup of the meetingplace. The leader and other group members should be aware of the subtle influences these factors have, so that they may use them to their advantage or counteract their deliberate or unconscious use by others.

LEADER PERFORMANCE

Leader Types

In what is now considered a classical study, Lewin, Lippitt, and White distinguished three different kinds of group climates produced by three types of leaders: the autocratic (or authoritarian), the democratic, and the laissez-faire.[37] Although the literature of leadership contains dozens of names to describe leader

[36]William H. Read, "The Decline of the Hierarchy in Industrial Organizations," *Business Horizons*, Fall 1965.

[37]This study is reported in almost every book dealing with leadership or group properties. Our source is Ralph K. White and Ronald Lippitt, *Autocracy and Democracy: An Experimental Inquiry* (New York: Harper & Row, Publishers, 1960).

types, styles and behavior, the terms used by Lewin and his associates adequately characterize the main differences between leader types. The original experiments used ten-year-old boys as subjects and adults as leaders who operated in the fashion described in Table 12.1.

As can be seen from the table, the laissez-faire leader is not what we usually call a leader for he does not exert much influence. The laissez-faire condition cannot be equated with the kind of leaderless discussion group mentioned earlier, because the laissez-faire condition sometimes results in what might be called a *leadershipless* group rather than a *leaderless* group. In the leaderless group, leadership functions are performed by no dominant person and no leaders can be singled out. In the laissez-faire condition described in this experiment, the leadership functions tended not to be performed by anyone. Perhaps because of the basic adult/child inequality or because of the boys' expectations for direction and guidance and their lack of experience in leadership, they did not assume the responsibility of performing the leadership functions neglected by the ostensible leader.

Autocracy and democracy are distinguishable by one criterion, the extent of control over *content* and *process* decisions. Content decisions are conclusions in the group's task area. They are decisions about the substance of the discussion. Process

TABLE 12.1.

Autocratic (or Authoritarian)	Democratic	Laissez-faire
1. All determination of policy by leader.	1. All policies a matter of group discussion and decision, encouraged and assisted by the leader.	1. Complete freedom for group or individual decision, with a minimum of leader participation.
2. Techniques and activity steps dictated by the authority, one at a time, so that future steps are always uncertain to a large degree.	2. Activity perspective gained during discussion period. General steps to group goal sketched, and where technical advice is needed the leader suggests two or more alternative procedures from which a choice can be made.	2. Various materials supplied by the leader, who makes it clear that he will supply information when asked. He takes no other part in work discussion.
3. The leader usually dictates the particular work task and work companion of each member.	3. The members are free to work with whomever they choose, and the division of tasks is left up to the group.	3. Complete nonparticipation of the leader in determining tasks and companions.
4. The leader tends to be personal in his praise and criticism of the work of each member, but remains aloof from active group participation except when demonstrating.	4. The leader is objective or fact-minded in his praise and criticism, and tries to be a regular group member in spirit without doing too much of the work.	4. Infrequent spontaneous comments on member activities unless questioned, and no attempt to appraise or regulate the course of events.

SOURCE: Ralph K. White and Ronald Lippitt, *Autocracy and Democracy: An Experimental Inquiry* (New York: Harper & Row, Publishers, 1960), pp. 26–27.

decisions are primarily concerned with the interpersonal area. They relate to how the content decisions are made. The best illustration of this difference is the elaborate set of rules of parliamentary procedure and the responsibilities and prerogatives of the chairperson. These rules are confined strictly to process matters. Who may make what kind of motion? When may motions be introduced? Who may speak? In what order? How long? These are the kinds of decisions that the chairperson may make within the bounds of parliamentary procedure. The rules are set up to reduce the influence that the chairperson may have over the content of the deliberations. When the chairperson wishes to speak on the content of a motion, he or she must relinquish the chair at least temporarily. Thus, the chairperson of a parliamentary group is a democratic leader even though many of the process decisions are quite arbitrary. These arbitrary decisions, however, are not the same as autocratic decisions because they are restricted to process only.

Undoubtedly, the manner in which process decisions are managed can influence content decisions. When leaders manage the process of deciding so that they restrict effective group control over the content of decisions, we call those leaders authoritarian. In the Soviet Union, for example, citizens regularly go to the polls in such large numbers they put United States citizens to shame. It looks very democratic, but the *process* of selecting candidates for the ballot leaves the voter no choice. Voting thus becomes a kind of patriotic observance, like pledging allegiance to the flag, instead of a decision-making process.

Since the quantity of control a leader exercises varies inversely with the quantity of control his or her group exercises, we can talk meaningfully about directive and nondirective democracy as well as about absolute and partial autocracy. The critical difference between democracy and autocracy, of whatever varieties, does not lie in the *quantity* of control but in the *kind* of decisions over which control extends. The autocrat's control extends over content decisions; he or she may or may not control the process. The democrat's control is limited to process decisions; and he or she may or may not share that control.

Although we have identified only three types of leaders in this section, there are many other possible points on the continuum from authoritarian to laissez-faire. Tannenbaum and Schmidt identified seven points on their continuum of leadership behavior, from *boss-centered leadership* to *subordinate-centered leadership*.[38] (These extremes have been dubbed *autocrat* and *abdicrat* by others.) Two other types of leaders that should be mentioned here are those described by McGregor as Theory X and Theory Y.[39] At the risk of over simplifying, let us merely say that Theory X leaders are the old-style authoritarian, paternalistic bosses and Theory Y are the newer-style developmental, participative leaders.

We are here describing both *types* of leaders and *methods* of exercising leadership. Ranges of behavior are possible and it would be a mistake to say that a given leader is always authoritarian without taking varying circumstances and other variables into consideration. We must also distinguish between a leadership style that a person would *like* to follow and the one he or she *must* follow. A person who would like to be

---

[38]Robert Tannenbaum and Warren H. Schmidt, "Choosing a Leadership Pattern," *Harvard Business Review*, March-April 1958. Reprinted in David R. Hampton, Charles E. Summer, and Ross A. Webber, *Organizational Behavior and the Practice of Management* (Glenview, Ill.: Scott Foresman & Co., 1973), pp. 620–29.

[39]McGregor, *The Human Side of Enterprise.*

a participative, free-rein leader may sometimes have to crack the whip because of task pressures and impending deadlines.

Leader types have been identified by the area of control—the autocratic leader controls content whereas the democratic leader controls process. Two principal methods of accomplishing an objective, open to either the autocratic or the democratic leader, are to *persuade* and to *dictate*. Yes, the democratic leader may sometimes behave in dictatorial ways. Examples of dictatorial democracy are not difficult to find. In our society we establish laws regulating the process whereby individuals are to conduct their affairs and we use force, if necessary, to compel them to obey the laws. The law itself was conceived democratically but its application may be quite dictatorial. Similarly, examples of persuasive autocracy are easy to find. Many parents, for example, do not punish their children; yet the children do not have control over the rules that govern their behavior. Rather, the parents establish the rules and persuade the children to accept them.

Effects of Leadership

When considering the effects of leadership, examine the effects of both the leader types and the leader methods on the task needs and on the interpersonal needs. The White and Lippitt study showed that democracy was superior to autocracy in getting both task and interpersonal needs solved. Autocratic groups did accomplish more *when the leader was present*, but their task accomplishment fell off sharply when the leader was absent. At the same time the authoritarian leaders produced among the boys considerable hostility and aggression that were sometimes directed at scapegoats in the group. Democracy, on the other hand, produced more originality, more individuality, and less leader dependence. When democratic leaders were absent, task accomplishment also fell off somewhat but maintained a relatively high level contrasted with task accomplishments in autocratic groups when the leader was absent.

An interesting finding emerged from research done by Wischmeier, who compared group-centered and leader-centered leaders. He found that although groups reported more satisfaction with the discussion process under a group-centered leader, they rated the leader-centered leader as the better leader.[40] The best explanation of this result is that the members were less sensitive to the actual contribution made by the persuasive democrat than to the more overt contribution made by the dictatorial democrat. Unwittingly they gave highest praise to the persuasive democrat or group-centered leader when they indicated greater satisfaction with the process itself.

SUMMARY

In this chapter we have shown that leadership is virtually synonymous with attempts to influence others by means of communication under circumstances that concede the right of the influencer to influence. A leader is thus a focal person whose contribution to the accomplishment of the group's goal, of its task needs, is sig-

[40]Richard R. Wischmeier, "Group-Centered and Leader-Centered Leadership: An Experimental Study," *Speech Monographs*, 22 (1955), 43–8.

nificantly greater than individual contributions by the majority of others in the group.

Leaders first emerge in groups that interact long enough to develop distinctive group characteristics. Although the trait theory is inadequate to explain the rise of leadership, it can identify, before the fact, which leaders are likely to emerge in a given situation. The need theory seems to be a better explanation of the rise of leadership. Leaders are identified by means of job, sociometric, or process analysis, or by a combination of all these methods.

Key dimensions of leadership discussed were power, personality, communication, structural rigidity, and spatial considerations. Under the heading Leader Types, authoritarian and democratic leaders were profiled. Their sharpest differences are in the kind and extent of their control over content and process areas in group deliberations. A distinction was made between persuasive and dictatorial leadership.

DISCUSSION QUESTIONS

1.   Discuss the opinion that the ability to lead and the ability to communicate are the same thing.

2.   Who are today's leaders and why?

3.   Why is it sometimes necessary to use autocratic methods to obtain democratic objectives?

4.   Are leaders really necessary?

EXERCISES

1.   Examine several definitions of the word *leader*. Consider carefully the full implications of each. Observe several groups of which you are a member, seeking to determine the extent to which the definitions (theory) reflect group leadership (practice). Choose a wide range of groups so as to have variety in such factors as formality, maturity, goals, status, and frequency of meetings. Prepare a report or plan a discussion of your observations.

2.   Select some relatively stable group with which the class is well acquainted, such as a student governing body. Attempt a comparative approach to identifying leaders by forming the class into three groups, each of which focuses on one method: job analysis, sociometric analysis, or process analysis. Each of the three committees should observe independently and formulate a short report for use as a basis for discussions among the members of the class.

3.   Arrange to have a group present a discussion before the class in which an expert on the problem chosen will be a participant. By prearrangement have the expert come about 30 minutes late so the group will already have begun. Meet the expert outside, inform him of the direction the discussion is taking and have him take an opposite view without regard to the fundamental merit of such a position. Provide opportunity for both the observers (class) and the discussants to analyze and discuss the effects.

4.   Leaders often influence groups by subtle and even subliminal reactions. Devise one or more experiments in which leaders deliberately attempt to exert influence in such ways. One possibility might be for the leader to first appear enthusiastic concerning a group's developing line of thought, followed by gradual withdrawal, silence, or change in tone of voice. Plan also for careful observation and reporting of results.

SELECTED READINGS

CARTWRIGHT, DORWIN, AND ALVIN ZANDER, *Group Dynamics: Research and Theory,* pts. IV, V. New York: Harper & Row, Publishers, 1968.

FIEDLER, FRED E., *A Theory of Leadership Effectiveness.* New York: McGraw-Hill Book Company, Inc., 1967.

FORD, R. N., "The Obstinate Employee," *Psychology Today,* 3, no. 6 (November 1969), 32–35.

LIKERT, R., *The Human Organization.* New York: McGraw-Hill Book Company, Inc., 1967.

PETRULLO, LUIGI, AND BERNARD M. BASS, eds., *Leadership and Interpersonal Behavior.* New York: McGraw-Hill Book Company, Inc., 1961.

SHAW, MARVIN E., *Group Dynamics: The Psychology of Small Group Behavior,* pt. III. New York: McGraw-Hill Book Company, Inc., 1971.

STOGDILL, RALPH M., *Handbook of Leadership: A Survey of Theory and Research,* pt. 1. New York: The Free Press, 1974.

chapter 13

Now we shift away from what a leader is and knows to what she or he *does*. Every group has certain functions that must be performed if it is to be successful. These functions may be performed exclusively by the elected or appointed leader, or they may be shared among group members, or they may be a combination of leader/ member responsibility.

TWO BASIC SETS OF GROUP NEEDS

No matter who performs the specific functions, every group may be said to have two basic sets of needs, both of which must be satisfied if the group is to operate successfully. These are *task needs*, or getting the job done, and *maintenance needs*, or building the group through effective interpersonal relationships.

A group's task needs are those that relate to the substance of the discussion. They include the need to define and assess the task, to gather information, to study the problem, to find criteria for solutions, and the like. Maintenance needs are those relating to the problem of organizing and developing the group so that tasks may be handled effectively and group members can realize personal satisfaction from their collective efforts. Among such needs are achievement of harmony, release of tension, and enhancement of status.

Often task needs can scarcely be distinguished from maintenance needs. This occurs when the group purposes are essentially personal, whether social, cathartic, therapeutic, or learning. However, in task groups, such as decision-making, action, advisory, and appraisal groups, the distinctions can and must be made if we are to diagnose accurately the circumstances affecting the group's deliberations. Although the task group must deal with matters that go beyond the personal requirements of its members, the personal requirements remain. (See Chapter 3 for a discussion of personal versus task purposes.)

Voluntary groups are subject to little pressure from outside the group; organizational groups feel considerable outside pressure. (See Chapter 3.) Since all groups are under some outside pressure, the principal question is where the main source of pressure comes from. Whether pressures for task accomplishment arise largely within or outside the group, task and personal pressures of the members create needs that the group, provided it is aware of them, will attempt to satisfy.

When discussing the problem of perception of group needs, we must consider the group itself, its leaders, and any outside agency or persons exerting pressure on the group. Considerable evidence suggests that the formal leaders of a group are the most sensitive to the task needs of the group, and outside agencies are almost always solely concerned with a group's task needs. Members of the group, however, are often not very sensitive to the group's task needs. Their sensitivity in this area is

Leadership Functions

primarily a function of their understanding of group problems and of their motivation with respect to group tasks. That is, the more the members understand how the group functions in general and in regard to a particular problem, the more highly motivated they are with respect to the group's goal and the more likely they are to perceive accurately the task needs that confront the group.

Maintenance needs, on the other hand, are more likely to be accurately perceived by the rank and file than by either those higher in status or those outside the group. For this reason so much of the literature on how to lead groups stresses the matter of interpersonal relations. The works of such authors as Gordon and McGregor illustrate this concern.[1]

Task and maintenance needs can be separately identified, as Bradford, Stock, and Horwitz have done in comparing a group to a machine or organism that (1) has something to do; and (2) must be kept running to do it.[2] But Cartwright and Zander have pointed out the difficulty of trying to make the two kinds of functions mutually exclusive:

> Any given behavior in a group may have significance both for goal achievement and for maintenance. Both may be served simultaneously by the actions of a member, or one may be served at the expense of the other. Thus, a member who helps a group to work cooperatively on a difficult problem may inadvertently help it to develop solidarity. In another group, however, an eager member may spur the group on in such a way that frictions develop among the members, and even though the goal is achieved efficiently, the continued existence of the group is seriously endangered.[3]

In addition to task and maintenance functions, Gulley proposed a third type, *procedural functions*. Principal activities are identified as (1) getting started and (2) controlling communication flow.[4]

Following are lists of specific task and maintenance functions, gathered from a variety of sources.[5] It matters little how these functions are labeled; what is important is the understanding that all these functions need to be performed if the group is to succeed.

[1]Thomas Gordon, *Group-Centered Leadership* (Boston: Houghton Mifflin Company, 1955); Douglas McGregor, *The Human Side of Enterprise* (New York: McGraw-Hill Book Company, Inc., 1960).

[2]Leland P. Bradford, Dorothy Stock, and Murray Horwitz, "How to Diagnose Group Problems," *Group Development* (Washington, D.C.: National Training Laboratories, National Education Association, 1961), p. 37.

[3]Dorwin Cartwright and Alvin Zander, *Group Dynamics*, 3rd ed. (New York: Harper & Row, Publishers, 1968), pp. 306–7.

[4]Halbert E. Gulley, *Discussion, Conference, and Group Process*, 2nd ed. (New York: Holt, Rinehart and Winston, Inc., 1968), pp. 192–93.

[5]See, for example, K. D. Benne and P. Sheats, "Functional Roles of Group Members," *Journal of Social Issues*, 4, no. 2 (1948), 41–49; *Adult Leadership*, vol. I, no. 8:2–23, "Spotlight on Member Roles," January 1953; J. R. Gibb and L. M. Gibb, *Applied Group Dynamics* (Washington, D.C.: National Training Laboratories, National Education Association, 1955); and many other publications of the National Training Laboratories in group development, sponsored by the National Education Association.

Task Functional Behavior

1. Clarifying or elaborating: interpreting or reflecting ideas and suggestions; clearing up confusions; indicating alternatives and issues before the group; giving examples.

2. Consensus testing: sending up trial balloons to see if the group is nearing a conclusion; checking with the group to see how much agreement has been reached.

3. Coordinating: showing relationships among various ideas or suggestions; trying to pull ideas and suggestions together; trying to draw together activities of various subgroups or members.

4. Evaluating: submitting group decisions or accomplishments to be compared with group standards; measuring accomplishments against goals.

5. Initiating: proposing tasks or goals; defining a group problem; suggesting a procedure or ideas for solving a problem.

6. Information or opinion giving: offering facts; providing relevant information about group concerns; stating a belief; giving suggestions or ideas.

7. Information or opinion seeking: requesting facts; seeking relevant information about group concerns; asking for suggestions and ideas.

8. Recording: writing down ideas, suggestions, and decisions for future reference.

9. Regulating: influencing the direction and tempo of the group's work.

10. Summarizing: pulling together related ideas; restating suggestions after the group has discussed them; offering a decision or conclusion for the group to accept or reject.

11. Testing feasibility: applying suggestions to real situations; examining practicality and workability of ideas; preevaluating decisions.

Maintenance Functional Behavior

1. Compromising: when a member's own idea or status is involved in a conflict, offering to compromise his or her own position; admitting error; disciplining self to maintain group cohesion.

2. Diagnosing: determining sources of difficulty, appropriate steps to take next, the main blocks to progress.

3. Encouraging: being friendly, warm, and responsive to others; accepting others and their contributions; agreeing with and praising others; giving others opportunity or recognition.

4. Expressing group feelings: sensing feeling, mood, relationships within the group; sharing individual feelings.

5. Following: going along with the decisions of the group; listening actively and responsively during group discussion and decision-making.

6. Gatekeeping: attempting to keep communication channels open; facilitating the participation of others; suggesting procedures to equalize participation opportunities.

7.   *Mediating:* harmonizing or attempting to reconcile disagreements; getting people to explore their differences and clarify their points of view.

8.   *Relieving group tension:* draining off negative feelings by putting a tense situation into a wider context; using humor to relax the group; sharpening the focus on ideas and away from personalities.

9.   *Standard setting:* expressing standards for the group to achieve; applying standards in evaluating group function and production.

10.   *Supporting:* creating an emotional climate that holds the group to gether; making it easy for members to work together comfortably.

SPECIAL FUNCTIONS AND PROBLEMS

Stimulating Involvement and Commitment

Probably the single greatest difficulty of voluntary groups is generating interest, involvement, and commitment. We've all attended meetings where the candidates for office outnumbered the voters. Door prizes, clever publicity, "name" attractions, fines for absence, and gold stars are among gimmicks used to get people to attend meetings. Sometimes they work; more often they are no substitute for more solid motivation. Techniques presented here are not those of the public relations specialist; they are techniques for ordinary leaders and group members. Moreover, they are techniques that are, for the most part, conceived as intrinsic, rather than extrinsic, to the group's actual work.

The problem of stimulating involvement is self-evident. Sagging and sporadic attendance, bored or uninterested participants, and poor or no preparation for meetings are among the symptoms of lack of member involvement. Even in groups such as school classes where attendance, participation, and preparation can be required, the lack of genuine involvement is often apparent. The problem is seen when students do as little as possible, speak only when spoken to, and set their sights on a passing grade rather than on accomplishment.

Demonstrate the Reason for Presence. The most indispensable of the techniques is to guarantee that each member perceives a reason for his or her presence. He or she must have a job to do, else why come? There must be something in it for the members and they must have a sense that they are needed and that their presence or absence makes a difference. Even assuming that the group has an appropriate reason for being, it may still mistakenly try to involve certain individuals by having them come to admire what others are doing. Here are two examples tied to reason for presence.

For a number of years we tried to secure involvement in meetings of a debate club. Our success was slight. We tried various techniques of publicizing and the like. We thought that getting to know one another and sharing experiences would help provide motivation for attendance. We should have known better (even before Hetlinger and Hildreth showed experimentally that debaters have less need for affiliation than nondebaters).[6] Attendance at work sessions and practice debates was al-

[6]Duane F. Hetlinger and Richard A. Hildreth, "Personality Characteristics of Debaters," *Quarterly Journal of Speech*, 47 (December 1961), 398–401.

ways better because in these meetings students had something specific to do. We finally gave up frequent general meetings and successfully used smaller groups working on projects and making decisions.

A group that was alleged to be the major student governing body of a sizable campus institution provides the second example. Actually, the group did little governing. Its chief tasks consisted of electing officers of the group itself and allocating to campus organizations a few office facilities. Fundamental decisions were made by others and occasionally explained to the group. When the group was conceived, membership was intended to be a "plum" for upperclassmen. Ultimately most of the positions were taken by freshmen and sophomores pressed into service.

Listing here all the kinds of jobs that individuals might be offered is pointless. Jobs depend on the nature and purpose of the organization itself. Be careful not to substitute make-work, however, instead of genuine individual jobs. Unless individuals can make a real contribution, they are unlikely ever to become involved in the group's work.

Provide the Opportunity to Participate. Part of the opportunity to participate may be secured by proper regulation of participation so that a few members do not dominate discussion. But if the group is too large and unwieldy, even the best attempts to regulate participation will be fruitless. For this reason large lecture sections in schools are broken down into smaller sections to give all students an opportunity to participate. Buzz groups and committees established to attack particular phases of a larger problem may also help accomplish this function.

Relate Individual Goals to Group Goals. Individuals may have a job to do and opportunity to participate, but their involvement will probably not be secured unless they perceive that their individual goals are somehow related to the goals of the group.

Many leaders mistakenly assume that individuals will discover this relationship for themselves. Since the nature and justification of the group's goals and the relationship of individual goals are so clear to them, leaders often assume that nothing need be said about goals. This assumption is not realistic. Individuals need to have group goals defined, defended, and related to their own.

One time we were conducting a training session for labor union leaders. We discovered that one of the main problems they confronted was securing attendance and involvement in union meetings and activities. Thus, we assigned a series of speeches to be presented as if the leaders were talking to union members and trying to urge them to participate. With only one or two exceptions the leaders stressed what the union members could do for the union, but they skipped blithely over group and personal goals or what the union could do for the members. Union members were given no basis for striking a bargain between themselves and the union; they had to figure it out themselves. They were not shown what they would receive, *in terms that were meaningful to them,* as a result of their involvement. Small wonder that they saw little reason to participate.

To perform this function, leaders and their groups must spend considerable time examining group goals. Next, leaders must be aware of the goals of potential members. Finally, leaders must take the initiative in tying group and personal goals together.

Listen Carefully with Understanding. The fundamental tenet of nondirective therapy demands that the therapist be a sympathetic and understanding listener. Listening is no less a requirement for the discussion group leader. Obviously, if leaders are to discover followers' goals, they must listen to them both during and between group meetings. Equally important, the very act of listening convincingly demonstrates that someone cares. Everyone needs sympathetic audiences. When we find someone who cares enough to listen, we can scarcely escape involvement in the group he or she represents.

Another advantage of real (as opposed to superficial) listening is that it facilitates evaluation of the group and its leadership. One of the reasons that some followers are not leaders is that they are not very articulate. Many a grievance, resentment, or aspiration lies buried for want of ability to command attention. Bottled up, such sentiment can become explosive, especially if an unscrupulous leader comes along and promises redress. If leaders are unapproachable or "hard of hearing," they may find themselves victims of revolutions.

Accept Contributions Without Evaluation. This is a necessary concomitant of the advice about listening. Sooner or later the contribution must be evaluated, but leave this to the other group members. As leader, you must help every group member to feel that he or she has a right to make a contribution and have it accepted for serious consideration. Nothing will cool the eagerness of a discussant more rapidly than having a contribution ignored or summarily dismissed. If the contribution is accepted for consideration, *and if the contributor participates in the evaluation of that contribution,* he or she will often be the one who rejects it if the idea cannot hold water.

It is true that contributions are not all equally valuable. But if an individual has a right to be a member, he or she has the right to be heard. If members are to become involved, they must know that their contributions will be accepted.

Be Stimulated Yourself. Member involvement is much easier to secure when the leaders are themselves involved and stimulated by what they are doing. The effective leader conveys personal enthusiasm for the group's activity.

Evidencing your own involvement means more than just acting excited. You must learn to communicate feelings as well as understanding. Your words are a part of this communication but everything you do is also a part of your communication. Is your speech lazy and indifferent? Do you sit in a semisomnolent position? Do your actions belie your words? You should be physically tired when you finish a good discussion because communicating enthusiasm requires energy—energy sufficient to stimulate yourself and a bit more to help stimulate others.

Follow Through. One reason for lack of commitment to a task or a group is that nothing seems to happen as a result of the meeting. People discuss, make proposals, offer solutions to problems—and then everyone goes away. Perhaps the problem was poor listening—suggestions and solutions might not have been grasped. Perhaps there was no or inadequate recording so people forgot what had been agreed to; or perhaps no one took the initiative to solidify agreements by summarizing or identifying the times the group reached consensus. Whatever the reason, a definite leadership function is following through. Make certain the group knows what it decided and what it accomplished at the end of the session. Good leaders do not leave next steps to chance. They make sure all group members have a progress report and a clear idea of what the next meeting will be about. Even groups that meet only once need a wrap-up or a summary at the end so that they have a feeling of closure and accomplishment.

Regulating Participation

When a group of even moderately stimlated discussants begins exchanging ideas, someone usually needs to regulate participation. Small groups of up to five participants, and even somewhat larger mature groups, often have less need for a given individual to assume this function. The group as a whole can, in these circumstances, do an adequate job. But even when everyone seems to be speaking whenever he or she wishes, someone may still need to be particularly concerned with regulating participation.

We will first of all discuss the objectives of regulating participation, and then discuss techniques that are useful means of achieving the objectives. Some people seem to think that participation is effectively regulated if everyone speaks about the same number of times and at about the same length. Unequivocally, balanced participation, as such, should *not* be the aim of regulating participation. Shelley, for example, found that spread of participation was negatively related to group cohesiveness.[7] Morton Deutsch used spread of participation as an index of the degree of competition in a group—the more balanced the participation, the more competitive the group.[8]

Why should this be? We can think of several reasons. First, potential contributions of group members are usually not equal. Democracy does not mean equal ability, but it does foster equal *opportunity*. Second, as we pointed out when describing the characteristics of a cooperative climate, one member need not duplicate the action of another, if the other member's action has moved both toward complementary goals. If they are competing, of course, one member cannot let another "get an edge." Finally, because of the status of some individuals or because of their involvement with a particular problem, others expect them to participate more.

If balanced participation is not the aim, what is? Actually, there are three aims or objectives:

> 1.   *To bring out the total resources of the group.* If the leader and the group have stimulated involvement and an individual wants to contribute, he or she may still need assistance to get the floor. Probably all of us have had the experience of engaging in animated conversation *after* the main discussion with people who spoke hardly at all during the meeting. When asked why they kept their interesting observations and ideas to themselves, they are apt to say, "I tried a couple of times, but the group was off on another track before I could get in," or "I wasn't sure the idea was appropriate at the

[7]Harry P. Shelley, "Focused Leadership and Cohesiveness in Small Groups," *Sociometry*, 23 (1960), 209–15.

[8]Morton Deutsch, "The Effects of Cooperation and Competition Upon Group Process," in *Group Dynamics: Research and Theory*, 3rd ed., eds. Dorwin Cartwright and Alvin Zander (Evanston, Ill.: Harper & Row, Publishers, 1968), pp. 461–82.

time." When an individual fails to bring out good ideas, the individual and those responsible for regulating participation—in essence, the whole group—have all failed.

2.   *To enable everyone to feel psychologically a part of the group's activity.* An opportunity to participate, as just seen, is necessary to secure individual involvement. Simply knowing that someone cares to hear an opinion may be sufficient for an individual to feel accepted. Even though the person may have nothing to add to what others have said, that individual should at least be given the opportunity.

3.   *To ensure reasonable deliberation.* In many ways the tyranny of the majority is worse than the tyranny of an individual. If no one regulates participation, a majority may brush aside or ignore the attempts of a minority. Maier and Solem found that leaders significantly improved the quality of group decisions by giving the minority a greater voice than was possible under leaderless conditions.[9] The size of their experimental groups was only five or six members. One might expect this advantage to be multiplied if group size is increased.

In employing techniques to achieve the foregoing three objectives, a leader must use tact and common sense. To a casual observer, one successful leader may appear almost brutal in curbing dominators, whereas another equally successful leader may seem to be gentleness personified. The leader must be particularly sensitive to how the group members react to direction. The techniques that follow should, therefore, be regarded as suggestions only. One additional note: Techniques of regulating participation must be preceded by, or accompanied by, *techniques of securing involvement.* After all, if a person does not want to participate, the leader has little need or opportunity to regulate.

1.   *Encourage informal, multidirectional participation unless the group is large.* Members should not normally raise their hands for recognition or direct their comments to one leader unless the group is too unwieldy for any other procedure. Most of the time the participation will take care of itself if the members are involved. Leaders need not feel that they must personally give the green light to each potential contributor. At first group members usually look to the leader for sanction to participate. As leader, you can simply acknowledge such requests as perfunctorily as possible. Others will soon learn that they need not secure leader approval every time they wish to speak.

2.   *Be hypersensitive to attempts to enter the discussion.* An alert leader will spot the individual starting to lean forward to make a contribution. If people are a bit shy or hesitant, they may never get a chance to enter the discussion without some help. We have observed dozens of groups in which one or more members made several unsuccessful attempts to get in. Sometimes we keep simple tallies of the numbers of contributions made by

[9]Norman R. F. Maier and Allen R. Solem, "The Contribution of a Discussion Leader to the Quality of Group Thinking: The Effective Use of Minority Opinions," in *Group Dynamics* (1953), Cartwright and Zander, pp. 561–72.

each individual. After the discussion we ask some of the more vocal members why others did not participate. "I guess they had nothing to say," is the usual reply. When we point out that some tried, but could not get a word in edgewise, the talkative ones confess that they had not noticed the attempts. A good leader *should* notice these attempts and help the member into the discussion.

3. *Warn the shy before directing questions to them.* If a member has appeared to be interested but has not made many contributions, you may be able to secure participation by asking for an opinion. However, if you bluntly ask, "What do *you* think, John?" you may receive nothing for your efforts because you caught him off guard. It may work, however, if you bring the discussion up short with some comment like "Before we go on, I want to make sure that we have heard all the ideas that people may have. Some of us haven't had a chance to say much and may have some ideas that haven't occurred to others. Let's summarize the ground we've been over and then see if anyone has anything to add." You have now warned everyone that you are going to solicit opinions, and you have given them time to arrange their thoughts by the simple expedient of requesting a summary. Now when you turn to the nonparticipant and ask if he has anything to add, you stand a better chance of securing a contribution.

We have been talking about helping shy people get into a discussion—but it would be a mistake to assume that all nonparticipants are shy. Some people withdraw from discussions because they are bored or angry or uninformed about the subject matter. We really don't know what kind of cure to apply for lack of involvement or participation until we know the why of the individual's behavior. In small, face-to-face groups, interpersonal interactions both in and out of the group should enable us to find out.

4. *"Slap wrists" cautiously, if at all.* Often one or two discussants monopolize the discussion, and leaders are sorely tempted to put them in their places. Think twice before you put them down, however. A person dominates discussion for one or more of several possible reasons. Once again, knowing the why must come before we can successfully treat the problem. Genuine involvement may be one of the reasons and so might a need for attention. Another possible reason is the feeling of not being listened to and so the individual keeps talking, hoping someone will respond. Use tact. You might say, "George, you have been pulling the bulk of the load so far. I wonder if others have some ideas to add." Or, if you have contributed quite a bit yourself, say, "George, if we're not careful, you and I will have a two-person group. What do you say that we sit back for a time and let other people get in the act?" In the first case you complimented George for his contribution; in the second, you shared the blame.

5. *Use private, between-discussion conversations.* Such conferences may often be used to sound out nonparticipants and to speak directly to dominators. By striking up a conversation with one of the quiet members, you can often discover clues to points in the discussion or topics likely to stimulate them to participate. Further, such conversations enable the

member to get to know you better and thus help them feel more at home in the group. Outside conversations are often the best way to learn the why behind both the undertalker and the overtalker.

6.   *Turn the whole problem of regulating participation over to the group.* The time may come for the group as a whole to give its undivided attention to the problem of regulating participation. If you believe that participation problems warrant, simply call a halt to the proceedings and announce, "I believe we have some serious problems of participation. What do you think?" And then keep still. If the participation problems are real, someone will surely pick up the discussion. However, there may be a long, painful silence before anyone musters enough courage to say what is troubling him or her. For this technique to work, you must resist the temptation to step in and begin explaining what you believe to be wrong. If you do step in, the other members are relieved of the responsibility of coming to grips with the problem. Once you pose the question, what had been a process matter now becomes the substance of discussion. You have confessed that normal means of regulating participation have failed, and, if other members agree that a problem exists, the group must seek the answer in their own emotions and actions.

One last word on this subject: Sometimes leaders who succeed in drawing out Silent Sam embarrass everyone by calling unwarranted attention to the contribution. You may have heaved an inward sigh of relief, but be sure to evaluate the contribution by the same standards you would use to evaluate the contribution of a more talkative member. To overpraise the contribution is to patronize the contributor. Accord the contribution no more or less than its due.

Building Cohesiveness

Cohesiveness was identified as an important group force in Chapter 5, and helping the group build cohesiveness, solidarity, or a team spirit is therefore a challenging problem to leaders. We say helping the group build because the leader cannot impose or coerce these qualities from the outside. Leaders need to create conditions that foster the growth and development of cohesiveness.

In a review of group communication research, Gouran reported that although studies have been made on how cohesiveness relates to such variables as interaction, productivity, and conformity, little is known of the actual determinants of group cohesiveness.[10]

Gulley, on the other hand, identified the following activities as contributing to the establishment of a group's solid front to itself and to outsiders: (1) Stressing the task's importance and the value of the outcome; (2) enhancing individual prestige by recognizing contributions; (3) emphasizing shared interests; (4) helping members accept group purposes and strive for objectivity; (5) encouraging reflective search and

[10]Dennis S. Gouran, "Group Communication: Perspectives and Priorities For Future Research," *Quarterly Journal of Speech*, 59, no. 1 (February 1973), 25. See also Marvin E. Shaw, *Group Dynamics* (New York: McGraw-Hill Book Company, Inc., 1971), pp. 192–205, 228–30.

the excitement of finding information and understanding; (6) planning programs with meticulous care; and (7) encouraging interaction in a permissive and accepting climate.[11]

The "we're in this together" feeling is, of course, easier to achieve in a smaller group where people can more quickly get to know and appreciate one another. Some leaders stress the "we versus them" kind of loyalty in competitive settings where small groups are working against each other or against a common outside "enemy." Once such loyalty is firmly established it becomes a formidable force.

In our discussion classes, for example, we insist on students shifting into several different small group combinations for group work even though the first small group identity is often so strong that they don't want to leave their newfound friends. We have found if we don't insist upon the reshuffling, the small group loyalties become so strong that building solidarity in the total class group is virtually impossible.

Handling Agendas

Perhaps the most widespread complaint about meetings concerns advance planning and the preparation of agendas. Students of discussion often disagree about methods of preparing agendas. The reason is that the items on the agenda constitute the goals to be achieved by the group. Thus, if leaders put down items *they* think should be discussed, they *may* be controlling the content of the discussion and thus may be depriving the group members of their democratic rights. If leaders list what they think the *group* wants to discuss, they may be reducing the involvement created by participating in the decision. At the other extreme, if the leader leaves the agenda planning to the group, the group may spend all its time creating agendas. This dilemma is in many ways reminiscent of the traditional–progressive controversy in education: Should the teacher plan the learning experiences or should the students decide what they want to learn?

In a large group that meets infrequently, failure to plan agendas can be disastrous. In a small, cohesive group that meets often, agenda planning is probably one of the least of the leader's worries. Since most situations fall between these extremes, the suggestions that follow are based on these assumptions: (1) We are talking about a small, ongoing group; (2) the group needs some sort of agenda to be prepared in advance of the meeting; (3) the leader assumes responsibility to see that an agenda is prepared either by doing it or delegating it to another; and (4) the leader wants the agenda to reflect genuine group concerns.

> 1.   *Start early.* The time to be thinking about next week's agenda is during this week's meeting. When issues come up in the discussion, when problems are uncovered, when hints of new directions are thrown out, note them immediately. Equally important, check with the group at the time. Toward the end of the meeting point out the items that seem to constitute the grist for next week's mill. Ask the group if they agree to these matters for the agenda. Also, ask if there are other items that you have overlooked. A minute or two stolen from one meeting to plan for the next may save much wheel-spinning later.

[11]Gulley, *Discussion*, pp. 233–36.

2. *Keep communication lines open.* Of course, issues will come up between meetings. Your agenda for the next meeting will seldom be neatly packaged at the adjournment of the previous meeting. Effective leaders need to be in constant touch with group members as well as with those over them in the organizational hierarchy. If group members feel they can talk to you between meetings, you have the opportunity to discover problems that they have encountered. You may also communicate to them issues that have come to your attention since the last meeting.

3. *Publicize agendas.* Let group members know as soon as possible what you believe should be covered during the meeting. If possible, put the agenda on paper and get copies into the hands of members before the meeting. Most certainly you should present the whole agenda to the group at the very beginning of the meeting. Do not disclose the list item by item as the group moves along. This practice is wrong for two reasons. First, group members have no basis for judging the relative importance of the several items. How much time should be spent on the first? Must we decide the matter now? These questions cannot be answered if the rest of the agenda is a mystery. Second, group members do not have opportunity to pass judgment on your agenda or suggest revisions.

4. *Consider your agenda as a starting point only.* As just pointed out, the group should be the final judge of the agenda. The first order of business should be acceptance of the agenda, either by formal vote or informal consensus. If people have revisions to suggest, the group may need to discuss these before going further. In any event, *your* agenda must be transformed into the group's agenda.

Executing Decisions

In the next chapter we will detail the various ways groups make decisions. Here, we discuss the leader's role in carrying out decisions.

Separate Legislative and Executive Functions. It is important that both you and the group understand the difference between policy making and policy implementing. The legislative or policy-making function is properly given to those most affected by the policy; the executive or implementing function is usually assigned to selected individuals or subgroups. Confusing these functions is a persistent source of group frustration and one of the easiest to remedy.

Many people equate democracy with collective action; unless the group does it, they feel that the action is authoritarian. A student did an extensive research project in which he studied in detail the leadership behavior of two ministers serving two different small churches. One of the ministers, he reported, was very interested in applying democratic principles to the management of church affairs, but he was becoming discouraged with the process. Questioning revealed why, and one instance was especially illuminating. The church's governing body had authorized the purchase of screens for the windows of the parsonage, but summer had come and gone and the screens were not yet installed. Why? The minister had not been able to get the group together to go downtown, purchase the screens, and install them! Apparently it had not occurred to anybody that, once the group had decided to purchase the screens they could give somebody the money and authorize the screens to be bought and installed. No wonder the minister was discouraged!

An effective group continually examines its behavior and asks this question: Does the activity involve formation of basic policy that requires group action or can the task be delegated to an individual or subgroup? Many groups will be amazed to discover how many hours can be saved by attention to this distinction.

Sometimes the problem stems from unclear goals and authority. For example, a task force was established to identify problems encountered by faculty and staff who were members of minority races at one university. The members of the group were far less effective than they might have been because they did not understand (or would not accept) that their job was policy making, or involving legislative rather than executive action. Their assignment was to *identify* and *provide evidence* for problems that were then to be communicated to the university administration; however, the task force persisted in wanting *to solve* the problems and to be given the authority to carry out their own unauthorized decisions.

Anticipate Scope of Authority. Insofar as possible get the group to set in advance the limits of their own and their leader's authority. Is there a maximum amount of money that can be spent? Are certain features essential? Can possible alternatives be ranked in order of desirability? Questions like these can be anticipated by the group and needed direction can thus be provided to their leader or representative.

Get group members to observe two important cautions, however. First, they should not spend time conjuring up all the improbable circumstances that might possibly affect the implementation of the decision. The group may just as well forget about delegation as to try to plug every single loophole. Second, they should not tie their representative's hands. The group must have some confidence in the judgment and integrity of the individual. If he or she sees an opportunity to strike a better bargain or pursue a different route that seems to be consistent with the group's basic intent, the representative should have that opportunity. One of the basic problems of bureaucracy is that individuals go by the book in order to avoid any blame for exceeding their authority, and while going by the book, they miss one opportunity after another to take more effective action. No one can anticipate everything, and the group that tries is simply penalizing itself.

Consult with Others When Interpretation Borders on Policy Making. If you are the leader or representative, and if you face a decision that seems to involve basic policy, you will usually have the opportunity to make a few telephone calls to key members of the group to check your assessment of the situation. Some leaders, however, overdo this because they are afraid to take responsibility for their decisions. Clearly, this practice is not recommended. You have no business undertaking executive responsibilities if you have no confidence in your judgment. The consulting we recommend is for the purpose of getting opinions from those who have some real insight into the kinds of decisions that you confront; it is valuable if you are genuinely unsure of the group's mandate.

Report to the Group Both Your Final Action and the Basis of Your Decision. The report to the group is obviously necessary; the group must know what was done. Reporting the *basis* of the decision is as necessary as the report of the action itself, not so much to praise or censure you for your interpretation but to form the basis for further implementation. If your interpretation coincides with the intention of the group at the time they drew up the policy, well and good; but if your interpretation departed from the group's intent or if you exceeded the bounds of your authority, the group has three alternatives. (1) They may decide that your action is an improvement over their previous intent and may, thus, establish policy after the fact. (2) They may prohibit such interpretation for future action. (3) They may decide that you are not competent to execute group policy. The last alternative will be seldom used, of course, if you and the rest of the group are conscientious about the previous steps in handling responsibility.

Either of the first two alternatives may be accomplished without acrimony or bitterness if these conditions prevail: (1) You have done your job well; (2) you have not tried to usurp group prerogative; (3) you have reported fairly and not defensively; and (4) the group is mature enough to understand what constructive criticism means. Only the third condition needs further comment here.

The faculty members of a graduate student's committee were deliberating whether or not to accept a thesis presented by the student as part of the requirements for an advanced degree. Everyone in the committee except the chairman was convinced that the thesis did not measure up to acceptable standards; they felt it should be thoroughly reworked before they approved it. The chairman and thesis director, in this case the person entrusted with implementing the group's standards, announced he would regard a vote against the thesis as a vote against him. He, after all, had originally approved the thesis. The committee chose what seemed the lesser of two evils. They decided to approve the thesis. No one was happy with the action, and needless to say, personal relations among committee members were strained for some time after. The thesis director's big mistake was not that he had submitted to the committee what proved to be an inadequate thesis. His problem was not being willing to admit that he had erred. Had he accepted the judgment of the committee, taken the thesis back to the student, and explained what needed to be done to bring it up to the department's research standards, both the thesis and group relations would have been improved. Moral: Don't undertake to perform executive functions if you are too insecure to admit a mistake.

Distributing Rewards

As group leaders, we may not think of ourselves as handing out rewards or favors but this is an important and inevitable aspect of leadership. Organizational leaders must recommend promotion, dismissal, and merit or other recognition. Much educational activity by parents and teachers involves praise and reinforcement on the one hand and the withholding of praise and reinforcement (punishment) to extinguish undesirable behavior on the other. In small group discussions, leaders (and other group members) can reward participation by acknowledging its effect on the group, by complimenting the author of an idea, and by according a sense of worth to individuals and to the group as a whole. Even subtle nonverbal smiles or nods of the head can serve as rewards. We have watched classroom teachers reward and punish entirely through the use of eye contact; students were rewarded by being seen and recognized, while others were punished by being ignored.

In Chapter 12 we pointed out that the rewards mediated by the leader constitute a considerable part of his or her power. The distinction was made between *intrinsic* rewards, or those inherent in the task the individual performs, and *extrinsic* rewards, those things that the leader can give or withhold from the follower. Here only the latter are considered because most of this book seeks to help individuals gain satisfaction *directly* from the discussion activity.

Though evidence shows the most significant rewards are those intrinsic to the discussion activity itself, extrinsic rewards are also meaningful, and their poor management may undo much of the best efforts of leaders. To prove this you need only recall what happened the last time someone's extra efforts went unnoticed or someone's name was omitted from a newspaper account of the group's activity.

Distributing rewards is probably at once the most gratifying and the most onerous task that leaders perform. Few teachers enjoy grading students and most students regard grades as both rewards and punishments. Certainly no decisions cause supervisors more anguish than the periodic evaluations of their subordinates. There is good reason for regarding the task as difficult and unpleasant; the means of measuring competence are crude at best. Teachers may use tests and student papers as means of assessing accomplishment, but we know that these are far from precise. Also, we know that results of our rewards can markedly affect those people we evaluate and reward. If one individual is promoted or singled out in some way, for example, but others whom group members regard as better qualified are not recognized, the effect on group morale may be devastating. Distributing rewards is thus difficult and thankless—no job for the incompetent or the weak-willed.

For one basic reason, no attempt is made here to list or rank the various rewards the leader may distribute. Aside from the broadest categories, rewards and the importance attached to them vary so much from one situation to another that ranking becomes impossible. You will discover the rewards available to you and the rewards you may create. You should also discover the meaning of the rewards *in the eyes of those who receive them.* Let us examine, therefore, some basic principles in the *management* of rewards.

Rewarding Should Be Realistic. That is, the evaluation should be as accurate as possible; evaluation and reward should be impersonal; and the reward should not purport to differentiate more closely than the evaluation scheme used. Each of these three characteristics of realism needs comment.

Evaluation should obviously be accurate, but more is implied by this criterion. Some leaders seem to feel that if they overevaluate followers, morale and consequent performance will improve. Thus, teachers may give higher grades than they think students deserve because they believe that the student will feel less threatened and will do better work. We do not agree with this approach because if individuals cannot accept a reasonably accurate evaluation of their performance, they have problems that will not be solved by receiving distorted evaluations from the leader (or the teacher).

The second criterion may seem confusing at first glance. Why should evaluation and reward be *impersonal* since many rewards such as praise and appropriate publicity seem so *personal?* Impersonal means that the evaluation and reward should, within limits of ability, be objectively determined. Personal factors, such as affection, should be minimized. Recall what happens to the teacher's pet. Maintaining proper psychological distance is the best way to achieve the perspective needed to be impersonal when evaluating and rewarding. It is virtually impossible to eliminate all personal factors—and it would be a cold, forbidding world if we could—but the good leader makes the effort to be as objective as possible.

The third criterion means that, if the evaluation methods are crude and likely to reflect the personal needs of the evaluator, only relatively gross differences in performance can be noted with any degree of certainty. Rewards should usually not, therefore, attempt to reflect small, precise differences. That's why many people oppose all but the simplest merit pay plans, and why most schools have abandoned numerical grades in favor of A, B, C, D, and F. Some schools have gone even further and use only two or three grades such as *superior, adequate, inadequate,* or a simple *pass/fail.*

From economic rewards and school grades, the principles may be extended for any kind of extrinsic reward that depends on the evaluation of a superior—a leader.[12] Realistic rewarding, then, means that the leader must try to be as accurate, objective, and impersonal as possible and the rewarding should indicate only those differences that can be clearly demonstrated and verified.

Standards Should Be Common Knowledge. If the rewards are to be meaningful to the recipient, and if individuals are to have any security in the group, the standards of both evaluation and reward should be known and *accepted* by all. If there is mystery about evaluation techniques or if members do not accept the evaluation standards, rewards are likely to produce tension and antagonism rather than satisfaction.

The best method is to have the group participate in determining what standards will form the basis of rewarding. If the larger organization does not permit the group to determine its own standards, the leader should at least discuss standards with the group so that members may accurately predict consequences of their own behavior.

The Right People Should Be Told. One of the most effective rewards is simple recognition of individual accomplishment. When the leader gives recognition, he or she must make certain that the right people learn about it. Sometimes letters of recommendation, personnel evaluation, and the like tell the right people. Another method is a short letter or memo to those concerned with the individual's accomplishment and whose opinion is important *in the eyes of the individual being rewarded.* For this reason house organs have become valuable as means of publicizing achievements of individuals within an organization. Praising people in the group at the time of achievement is the best means for most small group leaders.

Promote Your Group Members. When leaders find a valuable and productive group member, they are tempted to keep that person in the group and maintain the relationship. But people grow and must have head room. Often they cannot remain in the group because they can and should be allowed to go on to more significant and demanding roles. This is seldom a problem in classroom discussions but is a very real one in most voluntary and task-oriented groups that function within a larger hierarchical framework.

TOWARD A PHILOSOPHY OF LEADERSHIP

One cannot escape the requirement of thinking deeply about our fundamental assumptions concerning how we ought to influence and lead others. Anyone

---

[12]These extrinsic rewards may, of course, be symbols as well as rewards that have tangible value. Plaques, medals, and citations are examples of potential extrinsic rewards.

who leads is inevitably guided, consciously or more probably unconsciously, by a philosophy of leadership. The issue is not *whether* to hold a philosophy but rather what kind and, more important, what is the philosophy based on? A leader assumes an awesome responsibility because the heart of leadership is influence and control *of other human beings*. Similarly, the issue is not *whether* to control. Even though a democracy is based on individual freedom, which means being independent and *free* of control, its citizens do not have a choice of whether or not they will be led. As Haiman put it, "whenever two or more men form a society and live together there is no such thing as uncontrolled, unrestricted, uninfluenced behavior."[13]

Chapters 1 and 2 began the discussion of philosophy with the contention that the development of the individual is our prime concern. There the orientation was the relationship of individuals to others in collaborative action. Some of the questions whose answers have already been attempted are the following: For what purposes should individuals engage in collaborative action? What are the relative advantages and disadvantages of discussion? What effect will a given style of leadership have on the productivity and morale of the group?

In any thinking process, collective or individual, two functions must be performed—ideas must be created and ideas must be judged. Another conclusion is that in addition to the *task* goals and *maintenance* goals, there should be a third major goal: the *training* of participants. Each group experience can add to our store of knowledge about leadership, and we ought to get better and better at collaborative activity. No one is perfect so it is inevitable that we will make mistakes. But let's hope they are at least new mistakes as evidence of our growth.

Leader–Group Orientation

The leader's first task is to decide on a fundamental approach to a given group and a given set of circumstances. There is no need to repeat the distinctions between leader types and leader methods nor the philosophical issues already examined. But both the *quantity* and *kind of control* exercised by the leader are important. The assumption here is that the leader has decided to forego control over content as much as possible, wishes some form of democratic procedure, and will resort to authoritarian control only when absolutely necessary.

It is surely clear by now that we prefer the more democratic concepts of leadership on the grounds that persuasion rather than coercion is the better way of securing changed belief and action. Yet we are not indicting all authoritarian behavior as "bad." Sometimes strong control is the lesser evil. Moralizing about leadership is easy; practicing what we preach is more difficult. The leader who feels a need to use authoritarian means should not, therefore, always be made to feel guilty about the choice.

Again, the issue is the amount and kind of control over process. Some leaders will attempt too little control as often as others attempt too much. When working with peers, leaders often attempt too little control, as evidenced by the practice of most student leaders in our discussion classes. When rank, status, or age put something of

---

[13]Franklyn S. Haiman, "The Dynamics of Leadership," in *Small Group Communication*, eds. Robert S. Cathcart and Larry A. Samovar (Dubuque, Iowa: William C. Brown Company, Publishers, 1970), p. 358.

a gulf between leader and follower, leaders tend to exercise too much control. Each individual, of course, must determine his or her own proclivities.

Beginning teachers are usually advised to err on the side of too much control rather than too little. The reasoning is that it is far easier to give up control as the class matures than it is to regain it later. The basis of leader–group orientation should be solid respect for accomplishment. When leaders relinquish unnecessary control, therefore, they are subtly complimenting the group. But when leaders seek to impose order upon chaos, they often find themselves accused of tyranny.

The Philosophical Contradiction

Doubtless some conditions demand autocracy. We do not allow small children to discover by themselves that it is dangerous to run into the streets. We do not expect drivers at a crowded intersection to discuss the alternatives and create their own answers to the flow of traffic. We do not expect an orchestra conductor to call for votes during a performance of *Aida*. Such circumstances, and dozens of others that any of us could name, are so obvious that we tend to eliminate them when we are thinking about a philosophy of leadership. These are not to be included, we say, in our thinking about group discussion. But we cannot dismiss the matter so lightly. Children grow up, traffic laws must be enacted, and musical scores need interpretation.

Someone has to draw the line. Someone has to decide when children are old enough to assume responsibilities as well as when nascent nations are capable of self-government. Someone has to draw the line between those who have the right to create and decide and those who do not. It may be true that "no man is an island," but we do not expect to have a vote in the faculty meetings of other universities.

Our ways of drawing these lines are curious and often contradictory. Eighteen is now the legal voting age. Most states allow a 16-year old to have a driver's license. In some states girls can buy liquor when they are 18, but boys must wait until they are 21. The age at which young people can marry without parental consent varies from state to state.

Our ways of drawing the lines for those who have the right to decide are equally curious and contradictory. Corporations permit stockholders to vote in proportion to the amount of money they have invested, but employees who have invested their lives may have no vote. Membership in some organizations may be bought; in others it may be a right of family; in others simply attending a meeting and signifying intent may be sufficient; in still others membership selection is complicated and rigorous.

When we ask *who* draws either kind of line, we come face to face with the philosophical contradiction. It is the colonial power, not the colony, that decides when the colony is ready for self-government; it is the parent, not the children, who decides when the children may assume responsibility; it is the school administration, not the students, who decide what control and power the student government is to have; it is the teacher, not the students, who decides the amount of democracy that shall prevail in the classroom. True, in all the cases a revolution may force the prevailing power to relinquish some or all of the control, but the concept that authority stems from the top is unaffected.

If we contend that the end does not justify the means (more about this later in this chapter) and if we believe that authoritarian means are undesirable, we face the philosophical contradiction in two ways. First, as we have pointed out, there are circumstances that seem to demand authoritarian behavior. This is not a terribly severe contradiction in itself. It is the second that seems to be more contradictory. *Securing the right to create and decide depends on the benevolence of the authority—even in situations in which the leaders believe that they are behaving democratically.*

We are not necessarily dismayed by this contradiction, however. We believe in the concepts of democratic leadership, but we wish to recognize the fact that we, at least, are unable to piece together a single uniform philosophy out of one piece of cloth. We believe that a philosophy should be dynamic and growing as the holder grows in insight and understanding. Even though our own philosophy is not completely consistent, we hope that we are able to keep the aim of our behavior consistent. As we have said, that aim is enhancing the dignity of the individual.

Bases for Establishing Degree of Control

What, then, are some of the factors that condition the leader's choice of the degree of control?

Group Expectations of Structure. What the group expects of a leader is a function of the group's norms, climate, and degree of maturity. How does one gauge the group's expectations? Berkowitz found that most people seem to feel the leader should assume strong control over process *when task pressures are not perceived to be urgent.* [14] He included the qualification that group cohesiveness and satisfaction *decreased* as leadership sharing increased, although productivity remained about the same under both conditions. Apparently most people assume that the primary responsibility for group success rests with the designated leader.

In groups characterized by a competitive climate a strong leader must obviously control process. The leader becomes a kind of umpire or referee upon whom group members depend to ensure that one side does not gain some advantage.

Immature groups also expect leader control even though they may deny their desire. In books dealing with child rearing it has become commonplace to note that children actually desire clear, fair, and rigorously enforced rules. Immature groups of adults are similar. We recall an instance of a newly formed group that deliberated at length about whether to elevate one of its members to leader or to go outside the group's membership to seek a leader. This controversy occurred despite the fact that the group contained more than one leader of proven ability.

Another immature group was desperately in need of some structure, but the members persisted in believing that they liked their relaxed and informal manner. The group's process was so chaotic that one member actually did what many frustrated discussants have often wanted to do. He got up and punched another member on the nose. He also resigned. The leader came to us for guidance and we suggested that she begin extending control by carefully planning agendas, by securing individual commitments to provide evidence in advance of the meeting, and by physically arranging her living room to make herself the focus of attention. It worked. The

[14]Leonard Berkowitz, "Sharing Leadership in Small, Decision-Making Groups," in *Small Groups: Studies in Social Interaction*, rev. ed., eds. A. Paul Hare, Edgar F. Borgotta, and Robert F. Bales (New York: Alfred A. Knopf, Inc., 1965), pp. 675–87.

group began to accomplish more with greater leader control, and this level of achievement led in turn to greater solidarity and group pride.

The point of the foregoing analysis is that the leader should conform, at least initially, to group expectations of structure. It is true that imposing extensive controls on a mature group will almost certainly be resented. But allowing most groups to work out their own structure will generally prove disappointing unless members accept their task as urgent. As pointed out in the next chapter, the nature of the group cannot be modified if the leader refuses to accept the group as it is first.

Task Urgency. When group members perceive the task to be urgent, they worry less about how they think the leader should behave. The reason is obvious. If members are sufficiently concerned about the task, they do not care who does the job as long as the job is done. We have pointed out that in times of crisis, groups are willing to grant their leaders extraordinary powers. A group will also be more willing to share leadership.

Whenever possible, get members to perceive the task as urgent. Get them involved and concerned. Barnlund and Haiman felt so keenly about this point that they devoted an entire chapter of their book to the question of apathy and the problem of involvement.[15] How do leaders get members to perceive task urgency? First, they must stimulate involvement so that members come prepared to work. Second, they must initiate the task so that its urgency becomes apparent. But leaders should resist the temptation to arrogate control unto themselves, even though the group is willing.

Group Purpose. If the group's needs are personal, structure is less necessary than when the group is organized for task purposes.

Group Size. The larger the group, the greater the need for structure.

Leader Skills. Your own skills as a leader will affect the amount and kind of control you attempt. To attempt limited control and to share leadership functions are unquestionably difficult. Sharing requires insight, timing, and skill not usually possessed by beginning leaders. It is usually easier to do the job yourself than to get someone else to do it, but the easier way is seldom the best.

Attitude Toward Others

Are people basically good or basically evil? Are people naturally cooperative or competitive? Are people wise or foolish? These questions have troubled thinkers, theologians, philosophers, artists, poets, businessmen, politicians, and educators for centuries. We will now group together some of the positions that have been taken on the capacity of people, in general, to create and judge ideas.

Most People Can Neither Create Ideas Nor Judge Them. The fundamental position of authoritarians is that people in general are capable of neither creativity nor judg-

[15]Dean C. Barnlund and Franklyn S. Haiman, *The Dynamics of Discussion* (Boston: Houghton Mifflin Company, 1960), chap. 10.

ment. They must be told what to do and, if necessary, be compelled to do it. Plato put the issue squarely when he contended that the wisest should rule; the philosophers should be kings.

Most People Can Create Ideas But Cannot Judge Them. When the responsibility for a decision is levied specifically upon an individual rather than upon a group, there is evidence for the philosophy that most people can create ideas but cannot judge them. In any large organization, for example, the people at the top have the ultimate responsibility for the decisions that are made. However, their very position makes it difficult for them to create ideas, for they are apt to be isolated from the product, the equipment, and the average employee. They really don't know what is going on and must depend on subordinates to create ideas, which they will judge.

Some organizations that adopt this philosophy go to great lengths to stimulate creativity within the ranks. Suggestion boxes and bonuses are used to encourage employees to create ideas. Many of the brainstorming projects discussed in Chapter 10 reflect this point of view. The brainstorming group creates but does not judge the ideas. Out of the dozens of ideas produced, those responsible for the decision may find one or two that they deem usable.

Most People Can Judge Ideas But Cannot Create Them. Those who hold this point of view contend that is the responsibility of the leaders to supply the ideas and information and to communicate these effectively to the people, who can then judge. The argument for this particular stand is that most people do not have the training or experience to enable them to create many ideas, but they do have the capacity for judging the ideas of the experts. In any society that claims to be democratic, there must be this kind of confidence in the judgment of the people. From the distinction drawn in the previous chapter it is apparent that both the first and second points of view are usually associated with autocratic philosophies. The crucial aspect is the control over decisions and this third point of view places that control in the hands of the people affected by the decision.

Most People Can Both Create Ideas and Judge Them. In his book *Group-Centered Leadership* Thomas Gordon came directly to grips with these various concepts concerning the capacity of people.[16] He concluded that our inadequacies stem not from lack of capacity but from lack of opportunity.

Of course, this point of view must be based on a society in which people have access to information and education and are relatively free of tyranny. Personal security is required if people are to come forward with ideas that may or may not be successful. When people are fearful or threatened, they turn to authoritarian leaders and their own efforts at creativity grow fewer and fewer.[17] In many ways this is an idealized point of view that is possible only with many qualifications. Yet that does not mean it is unattainable.

Any of the four positions just discussed may be easily attacked by attempting to push an advocate into an all-or-nothing argument. Examples that seem to contradict each of these philosophies come readily to mind. Certainly one can find people who,

[16]Gordon, *Group-Centered Leadership*, chap. 2.

[17]See Stephen M. Sales, "Authoritarianism," *Psychology Today*, 6, no. 6 (November 1972), 94–98, 140–42.

even with all the opportunity and training in the world, will not be able to judge or create ideas. Certainly there are differences in the capacities of individuals, but such arguments miss the point. Let us examine these philosophies more closely in the framework of the ends–means dilemma.

Ends and Means

We have all heard people say, "I approve of his objective, but I don't like his methods." Usually this is an attempt to apologize for or rationalize a position. When college athletic directors are accused of under-the-table subsidies for promising athletes, they usually point to the fact that other athletic directors do the same thing and "If you want us to win, we have to compete for the best players."

It is easy to theorize and conclude that the end does not justify the means. The end inheres in the means employed. We have the formula and historical antecedents; Aristotle insisted upon the "right method"; Quintilian pointed out that the aim of the orator, a leader by our definition, was to speak well, for his *art* consists in the *act*, and not in the result. In modern times we see higher courts overturn convictions of patently guilty people because wrong methods were used to secure convictions. Yes, we have the theory. The only trouble is that it is very difficult to distinguish those ends and means.

The inner-directed man of an earlier day had an easier time of it. He knew what was right and what was wrong. His methods had the imprint of history and who could doubt their validity? His code of honor was secure. But our world is no longer so neatly ordered. Recent developments in fields from anthropology to zoology have changed our comfortably static world into a dynamic one in which ends and means become almost hopelessly entangled.

To illustrate, a cause of something is usually called the *means*, and the effect is usually called the *end*. We are disturbed about juvenile delinquency. This is a bad end, we say, and we are determined to discover and eradicate the cause. Some insist, "There are no juvenile delinquents, only delinquent parents." The parents must be the cause! But reason makes us ponder. Those parents must have causes for their behavior. Aren't people responsible for their behavior before they become parents? Or is parenthood an alchemy that transforms people into responsible citizens? Let us look further. The movies, TV, and comics display violence and lust. Perhaps they are the cause and we should rigidly censor them. But then someone points out that it is impossible to shield children from violence and lust. Some people tend to react to and distort these stimuli, although others are able to put them into proportion. Is the cause within the child? Can geneticists help us? No. They have also compounded the problem by discovering a seemingly infinite number of genes and an astronomical number of combinations that interact dynamically. Fortunately, we are a patient lot for the most part and we keep experimenting, trying, hoping, and working, for we do not like to admit defeat. And we make gains even when we are not quite able to explain why.

In our private dream worlds, most of us are like Thurber's Walter Mitty and we believe that, given the chance, we could come up with brilliant performances, even though we lack experience, as doctor, statesman, or trapeze artist. We know better, of course. We must learn; we must experience; or we are impotent. The squeaks from the violin are a necessary prelude to the proficient musician. Practice alone will not make us proficient for we can practice mistakes. ("Practice makes permanent.") We will undoubtedly need guidance as well as practice. Capacity in discussion is no different.

To the Extent That People Have No Opportunity to Create Ideas, They Become Incapable of Creativity. The requirements of creativity discussed earlier emphasized opportunity. In many organizations this opportunity is reserved for the few. "Stay out of trouble" is often the way employees describe how they may succeed. Even if an idea occurs to them, therefore, they will probably not consider it wise to express that idea. Even in groups that apparently encourage free expression of ideas, the prevailing norms may be such that ideas that deviate sharply from the accepted way of doing things may be rejected. Thus, the full range of creativity and opportunity to learn how to be creative may be denied.

In our school systems there are many pressures to restrict the creativity of students. Some of these pressures are well known. One example is manifest in the behavior of the child whose natural curiosity is discouraged by parents and teachers, who tell the child to stop asking questions. Another instance is the teacher who requires students to regurgitate his or her own lectures on the examination—a process that someone once described as the transference of ideas from the teacher's notes to the students' notes and back without having passed through the mind of anybody. Such practices obviously stifle creativity.

Today, the College Board Examinations, the National Merit Examinations, and other proficiency and personality tests are assuming great importance. By scoring well on such standardized examinations, high-school graduates receive scholarships, obtain advanced standing in college, and get admitted to special college courses designed for the superior student. By means of such tests, many businesses hire, classify, and promote their employees.[18]

There is considerable doubt about the merit of these tests as measures of superior ability[19] and severe criticism of their white, middle-class orientation, which systematically excludes nonwhite, non–middle-class students. For survival, many students who see these tests as the difference between open and closed doors and as their principal means of advancement become professional test takers. The point here is that learning to perform effectively on such tests may itself inhibit creative potential. Our hypothesis is that students' training in conventional test taking, whether accidental or designed, has all too often rendered them uncertain and unskilled when creativity is required.

To the Extent That People Have No Opportunity to Judge Ideas, They Become Incapable of Judgment. This conclusion is obviously analogous to the previous one about creativity, and the arguments in defense of it are similar. Most people are familiar with the story of the old farmhand who had worked hard and loyally for many years. His employer, seeking to give him a job that would not tax his failing strength but would

[18]William H. Whyte, Jr., *The Organization Man* (Garden City, N.Y.: Doubleday & Co., Inc., 1957), has an amusing and pathetic chapter, "How to Cheat on Personality Tests." It is amusing because of its style; pathetic because it may be all too true.

[19]See Paul B. Diederich, "Pitfalls in the Measurement of Gains in Achievement," *The School Review*, 64, (February 1956), 59–63. See also Jacob W. Getzels and Philip W. Jackson, *Creativity and Intelligence* (New York: John Wiley & Sons, Inc., 1962).

allow him to maintain his income and self-respect, set him to work sorting potatoes. The bad potatoes were cast aside, and the good ones were to be sacked for shipment. When the farmer came to check on the man's progress, he found him sitting exhausted and distraught with the work scarcely begun. "What's the trouble?" he asked. "Surely the work isn't too heavy?" "No, boss," the employee replied. "The work is light enough, but all these decisions are killing me!"

The story is a joke, but, like many jokes, it has a basis in fact. Those schooled solely in obedience usually make poor judges. Kurt Lewin put it well when discussing the effects of authoritarian, democratic, and laissez-faire leadership. "The change from autocracy to democracy seemed to take somewhat more time than from democracy to autocracy. Autocracy is imposed upon the individual. Democracy he has to learn."[20]

The problems many college students have in adjusting to the greater freedom of the college environment is illustrative. A dormitory counselor reported that many of the girls in her dormitory had never so much as decided, before they came to college, what clothes they would wear in the morning—let alone such matters as when, how, or if they should study. Since most college students are faced with making many more decisions than they had to make, or were allowed to make, in high school, we have the basis for the old dilemma facing counselors, teachers, and administrators. How much control over student behavior should be exercised? Should compulsory study hours be established? How much latitude should the student be given in choosing courses? What attendance policy should the teacher establish? On the one hand is the idea that the students should be on their own and not be spoonfed; on the other is the worry about students who fail or drop out but who might have succeeded had they been helped by being required to do certain things. All agree that much of the problem *for the college* would be solved if the students were more mature, if they had more experience in making responsible decisions, before they came to college.

It should come as no surprise that those who have observed only authoritarian structures, or people suddenly thrust into democratic structures, often believe that people in general are incapable of either creativity or judgment. When Alexander Hamilton uttered his famous statement, "The People, sir, are a great beast," he was not alone in his opinion. The men who framed our Constitution were generally chary of entrusting very much responsibility to the citizenry. The wonder is not that the vote was restricted to one adult in five; the wonder is that so much power was given to the citizens at all. Many argued for a monarchy, and the experiences in Europe seemed to support such claims. No one can say what kind of document might have resulted had our Constitution been drafted during the excesses of the French Revolution.

It also should come as no surprise that, even in democratic groups, most ideas are created by the leaders. As pointed out earlier, leaders feel most keenly about tasks to be performed. They thus apply themselves to the task more vigorously than those less involved. When the leaders create the ideas and when the group holds the final decision-making power, the leaders must persuade. Here again, however, we face the dilemma. If the leaders spend their primary energies creating ideas and persuading others to accept them, the creative capacity of the rest of the group may diminish.

[20]Kurt Lewin, "The Consequences of an Authoritarian and Democratic Leadership," in *Studies in Leadership*, ed. Alvin W. Gouldner (New York: Harper Brothers, Publishers, 1950), p. 417.

If the leaders spend their primary energies helping the others release their creative potential, they run the risk of not adequately coping with the task requirements.

The Case for Shared Leadership

Effective styles of leadership and business management must be reflections of changing needs, forces, and circumstances. It is best not to label leaders by terms like *permissive* or *strong*, but to think more in terms of flexibility and outcome.

Attitudes about work relationships and employer–employee roles have recently changed. *Job enrichment, work modules,* and *self-governing employee teams* illustrate the evolving trends. Employers and management consultants are collaborating to counteract some of the dehumanizing aspects of routine, assembly-line operations.

In their report, *The Changing World of Work,* the members of the Forty-third American Assembly noted:

> . . . Employees want challenge and personal growth, but work tends to be simplified and over-specialized. Employees want to be involved in patterns of mutual influence, but organizations are characterized by decision-making concentrated at the top. Employees want careers and self-development but organizations design rigid career paths that sometimes impede fulfillment of these goals. Employees want more opportunity to achieve self-esteem, but many organizations emphasize impersonality. . . . Employers should place the same emphasis toward the design of human work that they have long placed upon the design of the physical plant.[21]

Among the corporations that have responded to the need for a more creative approach to the world of work is General Foods, which replaced supervisors with team leaders and made the teams self-governing (they take care of their own maintenance and quality control, for example). The plan was so successful at its Topeka, Kansas, plant, that General Foods has redesigned other plants as well. Corning Glass in Medfield, Massachusetts, reorganized so that individual workers assemble and are responsible for complete products.

In his article, "The Work Module—A Tonic for Lunchpail Lassitude," Robert L. Kahn rejected the old notion of fitting individuals into jobs. His premise is that "workers are happier when they can construct the job than they are when the job constructs them."[22] Kahn's modules would permit employees at the bottom of the hierarchy some of the same flexibility that their bosses have in choosing what kind of work to do when. Alvin Zander found that "a worker may strive harder for the success of his group than for himself. A unified group that can set its own goals develops its own aspirations and will rise to meet them."[23]

---

[21]*The Changing World of Work,* Report of the Forty-third American Assembly (New York: Columbia University, 1973), pp. 4–5.

[22]Robert L. Kahn, "The Work Module—A Tonic for Lunchpail Lassitude," *Psychology Today,* 6, no. 9 (February 1973), 35–39, 94–95. See also William J. Roche and Neil L. MacKinnon, "Motivating People With Meaningful Work," *Harvard Business Review,* May-June 1970; and J. Richard Hackman and Greg R. Oldham, "Development of the Job Diagnostic Survey," *Journal of Applied Psychology,* 60 (1975), 159–70.

[23]Alvin F. Zander, "Team Spirit Vs. the Individual Achiever," *Psychology Today,* 8, no. 6 (November 1974), 64–68.

The concepts of team management and shared leadership are not new. We have already cited McGregor's famous Theory X and Theory Y styles of management. Rensis Likert, through his Institute of Social Research at the University of Michigan, has conducted many studies and accumulated much data to support the idea that employee-centered supervisors are more effective than production-centered supervisors. [24]

Despite the evidence to support the advantages of shared leadership, putting the concept into practice, particularly in large bureaucracies, seems to be as difficult as it has always been. Hampton, Summer, and Webber feel that managers go by intuition and ignore the evidence. Among the points they make are these:

> 1.   *We too often assume that organization change is for "those people downstairs," who are somehow perceived as less intelligent and less productive than "those upstairs."* . . .
>
> 2.   *We need to reduce our fond attachment for both unilateral and delegated approaches to change.* . . .
>
> The findings discussed in this article highlight the use of the more difficult, but perhaps more fruitful, *shared power* approach. As top managers join in to open up their power structures and their organizations to an exchange of influence between upper and lower levels, they may be unleashing new surges of energy and creativity not previously imagined. [25]

Although it must be apparent that we feel the case for shared and participatory leadership is a good one, we are not unmindful of the attendant problems. Jane Mansbridge identified time, emotion, and inequality as three distinct problems in participatory groups. [26] There is also the difficulty of training for leadership. Most people agree that leaders are made rather than born, but not all agree on how or even whether leadership training is possible. Fiedler, for example, has said the enormous investment organizations make in training leaders has produced little measurable return. [27]

But there seems to be no substitute for the satisfaction people get from sharing decisions, responsibilities, and work. Mansbridge concluded her article with the following statement:

> If an organization wants to govern itself as a participatory democracy . . . it won't be easy. The decision-making process will take much longer than in hierarchical, representational systems. It will be much more emotional than

[24]Rensis Likert, "An Emerging Theory of Organization, Leadership, and Management," in *Leadership and Interpersonal Behavior* eds. Luigi Petrullo and Leonard Bass (New York: Holt, Rinehart and Winston, Inc., 1961), pp. 290–309; and Rensis Likert, *The Human Organization* (New York: McGraw-Hill Book Company, Inc., 1967).

[25]David R. Hampton, Charles E. Summer, and Ross A. Webber, *Organizational Behavior and the Practice of Management*, rev. ed. (Glenview, Ill.: Scott, Foresman & Co., 1973), p. 910.

[26]Jane J. Mansbridge, "Time, Emotion, and Inequality: Three Problems of Participatory Groups," *Journal of Applied Behavioral Science*, 9, no. 2/3 (1973), 351–68.

[27]Fred E. Fiedler, "The Trouble With Leadership Training Is That It Doesn't Train Leaders," *Psychology Today*, 6, no. 9 (1973), 23–30, 92.

in impersonal, secret-ballot, strictly majoritarian systems. Ingrained inequalities will become apparent and will prove extremely frustrating and difficult to overcome. But the energy, creativity, excitement, and commitment generated in the process can be worth it. Once one has belonged to a good participatory group, it is hard to return to conventional, hierarchical decision making. [28]

We conclude with one final reference that whimsically (but truthfully) points out that shared leadership can be for selfish as well as altruistic reasons.

There is the matter of what kind of monarchy you are going to have. Pippin leaned strongly toward the constitutional form, not only because he was a liberal man at heart, but also because the responsibility of absolutism is very great. He owned himself too lazy to make all the effort for success and too cowardly to take all the blame for mistakes. [29]

SUMMARY

This chapter has dealt with leadership functions involved in getting the job done (task) and in interpersonal aspects (maintenance) and the following special functions and problems: stimulating involvement and commitment, regulating participation, building solidarity and cohesiveness, handling agendas, executing decisions, and distributing rewards. We then discussed some of the problems and dilemmas involved in developing a personal philosophy of leadership.

DISCUSSION QUESTIONS

1.   As our society becomes more complex, technical, and overwhelming, can we expect the average person to be able to cope with the critical issues of our times?

2.   Plan a discussion that explores the moral implications of some means-and-ends problems of leadership.

3.   Organize a small group discussion with other students to analyze how the task and maintenance functions have been handled in your class. What recommendations will you take back to the class as a whole?

EXERCISES

1.   Select two or three leaders you know and can observe over a period of 30 days. First engage each in a discussion designed to reveal a philosophy of leadership. Summarize the impressions you derive and check these for accuracy with the respective leaders. Then observe the leaders as they function. To what extent do the verbal statements agree with observed behavior? If there are significant differences, do you feel they are justified?

[28]Mansbridge, "Time, Emotion, and Inequality," p. 367.

[29]John Steinbeck, *The Short Reign of Pippin IV* (New York: The Viking Press, Inc., 1957), p. 57.

2.   Begin a systematic formulation and statement of your own philosophy of leadership by outlining on paper both its foundations and superstructure. Next consider the extent to which you have been guided by this philosophy in the past.

3.   In what ways has the leadership to which you have been subjected encouraged or retarded your personal growth and creativity? Consider relationships with parents, siblings, teachers, friends, and employers.

4.   Describe the person within your own acquaintanceship who is the most effective leader. Use some of the criteria from this chapter to evaluate as well as explain his or her attributes.

SELECTED READINGS

BORMANN, ERNEST G., *Discussion and Group Methods: Theory and Practice* (2nd ed.), chap. 11. New York: Harper & Row, Publishers, 1975.

CARLYLE, THOMAS. Several of Carlyle's writings reveal his point of view. They may be found in a variety of sources such as *The Works of Thomas Carlyle*. New York: P. F. Collier Publishing, 1897. Among the more important titles are: *Heroes, Hero-Worship and the Heroic in History* and *Past and Present*.

FISHER, B. AUBREY, *Small Group Decision Making: Communication and the Group Process*, chap. 5. New York: McGraw-Hill Book Company, Inc., 1974.

GORDON, THOMAS, *Group-Centered Leadership*. Boston: Houghton Mifflin Company, 1955.

JEFFERSON, THOMAS. Almost all Jefferson's writings are pertinent. An excellent single-volume collection is Adrienne Koch and William Peden, eds., *The Life and Selected Writings of Thomas Jefferson*. New York: The Modern Library, Inc., 1944.

STOGDILL, RALPH M., *Handbook of Leadership: A Survey of Theory and Research*, pts. V, VII. New York: The Free Press, 1974.

chapter 14

The finest leader may be frustrated if the group is inadequate—if group norms are unrealistic, if the group climate is competitive, if the group is immature, or if the other members have not begun to reach their potential. What you can do to improve the nature of your group is one of the subjects of this chapter.

The first question we address is, can the individual affect the nature of the group? The answer is *yes*. Throughout this book there has been evidence that the individual is not helpless. For additional evidence look at the results of an interesting experiment conducted by William Haythorn.[1] He found that *able* discussants could significantly affect the characteristics of small groups. The word *able* is emphasized because Haythorn found that successful individuals were described as cooperative, efficient, and possessed of insight. They were also mature and accepting individuals. These findings support the point made here from the beginning: that the dull and inarticulate can expect little success, but groups feel the impact of the able person.

Those who initiate change will probably be among the group's leaders, and members who have little influence will not be likely to accomplish very much directly. Nonetheless, the term *leader* is not used to designate the person who initiates or creates the change; instead, we use the term *change agent*.[2] This term may identify one who produces the change directly or one whose limited power compels her or him to operate indirectly. Still another reason for using the term is that it more accurately connotes the functions to be performed. No one can literally change another's belief or behavior. A change agent can, however, create circumstances that may induce another to change.

Introducing and effecting change or a new order of things are activities not everyone is willing to undertake. They involve risk and creativity—risk because the venture may fail and cause a blow to the ego, and creativity because not everyone sees the possibility of or the value in change. The person with a vision of how the group might be improved, the person with a sense of constructive discontent, is destined to be the change agent.

[1]William Haythorn, "The Influence of Individual Members on the Characteristics of Small Groups," in *Small Groups: Studies in Social Interaction*, rev. ed., eds. A. Paul Hare, Edgar F. Borgatta, and Robert F. Bales (New York: Alfred A. Knopf, Inc., 1965), pp. 287–98.

[2]Lippitt, Watson, and Westley used this term. Much of their theoretical and practical analyses is reflected in this chapter. See Ronald Lippitt, Jeanne Watson, and Bruce Westley, *The Dynamics of Planned Change* (New York: Harcourt, Brace & World, Inc., 1958); Warren G. Bennis, Kenneth D. Benne, and Robert Chin, eds., *The Planning of Change* (New York: Holt, Rinehart and Winston, Inc., 1964); and Everett M. Rogers, *Diffusion of Innovations: A Cross Cultural Approach* (New York: The Free Press, 1969).

Modifying the Group and Moving It to Action

Much of the literature about means of producing or engineering change causes considerable resentment because many people feel that engineering change means manipulating others. We all like to change, but not to *be* changed. Some feel the dignity of the individual is at stake. The change agent seems to array the forces in the group in such a fashion that individuals are changed without being aware of the fact, that individuals are pawns in the game of group discussion.

Because we have a keen awareness of this charge, the techniques in this chapter are all cards-on-the-table practices. Sometimes such techniques take more time than undercover manipulation, but consequences for both the group and the change agent are worth the added effort. The leader who is suspected of manipulation will confront an increasingly hostile and suspicious group; change produced by trickery can boomerang. But the line between facilitative leadership and manipulation is difficult to draw. We feel that the leader's intent is the key; it is never *our* intent to advocate that leaders manipulate people against their will or without their awareness.

CREATING NEW NORMS

When group operations are ineffective, inadequate norms are often to blame. Norms that emerge implicitly from group interaction and especially those based largely in social reality tend to cause groups the most trouble. The trouble arises because, first, the group is often unaware of either the existence or effect of such norms; and second, changing inappropriate norms based in social reality is more difficult than changing inappropriate norms based in objective reality.

That's why we now examine only those techniques for creating new norms to replace those norms both explicit and implicit based primarily in social reality. Little can be done about norms that are a part of the larger culture, and tools have already been presented for dealing with norms based in objective reality.

Inappropriate Norms

The norms identified here are representative of those that often cause trouble. The list is suggestive, certainly not exhaustive. Every individual must examine his or her own group to identify those norms that facilitate profitable discussion and those that hinder it.

Time-wasting norms. Many accepted norms may only waste time, but this charge alone justifies their examination. Simple lack of skill in discussion may perpetuate the norm—"That's how we've always done it." Often, however, the cause is at least partly rooted in personal insecurity. Let's look at some typical time-wasters.

> 1.   Using meeting time to report activities. "Everyone should be informed about what others have been doing since we met last," is often the defense for spending hours of group time listening to recitals of details. Of course we should be informed. But is the group meeting the best time or way to do it? It may be. Or would it be better to distribute written reports and save valuable time? When the group was new, small, and when it met often, written reports probably seemed unnecessary and even pretentious. Now

that the group is larger, the practice of oral reports persists simply out of habit. The norm is easily changed, however. In one group the chairman and other members recognized their problem and literally kidded themselves out of the practice by referring to the routine reports as show-and-tell functions. Occasionally routine reports were necessary, but the group was able to agree to avoid oral reports unless they were intended to form the basis for group action.

2.   Using the group to spread responsibility. This is a troublesome norm because it is difficult to decide when a particular problem is or should be an individual responsibility, a subgroup responsibility, or a responsibility of the whole group. The norm that everyone in the group should always bear the responsibility for decisions may well need to be changed. If the norm exists because people are too insecure to cope with personal responsibility, the issue may be individual or collective maturity and the norm is a symptom of the problem. But if the people have been simply distorting the "two heads are better than one" concept, norm changes may serve the purpose.

Time-wasting norms are legion, but these two will suffice to point out the problem. In general, whenever you feel that the group is taking too much time, ask yourself this question: Must we go through all these steps with all these people? In examining your own groups you may find several norms that serve no purpose other than delaying action. Sometimes, of course, such a practice was established for precisely the purpose of delay, in order to prevent hasty or ill-considered action. Bicameral legislative structures have this as one of their avowed objectives.

Talk–Action Imbalance. If we are to believe popular stereotypes, people of action in the business community scorn talk and make instant decisions. College professors, on the other hand, are supposed to seldom make decisions but cheerfully talk an idea to death. Probably neither stereotype is very useful, though not always unreal. If it seems that undue stress is put upon securing action, it is probably because we have been so frustrated by nonproductive talk in the past. If prevailing group norms favor one extreme or the other of the talk–action balance, they may need to be changed.

Unrealistic Standards. The standards by which the worth of our actions is measured are often unrealistic. Sometimes they are too high. Some students feel they have failed if they do not get an A; some teachers expect too much of their students; some managers in business drive subordinates toward impossible levels of achievement. However, most groups typically tend to set standards that are below their potential abilities.

The nature of the forces that restrain standards is much too complicated to explain in general terms. Each case must be examined to understand why standards are not higher, or lower, as the case might be. The framework for this analysis is discussed along with the procedures for producing change.

Opposition to Change Itself. This norm is widespread and pernicious. Browne put the problem clearly and identified an interesting antidote:

A change becomes terrifying when it is not expected and when it has not been taken into account in planning. Therefore, people don't want things to be different because no established plan of action will fit into the conditions which arise when differences are introduced into a situation. The development of "a set to be set for that which we are not set for" would take the terror and the dread out of change.[3]

Browne's advice that groups develop a "set to be set for that which we are not set for," suggests that some groups do develop a tolerance for change and may even welcome it. From Heraclitus to Korzybski great thinkers have insisted that the only constant is change itself; but far too many individuals and groups seek to freeze the present.

Genuine conservatism that insists on basing change on tested principles is, naturally, not out of date; nor are all who advocate change doing the group a favor. Any given change may be good or bad. It is just that the person who proposes the change has the burden of proof, as well as the responsibility for proving the change is an improvement. But change is inevitable and even the status quo must be considered dynamic. Thus, a group whose norms include resistance to change, come what may, is headed for trouble.

This list of inappropriate norms may help you perform the first step—discovering the norm(s) that may be causing trouble. Once you have done this, you are ready to begin the change process.

Changing Inappropriate Norms

Before you rush forth, determined to rid your group of its vanities, shibboleths, and crippling beliefs, remember that your task will be difficult and slow. Norms based on social reality are not easily changed. Moreover, a *direct attack* on such norms will probably have two consequences—the norm will become more firmly entrenched than ever, and you may find yourself a group outcast. Thus, take care to note both the techniques that follow and the sequence in which they appear. And remember that patience and persistence may well be your most important tools.

Accept the Norm. This advice has been given before. Accepting a norm involves at least three actions: (1) acknowledging the reality of the norm, (2) understanding the meaning and implication of the norm, and (3) subjecting one's self to the influence of the norm. There are two reasons for accepting the norm. First, it may be tactically necessary. In a classical study of the process of norm changing, Ferenc Merei demonstrated that would-be leaders who failed to accept the group's norms proved to be ineffectual and did not become true leaders.[4] Merei's experiments used children as subjects, but many other experiments and case studies, particularly those of therapists, confirm the point. He who would change another's belief must first accept that belief.

[3]C. G. Browne, "Leadership and Change," in *The Study of Leadership*, eds. C. G. Browne and Thomas S. Cohn (Danville, Ill.: Interstate Printers & Publishers, 1958), pp. 419–20.

[4]Ferenc Merei, "Group Leadership and Institutionalization," *Human Relations*, 2 (1949), 23–40.

The second reason for accepting the norm is that it subjects you to its influence. Once you have accepted the norm, you may be less inclined to want to change it because you may discover that it is much more appropriate than it seemed before. However, if you accept and understand the norm and still find it wanting, you will have experienced the total impact of the norm and will be in a better position to assess the scope of your task of changing it. You will be ready to take the next step.

Analyze the Norm. This step contains three parts. First, you must analyze the nature of the norm itself. Second, you must identify the actual effects of the norm on group process. (You probably began both these steps when you first determined that you had spotted an inappropriate norm.) Third, you should try to discover why the norm came into existence in the first place.

When you analyze the nature of the norm you should ask several questions. Is the norm broad and general, capable of infinite interpretations, or is it rigid and specific? If it is the former, you may not need to change the norm but merely alter the interpretation. You should also ask whether the norm is clearly perceived or whether it is distorted. In an intriguing set of experiments Tuddenham found that distorted norms produced less conformity than unambiguous norms, but they still affected the group.[5] For illustrations of the use of distorted norms, read some of the speeches that Mussolini and Hitler gave during their rise to power. These speeches are full of fascinating and horrifying examples of norms distorted to serve their purposes. Some of the finest norms of Christianity, national feeling, and pride were distorted into norms that apparently justified some of the most inhumane behavior the world has seen.

Knowing the cause of the norm is important. For example, the practice of oath-taking originated during a time when people believed that supernatural powers were invoked when certain words were uttered. If a person broke an oath, therefore, these supernatural powers would punish the transgressor. Today, however, there is no reason to hold such belief in the magic of words. Requiring loyalty oaths of college professors cannot be expected to keep presumably subversive individuals out of schools.

The very process of tracking down the cause of an undesirable norm may sometimes be sufficient to modify it. Usually you have to begin by asking other group members if they know why a particular norm was adopted. Often the others do not know either, and your question may stimulate their curiosity and cause an evaluation of the practice. For example, many organizations that insist on sharply limiting the term of office of chairpersons and prohibiting them from serving more than perhaps one term had at one time some unfortunate experiences with chairpersons who could not be controlled. Rules limiting tenure and succession were thus created to prevent anyone in the future from obtaining a stranglehold on the office. But these rules were applied after the fact and may also have the effect of turning a good chairperson out of office just about the time he or she begins to get the feeling of the job. The circumstances whereby a chairperson may be reviewed and appraised are different now from the time when the rules were adopted. If so, the process of change has begun.

[5]See Read D. Tuddenham, "The Influence of a Distorted Norm upon Individual Judgment," and "The Influence of an Avowedly Distorted Norm upon Individual Judgment," *Journal of Psychology,* 46 (October 1958), 227–41 and 329–38.

Analyze the Forces for and Against Change. There is no need for repetition of the forces and their interrelations set out in Chapter 5. That information should serve as a framework for determining the state of any given norm.

Condition the Group to Change. If you are in a position of leadership, you may make a variety of minor changes in the norm structure without causing resentment for having altered the basic norms themselves. Such minor changes serve the function of preparing the group to accept both other changes and change itself.

But be careful. This step in the change process is most susceptible of abuse. Dictators use this method. Every decline in standards that comes to mind began with a series of "insignificant" changes. Change for the sake of change is not desirable and neither is arbitrary tinkering that leaves group members confused, unable to predict next steps and increasingly dependent on the leader. As Merei demonstrated, you can change the basic norms this way,[6] but you may also subvert the democratic process. The group's energies will be spent attempting to counteract the various changes until out of the confusion one of two things happens. Either a revolution will oust the leader or the group will collapse from exhaustion and frustration. Neither outcome is desirable.

Improve Perception of Forces. As has been pointed out, the forces that operate on the group are conditioned by the perceptions of the members. If a person believes something exists, that "something" is real for that person whether or not it has any basis in fact. Thus, regardless of your objective determination of the forces that may be operating, you must consider how the members of the group may be perceiving the forces, and work toward improving the communication that determines perception.

The belief that others might not be ready to accept a change is often present. Not only does it make members less willing to express their true feelings, but it makes them resist attempts of others to effect the change because they believe that such pressures would disrupt group harmony.

Of course, there are dozens of other perceptual distortions of the norms themselves or the forces operating for or against change. University freshmen, for example, "hear" that their professors are unapproachable and will ridicule other students who seek assistance. Subtle forces are thus at work to keep students from getting help when they are having academic difficulty.

Fundamentally, the reasons for perceptual distortions are one or more of the following: communicative failure of the source of information, failure to receive accurately information that is sound, or incapacity to evaluate conflicting or contradictory information properly. When you suspect faulty perception is creating barriers to change, you should (1) find some means of discovering the correct information and (2) find some means of communicating this information to the others so that their perceptions may become more realistic.

Weaken or Eliminate Forces Against Change. One of the reasons that college professors are given tenure or continuous contracts is to remove the fear of dismissal that may act as a force to keep them from discovering or advocating new or controversial knowledge or insights. In the Lewin food experiments, discussed in Chapter 2, making a public decision removed a force against change—the fear of innovating

---

[6]Merei, "Group Leadership."

alone. Both the tenure practice and the food experiment are examples of weakening or eliminating forces against change.

As pointed out in Chapter 5, increasing the forces *for* change tends to produce greater tension; decreasing the forces *against* change tends to reduce tension. Thus, it is wise to first seek methods of decreasing forces against change. Unfortunately, most of us, when we are change agents, become so obsessed with the changed circumstances that seem to us to dictate the need for new norms that we fail to understand why others do not immediately adopt the change. If employees can get more money by working harder, why do they refuse to step up production? They may fear social ostracism. If restrictive management practices have been demonstrated as ineffective, why do many managers refuse to discard them? They perhaps feel personally inadequate in the new role. Since speeding is so obviously a cause of accidents, why cannot teenagers be persuaded to drive more conservatively? They may feel the need for opportunities to demonstrate courage and skill. In each of these instances experimentation has shown that norms can be changed when these forces against change have been eliminated.

Sometimes you personally will have the power to work directly on the force. Sometimes you will have to use the total resources of the group. Sometimes you will find it desirable to go outside the limits of the group to find people who have either the power, the perceptions, or the skill to effect changes. Sometimes you may have to relinquish power in order to remove some of the restraining forces. But whatever the means, remember that your task of changing norms will be much easier if you can remove or reduce forces against change.

Strengthen or Add Forces for Change. Too often the change agent who perceives the need for changing norms skips all the previous steps and begins to push the group into the change. It should now be clear that this step should be the last one. If possible, you should avoid it altogether since group members who are conscientious about their task should be themselves producing forces for change. If group standards are too low, for example, the more able members will surely become concerned. If you have been able to clear up inadequate perceptions of existing forces and have been able to remove some of the forces against change, the group may adopt higher standards and be almost unaware of the fact that they have changed.

Having properly managed the other steps, however, the change agent should not feel guilty at finding it necessary to strengthen or add forces for change. The group may well need prodding to overcome the inertia of established habit.

Strengthening or adding forces for change means simply that the change agent must use whatever powers he or she possesses that seem appropriate to the occasion. If the change agent does not possess the powers directly, he or she must persuade those who do hold power to use it. In either case beware of extremes. The dangers of overdoing are at least as great as the dangers of leaving the situation alone.

Punitive powers should obviously be avoided if at all possible. Positive rewards should be used. People will usually work much harder to get something than to avoid some kind of punishment. And the consequences for group harmony are much better if the change agent does not have to use threats or actual punishment. One motivation is worth any number of threats, pressures or reminders. We have discussed the application of these concepts with insurance agents. They tell us that the prevailing practice used to be "back the hearse up to the door" when selling life insurance. Today the basic practice is estate planning and "living insurance." The threat approach, they found, worked only with low-income, unsophisticated families. The practice changed when insurance agents discovered that they were much more successful using an approach that helped the buyer obtain a balanced program to manage his financial affairs effectively for the present as well as for the eventuality of death.

Once again, a reminder to be patient. Long-established norms may be extremely difficult to change, and even relatively newly established norms may already be deeply ingrained. Often the best that the change agent can hope for is a little less or a little more of a particular kind of behavior. Often we become impatient at what seems grossly inappropriate behavior, and, as mentioned earlier, because of the feeling that most people should become more capable of change. But when we reflect for a moment, we should be glad that people are not capable of being swayed by every breeze that blows. If they were, predictability would become only a dream. What was settled today would be discarded tomorrow. As it is, change is difficult but not impossible. The skilled and conscientious change agent *can* do much to improve the group's norms.

IMPROVING GROUP CLIMATE

If the group wishes to obtain the maximum benefit from collaboration, the group climate must be cooperative. The advantages of cooperation seem unequivocal, yet we have all observed groups whose climate was characterized by suspicion and competition rather than cooperation. Members have to "be on their toes" all the time lest another gain some advantage. When the discussion is over, everyone is exhausted and the only gains appear to be some shifting of the relative interpersonal standings.

The theory suggests that in most groups there are opportunities for both competition and cooperation. When the group goal is of overriding importance, the opportunities for competition may be sharply limited. But usually groups do not confront task demands of such magnitude that cooperation is virtually dictated. Thus, in most groups the climate will warrant attention, and often correction, *and the climate can be improved!* Specific experimental evidence shows that groups may be trained to make significant improvements in their group's climate.[7]

Let us look first at some common problems that may result in an unfortunate group climate and next examine a series of steps designed to harmonize interpersonal conflict in particular, and improve group climate in general. It is wise at this point to review earlier material about climate (particularly Chapters 4 and 5) and the chapter devoted to conflict (Chapter 11).

---

[7]The basis for most of the advice given here is research done by Harnack and reported in R. Victor Harnack, "An Experimental Study of the Effects of Training in the Recognition and Formulation of Goals upon Intra-Group Cooperation," *Speech Monographs,* 22 (March 1955), 31–38.

Common Problems

The objective here is the same as that of identifying some inappropriate norms. Some of the most significant problems that give rise to competitive behavior are identified.

Competition for Reward. This is an excellent method of stimulating individual effort, and our society makes considerable use of it. Prizes of one sort or another are eagerly sought in hundreds of contests. But when *collaborative* effort is required, competition for reward must be discarded. Teachers are aware of this when they arrange for group grades rather than individual grades for group projects. The group should be careful to see that rewards are determined on the basis of achieving overall goals and not on the basis of defeating one another.

Competition for Limited Resources. According to nineteenth-century Darwinism, this was supposed to account for intraspecies competition with the survival of the fittest being the result. Certainly, limited resources can give rise to competition, especially intergroup competition, but it need not. The fundamental fact is this: Resources are almost always limited, compared with an ideal. Individuals or groups may either compete for these resources or set up rules for equitable management of them. Thus, when competition for limited resources becomes troublesome, groups should establish rules to render wasteful competition unnecessary.

Failure to Distinguish Appropriate Areas of Competition. Competition, as already seen, may often be very good, but sometimes individuals find it difficult to judge where and when. One of the chief functions of the United States Chamber of Commerce, for example, is to help business people cooperate to promote the health of business in their communities. At the same time these business people compete for customers. Dozens of other organizations are established for similar purposes—to help people identify areas in which their goals are complementary and should thus stimulate cooperation. Often, however, individuals become so blinded by the pursuit of antagonistic goals that they miss opportunities to cooperate and to make substantial improvements in their lot. In adult training classes both business people and labor representatives, when asked whether they thought that the goals of labor were more complementary or antagonistic to those of business, were divided in their answers. It is obvious, however, that there are large areas in which cooperation makes more sense than competition.

Confusion of Competition and Controversy. It has already been noted that some people are incapable of handling controversy. When someone differs with them, they seem to assume that their critic is the embodiment of everything they do not like. Thus, personal defeat of the other person is mandatory. There is little that can be done about such people, so the real concern is with those who, when engaging in controversy, forget the prime goal (which is an examination of the problem), and substitute the goal of having their position adopted by the rest of the group. The line is difficult to draw. If we feel keenly about a matter, it is easy to begin to attribute personal malice to those who differ with us. The discussion becomes more heated, and soon any semblance of cooperation is gone. "Winning" such debates may be catastrophic, and particularly so for the "victor."

Confusion of Rivalry and Competition. Kept within appropriate bounds, rivalry is often a stimulating and effective incentive *within highly cooperative groups.* Often associates who are close personal friends and who exhibit every evidence of cooperation nevertheless stimulate each other by outstanding work. Probably all of us recall some instances of productive activity that would have been less satisfying without the stimulus of friendly rivalry. For rivalry to be effective, the rivals must be fairly evenly matched, and each party should take care that the rivalry does not get out of hand, for when it does energy and resources are wasted and an otherwise sound climate weakened.

Restructuring Goals

Whenever possible, we must restructure the situation itself in order to improve the group climate. If we can modify the bases of rewards or establish rules for managing limited resources, we can do much to improve climate. However, when the competition is the result of pursuing antagonistic goals *set by members themselves and not dictated by the situation,* we must start helping members restructure their own goals in order to create and emphasize complementary goals. As pointed out in Chapter 4, the multiplicity of problems and consequent goals present in any discussion allows opportunity for discussants to emphasize goal clusters that may be either complementary or antagonistic. What can we do about it?

The basic principle is to concentrate on *goals* and not on *motives* that may be impelling individuals toward those goals. We cannot deal directly with motives; they are complicated, personal, and usually a mystery even to the people driven by them. But we can identify and evaluate the goals for which people are striving. There may be dozens of reasons why a person wants to be promoted to a particular job, for example. Even if we were professional psychiatrists we would find it difficult to identify them all. But we can talk meaningfully about the nature of that job, its obligations and opportunities, its present and its future. Academic advisors do this all the time when they help a student choose a major field. Thus, each individual should wrestle with his or her own motives while other individuals should confine themselves to examining the goals that they seek. This examination of goals has four aspects.

Sensitize to the Effects of Goals. This brings us back to one of the basic considerations of problem solving discussed in Chapter 10. Since many people are simply unaware of the goals they seek, this lack of awareness hampers solving problems of interpersonal relations just as much as it hampers solving any problem.

First, you must become sensitized to your own goals; you must put yourself under the microscope and discover exactly what you are trying to accomplish. If you discover that some of your goals are antagonistic to the goals of others, you have at least three courses of action open to you. You may disregard the consequences and plunge ahead; you may bring the matter out into the open and indicate your desire to compete; or you may attempt to restructure your own goals so that they become predominantly complementary. If you choose the third alternative, you must abandon or suppress those goals that are antagonistic. In their stead you may emphasize existing complementary goals, substitute new complementary goals, or both.

Suppose that you want to be designated leader of a subgroup. Another member wants the same office. Your choice is clear. If you want the leadership badly enough, you may decide to compete even though you are likely to create animosities. For any of a number of reasons this may be your wisest choice. If, however, you decide that your reasons for selecting this goal are largely to obtain personal gratification and your opponent is better qualified or equipped, you may decide to give it up. You will then concentrate on doing a good job as a member. Some time later you may decide that a similar goal is important enough (or the circumstances are sufficiently different) to warrant fighting for. Then your previous action may have set the groundwork to avoid unfortunate repercussions.

Helping others to become sensitive to their own goals is not so simple. Asking leading questions is about the only way you can focus another's attention on the consequences of her or his behavior. Sometimes you may do this in the context of a discussion, and sometimes in between-meetings conversations.

Discuss Some Goals Openly. When an antagonistic situation has either developed or is developing, it is often wise to call a halt to the wrangling, summarize the positions, and describe what seem to you to be some of the goals of the competing individuals. This serves both to sensitize others to goals and to start an examination of at least some of them. Of course, when you are identifying goals, you will be careful to mention only those that are quite obvious and will not embarrass anyone involved. You may discuss goals as an integral part of your summary of what has been said. By beginning to consider content-problem goals, you may suggest the existence of personal goals that may be causing trouble. Possibly by this means you may stimulate others to discuss their goals openly; almost certainly you may start others thinking privately about their own goals and their effects on group climate.

Search for Substitute Goals. You cannot ask others, directly or indirectly, to give up some goals without helping them find some substitute goals. For example, if one member has been critical of some group projects, perhaps contending that action has been hasty and ill-considered, you may suggest that she head a committee to study means of developing efficient operating methods. The member's goals, whatever her motive, had been to block further action. Now she has an opportunity to set as a goal the streamlining of operating methods. Sometimes people will be able to see for themselves the wisdom of exchanging some antagonistic goals, but sometimes they will need help if they are to strike a reasonable bargain with the rest of the group.

Give Members the Opportunity to Change Without Losing Face. Often when antagonistic members become convinced of the desirability of restructuring some of their goals they find that they are not in a position to change. The group has been badgering them and ganging up on them. In short, the rest of the members have adopted the goal of defeating them. Now, if they change, they may appear foolish or weak-willed. They don't want to appear to be either and thus they may continue their antagonistic behavior for reasons other than those that launched them on the behavior. But whatever the reasons, the result is the same. They are balking, rather than helping, the group. And you and the rest of the group are to blame!

The remedy is simple. Leave them alone for a while. Let them change their behavior as unobtrusively as possible. Don't force them to admit publicly that they were wrong and intend to mend their ways. Allow that they may have misunderstood or have been misunderstood and that no dramatic change has taken place.

Often skillful leaders get a group to drop an issue and proceed on the tacit assumption that the differences have been resolved. When the issue finally comes up for a vote, the whole matter is quietly settled.

There is evidence that the foregoing procedure is often used in labor-management negotiations. When certain concessions are made, the other side prudently refrains from making an issue of the concession in order not to embarrass the negotiators in the eyes of those whom they represent.

Always remember that it is asking a great deal of people to ask them to admit that they were wrong. Count as your triumph not their changed behavior but the positive task accomplishment and the improved welfare of the group.

DEVELOPING GROUP MATURITY

Developing group maturity, like developing personal maturity, takes time. In both cases much maturation will take place without conscious effort on the part of anyone. But, just as a parent or teacher does not take the child's maturity for granted, neither do good leaders assume that groups will mature without paying attention to the process. What leaders do or do not do may hasten or retard development of group maturity. Some parents actually attempt to retard the maturation of their children, wishing to keep them dependent. So too, some leaders deliberately retard the maturation of their groups for similar reasons. After all, maturity implies greater independence, and the leader of a mature group is much more the servant than the master of it.

One of the quickest methods of developing group maturity is to weed out those clearly incompetent members and replace them. Of course, this is not always possible, and even when it is, it should be viewed as a last resort. But even if we are fortunate enough to have only exceptionally able individuals as group members, maturity is not automatic.

Provide Maturation Requirements

Chapter 4 listed four maturation requirements: a justifiable reason for being, realistic opportunities for progressive successes, promise of continuity, and promise of intergroup status. Here are some suggestions for achieving these requirements.

Justifiable Reason for Being. Every group should periodically reexamine its reason or reasons for existence. This activity is closely related to extending and defining the group's area of control and to the process of creating involvement by relating individual goals to group goals. The circumstances that originally called a group into being have a habit of changing and the group must change too, or go out of business. Further, new members may not be aware of some of the objectives that originally constituted the group's task. A whole new collection of members may have replaced the founders, and the new group may remain forever infantile if the members do not examine and accept as their own the main reason or reasons for the group's existence.

There is no better illustration of changing reasons for being and the consequent need for periodic reexamination than the role that fraternities and sororities play in most colleges. At one time such organizations provided the bulk of social opportunities on a campus. Further, they controlled campus politics in such a way that anyone who wished to "be somebody" simply had to belong, or be cast aside. Not infrequently job opportunities after college were enhanced by the individual's fraternal affiliations during college. Today, however, this preeminent position has largely disappeared. Highly organized programs in residence halls and university-wide groups make it possible for "independents" as well as "Greeks" to obtain many social, political, and professional opportunities. Fraternities and sororities have had to make noticeable changes.

Realistic Opportunities for Progressive Successes. Success is meaningless, of course, unless there is some possibility of failure. Cooperative groups, moreover, are less likely to be crippled by early failures than individuals working alone. Thus, leaders should not set up straw men for their groups to conquer; this will defeat the objectives of involvement and creation of a justifiable reason for being. But by the same token, the leader should not confront the group with the toughest task at the outset.

Enhancing success probability is partly a problem of both long-range and short-range agenda planning. Long-range planning suggests that the leader set not only simpler tasks in early meetings but tasks that may be completed and their effects observed rather quickly. With a history of demonstrable successes behind it, a group may approach more complicated and drawn-out tasks with more assurance. Short-range planning concerns the order of the items on the agenda for a given meeting. Place first on the agenda items that are least likely to arouse controversy and may be handled with dispatch. Place the longer (not necessarily the more difficult or important) items further down the list.

The time-wasting practice of using group meetings to make routine reports was mentioned earlier. One way to modify this norm, and to hasten maturity at the same time, is to place such routine reporting toward the *end* rather than the beginning of an agenda. If the group runs out of time, such reports may be either abbreviated or circulated in written form after the meeting. This is an example of a minor change that may lead to major changes. By the simple expedient of allowing more time for group deliberation on those items that really merit group action, the change enhances the possibilities of success. Nothing is more frustrating than spending half a meeting with routine matters and then having to stop some significant task short of accomplishment because time has run out.

Finally, some problems cannot be solved at one sitting. Let members know when you believe that the task will require more than one meeting. Then set specific goals to be accomplished during the meeting, such as preliminary examination of the problem, assignment of research responsibilities, and brainstorming potential solutions. Recognize that, though the group needs to feel a sense of accomplishment, such accomplishment does not necessarily mean the completion of an entire task.

Promise of Continuity. You can do nothing on this score if the group is to disband when a particular task is completed. However, if there is honest justification for continuing the group and if there is a possibility of its making additional positive contributions, you should do everything in your power to obtain assurances of continuity from those responsible for creating the group. Nonetheless, the continuity of a group is a situational factor that you may or may not be able to affect.

Promise of Intergroup Status. In addition to emphasizing the significance of the members' work, you must keep reminding the group of its potential intergroup status. You should also point out evidences of success and recognition. Discovering that others are taking note of the group's accomplishments is a strong force for producing a cohesive and cooperative climate. Reminding the group of past accomplishments may be just the spur needed to overcome discouragement when the group is embroiled in a particularly difficult task.

Share Leadership

If you do not share leadership, you keep members overly dependent on you. The group in which leadership is limited to one or two individuals will remain immature, and members who never have the opportunity to exercise leadership, are not likely to develop their leadership potential.

For leadership to be shared, the members must see the task as urgent and they must have the opportunity to perform functions in keeping with their ability. We were told about a volunteer worker with the NAACP who was subtly but deliberately tricked into developing her leadership abilities by a group leader who believed in sharing responsibilities. The worker had little education or sophistication and was both shy and unsure of herself. The leader managed a series of "emergency" situations in which the worker's skills were immediately needed by the group. At first, they were small tasks and of brief duration. She was asked to take over the recording duties when the group secretary was called out of the room; she was asked to get some specific material the group needed for its deliberation. As the woman gained experience and confidence, the tasks became greater and she was eventually asked to fill in for the leader who was suddenly needed elsewhere. The former small-town community worker is now a highly effective member of the NAACP national staff.

This example shows some of the ways a leader can share responsibility and at the same time help develop leadership in others:

1. Appoint others as heads of subgroups and delegate duties.
2. Let the group meet without you (whether the reason for your absence is real or manufactured).
3. Obviously restrict the scope of your functions.
4. Occasionally, sit back and wait.

Encourage Reasoned Controversy

We have repeatedly emphasized the value of controversy. We do not wish to belabor the point, but we want to make one more suggestion for developing the group's capacity for controversy and thus hastening maturity.

In the early stages of a group's development it often discusses a matter, discovers no apparent disagreement, and proceeds rather blandly to a conclusion. Before the group accepts the conclusion, however, you might offer to play the role of devil's advocate and raise all the arguments you can think of against the prevailing group sentiment. As a result the group may witness a demonstration of the use of controversy to illuminate an issue rather than defeat an opponent. All the benefits of role playing are apparent here. Further, the group may discover that its previous examination was superficial and that the conclusion needs reexamination. Still further, you may discover that not everyone was really in accord. Some may not have liked the conclusion but did not know why, or did not know how to make their feelings known. Of course you must restrict your use of this approach to issues wherein genuine controversy is possible, but if it is, this can be a potent means of aiding group maturity.

MATCHING PEOPLE, ROLES, AND FUNCTIONS

Another important way to modify the group is to make certain that all necessary roles and functions are being performed adequately and that the talent available within group members is being used where it is most needed and where and how it can be most effective. We discussed roles and functions as a part of group forces (Chapter 5) and will discuss them again in connection with evaluating and improving the group (Chapters 15 and 16). Our purpose here is not to delineate functions but to point out the critical nature of the right "fit." It may not be nearly so crucial that a given leader has an authoritarian style as it is that we give him or her followers whose personality structures and abilities permit them to be comfortable while working with an authoritarian leader. Equitable and efficient division of labor is, of course, a requirement for group success and member satisfaction. As we have said previously, functions are apt to be duplicated rather than spread around in the immature group.

One means of finding out if our group members are performing those roles and functions they are best suited for (and enjoy most doing—which are not necessarily the same) is to ask them. Another way is to observe, either ourselves or with the aid of official observers, and open the findings of the observation to group analysis and discussion. A third way is to provide the opportunity for people to swap roles occasionally and try out other kinds of behaviors than those to which they are most accustomed or into which the group has positioned them. The more mature the group, the more able we are to experiment while we work toward group development and improvement.

Fiedler and his associates searched for the most effective leadership style to fit circumstances as well as the task.[8] They devised an interesting dimension based on the "least-preferred co-worker" or the person with whom the leader felt least effective. The better leaders described their least-preferred co-workers in favorable terms, indicating they were more relationship than task oriented, and also that they could view the transaction between themselves and the least-preferred person, rather than the person, as the problem.[9]

PLAN FOR GROUP DEVELOPMENT AND INDIVIDUAL GROWTH

It may be a cliché, but the most effective leaders are those who eventually work themselves out of a job. They deliberately plan for the sharpening of leadership

---

[8]Fred E. Fiedler, "Style or Circumstance: The Leadership Enigma," *Psychology Today*, 2 (March 1969), 38–43.

[9]This last point is our inference and not a reported conclusion of the research.

skills among as many group members as is feasible. If the rising young executive is wise, he or she sees value rather than threat in training a successor.

The group leader can set an example of wanting to improve by asking for, and responding to, feedback. With the aid of the group, the leader can establish his or her own goals for personal development and encourage group members to follow suit. Opportunities for both informal and formal education and experiences can be arranged. The mature and effective group makes maximum use of all its resources, and the leader of such a group can count on support if the group has been through experiences sufficiently similar to the leader's to have brought them to similar conclusions. Group members, as well as the leader, must be open to change and courageous enough to try to unlearn old habits and acquire new skills that will make them more congruent in their personal expression.

The group leader who tries to keep group members dependent, uninformed, or blocked from personal or group progress is a boss rather than a leader. To paraphrase one of Tead's premises: A leader is known by the people he *develops*, not those he *dominates*. [10]

INITIATING ACTION

The advice we give in this section is directed toward the group's leaders, since they normally have sufficient influence to affect the behavior of the other group members. For the purposes of our example, we assume that the task requirements have not been levied upon, or created by, the group as a whole. That is, whether the task requirement originated outside the group or within it, relatively few members fully appreciate the significance of the task and the desirability of having the group undertake the task. We also assume that the group's leaders are among those who appreciate the significance and intensity of the task requirements—and that the task is indeed significant and not simply a personal "pet" of one of the leaders.

The fundamental premise underlying the advice given here is that group members must adopt for themselves the goal of accomplishing the task. If they simply go through the motions of complying with a task requirement, the values of group participation will be sharply limited. If the goal of task accomplishment becomes every member's goal, quality of participation will be improved and problems of successfully terminating action will be greatly reduced. Thus, simply getting the group to start work on a task is not sufficient. Failure to secure commitment often causes drawn-out arguments and watered-down compromises.

Chapter 5 showed that some of the aspects by which a task may be characterized are its stability, complexity, intensity, and attractiveness. These characteristics form the framework for the discussion in the pages that follow. These methods are not arranged in a time sequence; nor must leaders use each one. Each leader must judge in each situation which methods are needed and which will have the fewest repercussions.

Stabilize Task Requirements

The leader must be careful to avoid jumping from one task to another. Giving groups tasks and then pulling them away before the tasks are completed is

[10]Ordway Tead, *The Art of Leadership* (New York: McGraw-Hill Book Company, Inc., 1935).

also a sure way to create tension. A wiser practice is to be more selective and to confront the group with only those tasks that are clearly significant and within the province of the group's control.

Some otherwise capable groups fail because they take up tasks one by one as the tasks are given to the group, either by outside forces or by group members themselves. A much better procedure is for the group to list all tasks in order of priority. The leader might ask, "Since we may not have time to accomplish all these items, which are the most important for us to finish at this meeting?"

Emphasize Success Potential

Two issues are important here. First, the group must perceive that its abilities and skills are equal to the task. Second, the group must perceive that it has, or can obtain, the necessary resources to accomplish the task. Recall from the previous material how early successes can be used to hasten group maturity. Here the concern is with helping groups to perceive accurately their chances of success.

Before attempting to convince others of the success potential of the group, however, the leader should check the accuracy of his or her own perceptions. Evidence suggests that leaders tend to overestimate their own capacity, while those lower in status tend to overestimate the leader's capacities by *underestimating* their own. Typically, then, leaders will tend to be overambitious for themselves and their groups whereas followers will tend to be overcautious. With this warning in mind, the leader should seek to help others accurately perceive the group's success potential by (1) praising individual abilities and (2) assessing existing and potential resources.

Praise Individual Abilities. Few people are not pleased to be praised, if it be genuine praise and not mere flattery. Such praise can help others to raise their sights. Focus on those skills that are relevant to the task. Don't forget that people deserve praise for their performance of maintenance as well as task functions.

Assess Existing and Potential Resources. What is needed to accomplish the task? Information? Special facilities? Special equipment? Money? Cooperation from other groups, institutions, or individuals? Your group must know that these and other needed resources are available or can be secured before they can feel confident about the group's success potential. You can assess these existing and potential resources in at least three ways. Obviously, you can look them up yourself. You can ask other group members (not necessarily the whole group) to assess the resource possibilities. Or you can bring in an outside resource person.

Because of the leader's position in the group and greater access to communication channels, he or she may be aware of resources and assume that everyone else knows about them. Under these conditions, the leader may become frustrated because the group balks at undertaking what it regards as an impossible task. Unless you are completely certain that others know all that you know, take a minute to review the information about resources. Even if most of the members know of the existence of the resources, the review will often serve to reinforce confidence in the group's success potential.

Spread Task Pressures

Spread Task Pressures Among People. The more members you are able to fire up before the task is presented to the group as a whole, the more likely are your chances of success. Thus, talk to as many members as possible before the group formally convenes. First, you have an opportunity to check your perceptions of the desirability of undertaking the task. You may find your perceptions are totally unrealistic, and these premeeting conferences may help you avoid taking up group time fruitlessly. Second, you will, at the very least, reduce resistance caused by novelty.

When possible, have someone other than yourself present the task to the group. Then you can support others rather than be the prime mover. Sometimes the presentation can be collectively handled by several members. Regardless of the mode of presentation, the principle is the same: The broader the base of presentation, the more likely is the acceptance by the rest of the group. In your efforts to spread task pressures among group members, beware of creating special subgroups or cliques and be equally cautious of leaving the *impression* that you have done so.

Spread Task Pressures over Time. Remember the virtues of carefully planned and publicized agendas. If members know in advance what tasks are going to be undertaken, they will have time to do some thinking about them. One reason behind this practice is that it guarantees that groups will not be surprised by action they have not had time to consider. Whether or not your group adopts some formal procedure of giving notice of motion is not the issue. The issue is the amount of time that you allow between the first application of task pressure and the point that you hope the group will begin actual work on the task.

Sometimes it is desirable to set aside an entire meeting, or at least part of a meeting, to describe tasks you intend to urge upon the group at a later time. As an example, the President's State of the Union address serves primarily the purpose of alerting Congress to what the President considers "must" legislation.

Intensify Task Pressures

Observe the same caution here as when intensifying pressures to change norms. If you must increase pressures beyond the levels already perceived by group members, you are certain to increase tension and you may create resentment. Don't be panicked by an initial lack of enthusiasm on the part of group members. They may just be evidencing normal inertia that will be overcome as they perceive the significance of task commitment. Unnecessary intensification of pressures may cause members to feel that they are being railroaded into something against their better judgment. Members may refuse the task because they do not want to be pushed around. However, just as there are reasons for increasing pressures to change norms, there will often be reasons for intensifying task pressures. Tactful and judicious use of the following methods may be an essential part of securing task commitment.

Pressure from Authority. Organizational groups are forever subjected to pressure from individuals or groups above them in the organizational structure. Deans exert pressure on academic departments in universities and in corporations vice-presidents exert pressure on divisional managers.

This pressure from above may be a boon to harassed group leaders because it lets them shift the blame for the pressure from themselves to their superiors. "The boss says we have to get this done by next week" is far easier to present than "I want this done by next week." But although it's tempting to place the responsibility elsewhere, use caution. Make sure you are willing to face up to your own share of the responsibilities.

For the pressure from authority to be effective at least two conditions must prevail within your group. First, the group must believe that the superior has the *right* to levy such pressures. If they perceive the superior is trying to extend control in an unwarranted fashion, the consequences will be what one may expect from any kind of authoritarian leadership. Second, the group must perceive that you are reporting the levying of pressures from above without exaggeration or distortion.

Pressures to Cooperate with Other Groups or Individuals. Both organizational and voluntary groups are subject to this pressure. Whenever your group members perceive that their group goals complement another group's goals, pressures are created for your group to undertake tasks that help the other group attain its goals. For example, the English departments of colleges and universities have repeatedly diagnosed and analyzed the English background and abilities of entering freshmen. Such activities help the departments handle problems in curriculum planning, but they also help high-school English teachers assess the methods they use in preparing students for college work.

Intergroup Comparisons. A group need not be engaged in a competitive struggle with another group for relevant comparisons to be an effective pressure for task commitment. What other groups are doing is a legitimate question to raise, whether or not one group wishes to emulate another. If a bit of healthy rivalry exists between the groups, so much the better.

Desire to Obtain Extrinsic Rewards. Just as individuals can be stimulated to work to gain rewards or avoid punishment, so groups can be stimulated by the promise of recognition, improved intergroup status, or extended area of control. You will probably not be in the position to mediate the group rewards, but you should know what rewards are available and the procedures necessary for placing your group in line to receive such rewards.

Personal Influence. Assuming that you are a real group leader, and not simply a figurehead, your own personal influence may well be the second most potent force for task commitment. (The most potent is task attractiveness, to be discussed next.) The leader's control of both extrinsic and intrinsic rewards coupled with the sources of personal power combine to make personal influence quite powerful. People will do any number of things to please their leaders, and undertaking tasks recommended by their leaders is a common way of pleasing them. If you possess strong personal influence on your group, you can often significantly intensify task pressures by simply indicating, without giving further reasons for your assertion, that you personally believe the group should accept the task.

You will seldom be able to eliminate personal influence from the task pressures that are levied upon the group. However, use it as sparingly as possible. You can use it like money in the bank, trading on it for a variety of things that you want done. But you can deplete that store of influence and cause resentment stemming from others' dependency on you. Leaders can neither avoid using personal influence nor escape the consequences of its use. But the leader's productive tenure can be prolonged if personal influence is used with discretion. The consequence of the use of personal influence is one reason why many organizations make a practice of changing their leaders periodically.

Emphasize Task Attractiveness

> Without the job that comes from doing and making, from having a creative purpose, from working with others toward a common goal, he [man] is less and less satisfied with having more and more. [11]

Magda Arnold reached this conclusion in her book *Emotion and Personality*, and we agree completely.

On the surface, emphasizing task attractiveness seems easy— point out the pleasure from doing whatever needs doing. Unfortunately, it is not that simple. Some tasks are difficult to enjoy; they are monotonous, repetitious, or otherwise beneath the dignity of the doer. Dozens of external pressures, such as need for haste, may rob the doer of much of the pleasure. Many people have never learned to enjoy work; their lives are measured by clocks and compulsions; for one reason or another their creative capacities have been stifled. For such people, work could never be fun nor can there be joy in accomplishment. But some leaders make a serious mistake in not communicating the inherent rewards in the doing.

Learning, for its own sake, is perhaps the most exciting and rewarding activity we know of. Yet far too many students at all levels of education regard learning, as it takes place in schools at any rate, as a distinctly unpleasant chore. Part of the blame must rest upon teachers who either never discovered the joy of learning for themselves or are incapable of communicating it. For such students the task of learning is solely a means to an end (a grade, a degree, sports eligibility, a job) rather than an end that is worth pursuing for itself. The teacher, like any other leader, has the responsibility of helping students discover rewards in the learning activity.

Almost all the means of stimulating involvement are also applicable for emphasizing task attractiveness. The leader must be certain that the task is worthwhile, that members have ample opportunities to participate, that individual goals are related to group goals, that communication channels are open for both sending and receiving, and that the leader is also stimulated and enthusiastic. In short, the leader must motivate the other members.

But as Smith and Scott have pointed out, motivation is not a kind of push-button activity. [12] One does not select some emotional appeals, or a few drives or needs such

---

[11]Magda B. Arnold, *Emotion and Personality: Neurological and Physiological Aspects* (New York: Columbia University Press, 1960), II, 306–7.

[12]Donald K. Smith and Robert L. Scott, "Motivation Theory in Teaching Persuasion: Statement and Schema," *Quarterly Journal of Speech*, 47 (December 1961), 378–83.

as the need for status, or power, or prestige, and then say in effect, "Do this task and you will obtain status, power, or prestige." Rather, problem-solving is a more appropriate framework for communicating task attractiveness. Doing the task well becomes the solution to problems facing each participant. The goals may be different for each individual, and the tensions that are relieved as a result of performing the task may vary. But it is possible for each one to discover pleasure in the task.

Suppose that a group of students has been appointed to study a college's admissions policies with its primary task being to determine if women and members of minority races have had equal opportunities for admission in all departments. Suppose, too, the group is asked to make recommendations for future admissions policies on the basis of its findings. It may decide that there is no evidence of deliberate discrimination, yet the effects of present practices—in the form of fewer minority and women students—indicate a problem that needs correction. Some students in the group may be stimulated by the prospect of learning about the inner workings of school administration; others may become intrigued by the intricacies of civil rights legislation and affirmative action programs; still others may become involved in trying to untie the knots caused by disparate education programs and grading procedures at elementary and secondary levels. Even though there are long-range rewards from the experience and status gained from working on the project, at least some of the motivation for accepting the assignment may be found in the task activities themselves.

TERMINATING ACTION

Our worries do not end once the group is committed to action. Getting the group to terminate action with some reasonable conclusion is often at least as difficult as initiating action is. As individuals we are prone to procrastinate and we hate to commit ourselves to any course of action until we are forced to do so. We don't improve when we get into groups. In fact, as we have already shown, forces are created that aggravate rather than improve this factor. We know that reasonable people can become quickly disillusioned about the values of group discussion when their groups talk endlessly and come up with watered-down compromises instead of effective plans of action. What can we do about it?

Before we give suggestions for terminating action, we need to state some assumptions. One is that you have done a good job of initiating action. If members are concerned about the task and have undertaken their work cheerfully, you have set in motion a powerful force for concluding the task with dispatch. Of course, another assumption is that the group has been progressing with all the characteristics of a first-rate group. A very important assumption is that the group does have some requirement to arrive at a *group* decision. Social, cathartic, and therapeutic groups seldom have to reach group consensus; learning, advisory, and appraisal groups can often agree to disagree and present a divided report or simply terminate action when the problem has been adequately explored; but decision-making and action groups must reach a group decision.

Set Deadlines

Once the group has committed itself to the task and has surveyed the requirements of solving the problem, the group as a whole should begin to set deadlines. If the task is large, it should be broken into subproblem areas and a deadline should be set for each. All deadlines should be flexible, of course, since it is impossible to foresee exactly what must be done to accomplish any given task. But being flexible is different from being spineless. Deadlines serve no purpose if they can be abolished by complaints of the lazy.

Deadlines are often set by authorities outside the group, such as when the discussion instructor sets the date when the group project is due. But the group members must make the deadlines their own. If members agree that the deadlines are reasonable and if they agree publicly to attempt to meet them, the first step toward terminating action has been taken. Take some time to get the group to make deadline decisions; it will save time in the long run and provide an invaluable focus on potential accomplishment.

Provide Resources

The procedures given earlier for how the group can see that necessary evidence and other resources can be made available should suffice; however, some people will still protest, "We can't make any decisions until we have all the facts." We can *never* have all the facts. We must abstract information that seems important; we can't get it all. To say that we should not do anything until we can be *certain* that it will work means nothing will ever get done.

The best way to cope with the caution of those who want to be certain is to urge the group members to consider the probable consequences of their action or lack of action. If the group does take a particular course of action, what does it stand to gain and what does it stand to lose and what are the probabilities of each? In some situations the possible loss is so great that prudent people will refuse the hazard. Most of us refuse to drive automobiles unless we are covered by liability insurance. We are not really insuring ourselves against probable loss; we are trying to protect ourselves against that *improbable* instance when a judgment of thousands of dollars may be returned against us. At the other extreme, we may decide that the present situation is so bad that almost any action will be an improvement. During the depression of the 1930s, for example, Congress passed all kinds of legislation with little caution. Many acts were later declared unconstitutional, and many others proved to be hasty and ill-considered. But the economy was in a critical condition, and potentially constructive change and immediate action were imperative.

Most of the time, however, the choices are not so clear-cut. We must decide whether or not we have sufficient information to predict reasonably well the consequences of proposed action. If we have taken the necessary steps to ensure that pertinent resources are available, and if we urge the group to consider the possible gains and losses, we increase the probability that the group can take positive action.

Maintain Objectivity

We should seek to maintain objectivity for a number of reasons, but two apply particularly to the problem of terminating action. First, objective discussion helps avoid emotional commitments that can prove embarrassing. If, for example, a discussant gets carried away in espousing a position that others will not accept, he or she may be unable to accept an alternative action gracefully. Second, frankness, as an essential part of objectivity, helps clear away confusion about where people stand. After many unduly prolonged discussions, a substantial majority of the group members may admit they were ready to take action long before the group finally stopped talking, but because they felt that others were not ready, they said nothing. Frankness would have shortened the decision-making time.

Means of developing and encouraging objectivity have been examined already. Here is just one more suggestion: After the problem has been thoroughly explored, some members may still offer reasons against a proposal for action or against taking action at the time suggested. Simply ask whether they are expressing their own feelings or whether they are offering arguments they think others hold.

We recall an individual who kept reopening the question for more discussion every time the group seemed ready to decide. When pinned down, he admitted that he was ready to act but he was afraid that *others* might still have reservations. This kind of behavior is typical of the peer-oriented individual who is so worried that everyone will not be in perfect accord that she or he invents excuses to prolong the discussion.

The devil's advocate role was suggested earlier as a way to raise arguments when the group seemed to have come to a conclusion too casually or superficially. That advice is not contradicted here, but when the discussion has been thorough and complete, why prolong it because some people hesitate to be frank about their own feelings or are guessing at other people's positions? People with genuine reservations should be encouraged to voice them but not to the point where reasoned controversy ceases to be productive.

Summarize and Review

In a typical discussion, members reach a point where they begin to repeat their arguments. Although this is sometimes a deliberate delaying tactic, members are often not aware that it is happening. Some people act as if they believe an argument can be proved by repetition. Effective summaries and reviews can help minimize the problem of sterile repetition.

Summary and review are effective if conflicting lines of argument are stated with scrupulous fairness, points of agreement are clearly identified, and logical consequences of unresolved lines of argument are stated. Then, two more important steps must be taken. First, *get the proponents of the conflicting positions to agree that your summary is accurate.* If necessary, keep rephrasing until everyone can agree that the arguments have been fairly stated. Next, ask the members if they have anything to *add*, and underscore the word *add* when you make the request. If some members persist in going back to old arguments, the rest of the group may now help you remind them that the ground has been covered. If members have nothing to add, further talk is unnecessary and you are ready to move to something else.

Provide Time to Think

Several times we have cautioned against attempting to cram everything into one meeting. Most problems of any consequence require at least three meetings. A typical time apportionment would be one meeting for preliminary analysis and division of research assignments, a second meeting for actually working through the problem, and a third for recapitulating and making the decision.

Providing this time to think is obviously advantageous because it can be used for individual thinking and research. If legitimate arguments have been overlooked, they may be discovered and brought to the group's attention at the next meeting. The delay also provides a face-saving device for those whose positions are not accepted. Somehow it is much easier for people to concede a point or modify a position after time has elapsed. Moreover, the time to think alleviates many of the unfortunate pressures for conformity.

Some may contend that the additional time simply provides those who wish to block action with the opportunities to think up additional strategems. For the most part, experience proves otherwise. This method allows many groups to make decisions calmly and rationally, although in an earlier meeting the members may have been at each other's throats. When groups press for decision hard on the heels of vigorous debate, there are apt to be charges of railroading, failure to carry out decisions, and even worse, later rejection of the whole plan or policy.

Decide

The processes of decision-making and problem-solving were discussed in Chapter 10. Now it is time to consider ways to help a group come to a decision and closure.

Groups make decisions in four ways: by force, by arbitration, by majority vote, or by consensus. Let's look at each of these ways in more detail.

Force. The application of force is usually the result of lack of action or decision by a group. If a decision must be made and the group is unable to make it, a higher authority may hand a decision down. Fortunately, this is rare but when it occurs it is more of a default than a decision and should be used as a last resort.

Arbitration. If the group is hopelessly and bitterly split and if the group members see no way to resolve differences, the group may have to resort to arbitration. When this happens, the group brings in a disinterested third party to make the decision. Labor–management disputes are often turned over first to a mediator; if the mediator cannot help the group resolve its differences, the problem is then turned over to an arbitrator. Just as with decision by force, the decision is made not by the group but by someone on the outside.

Majority Vote. Voting is a way of life in a democracy, as is the principle of majority rule. But for small group operations there may be times when voting is more of a hindrance than a help. We would recommend the use of both parliamentary procedure and voting for groups that are so large (let's pick 20 or more as an arbitrary figure) that not everyone can speak at will. Voting under parliamentary procedure is much more efficient for larger groups and has the virtue of protecting any minority viewpoint.

Other advantages of voting are these: Individual positions on an issue are made clear and can be made part of the record for later reference; the majority vote offers the finest face-saving device because people can say, "I do not agree with the decision, but I will do all I can to support it." If the decision proves to be wise, they can always say, or imply, "I was wrong to oppose the plan but right to agree to help carry it out." If the decision proves to be unwise, they can be pardoned for a tactful, "I told you so."

But under certain circumstances both of these last two advantages can work to the detriment of the group. The very fact that people go on record with their ayes and nays makes modification of their position more difficult. We all like to stand by a commitment once it has been made public. But perhaps the most serious indictment against voting is that it turns a group into winners and losers. Losers may not feel committed to carry out a decision they voted against, and they may be tempted to start to work immediately to line up people and arguments to get the decision overturned.

Barnlund and Haiman put it this way:

> Finally, and most important of all, the decision rests on a quantitative rather than a qualitative basis—the number of votes that can be marshaled by either side. A decision means that a powerful majority has brought a minority to its knees, or that a compromise between competing factions has been arranged. Settling disputes through voting does permit a group to act (and this is often important), but it does not really resolve the differences nor change people's minds about the nature of the problem.[13]

Consensus. For some people, consensus means a *unanimous agreement*. Leaders sometimes push their groups toward this unanimity to the point of coercion. We prefer the definition of consensus as *general agreement or concord*. We believe this is an important distinction.

For some, the concept of compromise takes on a connotation of weakness. "This is my position; I will not compromise; my demands are 'nonnegotiable.'" For such people, compromise means giving up at least part of what they want. As an example, when a labor union asks for 60 cents more an hour and management offers 30, both labor and management must give up part of what they want in order to compromise on 45 cents an hour. When an honest consensus is arrived at, by contrast, the group product is *added to* by group members and no one is positioned into having to give up something.

Let's look at how this might work in a group of eight people. Member A suggests a policy that could be formulated to solve the problem under discussion. Member B agrees with most of it but asks the group's permission to change part. Member C wants still another modification, which is partly contradictory to what B wants. Member D proposes a change that accommodates both B and C and also includes an aspect about which D is concerned. Member E persuades the group to delete a troublesome phrase. After more discussion, Member F calls for a restatement and summary of what has been agreed to so far. The attempt at restatement brings out some avenues that Members G and H want clarified and amended. Then the entire group agrees to the statement of policy as amended.

This was a consensus because by the end of the process, no one remembered or cared who made the initial statement; each person *added* something to the formation of the adopted policy. Because the amended policy belonged to the group rather than to an individual proponent, no one felt called upon to attack or defend. All could concentrate instead on improving and clarifying. The leader of a group that is working toward consensus would not call for agreement or disagreement, *yes* or *no* votes,

---

[13]Dean C. Barnlund and Franklyn S. Haiman, *The Dynamics of Discussion* (Boston: Houghton Mifflin Company, 1960), p. 159.

but would, instead, ask something like, *"Are there any objections* to the policy in its revised form?" If the leader hears objections, more discussion is needed. If there are no objections, then consensus has been reached.

Making decisions by consensus is an ideal method but far more difficult than voting. It takes longer and requires sensitivity to both verbal and nonverbal communication. It also demands a sense of timing, to know when the right moment to culminate the integration of ideas has occurred. Consensus seeking works best in small, mature groups whose members understand how the process works.

Some groups appear to have consensus but it is what Keltner calls *phony* when some in the group capitulate just so the group can move on.[14] This is the problem Janis is concerned with when he points out the dangers of groupthink, which occurs when *concurrence seeking* becomes so dominant in a cohesive ingroup that it tends to override realistic appraisal of alternative courses of action.[15]

The search for consensus should not be overworked, as Cortright and Hinds have advised:

> When discussion does not lead to unanimity within the time limits which are practical, the democratic process calls for decision or action by majority rule. Discussion ought not to become an instrument of endless delay foisted upon a majority by a willful minority.[16]

Before we leave this section on how groups make decisions, it is important to stress that all group members should be aware of how decisions are usually made, and how they might be handled in a particular group. Jo Freeman pointed to *structurelessness* as a severe handicap to the success of the Women's Movement. She explained that early consciousness-raising discussion groups lacked structure because they were a "natural reaction against the overstructured society in which most of us found ourselves, the inevitable control this gave others over our lives." But there are severe limitations to structurelessness and one, according to Freeman, is that it masks power:

> As long as the structure of the group is informal, the rules of how decisions are made are known only to a few and awareness of power is curtailed to those who know the rules. Those who do not know the rules and are not chosen for initiation must remain in confusion, or suffer from paranoid delusions that something is happening of which they are not quite aware. For everyone to have the opportunity to be involved in a given group and to participate in its activities, the structure must be explicit, not implicit. The rules of decision-making must be open and available to everyone, and this can happen only if they are formalized.[17]

---

[14]John W. Keltner, *Interpersonal Speech-Communication* (Belmont, Calif.: Wadsworth Publishing Company, Inc., 1970), p. 302.

[15]Irving L. Janis, "Groupthink," *Psychology Today*, 5 (November 1971), 43–46, 74–76.

[16]Rupert L. Cortright and George L. Hinds, *Creative Discussion* (New York: The Macmillan Company, 1959), p. 14.

[17]Jo Freeman, "The Tyranny of Structurelessness," *Ms.*, 2 (July 1973), 76–77, 86–89.

SUMMARY

Able individuals *can* affect the nature of their groups, but they should be careful to avoid trickery or manipulation as they attempt to change others. In this chapter we have focused first on ways to modify the group, such as creating new norms or changing inappropriate ones, improving group climate, restructuring goals, and developing group maturity. Next we pointed out ways groups can be helped to initiate and terminate action.

DISCUSSION QUESTIONS

1.   What is the most difficult problem in modifying the nature of a group? Why?

2.   Why is it impossible to change group norms from outside the group?

3.   How can students modify the nature of their classroom groups? What norms would need to be changed?

4.   In what ways can a group prevent the steamroller effect caused by pressures for premature decisions or closure, and the tendency to choose up sides and vote?

EXERCISES

1.   Analyze the stated or implied norms of two or three groups to which you belong. Which norms do you judge to be inappropriate? How could you proceed to effect a change?

2.   Compare two or more groups of widely different age levels in their resistance to change. What factors do you feel contribute to rigidity or flexibility? How would you suggest group leaders or members proceed in each case? To what degree are we justified in generalizing concerning the relationship between age and change?

3.   Select two groups that you belong to that differ markedly in willingness to reach decisions and take action. Analyze and compare these groups on the bases of (a) nature and importance of objectives and specific tasks, (b) group maturity and commitment to common interests, and (c) the potential for using suggestions offered in this chapter for moving the group to action.

4.   Think back over a number of the groups you have been a member of. Analyze how each reacted when faced with the need for a decision. Make one list of those decisions where all seemed to proceed effectively and constructively (not necessarily harmoniously or to full consensus). Make another list of those situations where decision was difficult, led to unhappy results, or was avoided. Is it possible to identify success or failure with the presence or absence of any of the factors discussed in this chapter? Consider how the final result might have been affected by the presence or absence of such factors.

SELECTED READINGS

BENNIS, WARREN G., KENNETH D. BENNE, AND ROBERT CHIN, eds., *The Planning of Change*, chap. 12. New York: Holt, Rinehart and Winston, Inc., 1964.

FISHER, B. AUBREY, *Small Group Decision Making: Communication and the Group Process*, chap. 7. New York: McGraw-Hill Book Company, Inc., 1974.

GOURAN, DENNIS S., *Discussion: The Process of Group Decision-Making*, chap. 9. New York: Harper & Row, Publishers, 1974.

JANIS, IRVING L., "Groupthink," *Psychology Today*, 5 (November 1971), 43–46, 74–76.

PART SIX

One of the most effective ways to improve group discussions is to build in opportunities and make plans for systematic evaluation. Chapter 15 is intended to help students better observe and evaluate both the groups of which they are a part (in and out of the classroom) and those groups of which they have only a sideline view.

Many discussion textbooks avoid the subject of evaluation, partly because it is hard to grasp anything so complex. Another reason evaluation is not included, we suspect, is that it has generally been accepted as being only within the teacher's province; the subject therefore becomes confined to teachers' manuals. Obviously, we disagree with this view; we feel that all students of discussion and small group communication should know at least some of the ways in which groups can be analyzed and rated. We advocate that students and teachers, individually and collectively, design their own evaluation instruments so that the group's attention can be sharply focused on the most relevant and timely specific problems, as well as general ones.

Evaluating the group we are a part of is extremely difficult. To do so means stepping outside ourselves as participants and taking on the role of observer and critic. What's more, groups should not accept everything even an outside evaluator says as absolute truth, particularly if the evaluator is inexperienced or sees the group for only a short time. The effective evaluator will emphasize the *description* of what she or he saw and heard and will allow the group to participate in the interpretation or the meaning of the events. A single evaluator provides us only with *one person's version* of what happened; remember that the group members' evaluation and interpretation is of equal value—even if it contradicts the outside evaluator. The "truth" is probably a synthesis of the varying viewpoints.

Chapter 16, "Improving Small Group Discussion," summarizes what individuals can do to improve themselves and their groups. At the end of the chapter is a checklist that shows where in earlier chapters you may find additional material on specific points covered in the chapter.

MAXIMIZING
EFFECTIVENESS

chapter 15

How can our discussion be improved? is a question every group should be seriously and continually concerned about. If a group experience frustrates, disappoints, or angers us, we have a responsibility not only to make our feelings known but also, and more important, to motivate other group members to work with us in diagnosing and curing whatever ails the group. Successful discussants don't put the blame on other people, but approach the situation as a shared problem that all need to work on.

Because of the complexities of small group communication, it is impossible to devise a simple, one-two-three method of evaluating group performance. For example, each time there is a shift of topic or a change in patterns of interaction, the group has, consciously or unconsciously, evaluated the former topic or interaction as completed or unprofitable. This chapter will not attempt to define or categorize all the possible subtle and informal ways and means of evaluation but will look at major aspects only.

Keep in mind that the very act of evaluating can be destructive. Mature individuals in mature groups can effectively evaluate themselves as long as they use great skill, care, and tact. Immature individuals in beginning groups can ruin all hope of solidarity, cohesion, or successful outcomes by inept handling of evaluation.

As groups struggle to build a cooperative climate, any factor that pits one individual against another (or even appears to) introduces a competitive element that may destroy the previously hard-won cooperative spirit. As an example, if an instructor makes a group assignment but awards individual grades, students are forced to compete with one another and the grade can become more important than the group's work or accomplishments.

For many years those interested in interscholastic communication activities at both the high school and college levels tried to design discussion events to parallel the extensive efforts that have been devoted to debate over the years. Some good came of the efforts because students became knowledgeable about the discussion process and learned to handle problem-solving and evidence and reasoning in ways different from the pro-and-con debate format. But the discussion events themselves were failures because the speech festival or tournament was built on competition for trophies, certificates, or ratings; students vied with each other to talk the most or produce the most evidence in order to impress the judge or critic. Getting a top rating was inevitably the goal, not engaging in successful group discussion. Even when festival directors did away with individual ratings and substituted a group award, the intergroup competition was still there. Under pressure to "be the best group," students were tempted virtually to script their discussions ahead of time so that they ran smoothly and met all the judge's criteria. Whereas individual ratings produced interpersonal competition, group ratings produced artificial going-through-the-motions. Neither type educated the students for a real discussion.

Evaluating
Small Group Discussion

Yet, despite the difficulties and complexities, it is necessary to learn how to evaluate group discussions in order to improve them. Experiential learning, or learning by doing, is a popular educational practice but unless we are careful we merely spend time on the experience without being sure what it was we learned. As Brilhart put it,

> Unless practice is constantly evaluated, it may result in bad habits. The means to learning is practice with analysis and evaluation leading to change in future discussions.
>
>   Constructive evaluation depends on observation and feedback of information about how a discussion group is doing.[1]

It is always valuable for a group to allot time to study its own operations. Many unsuspected problems can be uncovered this way. A means to accomplish this that we have used in our classes involves asking each group member to put down in one word how he or she feels about the group at that moment. The scraps of paper (members' names not on them) are collected, scrambled, and then read aloud. It comes as a revealing surprise to the person who wrote "pleased" or "satisfied" that others are feeling confused or bored. Trying to identify the whys behind the choices of words becomes a first step in evaluation.

Too often, however, groups conduct an unstructured, open-ended "How are we doing?" session as their only means of evaluation. Unless the group has developed some criteria against which to judge itself, its analysis is apt to be shallow and unproductive. If we merely smile and say "Fine" in response to "How are we doing?" we have learned nothing.

One of the keys to successful evaluation is to focus on individual and group *behavior*, not the person or the personality. "Is our participation out of balance?" is a better approach than singling out individual undertalkers or overtalkers. Another key is to establish ground rules on how and when evaluation will occur. Regular procedures are less threatening than unexpected forays. One ground rule we have found helpful, for example, is that the individual participant must focus on his or her own feelings or reactions rather than attempt to guess at or criticize someone else's feelings or reactions. As an illustration, it is more effective for a discussant to say, "Judy, when you made that statement *it made me feel* uneasy and confused about where you wanted the group to go," than "Judy, that was a dumb thing to say." In the first statement, the speaker is offering feedback to Judy. She can then evaluate it and use or not use it as she sees fit. She also has the opportunity of going back to her own statement and clarifying it or her intention. The second statement is so flat-footedly critical that Judy would be put on the defensive and would have no motivation to try to clarify or improve.

Before we move to specific subjects for and means of evaluating, one last point needs to be made. There is considerable difference between how we evaluate groups for *educational* purposes and how we conduct *research* on groups. Observations, experiments, and activities carried on to advance the scientific understanding of small group research must be more carefully controlled than those used for educa-

---

[1]John K. Brilhart, *Effective Group Discussion* (Dubuque, Iowa: William C. Brown Company, Publishers, 1967), p. 94.

tional purposes. We need to distinguish between independent and dependent variables; we also need to test the reliability of observers and observing tools and instruments. Although some class groups have been (and undoubtedly will be) used for research, most learning groups can evaluate themselves and be evaluated by their teacher and other observers without undue concern for rigorous validity and reliability measures.[2]

SPECIFIC EVALUATION SUBJECTS: WHAT CAN BE EVALUATED

Discussion evaluations can be conducted on two levels: We can evaluate the individual participants or we can evaluate the group as a whole.

Individual Participants

Ideally, individual participants should be evaluated on the basis of their own needs and goals. Self-evaluation, as long as it is based on appropriate standards and criteria, can be the most productive. Teachers can help individual students establish goals for their own development and students and teachers together can decide what *cognitive* and *behavioral* learning should take place by a given time.

Depending on the individual's own goals for development and on the group's learning goals, a variety of individual learning and behavior aspects can be evaluated. Some of these might be communication ability, quality of contributions, ability to use conflict constructively, and ability to help the group integrate ideas. (Sample individual evaluation forms are included toward the end of this chapter.)

The Group

We will now identify five aspects of the group that can be analyzed. We selected these five properties because they seem to be the most important and productive for study. Now let us look at each of them.

Structure. Davis defined structure in the following ways:

> The pattern of interpersonal relations is called *group structure.* In this sense, structure is a picture of interpersonal processes taken at a particular point in time. A particular structure may be relatively enduring or emerge only briefly, depending on a number of factors such as task demands, physical surroundings, motivation, and the life expectancy of the group. Long-term groups are obviously the sort most likely to yield a well-defined structure, but even the *ad hoc* group typical of the laboratory ordinarily displays a detectable structure that is an important determinant of performance.[3]

[2]For a critique of small group research subjects and methods, see Arthur P. Bochner, "Task and Instrumentation Variables As Factors Jeopardizing the Validity of Published Group Communication Research, 1970–1971," *Speech Monographs,* 41 (June 1974), 169–78.

[3]James H. Davis, *Group Performance* (Reading, Mass.: Addison-Wesley, Publishing Co., Inc., 1969), p. 88.

There appears to be no disagreement that groups have structure but there is confusion on what is meant by structure and how to depict it. Some people refer to an *unstructured* group or class; they mean that individuals are allowed to set their own rules and procedures rather than having them imposed by a leader or a teacher. Unstructured in this sense means informal with perhaps an element of freewheeling.

Freeman stated that "any group of people of whatever nature that comes together for any length of time for any purpose will inevitably structure itself in some fashion."[4] She was referring primarily to the decision-making structure. But other people look at group structure in terms of communication networks (who talks to whom and with what effect?); others think about sociometric graphs and diagrams (who is most liked or respected by the group and which people are most attracted to each other?); still others focus on leadership and the analysis of task structure (whose ideas are most often accepted and who seems most responsible for moving the group forward?).[5] In order to evaluate structure effectively, we need to define carefully which type or types we intend to analyze.

Leadership. As we have already seen, definitions of leadership are varied and often elusive. To evaluate a group's leadership, we must first decide what we mean by leadership and how we will know when it happens. Do we want to examine only the behavior of the person with the title of leader, or do we agree with Smith, who said,

> Evaluation should not concentrate on the "leader" alone, for leadership in discussion is a group function; a leader is named only in order to help the group develop its own leadership. Theoretically, at least, leadership in the group may receive a low rating even when the named leader has done everything possible to facilitate the work of the group.[6]

Gulley has developed nine criteria for the evaluation of leadership: knowledge of group process, knowledge of problem, reasoning ability, respect for others, language and speech skills, guiding the discussion, regulating the discussion, introducing the discussion, and ending the discussion.[7] Other people, including Smith, would add the elements of order, atmosphere, mechanics, and summaries.[8]

Since leadership has little meaning except in relation to the attainment of the group's goals, evaluators must know what the group's objectives are. What may appear to be lack of leadership could really be lack of clear-cut group objectives.

Climate and Cohesiveness. We can observe and sense esprit but it is difficult to measure in specific or even relatively objective ways. The best criterion seems to be how group members feel about their group and its accomplishments. One exercise

[4]Jo Freeman, "The Tyranny of Structurelessness," *Ms.*, 2 (July 1973), 77.

[5]For more on task structure, see Gordon E. O'Brien, "Leadership in Organizational Settings," *Journal of Applied Behavioral Science*, 5 (1969), 45–63.

[6]William S. Smith, *Group Problem-Solving Through Discussion*, rev. ed. (Indianapolis: The Bobbs-Merrill Company, Inc., 1963), pp. 161–63.

[7]Halbert E. Gulley, *Discussion, Conference and Group Process*, 2nd ed. (New York: Holt, Rinehart and Winston, Inc., 1968), p. 313.

[8]Smith, *Group Problem-Solving*, pp. 164–65.

we have used in discussion laboratories is aimed at evaluating the participants' commitment to the group. This can be done in either or both of two ways: (1) Select a spot on the floor that represents high commitment and ask group members to position themselves at whatever distance from the spot they feel best depicts their individual commitment at the time. (2) Ask each group member to position the others in relation to their *perceived* commitment. This exercise can be illuminating, and it can form the basis of an effective evaluation of climate and cohesiveness.

Communication and Interaction. It takes both skill and practice to be able to follow the communication in a fast-moving discussion. (A glance at some of the sample interaction forms found toward the end of this chapter will show why.) Begin by noting only the number of contributions each participant makes; next, add estimates of the length of time of each contribution; finally, show to whom each contribution was directed (an individual, a subgroup, or the group as a whole). The value of simply noting how many times individuals speak is obviously limited. But, as a beginning evaluation step, it can help point out communication patterns. It can also reveal participants' tendencies to monopolize on the one hand or withhold participation on the other. Reporting the tallies to the group can also serve as a springboard to a more thorough analysis.

Starting with Bales' well-known *interaction process analysis*,[9] which includes problem-solving and socioemotional responses, and continuing with more recent process analysis systems,[10] the emphasis has tended to be on the process of communication rather than its content. Two methods that do include content are those developed by Ober, Bentley, and Miller[11] and Mills.[12] Two other aspects that can be included in the evaluation of communication are the handling of evidence and reasoning. Smith has also developed an evaluation form to note digressions and to measure how well the group follows a pattern of constructive thinking.[13]

In connection with their experiments with self-directed therapy groups, the research staff of the Western Behavioral Sciences Institute developed Interpersonal Responsibility Scales.[14] The scales measure both the therapy group member's *intrapersonal exploration* (being open to discovering new depths in one's own feelings) and *facilitative behavior* (being authentic, responsive, and collaborative).

Product and Outcomes. Sometimes a group will arrive at a specific product (a report, a problem solved) and sometimes the outcome is less tangible (internalized learning,

---

[9]See Robert F. Bales, *Interaction Process Analysis* (Cambridge, Mass.: Addison-Wesley Publishing Co., Inc., 1950).

[10]See E. J. Amidon and J. B. Hough, *Interaction Analysis: Theory, Research and Application* (Reading, Mass.: Addison-Wesley Publishing Co., Inc., 1967); and E. J. Amidon and N. A. Flanders, *The Role of the Teacher in the Classroom*, rev. ed. (Minneapolis: Association for Productive Teaching, 1967).

[11]R. L. Ober, E. L. Bentley, and E. Miller, *Systematic Observation of Teaching* (Englewood Cliffs, N.J.: Prentice-Hall, Inc., 1971).

[12]Theodore M. Mills, *Group Transformation* (Englewood Cliffs, N.J.: Prentice-Hall, Inc., 1964).

[13]Smith, *Group Problem-Solving*, pp. 161–62.

[14]Betty Berzon and Lawrence N. Solomon, "Research Frontiers: The Self-Directed Therapy Group: Three Studies," *Journal of Counseling Psychology*, 13 (1966), 491–97.

increased awareness). Even when the group does its own evaluating, the subjective, intangible outcomes are difficult to pin down. It is especially difficult for the outside observer to identify the less tangible results, unless the group makes a point of verbalizing them as a part of its own process.

For a problem-solving discussion, it is possible to keep a running record of such things as who introduced certain topics and who proposed new solutions. Gulley advocated this method as well as rating the following attributes of the ultimate group decision: quality of decision reached, extent to which the decision was based on the substance of the entire discussion, extent of member agreement, and extent of member satisfaction and commitment.[15] Citing the work done by Webb and associates,[16] Davis called attention to another possible group product in "the 'traces' left behind by the interaction itself."[17]

EVALUATION WAYS AND MEANS: HOW TO EVALUATE

Now that we have examined some of the subject matter for evaluation, let's look at some of the evaluation methods available to us. The forms and instruments reproduced in this section are intended to serve as samples only. We repeat our earlier advice that it is better for each group to devise its own forms according to its own needs and goals.

Of necessity, evaluation involves the collection of data and the interpretation of the data. According to Potter and Andersen, methods of analysis of discussion cover a wide range, from the actual counting of the number of times a person spoke to the subjective guessing of what a person intended when he talked.[18]

Individual Self-Reports

One technique some teachers use to help their students better evaluate their own progress in a discussion class is to ask the students to keep a journal throughout the life of the class (or of a specific subgroup). Students are asked to record experiences and perceptions and keep track of their own and their fellow students' growth and development. Most diaries or journals are kept confidential in order to encourage frankness, and they can serve as a private means of two-way communication between the teacher and the individual student if the teacher will provide written or oral responses.

Keltner advises the use of final-examination questions based on the journal and on readings and experiences as an aid in self-analysis. Here are some potential examination questions adapted from Keltner: (1) Trace the changes that have taken place in your own perceptions of other people as communicators during the course. (2) Trace the changes you have made in your speech communication during this course. Identify when possible when and where specific events that opened up some change

[15]Gulley, *Discussion*, pp. 300–302.

[16]E. J. Webb and others, *Unobtrusive Measures* (Chicago: Rand McNally & Company, 1966).

[17]Davis, *Group Performance*, p. 7.

[18]David Potter and Martin P. Andersen, *Discussion* (Belmont, Calif.: Wadsworth Publishing Company, Inc., 1963), p. 191.

development for you took place. How do you account for these changes? (3) From your journal accounts, summarize the development of the class as a working group. (4) What evidence have you collected during the period of your work in this course that shows that you have been increasingly effective in your group discussions outside this class?[19]

Recall our earlier assertion that ideally, individual participants should be evaluated on the basis of their own needs and goals and wherever possible they should evaluate themselves. Figure 15.1 is designed to help students determine their own goals with the aid of constructive feedback from other group members.

Participant Reports on the Group

An effective tool to help groups evaluate themselves is to ask individual participants to complete a post-meeting reaction form (PMR). This can be detailed or brief. It can include a continuum or scale for scoring, or it can be open-ended or call for filling in the blanks. The following two forms (Figures 15.2 and 15.3) are simplified versions, which allow participants to include as much detail as they wish. Unless the group is too small to make it practical, we recommend that PMRs be completed anonymously.

Results of PMRs can be fed back to the group either by handing them around for general reading or by having them read aloud. Another method is to select a group member or someone outside the group to tabulate and summarize the responses, which can then be reported to the group. For example, in a group of eight people it would be useful to know that no one was very satisfied, that two were fairly satisfied, three were slightly more satisfied than dissatisfied, two were slightly more dissatisfied than satisfied, and one was very dissatisfied. The range of responses, in this case, is probably as significant as the answers themselves.

More specific participant reports on the group can evaluate what was learned from the group experience, with respect to information and skills. It is interesting to compare the learning acquired through the discussion method with that acquired from lecture or from working alone.

Participant Reports on Others in the Group

Asking group members to evaluate each other provides feedback and gives participants a means of evaluating themselves in relation to their peers. If a participant's behavior is revealed to be a continual source of irritation (perhaps because the person always seems to take the group off on tangents or doesn't do an equal share of the work), identifying the source of the problem can cause the other members to take a closer look at their own behavior. Are we perhaps guilty of the same fault? Or is there something that we do or say that contributes to or causes the problem behavior in the other person? Needless to say, evaluation is always relative, and a comparison with others' strengths and weaknesses is an effective way of evaluating one's own.

There are two difficulties associated with small group members evaluating each other. First, it isn't easy to be an effective participant and an effective observer (and

[19]John W. Keltner, *A Teaching Guide To Interpersonal Speech-Communication* (Belmont, Calif.: Wadsworth Publishing Company, Inc., 1970), p. 79.

GOALS FOR PERSONAL DEVELOPMENT

Please help me set my personal/professional goals for development by giving me feedback on this form. Base your responses on my relationships with you and with others, and mark each item according to whether you feel I'm doing all right, need to improve, need to do more, or need to do less. If you think some important goals are not listed please write them on the blank lines. Finally, please go over the whole list and circle the numbers of the three or four activities that you feel are the most important for me to work on. Thank you.

	Doing All Right	Need to Improve	Need to Do More	Need to Do Less
Communication Skills				
1. Amount of talking in group	___	___	___	___
2. Listening alertly	___	___	___	___
3. _____	___	___	___	___
Observation Skills				
4. Sensing others' feelings	___	___	___	___
5. Noting reaction to me	___	___	___	___
6. _____	___	___	___	___
Problem-Solving Skills				
7. Evaluating ideas critically	___	___	___	___
8. Clarifying issues	___	___	___	___
9. Summarizing	___	___	___	___
10. _____	___	___	___	___
Morale-Building Skills				
11. Harmonizing, helping people reach agreement	___	___	___	___
12. Upholding rights of individuals under group pressure	___	___	___	___
13. _____	___	___	___	___
Emotional Expressiveness				
14. Being authentic	___	___	___	___
15. Being tactful	___	___	___	___
16. _____	___	___	___	___
Ability to Handle Emotional Situations				
17. Ability to face conflict, anger	___	___	___	___
18. Ability to stand tension	___	___	___	___
19. _____	___	___	___	___
General				
20. Understanding why I do what I do (insight)	___	___	___	___
21. Encouraging comments on my own behavior (feedback)	___	___	___	___
22. _____	___	___	___	___

FIGURE 15.1.   Feedback-Eliciting Evaluation Form

POST-MEETING REACTION—CONTENT

1. How satisfied were you with the material covered by the group? (Check one.)
    _____ Very satisfied
    _____ Fairly satisfied
    _____ Slightly more satisfied than dissatisfied
    _____ Slightly more dissatisfied than satisfied
    _____ Fairly dissatisfied
    _____ Very dissatisfied

2. What seemed to you to be the most useful idea or ideas discussed? (Write in.)

3. What seemed to you to be the least useful idea or ideas discussed? (Write in.)

4. What suggestions do you have for future subject matter or material? (Write in.)

5. Other comments:

FIGURE 15.2   Participant Report Form: Discussion Content

evaluator) at the same time. If we really get involved in the interaction, we can easily forget to reserve part of our attention for the "big picture" of the task and maintenance functions of the whole group. It is hard to be simultaneously group-minded and an individual participant following the trend and thinking of what we want to say next. Second, as the group becomes more effective as a team, its members become better acquainted and generally more fond of each other. Some may find it repugnant to be critical of friends, especially if the criticism is to be reported to an outsider, such as the teacher. We recognize these difficulties as facts of group life that must be taken into account. Yet we deplore their being used as excuses to avoid individual evaluations.

Figures 15.4 and 15.5 are sample evaluation forms for individuals and groups. (See also Brilhart,[20] who uses a form on which a participant's use of task and maintenance functions can be tallied, and Barnlund and Haiman,[21] who have developed a well-known Leadership Rating Scale.)

[20]Brilhart, *Effective Group Discussion,* p. 104.

[21]Dean C. Barnlund and Franklyn S. Haiman, *The Dynamics of Discussion* (Boston: Houghton Mifflin Company, 1960), pp. 401–4.

POST-MEETING REACTION—PROCESS

1.   How satisfied were you with the performance of your group? (Check one.)
    _____   Very satisfied, accomplished a lot
    _____   Fairly satisfied
    _____   Slightly more satisfied than dissatisfied
    _____   Slightly more dissatisfied than satisfied
    _____   Fairly dissatisfied
    _____   Very dissatisfied, accomplished nothing

2.   What seemed to you to *help* the group the most? (Write in.)

3.   What seemed to you to *hinder* the group the most? (Write in.)

4.   What suggestions do you have for improving the group's performance? (Write in.)

5.   Other comments:

FIGURE 15.3   Participant Report Form: Discussion Process

Observation

Although a certain amount of observation is required in order to prepare the individual reports just discussed, we now move to the *role of observer* as an evaluation means. There are essentially four ways in which observers can function:

1.   *Participant as observer:* A group member may be assigned to observe the group or someone may decide to do it on his or her own. Because of the difficulties already delineated, we recommend that group-member evaluators keep their assignments simple if they are expected to be fully functioning group members at the same time. One possibility would be to watch for and note which people provide summaries.

2.   *Group member as temporary outside observer:* In this role, the group member *moves outside the group* temporarily so that he or she can devote full attention to being an observer. We recommend that observers sit outside the group and position themselves so that they can witness as much verbal and nonverbal communication as possible. One activity we have used

INDIVIDUAL EVALUATION FORM

Discussant's name _____ Date _____

Rating scale: 1. Poor   2. Below average   3. Average   4. Excellent
                5. Superior

Criteria	*Evaluation*	*Comments*
1. INFORMATION: Did the discussant show evidence of background reading, knowledge of the subject, and analysis of the problem?		
2. REASONING: Did the discussant show evidence of critical thinking? What were the quality and relevance of the contributions?		
3. COOPERATION: Did the discussant help the development of ideas and logical progression of group thinking? Did the discussant support and encourage other members and accept and adapt to their ideas?		
4. LEADERSHIP: Did the discussant show initiative and share the responsibility for stimulating discussion, summarizing, and resolving conflict?		
5. COMMUNICATION: Was the discussant a critical listener? Were contributions clear and to the point? Was the discussant able to explain complex ideas and help clarify meaning?		
6. OVERALL EFFECTIVENESS:		

Note: Because numbers and scales are meaningless unless we know what they're based on, comments are especially important. If for some reason a discussant's participation was not sufficient to warrant a rating, leave the form blank and place a check here: _____

_____
                                            Evaluator

FIGURE 15.4.   Sample Evaluation Form, to Be Filled in for Each Group Member by Others in the Group

GROUP EVALUATION FORM

Group _____ Date _____

	Rating scale				
Criteria	Poor	Below average	Average	Excellent	Superior
Clarity of Goals					
Problem-Solving					
Organized Group Thinking					
Evaluation of Ideas					
Equal Opportunity to Participate					
Mutual Respect					
Listening					
Leadership					
Conflict Resolution					
Effective Atmosphere					
Summarizing					
Final Decision, Product					

Comments:

Note: Because numbers and scales are meaningless unless we know what they're based on, comments are especially important.

_____

Evaluator

FIGURE 15.5.   Sample Evaluation Form, to Be Used by Group Members in Evaluating the Group as a Whole

in discussion classes is to form a "group within a group," in which each participant has an observer who can later provide private feedback in a dyad.

3. *Outside observer:* Here someone who is not a group member is asked to be an observer. This person may be an expert, a consultant, or perhaps a student from another class. There are obvious advantages in the use of a relatively objective, uninvolved outsider. But a cardinal disadvantage is the

stranger's lack of understanding of the group's growth and past history (unless of course the group is meeting for one session only). We can either recognize that the outside observer is able to provide us with an evaluation of only a slice of the group's life or we can make provisions for him or her to observe the group from its beginning.

4. *Unseen observer:* For some purposes, notably for laboratory experiments and research, the observer is behind either a screen or a one-way mirror. The observer may be present either with or without the group's knowledge.

The observer must first be sufficiently sensitive to people and groups to *be aware* of observable events. Second, he or she must be able to *describe* what is observed. Third, the observer must be able to *interpret* what has been observed and described. The last step is, of course, the most troublesome; even when we have what appears to be sound and objective data, more than one interpretation is usually possible. Observers, therefore, are cautioned to focus on *describing* events as they see them and then presenting interpretations tentatively for the group's acceptance or rejection.

Naturally, the range of possible observer subject matter is very wide, as was indicated by a previous section of this chapter. Brilhart[22] and Patton and Giffin[23] have included additional pointers for observers as well as detailed checklists of possible subjects.

Group Records

Another source of material for evaluation comes from group records kept during sessions. The most effective means is a *videotape recording,* which the group and/or observers can evaluate after the meeting. If more than one camera is available, it is possible to record nonverbal communication of all members even though they are seated around a table or in a circle. If a single camera is used, either the group will have to be in a semicircle or some facial views will have to be sacrificed.

Audiotape recordings are an effective means of reviewing who said what and with what effect—although nonverbal communication is sacrificed. The recordings can be played again and again for many different purposes.

Verbatim transcripts of group sessions are valuable but very time-consuming when they have to be transcribed from a recording and then reproduced. Moreover, it is sometimes difficult for the transcriber to identify individual speakers, particularly if he or she is not a group member.

Informal process analyses are sometimes useful when an observer or participant keeps track (usually in specific time blocks) of the group's major events. Highly significant contributions, as well as turning points in the discussion, can be noted. Figure 15.7 is an example of this method.

Recorder's notes are still another source for evaluation. Depending on the skill of the person elected or assigned to keep track of what happened, this method can be useful. The recorder might concentrate on decisions or points of consensus or merely on the principal ideas the group discussed.

[22]Brilhart, *Effective Group Discussion,* pp. 95–97.

[23]Bobby R. Patton and Kim Giffin, *Problem-Solving Group Interaction* (New York: Harper & Row, Publishers, 1973), pp. 250–53.

Sociometry

Sociometric tests and charts are another means of securing data for evaluation. In Chapter 12, we discussed the use of sociometric analysis as one means of assessing leadership. It can also be used to study "liking" relationships (rank the three group members you would most like to work with) and such aspects as communication skills (rank the three group members who are the best communicators). Sociograms are usually pictures in which circles are used to represent people and arrows are used to represent the relationships based on their choices. Some therapists and other group leaders ask each group member, following each group session, to make a drawing that shows, by distance between the circles, the current status of their like or dislike of other members.

In addition to the sociogram, sociometric data can be treated in three other ways, according to Hare: in an *index*, formed by adding the numerical ranking values; in a *statistical analysis;* and by the use of *matrix algebra*, which can demonstrate mutual and reciprocal choices.[24]

Although some interesting data can be acquired through the use of sociometry, we remind you of its limitations and drawbacks, discussed in Chapter 12.

General Communication Analysis: Content

Observers can assist a group by evaluating the content of its communication. What are the ideas introduced into the discussion and by whom? What happened to the ideas? How are varying viewpoints integrated into the final conclusions? It is very difficult to keep track of idea formulation, progression, and development, even if you are an observer with this as your only task. We recommend that observation be supplemented by recordings, which can be replayed.

Just as the classification of a contribution into task-oriented or maintenance-oriented categories is made difficult by the fact that comments can often serve both purposes, so is it often hard to separate communication content from the interaction process. Liebowitz found this to be true in his study of the thematic structure of sensitivity groups, where the content for discussion *is* group process and interpersonal problems.[25] It is interesting to note that National Training Laboratory staff members are advised that the content of the conversation taking place in a T-group is often the best clue as to what process issue may be on people's minds when they find it difficult to confront the issue directly. For example, "talking about problems of authority back home may mean that there is a leadership struggle going on in the T-group."[26]

There is also ambiguity in attempting to analyze the nonverbal communication of a group discussion. Group members incorporate many nonverbal cues (a frown, head nodding, a jiggling foot) into communication content. It is best for group members to check out the meaning of nonverbal communication with each other rather than-

---

[24]A. Paul Hare, *Handbook of Small Group Research* (Glencoe, Ill.: The Free Press, 1962), p. 409.

[25]Bernard Liebowitz, "A Method For the Analysis of the Thematic Structure of T-Groups," *Journal of Applied Behavioral Science,* 8 (1972), 149–73.

[26]National Training Laboratories Institute For Applied Behavioral Science, *Laboratories in Human Relations Training Reading Book,* rev. ed. (Washington, D.C.: National Education Association, 1969), p. 21.

make unwarranted assumptions. Group evaluators can report what nonverbal communication *they saw* but they are on dangerous ground if they proceed to what it means. As Flynn and LaFaso pointed out:

> It is not a wise procedure for a discussion group to appoint an observer to watch for "unexpressed emotion." His reporting to the group after the discussion would inevitably have a judgmental character and his interpretations of what he saw, heard or felt are very subjective and may easily be incorrect. . . . What might appear to an observer as an "emotional reaction to member X's contribution" might, in fact, be a "bit of undigested cheese."[27]

Interaction Analysis: Process

Most of the research and development of evaluation tools has centered on interaction analyses. We have chosen two original forms (Figures 15.6 and 15.7) as examples of simplified process analyses and are reprinting two (Figures 15.8 and 15.9) as samples of those developed by others.

The kind of analysis depicted in Figure 15.6 is good for beginning discussants and evaluators to use. The direction of the arrow indicates whether the contribution is addressed to an individual or to the group as a whole and the "hash marks" show how many contributions were made in this direction. The inverted arrow indicates the participant asked a question.

From looking at Figure 15.6, we can analyze each member's role in the group. Beth was obviously a strong member not only because of the number of statements and questions she addressed to the whole group but also because Andy, Fay, and Phil apparently reacted most to her contributions, possibly looking to her for leadership. Andy made only one comment to the total group and directed the rest of his attention to Beth. Carlos and Fran participated the least, with Carlos communicating to the whole group twice and asking the group one question. Fran only asked one question, of Phil. Fay was the most vocal participant, dividing her contributions between the total group, Beth, and Phil; she asked no questions and received no communication directly. Phil spoke primarily to the participants on each side of him and also asked no questions.

This is obviously a superficial analysis and should be treated as such when shared with the group. It makes no attempt to analyze content or quality of communication. If the same analysis were made for several meetings, however, it would be possible to begin to identify the quantity and direction of communication flow, which could provide preliminary feedback to the participants and data for their own further analysis.

Another kind of process analysis that keeps a running account of interactions is illustrated in Figure 15.7. This method can be as detailed as the evaluator wishes and can be used to keep track of one or many different aspects. It is similar to a transcript except that it makes no attempt at verbatim comments, reporting only the gist or sometimes the purpose of the comment. Both verbal and nonverbal behavior can be summarized and reported.

---

[27]Elizabeth W. Flynn and John F. LaFaso, *Group Discussion As Learning Process* (New York: Paulist Press, 1972), p. 77.

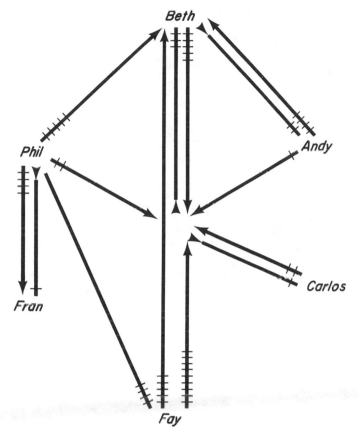

FIGURE 15.6.   Interaction Analysis Diagram

Because of the importance of feedback in group discussions and the fact that most contributions are in response to other comments, Leathers developed a Feedback Rating Instrument.[28] Maintaining that the feedback instrument has particular relevance for teachers' evaluation of discussion, Leathers said,

> The nine-factor Feedback Rating Instrument is based on the assumption that effective and efficient communication in discussion demand that the sender of a message receive feedback of maximum "self-correcting" potential if the sender is to possess the flexibility of response so necessary in small group communication. The instrument is designed to provide an accurate quantitative reading of the feedback dimensions which characteristically follow a given type of message.[29]

[28]Dale G. Leathers, "The Feedback Rating Instrument: A New Means of Evaluating Discussion," *Central States Speech Journal*, 22 (1971), 32–42.

[29]Leathers, "The Feedback Rating Instrument," pp. 36–38.

PROCESS ANALYSIS
SIGNIFICANT EVENTS

Time	*Contribution*	*Event/Comments*
10:00 a.m.	Mary opens discussion by reminding group their project report on conflict is due in three days. General discussion of work left to be done and who will do it. Lee asks about absent members. Bob says the same two are always late or absent and it makes him angry. General agreement that the missing two have made little effort. Gail asks if anyone has tried to contact them. No one has.	Six members present
10:10	Group decides to get back to project. Mary distributes outline of what she thinks should be in report. General discussion of outline. Paul wants to substitute a new point for item three.	
10:20		Mark comes into room, joins group, which looks at him in silence.
	Mark apologizes for being late. Paul continues talking about his substitution.	Group ignores Mark, who is looking puzzled.

FIGURE 15.7.   Sample Process Analysis Report

The pioneering effort was the previously mentioned interaction process analysis devised by Bales.[30] Figure 15.8 is an adaptation of Bales' categories by Barnlund and Haiman.[31] This is still a useful evaluation method but it requires practice and skill. Even when the evaluator has a tape or a transcript for reference, it is difficult to decide exactly which category is most appropriate. The use of Bales' and others' process analyses, particularly when they involve as many as 10 or 15 categories, is much more reliable when several evaluators are used and their results are either compared for reliability or averaged.

Another weakness of interaction process analysis was pointed out by Stech and Goldberg: "There is something about the social interaction process that makes sampling more error prone than one might expect." They concluded that "sampling small group interaction over short periods is not feasible."[32]

McCroskey and Wright developed an Interaction Behavior Measure, which is re-

[30]Bales, *Interaction Process Analysis.*

[31]Barnlund and Haiman, *The Dynamics of Discussion,* p. 400.

[32]Ernest L. Stech and Alvin A. Goldberg, "Sampling Discussion Group Interaction," *Speech Monographs,* 39 (1972), 314.

PARTICIPATION RECORD

Category of Interaction	Name or Number of Participant							Totals
1. Expresses Support, Releases Tension								
2. Agrees or Accepts Conclusion								
3. Gives Information								
4. Gives Opinion or Idea								
5. Gives Argument, Reasons								
6. Defines or Clarifies Remark								
7. Offers Procedural Help								
8. Asks for Procedural Help								
9. Asks for Clarification								
10. Answers Argument, Refutes, Criticizes								
11. Asks for Opinion								
12. Asks for Information								
13. Disagrees, Objects, Blocks								
14. Expresses Antagonism, Tension								
Totals								

FIGURE 15.8. Participation Record Form. From Dean C. Barnlund and Franklyn S. Haiman, The Dynamics of Discussion (Boston: Houghton Mifflin, 1960), p. 400.

produced as Figure 15.9.[33] They advocate that it be used by a panel of evaluators at specified intervals, with each evaluator rating all group members on all 12 dimensions. Results can then be compared or averaged.

[33]J. C. McCroskey and D. W. Wright, "The Development of an Instrument for Measuring Interaction Behavior in Small Groups," *Speech Monographs*, 38 (1971), 335–40.

INTERACTION BEHAVIOR MEASURE

Participant _____ Period _____

(Place a mark in whichever space best represents how closely one of the adjectives describes the observed behavior.)

Relevance

Relevant:	___	___	___	___	___	___	___	:Irrelevant
Related:	___	___	___	___	___	___	___	:Unrelated

Flexibility:

Flexible:	___	___	___	___	___	___	___	:Inflexible
Changeable:	___	___	___	___	___	___	___	:Unchangeable

Tension

Bothered:	___	___	___	___	___	___	___	:Cool
Tense:	___	___	___	___	___	___	___	:Relaxed

Orientation

Task:	___	___	___	___	___	___	___	:Social
Ideational:	___	___	___	___	___	___	___	:Personal

Interest

Interested:	___	___	___	___	___	___	___	:Apathetic
Involved:	___	___	___	___	___	___	___	:Withdrawn

Verbosity

Wordy:	___	___	___	___	___	___	___	:Short
Brief:	___	___	___	___	___	___	___	:Lengthy

FIGURE 15.9　Interaction Behavior Measure Form. From J. C. McCroskey and D. W. Wright, "The Development of an Instrument for Measuring Interaction Behavior in Small Groups," *Speech Monographs*, 38 (1971), 338.

We want to stress again the overall importance of evaluation as a means to individual and group improvement. It is our advice that evaluators begin with only one or two aspects that they can evaluate in depth, rather than try to watch for too many facets at once. Even better, follow the same one or two aspects over several meetings to avoid the criticism of too short or too isolated a sample.

One of our principal means of learning is to evaluate our own efforts in relation to the efforts of others and especially to try to emulate those attitudes, thoughts, and behaviors of others that we decide are more effective than our own.

SUMMARY

In this chapter, we have discussed some of the ways all kinds of groups (but primarily learning groups) can evaluate themselves or be evaluated by others. We first presented *what* can be evaluated and followed with various methods of evaluation, or the *how*. Nine sample evaluation tools were included.

DISCUSSION QUESTIONS

1.   Which criteria should be used first by beginning discussants as the subjects for their first evaluations? Why?

2.   How would you evaluate your current classes in terms of their suitability for discussion and/or lecture methods?

3.   Using the criteria in Figure 15.1 as a start, what other aspects should be included in the feedback you request from others?

4.   What are the ethical implications of observing groups without their knowledge? Under what situations and factors would you feel the ends (training for the evaluators and feedback for the group) justify the means (unseen and unknown observers)?

EXERCISES

1.   Assume that you are a member of a newly formed discussion group and are serving as leader for the first few meetings. How would you go about getting the group to accept the idea that they are to evaluate themselves and each other? What would you do to persuade the group members that allotting time for group evaluation will be a time-saver in the long run?

2.   Describe the manner in which your teachers use evaluation and give you feedback. Is it adequate? If not, how can you make the teacher more aware of your needs?

3.   For your next small group discussion, provide enough copies of a form something like that in Figure 15.4 so that after the session participants can evaluate themselves and all other group members. Keep the forms anonymous (they can be taken away and typed if handwriting might be recognized). Discussants should compare the other evaluations received with their own. In addition to studying the individual ratings and comments, determine the mean and the median of each criterion. Discuss your comparisons with the group and/or the instructor.

4.   Select some group of which you are a continuing member and make a self-evaluation of your group and your participation. What do you perceive to be the group's unmet needs? What functions have you been performing? What, if anything, can you do at once to improve group functioning? What can you train yourself to do that will help the group? To what degree would this evaluation differ for another group of which you are a member? Why?

SELECTED READINGS

AMIDON, E. J., AND J. B. HOUGH, *Interaction Analysis: Theory, Research and Application*. Reading, Mass.: Addison-Wesley Publishing Co., Inc., 1967.

BION, W. R., *Experiences in Groups*. London: Tavistock Publications, Ltd., 1961.

BRILHART, JOHN K., *Effective Group Discussion*, chap. 8. Dubuque, Iowa: William C. Brown Company, Publishers, 1967.

FISHER, B. AUBREY, *Small Group Decision Making: Communication and the Group Process*, appendix 2. New York: McGraw-Hill Book Company, Inc., 1974.

PATTON, BOBBY R., AND KIM GIFFIN, *Problem-Solving Group Interaction*, chaps. 12–14. New York: Harper & Row, Publishers, 1973.

POTTER, DAVID, AND MARTIN P. ANDERSEN, *Discussion*, chap. 9. Belmont, Calif.: Wadsworth Publishing Company, Inc., 1963.

SMITH, WILLIAM S., *Group Problem-Solving Through Discussion* (rev. ed.), chap. 9. Indianapolis: The Bobbs-Merrill, Company, Inc., 1963.

TORRANCE, E. PAUL, "Methods of Conducting Critiques of Group Problem-Solving Performance," in *Small Groups: Studies in Social Interaction* (rev. ed.), eds. A. Paul Hare, E. F. Borgatta, and R. F. Bales, pp. 692–99. New York: Alfred A. Knopf, Inc., 1966.

chapter 16

Although the group and its leaders have responsibilities for helping group members become better participants, *the ultimate responsibility rests with the individual.* Time and again students complain that they do not seem to have a chance to perform well. "I can't make myself heard. The rest of the group just ignores people like me. They won't give me a chance." The rest of the group can undoubtedly make the work of learning to participate easier for the individual but they can't do it *for* the individual.

People will forgive novices almost any lack if they are genuinely trying to make a contribution. But if all they seek is sympathy or affection, if they make no earnest attempt to contribute and help the group toward its goal, they usually receive short shrift. If the group is split into factions, their votes may be counted. But there is no real membership; that must be based on solid contribution.

This chapter is based on the assumption that the student is making an earnest attempt and has already read and experienced much of the rest of the book. Now the student comes to a place in her or his development where she or he says, "Our group has this problem. What can I do to help?"

The first step is to analyze your individual strengths and needs as a person and as a discussant and to plan ways to improve. Next, analyze the group's needs. Finally, try to figure out how to help the group meet its needs.

FIRST STEP: SELF-ASSESSMENT

Attitudes

Attitudes affect perception of evidence, group climate, maturity, norms, and leadership. Attitudes also form the basis for choice of leadership methods. Where do our attitudes come from? We aren't born with them. Obviously, we acquire them from people who have influenced our lives (parents, teachers, friends), from exposure to the ideas of others via the media (newspapers, magazines, television), and from the very process of living and experiencing and learning.

Behind our attitudes are some deeply rooted convictions sometimes called *values.* In today's world it is not enough to accept values handed down to us as so many heirlooms to be preserved. Today we think more in terms of a *process of valuing;* we have learned how important it is to identify and clarify our own belief systems and priorities in order to give shape and meaning to our lives.[1]

---

[1]For some excellent suggestions on how to clarify values, particularly for classroom use, see Louis E. Raths, Merrill Harmin, and Sidney B. Simon, *Values and Teaching* (Columbus, Ohio: Charles E. Merrill Publishing Co., 1966).

Improving Small Group Discussion

Attitudes Toward Self

In Chapter 1 we discussed the importance of understanding oneself. Psychologists tell us that of the many ways in which we differ, it is in our self-images that we differ most. Our assessment of personal identity, potential, status, assets, and limitations may be quite realistic, or it may be grounded in fantasy. Although none of us can hope, or perhaps bear, to see ourselves with full clarity, or even come close to the perceptions others have of us, our contributions to a group are related to the way in which we see ourselves, find satisfaction for our needs, and become active in the work of the group. Insofar as the member increases understanding and objectivity regarding self, he or she may be more effective and may help others function better.

We have stressed the concept of personal security that results from an appropriate assessment of ourselves. The issue here is this: How can we learn to improve our assessment of ourselves? Although some of us may need professional help from therapists, psychiatrists, or ministers, most of us can use more conventional channels. Four suggestions for taking stock of ourselves and doing something about our attitudes follow.

Use Tests. Our faith in standardized tests is not unbounded, but attitude, aptitude, achievement, and ability tests may be helpful if wisely used. Students in school will take many such tests as a matter of course. Others may take them with nominal or no fees from school guidance or other public service centers. Many businesses make provision for testing as a part of their personnel programs.

Evaluate Your Own Work. Like most teachers, we encourage our students to come to our offices to discuss their performances in class. With distressing frequency students come in and ask, "How am I doing in class?" or "What was wrong with that last paper?" When we try to turn the question around and ask, "How do *you* think you are doing?" or "What do *you* think was wrong with that last paper?" the students are often nonplussed. "You are the expert," they say, "what do you think?" These students miss the point. They are the ones who must ultimately set the value upon their work; they, not we, must live with themselves. They cannot be helped until they begin to evaluate and help themselves.

But sometimes the student begins the discussion this way: "Last Tuesday when we were discussing such and such, I did such and such. At the time I thought it was a pretty good idea, but it didn't go over. Was it poorly timed?" Now we can go to work! The student's diagnosis is probably sound since he or she has gone to the trouble of thinking it out beforehand. But right, wrong, or indifferent, we now have a basis for an effective analysis.

Use Learning and Therapeutic Discussions. If you are taking a course in discussion, you probably know other students whose participation problems and self-attitudes are similar to yours. If you are not taking a course, you may know or be able to find others who have similar problems or concerns. There is no particular mystery about learning and therapeutic discussion. Sharing experiences and feelings with others is a great help in self-understanding, provided the sharing is both reciprocal and objective.

We often make this recommendation to students who seek assistance in improving their understanding of themselves. When they follow this advice, their participation often improves dramatically for at least two reasons. They have gained greater insight into their own problems by discussing them with others. Also, they feel more confident when they speak up in discussion because they know they have the sympathy and support of at least some of their colleagues.

Talk to Yourself. Some people need to get better acquainted with themselves. Some reflection, meditation, and private introspection may be necessary. Using information gleaned from tests, observations of professionals and others, as well as our own experiences, we can examine our own self-attitudes and their reasonableness. As we go from group to group and adapt to first one norm and then another, it becomes very difficult to maintain a sense of identity. Occasional reflection in depth and in privacy, therefore, may be the answer.

Attitudes Toward Others

To separate attitudes toward ourselves from attitudes toward others is difficult. We tend to blame others when we are unable to face up to an understanding of our own feelings and desires. If we feel insecure, we tend to see the rest of the world as hostile. On the other hand, if we feel secure, we tend to see the rest of the world as friendly.

Understanding Others. After explaining the difficulties and hazards of understanding the personality of another, Allport concluded, *"A major task in life is to achieve increasing success in our perception of one another."*[2] We can scarcely disagree with this conclusion, but we caution against becoming preoccupied during a discussion with subtle analyses of other group members. We make this caution not solely because the business of understanding others is difficult (and it *is* difficult) but primarily because preoccupation with the character, feelings, emotions, and attitudes of others can be positively damaging to interpersonal relationships. Let us illustrate.

If we tend to focus upon an analysis of the personality of others, we may find ourselves thinking something like this when we listen to someone else talk: "I'll bet he said that just to bolster his own ego. Is it good for him to have his ego bolstered, or should I give him his comeuppance?" What was the idea he expressed? Did we agree with it? How was it supported? No matter. Our minds are fixed on his personality and our diagnosis of what is good for him.

"Wherein thou judgest another, thou condemnest thyself," is a good motto for a number of reasons. The first reason is the old inability to see the mote in one's brother's eye because of the beam in one's own. The second is that for philosophical reasons we do not believe we have any right to determine what is right or good for others and, thereby, manipulate or coerce them except when their actions are causing harm to others.[3] Finally, practical reasons indicate that interpersonal relations should rest on a fundamental basis of respect for substantive accomplishment. Thus it is better to concentrate on what other discussants say and the goals they seek rather than on our *judgment* of their *motives.*

[2]Gordon W. Allport, *Pattern and Growth in Personality* (New York: Holt, Rinehart and Winston, Inc., 1961), p. 522.

[3]John Stuart Mill in his famous essay, "On Liberty," defined this position very well.

The Charitable Assumptions. In place of attempting to become amateur psychiatrists each discussant should make, at least initially, the "charitable assumptions" about the motives of others. These assumptions are as follows: *The other participants want to reach a reasonable solution; they want to reach that solution in a reasonable fashion.* These assumptions are very much like the familiar "innocent until proven guilty" assumption of our courts. Until we have clear evidence to the contrary, we should assume the better motive.

Making charitable assumptions does not mean that we abandon reasonable precautions. We assume that most people are not criminals, but we still lock the door at night. There are, of course, unscrupulous discussants and, despite our precautions, we may occasionally be injured by making the charitable assumptions. Still the advantages clearly outweigh the dangers.

There are two principal advantages. First, we can concentrate on the substance of the discussion rather than becoming overly concerned about the motives of discussants. Second, people have a habit of behaving as others expect them to behave. If we assume that we are working with people of integrity, they will more often than not live up to the assumption.

I, You, and We. We already made the point that ideas should become group property so that their originators don't have to defend them. An example of how this worked was in the atomic energy committee headed by David Lilienthal. Here is how one of the members pinpointed a major reason for the success of the committee:

> Our first joint decision, then, was to liberate all our discussions from idea-possessiveness. No point would be argued down; we agreed that we would attack the problem inductively, working from the ground up, assembling all the facts pertinent to the problem as a basis for conclusions, implied or explicit. We agreed that all questions coming up were to be considered as being brought up by the group as a whole rather than by any single member. If a member had an objection to any one point, it was to be regarded as something that troubled the group as a whole.[4]

How different is this approach from the "*I* thought up this idea and now *you* are opposing it," attitude. Saying and meaning *we* is not easy. Some use it as a gimmick to conceal differences that matter, as a technique to fool people into believing that harmony prevails. The genuine use of *we* is based on the foundations of respect and affection for others that come from placing task accomplishments above petty jealousies and rivalries. Was there conflict in the Lilienthal committee? Of course. Did the originator of the idea defend it? Sometimes, but once the members learned how to think as *we*, the originator of an idea seldom defended it solely because it was his.

Attitudes Toward Task

Objectivity. Objectivity does not mean that an individual has no convictions. The way the terms *objectivity* and *open-mindedness* are used by some people may lead

---

[4]Norman Cousins and Thomas K. Finletter, "A Beginning for Sanity," *Saturday Review of Literature,* 29 (June 1946), 9.

us to suspect that an open-minded individual is an empty-minded one. Not so. The issue is how we handle our beliefs concerning the group's task. Two criteria distinguish the individual's degree of objectivity.

Frankness with ourselves and others is the first criterion. Frank individuals will, within the limits of tact and common sense, confess, rather than conceal, their beliefs. When discussants conceal their beliefs, it is bad enough; but when individuals manage to conceal their beliefs even from themselves, it is worse. And this happens, probably to everyone at some time or another. All are familiar with the "liberal" who loudly denounces discrimination against minorities but who becomes upset when a black or Chicano wishes to move into the neighborhood. "I'm not prejudiced," he or she says, "I'm just afraid that property values will fall."

Respect for evidence and reason is the second criterion. "My mind is made up; don't confuse me with the facts," may be a humorous slogan to paste on our desks, but it is hardly a motto to live by. Great men and women have always had respect for evidence and reason. Albert Schweitzer placed respect for truth with reverence for life as the two cardinal points of his own philosophy of life.

How do we acquire this objectivity? We must confess that we are not sure. The literature is rich with procedures for *distinguishing* the open from the closed mind and *predicting* the consequences of either.[5] There are many techniques for changing beliefs themselves. But how do we modify tendencies toward nonobjectivity in general?

Just how difficult changing tendencies toward nonobjectivity can be was once brought home forcibly to us. We were preparing a discussion group to present a public program before a service club. The subject for discussion was the United States' relations with Cuba. When the students gathered to explore ideas and plan their presentation, one of the students presented nothing but a series of glittering generalities about friendliness, mutual respect, and similar abstractions, without including any evidence from any source that even pretended to know about the Cuban situation. After some conversation, we discovered that he had taken a popularized non-university course in "personality development." He learned in that course, he said, that people do not want to listen to "dry" facts; they want speakers to present their own thoughts and feelings. He had done just that. We tried every way we knew to convince him that mouthing personal prejudices and abstractions was no substitute for sound evidence and reasoning. We failed. We excused him from participation in the project and sometime later received a "Thank-you-gram" for our efforts. We were thanked for having further confirmed him in his beliefs!

This case is, of course, extreme; and, after all, at the moment we are concerned with improving our own objectivity, not that of others. The best way to improve our own objectivity is to first surround ourselves with as rich, varied, and able a collection of people and ideas as possible. If we allow ourselves to be affected by this environment, it will not allow us to retain myopic beliefs that ignore evidence and reason. The stimulation afforded by the challenge of others may help us modify our basic belief systems. This is the very essence of a liberal education.

Another way to improve objectivity is to become as familiar as possible with the nature and use of evidence and reasoning. The causal connections are not as conclusive as might be hoped, but many reports from teachers contend that students

---

[5]See particularly Milton Rokeach, *The Open and Closed Mind* (New York: Basic Books, 1960).

trained in the use of evidence and reason seem capable of more objectivity than those not so trained. Whether such people are capable of compartmentalizing themselves so that they become objective in one or more areas of behavior while remaining rigidly closed in others is uncertain. Further, it is not known whether a disproportionate number of objective people expose themselves to training in the use of evidence and reason while disproportionately fewer nonobjective people expose themselves to the same training. Nonetheless, these two methods still appear to offer the greatest promise for attaining that elusive goal, objectivity.

Involvement. Involvement in the task means simply that we care about (are concerned with) task accomplishment and further that we are actively participating in task accomplishment. The participation may be vicarious. But usually the participation is and should be direct.

Some people seem to go through life without ever allowing themselves to become involved, except peripherally, in anything besides their own births and deaths. Yes, they participate in various tasks in order to exist. But their participation is bland because they have committed little of their personal concern to the task. Progress was never moved forward by blandness. As Lincoln Steffens wrote long ago:

> I teach my child and I tell other children of all ages—pre-school, in school, in college, and out:
>> *That nothing is done, finally and right.*
>> *That nothing is known, positively and completely.*
> That the world is theirs, all of it. It is full of all sorts of things for them to find out and do, or do over and do right. . . . Young people are glad, as I am, that there is something left for them to discover and say and think and do. Something? There is *everything.* [6]

Burgoon, Heston, and McCroskey applied this idea of commitment to small groups:

> The good group member is willing to commit himself to the group process and product, whatever the outcome (assuming it doesn't violate his personal ethics). He is willing to devote time and energy to the group's activities. He gives as well as takes. This is basically a question of loyalty. Prior to any particular group meeting, each member should determine for himself if he is really committed to the group's membership and activities. The individual who has no initial commitment to a group, whose entering attitude is one of "wait and see," is not likely to be an asset. In times of stress, he is more likely to "abandon ship" than to address the problems seriously. If a person voluntarily chooses to be a member of a group, he has an obligation to maintain a commitment to it in return for the benefits he gains by membership. [7]

[6]Peter Steffens, *Lincoln Steffens Speaking* (New York: Harcourt Brace Jovanovich, 1936) by permission of Harcourt Brace Jovanovich, Inc. Reprinted in *Reader's Digest,* 105 (December 1974), 253–54.

[7]Michael Burgoon, Judee K. Heston, and James C. McCroskey, *Small Group Communication, A Functional Approach* (New York: Holt, Rinehart and Winston, Inc., 1974), p. 159.

If you want to become involved in group task accomplishments, participate actively and *accept some personal responsibility for task accomplishment.* Simply attending meetings, sitting there, and speaking only when spoken to won't do. The task won't seize you; you must seize it. Do you lament your lack of involvement in politics? Attend a precinct caucus of your party and volunteer to distribute campaign literature or become a block worker. You will be warmly welcomed because there are never enough such workers to go around. Do the conferences at your place of employment leave you cold? You might try volunteering for something other than what you are told to do. In short, if you wish to become involved, stick your neck out and *do* something.

SECOND STEP: GROUP ASSESSMENT

Throughout this book we have dealt with characteristics and forces within groups and have pointed out a wide variety of potential problems and solutions. The more experience we have with groups the better able we are to evaluate, diagnose, and help cure. Whatever is wrong with our group or needs improvement may be so subtle we have only a vague uneasy feeling as a symptom or it may be a blatant problem that is obvious to everyone. We therefore cannot offer a cookbook recipe on how to assess your group. We *can* steer you to help within this book.

Review Chapters 4 and 5 on group characteristics and forces for possible clues and then follow the suggestions outlined in Chapter 15. Once you have located what you believe to be the troublesome aspect, both the overall index at the end of the book and the checklist at the end of this chapter should assist you in locating relevant material on that aspect.

THIRD STEP: HELP YOUR GROUP MEET ITS NEEDS

You have carefully assessed your group's needs, structure, climate, communication, and leadership. You have also evaluated strengths and weaknesses. The next logical procedure is to try to help your group meet its needs. Have you decided, for example, that your group's communication is at fault, that people are not really listening to each other? Then what can you do about it?

One thing you can do is examine your own capabilities, as was suggested earlier in this chapter, and put them to work. Could you help your group's communication by working harder at your own and thereby providing a model of successful interaction that others can emulate? If you feel inadequate to the task, then better preparing yourself will eventually help the group. This may involve no more than reading and obtaining some new insights or evidence needed by the group; or it might involve your launching a more ambitious program to help you become more knowledgeable and skilled in the areas in which you feel inadequate.

Another thing you can do is enlist the aid of one or two other group members. If their assessments and evaluations are similar to yours, you might have more success meeting the group's needs as a coordinated subgroup. We had an example of this in a large discussion class where we had given the total group an assignment. Group members found it impossible to stick to a point long enough to see it through and the group badly needed someone to regulate participation, maintain individual recognition, and improve group climate. About halfway through one meeting, a member announced that he had a plan he thought would work. Because of all its pressing needs, the group did not allow him even to present his plan. Then three other members got together between meetings, worked out a plan, and agreed to have one of their number present the plan while the other two fended off critics until the plan could receive a fair hearing. When the class next met, the three announced exactly what they had in mind and proceeded to do it. Within minutes the plan, with modifications suggested by others, was adopted. For the first time the group began to make significant progress. Working alone, none of the three could have succeeded; working together, they made an important contribution.

Another means of helping your group meet its needs is to think about what training would help other group members and whether you can provide it. Your opportunities for training others are probably far greater than you imagine. Suppose that another member of the group says she doesn't know where to find some information she has been asked to locate. You do know and you tell her. You are performing a training function. If you go one step further and show her, perhaps after the discussion, how to find *any* information of this kind by using some standard reference such as the *Readers' Guide*, you are doing an even better job of training because you are making her less dependent upon others.

You don't have to be an expert in a field in order to train. You simply have to be able to detect some area of behavior in which you can be of assistance, and then guide the other person to perceive what you have to offer.

It is possible, of course, that your assessment of training needs will indicate that your group needs the services of an expert. Suggesting that your group invite a guest lecturer or an outside evaluator who can provide training for the whole group may be the answer. Don't forget that your instructor is an expert and can also help supply this need.

Try Role Playing, Games, or Simulations

One last suggestion on a means to help your group improve is to arrange for role playing, games, or simulated activities. In *role playing*, people try to behave as another person would in a given set of circumstances. Sometimes the role given is merely functional ("You are a person who continually takes the group off on tangents"). Sometimes a detailed background of the individual to be portrayed, including how the person feels about the issue under discussion, will be included in the role. *Games* are group activities that are usually based on competition and winning and losing and have more elaborate rules and procedures. Games such as Ghetto and Blacks and Whites are designed to develop awareness of what it is like to be someone else, economically and socially, and struggle against heretofore unexperienced odds. *Simulations*, which are often based on case studies, place the individual or the group in a mock situation to which people respond as they would in real life. Commonly used as a diagnostic tool to assess and evaluate management and leadership potential, simulations such as the In-basket Exercise[8] demonstrate how well a person can quickly solve problems, organize materials, and establish priorities.

---

[8]Norman Frederiksen, "In-basket Tests and Factors in Administrative Performance," *Simulation in Social Science: Readings*, ed. Harold Guetzkow (Englewood Cliffs, N.J.: Prentice-Hall, Inc., 1962), pp. 124–37.

The group may plan for role playing in several ways. If group members discover a need to develop an insight into some problem, roles may be created spontaneously. If the group wishes to learn how to cope with particular forces or circumstances, someone must usually create the roles beforehand. If the nature of the role playing demands that the role players have incomplete knowledge of other's roles, someone else must create the roles.

Although playing roles is not difficult and most people enter into the spirit enthusiastically, you should nevertheless observe two cautions. First, when drawing up the roles, be careful to avoid caricaturing. Many people tend to draw roles in a right-or-wrong, hero-or-villain fashion. The dominator is drawn as a perfect tyrant, the submissive person as completely spineless, and so on. People are seldom like that, so roles should enable the participants to reflect, as much as possible, real people. Second, when you are a role player, avoid overdoing the role. Sometimes people begin having so much fun they forget why they are playing the role and get carried away with their own histrionics.

SUMMARY

This chapter has given an overview of how the individual can help improve the group. We looked first at attitudes toward self, toward others, and toward the task. Next we advocated a thorough assessment of the group and its needs and offered the following suggestions for ways to help your group meet its needs: (1) Assess your own ability to meet the needs; (2) better prepare yourself if you don't feel up to the task; (3) join with one or two other members and work out a plan; (4) provide training for other group members; (5) get outside, expert help if necessary; and (6) try role playing, games, or simulations.

To further assist you in finding ideas and suggestions to help improve your group, we are providing a checklist organized by subject matter to show where you can find additional material on the main points of this chapter.

CHECKLIST:
WHERE TO FIND ADDITIONAL MATERIAL ON THE MAIN
POINTS OF THIS CHAPTER

Subject	Chapter
Self-assessment	
Attitudes about self, others, and task	1, 2, 5, 13
Group assessment	
General	2, 4, 5, 15
Structure	5, 13, 15
Leadership	5, 12, 13, 15
Climate and cohesiveness	4, 5, 13, 14, 15
Communication and interaction	1, 5, 6, 7, 12, 15
Product and outcomes	10, 15

Subject	Chapter
Ways to help the group meet needs	
Evaluate	15
Put suggestions into action	13
Training	14
Get outside help	15
Role playing, games, simulations	3
Most important membership and leadership functions	
Managing problems	
Discovering problems	10
Handling agendas	13
Initiating action	14
Balancing task and maintenance orientations	5, 13
Terminating action	14
Generating ideas	
Stimulating thought	11
Creating hypotheses	10, 11
Testing ideas	
Diagnosing need for evidence	8
Stimulating research	8
Supplying evidence	8
Criticizing and reasoning	9
Preserving ideas	
Recording	13
Summarizing	13, 14
Reporting progress	13
Handling participation	
Stimulating involvement	13
Equalizing opportunities for participation	13
Regulating participation	13
Using and resolving conflict	4, 10, 11, 14
Building the group	
Diagnosing process needs	5, 12, 13
Understanding norms and creating new ones	4, 14
Improving group climate	4, 5, 13, 14, 15
Developing group maturity	4, 5, 14
Problem-solving and decision-making	
Developing and identifying goals	4, 5, 10, 14
Synthesizing and integrating ideas	14
Reaching a decision	5, 10, 14
Handling pressure for conformity	5, 11
Protecting the minority viewpoint	13, 14
Providing satisfaction for the individual	
Distributing rewards	13
Expressing appreciation	14
Stimulating commitment to the group and task	2, 5, 13, 15
Providing opportunities for improvement, training	2, 14

DISCUSSION QUESTIONS

1.   In what ways can a group instill a lasting sense of commitment and personal responsibility in its members?

2.   Is there a danger in too much cohesion? Why?

3.   How much responsibility does each group member have for the improvement of the group?

EXERCISES

1.   Using an evaluation form from Chapter 15 or one of your own design, arrange for several class members to evaluate the same group. Have each evaluator put the group's most critical needs in rank order. Hold a discussion in which the evaluators compare notes and try to reach a consensus. What do you conclude, from both a content and a process standpoint?

2.   Plan a role-playing demonstration of participation in which some particular problems or needs are illustrated and some positive solutions are included. Provide only the general structure in a realistic framework for all participants, but provide each role player with specific suggestions or descriptions of his or her role and goals. Some possible situations might be (a) a group whose members have a wide variety of interests and levels of maturity, (b) a young leader in a situation where established and high-status individuals are members of the committee, or (c) a group where several individuals are concerned with their personal hidden agendas.

3.   Divide the class into small groups and ask the instructor to evaluate each group in a different way. For one group, have the instructor participate as a member; for the second group, have the instructor serve as observer/evaluator; for the third group, have the instructor evaluate only the end product or final report. Compare evaluations with the whole class. Ask the instructor to report on the quality of the separate evaluations and how he or she felt about the different methods. Which was the most thorough? Which was the most objective? Which was the most helpful to the group?

4.   Conduct a brainstorming session with other class members to identify in what ways role playing, games, or simulations could be of most benefit to a class in discussion. What are the problems and what are the situations that can most beneficially be used in these ways? Why?

SELECTED READINGS

Boocock, Sarane S., and E. O. Schild, *Simulation Games in Learning*. Beverly Hills, Calif.: Sage Publications, Inc., 1968.

Elms, Alan C., *Role Playing, Reward, and Attitude Change*. New York: Van Nostrand Reinhold, 1969.

Flynn, Elizabeth W., and John F. LaFaso, *Group Discussion As Learning Process*, chap. 14. New York: Paulist Press, 1972.

PFEIFFER, J. WILLIAM, AND JOHN E. JONES, *Structured Experiences for Human Relations Training.* Iowa City, Iowa: University Associates Press, 1971, and later editions.

POTTER, DAVID, AND MARTIN P. ANDERSEN, *Discussion,* chap. 6. Belmont, Calif.: Wadsworth Publishing Company, Inc., 1963.

ROGERS, CARL R., *Freedom to Learn.* Columbus, Ohio: Charles E. Merrill Publishing Co., 1969.

Name Index

Subject Index